PAKISTAN'S POLITICAL PARTIES

PAKISTAN'S POLITICAL PARTIES

Surviving between Dictatorship and Democracy

Mariam Mufti
Sahar Shafqat
Niloufer Siddiqui

Editors

Georgetown University Press
Washington, DC

The publisher is not responsible for third-party websites or their content. URL links were active at time of publication.

Library of Congress Cataloging-in-Publication Data

Names: Mufti, Mariam, editor. | Shafqat, Sahar, editor. | Siddiqui, Niloufer, editor.
Title: Pakistan's Political Parties : Surviving between Dictatorship and Democracy / Mariam Mufti, Sahar Shafqat, Niloufer Siddiqui, editors.
Description: Washington, DC : Georgetown University Press, 2020. | Includes bibliographical references and index.
Identifiers: LCCN 2019028852 (print) | LCCN 2019028853 (ebook) | ISBN 9781626167704 (hardcover) | ISBN 9781626167711 (paperback) | ISBN 9781626167728 (ebook)
Subjects: LCSH: Political parties—Pakistan—History—21st century. | Pakistan—Politics and government—21st century.
Classification: LCC JQ629.A979 P35 2020 (print) | LCC JQ629.A979 (ebook) | DDC 324.25491—dc23
LC record available at https://lccn.loc.gov/2019028852
LC ebook record available at https://lccn.loc.gov/2019028853

∞ This book is printed on acid-free paper meeting the requirements of the American National Standard for Permanence in Paper for Printed Library Materials.

21 20   9 8 7 6 5 4 3 2 First printing

Printed in the United States of America.

Cover design by John Barnett.
Composition by Paul Hotvedt at Blue Heron Publishing Services

The map on the book's cover depicts political representation in Pakistan's National Assembly. Gilgit Baltistan and Azad Jammu and Kashmir are not denoted with party banners because they do not send representatives to the National Assembly. The image is not intended to be a commentary on the territorial status of any part of the country.

To Alexis. —M. M.

To Sapna and Saira Kiran. —S. S.

To my parents. —N. S.

Contents

List of Illustrations   *ix*

Acknowledgments   *xi*

List of Abbreviations   *xiii*

**Introduction: Pakistan's Political Parties in an Era
of Transition**   1
Niloufer Siddiqui, Mariam Mufti, and Sahar Shafqat

Part I: The Form of Pakistan's Party System

1   The Formation, Development, and Decay of the Pakistan
    Muslim League-Nawaz   23
    Saeed Shafqat

2   Pakistan People's Party: From Populism to Patronage   41
    Philip E. Jones

3   Pakistan Tehreek-e-Insaf: From a Movement to a
    Catch-All Party   60
    Tabinda M. Khan

4   What Remains of the Muttahida Qaumi Movement   76
    Tahir Naqvi

5   Leftist Parties in Pakistan: Challenges and Limitations   90
    Anushay Malik

6   Religious Parties: The Politics of Denominational Diversity
    in an Islamic Republic   105
    Johann Chacko

Part II: The Functions Served by Pakistan's Party System

7 Who Do Politicians Talk To? Political Contact in Urban Punjab 125
ASAD LIAQAT, ALI CHEEMA, AND SHANDANA KHAN MOHMAND

8 Candidate-Party Linkages in Pakistan: Why Do Candidates Stick with Losing Parties? 144
HASSAN JAVID AND MARIAM MUFTI

9 Women in Electoral Politics: An Account of Exclusion 162
SARAH KHAN

10 Governance Amid Crisis: Delegation, Personal Gain, and Service Delivery in Pakistan 178
SAMEEN A. MOHSIN ALI

11 Opposition Parties and Regime Uncertainty in Pakistan 195
SAHAR SHAFQAT

Part III: The Survival of Pakistan's Party System

12 The Kingmaker: Pakistan's Military and Political Parties 215
AYESHA SIDDIQA

13 Judicial Politics in a Hybrid Democracy: Pakistan's Judiciary and Political Parties 235
YASSER KURESHI

14 Parties and Foreign Policy in Pakistan 253
CHRISTOPHER CLARY

Conclusion: Political Parties in an "Establishmentarian Democracy" 272
MOHAMMAD WASEEM

Appendix: Pakistan Electoral Results, 1988–2018 282
References 285
About the Contributors 307
Index 309

Illustrations

Tables

7.1 Correlates of politician–voter contact   136
8.1 The distribution of different types of candidates as a percentage
     of total candidates from a given political party in the 14th
     National Assembly   158
13.1 Summary of reported judgments by high courts on rulings
     by military courts and martial law administrators, 1978–79   243
A.1 Pakistan electoral results, 1988–2018   282

Figures

7.1 Extent of campaign contact between voters and politicians   138
7.2 Extent of voter-initiated contact with political parties   139
7.3 Closeness between UC chair and citizens   140
8.1 Typology of candidates   147
9.1 Women as a percentage of total candidates fielded on general
     seats for the national and provincial assemblies in 2018, by party   165
9.2 Women as a percentage of total candidates contesting election
     to general seats in the National Assembly and as a percentage of
     all sitting legislators in the National Assembly, 1977–2018   169
9.3 Proportion of winning candidates, in general elections to
     national and provincial assemblies, who are dynastic, 1985–2008   173
9.4 Proportion of respondents, by country, who agree or strongly
     agree with the statement: "On the whole, men make better
     political leaders than women do."   175
13.1 Percentage of Supreme Court judges recruited from the bar
     of professional lawyers   241
14.1 Distribution of attitudes toward foreign entities by partisan
     affiliation   264

Acknowledgments

This book would not exist without the contributions and assistance of several people. First and foremost we thank all of our distinguished contributors, who have been generous and good-humored throughout this process. We have learned a lot from their work and hold them in high regard as colleagues and as valuable scholars. Thanks go to Christine Fair for encouraging the project and connecting us with Georgetown University Press. At Georgetown University Press, we thank the entire editorial team, particularly Don Jacobs, for supporting the project and shepherding it through the editorial and production process. We are also grateful for other colleagues who provided feedback, most notably Meredith Weiss at the University at Albany and Colin Cookman and Jumaina Siddiqui at the US Institute of Peace, as well as two anonymous reviewers, for their valuable comments. Big thanks also go to Johann Chacko and Alexis Blondin for their help with the concept and execution of the book cover design. We are also grateful to our respective institutions for their support during this project.

Sahar and Niloufer also thank Mariam for envisioning this project and approaching them with the idea back in 2015. Her persistence was pivotal to the completion of this book, which saw countless hours of editing, innumerable messages, hundreds of emails, and dozens of conference calls but also one wedding and the arrival of three babies. For supporting us as we pursued this passion project, we thank our families, and for inculcating in us a love for Pakistan, we thank our parents: Sameera and Anjum Mufti, Sarah and Hamid Shafqat, and Farzana and Tayyab Siddiqui.

Finally, and most importantly, we are grateful to all the party activists, organizers, and leaders who took precious time out of their busy schedules to grant us interviews, brought us along on the campaign trail, and allowed us to observe their interactions with constituents. Without their cooperation, generosity, and receptiveness, fine-grained field research like the kind presented in this book would not be possible.

Abbreviations

AAT	Allah-o-Akbar Tehreek
ANP	Awami National Party
APP	Azad Pakistan Party
ASWJ	Ahle Sunnat Wal Jamaat Party
AWP	Awami Workers Party
BAP	Balochistan Awami Party
BISP	Benazir Income Support Program
BLA	Baloch Liberation Army
BNP-A	Baloch National Party-Awami
BNP-M	Baloch National Party-Mengal
CENTO	Central Treaty Organization
CII	Council for Islamic Ideology
COAS	chief of army staff
CPEC	China-Pakistan Economic Corridor
CPI	Communist Party of India
CPP	Communist Party of Pakistan
DCO	district coordination officer
DMG	district management group
ECP	Election Commission of Pakistan
FSF	Federal Security Force
GDA	Grand Democratic Alliance
GHQ	Army General Headquarters
IJI	Islami Jamhoori Ittehad
IJT	Islami Jamiat-ul-Tuleba
IPE	Intra-Party Election
ISF	Insaf Students Federation
ISI	Inter-Services Intelligence
JI	Jamaat-e-Islami
JIT	joint investigation team

JUH	Jamiat Ulema-e-Hind
JUI	Jamiat Ulema-e-Islam
JUI-D	Jamiat Ulema-e-Islam-Darkhwasti
JUI-F	Jamiat Ulema-e-Islam-Fazlur Rehman
JUI-S	Jamiat Ulema-e-Islam-Sami-ul-Haq
JUP	Jamiat Ulema-e-Pakistan
JWP	Jamhoori Wattan Party
KNM	Khatm-e-Nabuwwat
KP	Khyber Pukhtunkhwa province
LeT	Lashkar-e Tayyaba
MKP	Mazdoor Kissan Party
MMA	Muttahida Majlis-e-Amal
MML	Milli Muslim League
MNA	member of National Assembly
MPA	member of Provincial Assembly
MQM	Muttahida Qaumi Movement
MQM-Haqiqi	Muttahida Qaumi Movement-Haqiqi
MQM-P	Muttahida Qaumi Movement-Pakistan
MRD	Movement for the Restoration of Democracy
NA	National Assembly
NAP	National Awami Party
NP	National Party
NRO	National Reconciliation Ordinance
NSC	National Security Council
NWFP	North-West Frontier Province
PAS	Pakistan Administrative Service
PAT	Pakistan Awami Tehreek
PCO	provisional constitution order
PIA	Pakistan International Airlines
PKMAP	Pukhtunkhwa Milli Awam Party
PML-F	Pakistan Muslim League-Functional
PML-N	Pakistan Muslim League-Nawaz
PML-Q	Pakistan Muslim League-Quaid
PNA	Pakistan National Alliance
PPP	Pakistan People's Party
PSP	Pak Sarzameen Party
PTI	Pakistan Tehreek-e-Insaf
SEATO	Southeast Treaty Organization
SMT	social movement theory
TLP	Tehreek-e-Labbaik Pakistan Party
TTP	Tehreek-e-Taliban-e-Pakistan
UC	union council
UML	United Muslim League

Introduction
Pakistan's Political Parties in an Era of Transition

Niloufer Siddiqui, Mariam Mufti, and Sahar Shafqat

Pakistan has long had a turbulent relationship with democracy. Since its independence in August 1947, the country has experienced four military coups, ratified three constitutions, experimented with both presidential and parliamentary forms of government, and held ten general elections. In addition to dismissing elected governments, the military has engaged in a range of "soft coup" behaviors, such as supporting new political actors, to make dents in the vote banks of existing parties, particularly those that have fallen out of favor.

General elections held in 2013 marked Pakistan's first transfer of power from one elected civilian government to another. In the sixty-six years of the country's independence, this was the first time a civilian government had completed a full five-year term in office. Prior to this watershed moment, popularly elected governments had been unceremoniously dismissed by the military, often with the support of opposition parties concerned with short-term gain. The 2018 elections marked yet another successful transfer of power and have led some to believe that the country is now firmly on a path toward democratic transition and consolidation.

However, long-term observers of Pakistan are celebrating this development in circumspect fashion. Indeed, even though two parliaments have now completed their full tenures in office, no prime minister has had the honor of doing so. The last prime minister, Nawaz Sharif of the Pakistan Muslim League-Nawaz (PML-N), was disqualified by the Supreme Court in June 2017 for misdeclaration of assets. This happened approximately a year before Sharif was set to complete his term and was the third time Sharif found himself sacked prematurely (he was previously dismissed in 1993 and 1999). The 2018 elections were also marred by allegations of pre-poll and post-poll rigging. Corruption and criminal cases against PML-N leaders and members, asymmetric application of the *sadiq aur ameen* (truthful and righteous) clause of the constitution, and apparent pressure by the military on party members to switch their allegiance to the Pakistan Tehreek-e-Insaf Party (PTI), as well as on the media to mute coverage of the PML-N, raised questions about the free and fair nature of the elections.[1] Similarly, the military's concerted campaign against the Karachi-based Muttahida Qaumi Movement (MQM) ensured that the electoral prospects of this once-dominant party were significantly curtailed.

Despite these hurdles—and in some ways *because* of them—the role of political parties in Pakistan is more significant than ever before. Until now, the central preoccupation of scholars has been to explain the country's lack of democracy by focusing on the undemocratic institution of the military, which has served to limit the range of options available to civilian actors. However, as we argue in this book, scholars and policymakers stand to gain far more from examining institutions that in the West have been integral to the process of democratization, namely political parties, elections, and legislatures. Indeed, E. E. Schattschneider (1942, 1) has famously argued, "Political parties created democracy and modern democracy is unthinkable save in terms of parties." Susan Stokes (1999, 245) has similarly written, "Political parties are endemic to democracy." Understanding the role of political parties in Pakistan is therefore essential to determining its prospects for future democracy.

Rather than being an indication that parties do not matter, the precarious and constantly shifting power balance between the military and political parties serves instead to highlight the importance of parties to Pakistani politics and society. If parties were unnecessary, activists would not bother to join them or sustain local party organizations during non-election years. Parties would not receive donations from supporters, nor routinely submit statements of party accounts to the election commission of Pakistan, nor issue party manifestos. Furthermore, the military establishment would not expend so much energy attempting to mold and control the parties' leaders or the parties' cadres. Political parties are not always alternative contenders for power; they have also acted as conduits through which successive military governments have ruled. Field Marshal Mohammed Ayub Khan (1958–68), Gen. Muhammad Zia-ul-Haq (1977–88), and Gen. Pervez Musharraf (1999–2008) all undertook a series of steps to co-opt political parties.

Political developments in Pakistan are taking place against a backdrop of continuing democratization around the world. As new democracies emerge, the role of political parties is being continuously redefined. In these contexts the parties do not follow the patterns that literature on Western Europe would predict. Using the experiences of parties in well-established democracies to elucidate the role of their counterparts in developing countries today represents "an effort to cram square pegs into round holes" (Gunther and Diamond 2003, 168). In established democracies, relatively fixed partisan identities have developed as a result of socioeconomic cleavages already existent in society (Lipset and Rokkan 1967) or along cleavages created by the parties themselves (Sartori 1969). In newer democracies, however, programmatic and ideological appeals are often rare and electoral volatility is high. Linkages are largely formed instead on the basis of material transactions or exchange or on the basis of ascriptive characteristics such as ethnicity or religion (Kitschelt and Wilkinson 2007).

In recent years, a burgeoning literature (Mainwaring and Scully 1995; Hicken and Kuhonta 2011; Lupu and Riedl 2013) has started to question the application of Western theories about party systems and political parties onto developing democratic contexts. In particular, Lupu and Riedl (2013) argue that three types of uncertainty—regime, institutional, and economic—shape the behavior of individual political parties and their interactions with one another, with voters, and with other societal institutions. In such settings, political parties are unable to accurately gauge the types of future interactions because the rules and players involved are subject to frequent change. Parties are thus forced to make decisions and policies accordingly. Despite this, a slew of research demonstrates that, even in these party-averse environments, parties and partisanship matter for a range of outcomes (Merolla, Stephenson, and Zechmeister 2008; Brader and Tucker 2012; Elischer 2013; Samuels and Zucco 2014).

This book contributes to this literature by examining the role of political parties in a particular context in which other institutions—such as the military—have an outsize role in governance. In these circumstances, political parties are forced to compromise, accommodate, and adjust their own strategies and internal workings in order to carve out a political space for themselves. And they have done so in a number of different ways in Pakistan. Parties have proved to be not only representatives of citizen interests in legislative assemblies but also important actors outside the legislative process, where they often function as pressure groups. Governing parties are also representatives of the state in the international system, making them critical given Pakistan's key global role. Studies have further shown that parties in Pakistan matter in a wide array of local outcomes that have historically been thought to be under the purview of the military, such as level of violence (Nellis and Siddiqui 2018; Mir and Moore 2017). Additionally, research has demonstrated that increased political competition can create incentives for elected legislators to respond to citizen needs, such as providing urban residents with access to services (Cheema, Khan Mohmand, and Liaqat 2017).

This edited volume seeks to illuminate three key research areas related to party politics in the country: what makes up the party system in Pakistan (form); what purpose the party system serves in this hybrid political context (function); and how the party system responds to a dominant military and multiple crises of legitimacy (survival). The book is divided accordingly into three sections: in the first we provide critical overviews of the main political parties in Pakistan, in the second we examine the role that political parties play in Pakistan's fractured political system, and in the third we explore the challenges that parties have faced from other state and nonstate actors and the manner in which they have responded to these challenges. In short, this book seeks to rescue Pakistani political parties from perceived irrelevance.

Existing Literature on Parties in Pakistan

Electoral politics were key to the very creation of Pakistan (Wilder 1999). Pakistan emerged as a state in part because of the 1946 elections in British India, in which the Muslim League was able to gain support through communal appeals to the Muslim population. Winning a large number of seats allowed it to gain the negotiating power necessary to begin the process of Partition. However, since then political instability has meant that the country has neither convincingly settled into a military dictatorship nor embraced democracy and instead finds itself in the "gray zone" of a hybrid regime (Carothers 2002, 9) manifesting various combinations of authoritarian and democratic practices (Mufti 2011; Adeney 2017).

The most commonly cited reason for Pakistan's uneven path to democracy is the complex interaction between the country's two dominant political forces: the military bureaucratic elite (also referred to by domestic observers as "the establishment") and the political elite. The former, citing the ineptitude of the latter, have claimed to be the defenders of Pakistan's territorial integrity, the guardians of Islam, and the protectors of citizens' interests. The political elite, comprising political parties and their leaders, has vied for political power instead by relying on the electoral process for elites' succession and the Parliament for influencing policy.

However, analyses of Pakistan have overwhelmingly focused on the former at the expense of the latter. Much of the literature on the political elite that does exist focuses on how parties have responded to major events in the political system rather than providing an in-depth look at the inner mechanisms of political parties (Sayeed 1968). Indeed, few attempts have been made to study the dynamics of political parties after military rule ended in 1988, with existing studies assessing only the results of general elections (Waseem 1994, 2006; Wilder 1999). The last comprehensive works to be written on Pakistan's political parties have been historical and descriptive accounts of individual parties, and those analyses end in 1977 (Aziz 1976; Afzal 1987, 1998). One notable exception is Andrew Wilder's (1999) *The Pakistani Voter,* which provides a comprehensive overview of voting determinants in Punjab province but ends its analysis at the 1993 elections. To our knowledge there is little work that analyzes the critical "decade of democracy" of the 1990s (see Nasr 1992 and Mufti 2015b for two notable exceptions), the

2002–8 period of military-backed party rule, or the post-2008 return to democracy. Further, while there have been books written about some of the country's major political parties, most notably the MQM (Verkaaik 2004; N. Khan 2010; Gayer 2014) and various religious ones (M. Ahmad 1993; Nasr 1994; Pirzada 2000; Ullah 2013), there are still large gaps in the literature on individual parties. For example, no English-language books exist about the PML-N, a striking omission given that this party has operated in government for a significant portion of the last twenty-five years. Only one book about the Pakistan People's Party (PPP) exists (Jones 2003), and it ends its account in the 1980s. Similarly, the only account of the Awami National Party (ANP) is a biography of its leader (Easwaran 1984).

Form: What Do Pakistan's Political Parties Look Like?

A party system is the "set of parties that interact in patterned ways" implying "continuity" in the way political parties interact with each other and the regulations and norms to which they abide (Mainwaring 1999, 24). The most commonly used variables to classify party systems are the number of political parties and the ideological distance between them (Sartori 1969). In 2018 there were 120 political parties registered with the Election Commission of Pakistan (ECP).[2] However, only 12 parties won at least one seat. Thus, while Pakistan is clearly a multiparty system, the number of effective parties (Laakso and Taagepera 1979) is lower than the number of registered parties might suggest.

Pakistan's electoral system has gone through many manifestations over the years since its independence. Elections have been held through an electoral college structure comprising members of local bodies; through nonparty means, only at the provincial level; and on the one person–one vote basis of today. It should not therefore be surprising that parties in Pakistan have sought to keep up with these changes, adjusting their tactics and policies in order to achieve the greatest electoral success. For example, nonparty local elections introduced under General Zia-ul-Haq disadvantaged the popular PPP by privileging local—and patronage—politics over national politics. Concerning this period, Wilder (1999, 133) writes that "representing personal and constituent interests became more important for legislators than representing national interests." A senior PPP leader admitted in an interview that the party has been forced to make a number of compromises since its founding, including relying on local elites and notables despite the party's ostensibly leftist ideology. "My choice is that if I don't take them along, they go to the army. Can I afford it?"[3]

Given these circumstances, how can we categorize political parties in Pakistan and across which cleavages and platforms? Parties in Pakistan are often informally grouped into three categories: mainstream, ethnic, and religious. Mainstream parties, most akin to Kirchheimer's (1966) catch-all party, appeal to voters across a number of different social and ethnic groups and across different regions. Ethnic parties appeal primarily to voters belonging to a specific ethnic group or in a geographically defined area, while Islamist or religious parties contest elections on the basis of support of *sharia* (Islamic law) and other markers of cultural conservatism.

These categories have proved to be instructional, as the remainder of this introduction demonstrates, but they should nonetheless be analyzed with caution as they undervalue many of the similarities across types of parties and obfuscate important differences within groups. For example, even mainstream parties in Pakistan tend to have geographically and sometimes ethnically defined support bases, and many ethnic parties have made efforts at expanding their support bases beyond their ethnic communities. Additionally, many prominent mainstream, ethnic, and Islamist parties have originated from social movements (similar to the experience of many Western parties; see Michels 1915). For example, the PPP emerged out of protest movements galvanized by the Left against Field Marshal Ayub Khan, while the MQM, which grew out of a student movement, drew enormous crowds of disgruntled Muhajirs in search of representation. The line between the electoral and legislative priorities of political parties and their "street politics" continues to remain blurred. For example, between 2013 and 2018 the PTI orchestrated large-scale protests against corruption and alleged electoral rigging at the same time as it formed the provincial government in Khyber Pakhtunkhwa. Similarly, Tehreek-e-Labbaik Pakistan (TLP) emerged in 2017 directly out of protests around the blasphemy law, and, despite contesting and winning seats in 2018, it continued its tactics rather than seeking to instill change solely through legislative politics.

In addition to similarities across categories, important differences exist within party types. Many mainstream parties differ along ideological lines. While parties in advanced industrialized countries are often distinguished from one another on the basis of ideology, in Pakistan and other developing nations it has long been assumed that the vast majority of voters are not ideologically motivated. (See Elischer 2013 on similar assumptions about political parties in African countries.) Rather, parties are thought to make appeals to voters primarily on the basis of local issues, such as assistance in solving problems related to *thana-katcheri* (police-courthouse) or the provision of goods and services such as electricity and jobs. Yet parties invest time and resources in identifying policy positions, in making explicit particular ideologies, and often in campaigning on these grounds.

How can we reconcile the pervasive patron-client relations that undergird the party system with this attempt at ideological differentiation? Waseem (2016, 67) argues in favor of the ideological distinction between parties, writing, "It is the expression, projection, and manipulation of profile and policy in a non-electoral context that brings out the internal and lasting dynamics of political parties." Parties in Pakistan are often colloquially grouped as being right-of-center or left-of-center, or as being pro-establishment (closely allied with the interests of the military-bureaucratic axis) or anti-establishment. Nellis and Siddiqui (2018) find that the secular or nonsecular nature of the parties to which members of the National Assembly (MNAs) belong determines the extent to which they crack down on Islamist or sectarian violence occurring in their constituency. These findings suggest that the ideological orientations of political parties *do* matter in Pakistan, at least among particular subgroups of the populace, but further work remains to be done in identifying the precise ways in which this importance is manifested and how it ranks alongside other party attributes.

Each chapter in the first section of this volume examines the major Pakistani political parties and focuses on the circumstances under which they came into being, their internal organizational structures, and their interactions with voters and other state and nonstate actors.

Mainstream Parties

From 1988 until approximately 2013, two political parties—the PPP and the PML-N—dominated political competition in Pakistan. More recently, the PTI, which received the largest number of votes in 2018, has proved to be a viable third-party option. Together, these parties can be thought of as the primary "mainstream" parties in Pakistan's political system, distinct from those parties that appeal primarily to one ethnic group or region or those that are avowedly Islamist in nature. All three of these parties have in common a weak organizational structure and an overreliance on local notables or elites in lieu of party workers.[4] While the PML-N and the PTI are considered right-of-center, particularly in comparison to the left-leaning PPP, this ideological positioning has not prevented electoral candidates and party members from switching across the three parties.

The PML-N inherited its legacy from the All India Muslim League, whose struggle led to the establishment of a separate homeland for Muslims in 1947. But, as Saeed Shafqat writes in chapter 1, rather than seeking to institutionalize a democratic party system with itself at the helm, the PML-N was initially vulnerable to factionalism and co-optation by the military. Indeed, the PML-N, led by former prime minister Mian Nawaz Sharif, is made up of politicians who began their careers during General Zia-ul-Haq's tenure. However, since General Musharraf's 1999 military coup, and notably again in 2018, the party has found itself on the receiving end of the military's interventions. Shafqat argues that the PML-N's formation and development over the years and the personal rise of Nawaz Sharif is a story of the changing dynamics of civil-military relations in Pakistan more broadly.

The PPP has much in common with the PML-N, even while it remains its erstwhile enemy. In chapter 2 Philip E. Jones explains how the party has been shaped by political events dominated by a powerful military-bureaucratic establishment. Jones describes the evolution of the PPP following the historic 1970 election, when it successfully campaigned to win a landslide victory on the populist mantra of *roti, kapra, aur makaan* (food, clothing, and shelter) and its heavy reliance on the Bhutto family and the land-owning elite to its current electoral decline. Jones argues that the PPP's decline is due to the personalistic leadership of the Bhutto family, which compromised its organizational ability in order to counter the challenges posed by the military establishment.

Although the PTI was founded in 1996 by cricketer-turned-politician Imran Khan, it did not register its presence in Pakistan's electoral politics until 2011. Khan is a controversial figure who attracts vitriol and adulation in equal measure. He has been referred to simultaneously as a rebel, a Taliban sympathizer, and a Jewish agent. In 2013 the PTI formed the government in Khyber Pakhtunkhwa province (KP) but continued its oppositional politics centered on accusations that the elections had been rigged and the governing PML-N was corrupt, before winning in the center in 2018. In chapter 3 Tabinda M. Khan examines whether the PTI truly marks a departure from the norm of patronage-driven and elite-run political parties or if it is a continuation of traditional Pakistani politics. As a former member of the PTI herself, Khan offers a unique perspective as both an insider and an outsider—a perspective that she acknowledges and engages with critically.

Ethnic/Regional Parties

An ethnic party has been defined as one that "derives its support overwhelmingly from an identifiable ethnic group (or clusters of ethnic groups) and serves the interests of that group" (Horowitz 1985, 291), as "a party that overtly represents itself as a champion of the cause of one particular ethnic category . . . and makes such a representation central to its strategy of mobilizing voters" (Chandra 2004, 3), and "as an organization authorized to compete in elections, the majority of whose leaders and members identify themselves as belonging to a nondominant ethnic group, and whose electoral platform includes among its central demands programs of an ethnic or cultural nature" (Van Cott 2005, 3). A party may be classified as an ethnic party at one point in time but may not always remain an ethnic party. Indeed, parties may make ethnic appeals in some locations but not in others.

According to these definitions, the MQM and the ANP are ethnic parties. They have been relevant both as coalition partners of mainstream parties and have held important roles in provincial governments. Even though their electoral fortunes have waxed and waned, they have largely preserved their electoral support bases, rooted in distinctive ethnic groups.

The MQM, a Karachi-based political party, has represented the interests of the Muhajir ethnic group since the early 1980s. The party's strong organizational structure has attracted the attention of many scholars (Verkaaik 2004; N. Khan 2010; Gayer 2014; N. Siddiqui 2017). Two features in particular made the MQM unique not only by Pakistani standards but by those of the developing world more broadly: the outsize role of Altaf Hussain, the party's London-based founder, and its city-wide organizational structure. In recent months—culminating in its disastrous showing in the 2018 elections—the party has faced significant challenges, with splinter groups forming and Hussain facing legal troubles in the United Kingdom. In chapter 4 Tahir Naqvi nests his contemporary analysis of the party within a historical overview of its cultural appeal for the Muhajir community. Naqvi argues that while the party may face organizational challenges in the near term, the demand for a Muhajir political formation will continue to exist in some form.

Little has been written about the Pashtun nationalist ANP in Pakistan, despite the party being an important actor in the politics of KP. In addition to representing Pashtun interests, the ANP is also essentially a leftist party that traces its origins to Bacha Khan's party, the Khudai Khidmatgar (Servants of God), in the 1930s. In chapter 5 on the party and the leftist movement more broadly, Anushay Malik examines the ANP as a secular, left-leaning organization that has not experienced consistent electoral success. She explains that the ANP has traditionally banked on its Pashtun voter base to win elections in Pakistan's First Past the Post system, both provincially and nationally. But tying their regional interests with leftist political ideals has made the ANP the target of state repression, which in turn has inhibited the party's organizational capacity to mobilize electoral support outside the Pashtun belt. Its ineffective governance of KP province from 2008 to 2013 further led to the party being sidelined by PTI's rise in subsequent elections.

A number of ethnic political parties also exist in Balochistan province. Among these are four Baloch parties—the Jamhoori Wattan Party (JWP), the National Party (NP), the Baloch National Party-Awami (BNP-A), and the Baloch National Party-Mengal (BNP-M)—as well as a Pashtun nationalist party, the Pukhtunkhwa Milli Awam Party (PKMAP). The Baloch parties have had a turbulent history of splits and mergers instigated by both tribal family politics among the Bugtis, Mengals, Bizenjos, and Marris and differences over how to negotiate with the central government. Although the parties have been united in their pursuit of Baloch nationalism, they have disagreed on the strategies used to achieve it. The JWP vociferously championed the goal of attaining control over natural resources but, unlike other parties, has not extended this claim to self-determination for the Baloch. After party leader Nawab Akbar Bugti's death, caused by a military operation in 2006, the party split into two factions, one led by Bugti's brother and the other by his grandson, with the latter leading an anti-government insurgency. In contrast, the NP—born out of a merger of the left-leaning Pakistan

National Party and the Balochistan National Movement—is self-styled as a "moderate, middle-of-the-road" political party (Waseem and Mufti 2012, 58) that aims to achieve provincial autonomy through the democratic process under the leadership of the Bizenjos. The BNP-M also traces its origins to the Balochistan National Movement. It was originally conceived as a party that would unify the disparate Baloch parties and uphold a progressive agenda against the domination of the *sardars* (tribal chiefs). It experienced short-lived electoral success in 1997 but also failed to achieve its stated goals due to the centralized leadership of Sardar Attaullah Mengal and his son, Sardar Akhtar Mengal. The Baloch Liberation Army (BLA), led by the Marri tribe, strives for Baloch self-determination at all costs and engages in violence against the Pakistani state. Finally, in keeping with the dizzying array of splits and mergers in Baloch politics, defectors from the PML-N and Pakistan Muslim League-Quaid (PML-Q)—closely aligned with the Center—formed the Balochistan Awami Party (BAP) in an effort to boost their election prospects. The BAP subsequently joined the PTI-led coalition government in 2018.

Islamist Parties

A number of Islamist parties, which range in their commitment to the democratic system and in their sectarian affiliations, have played a key, albeit supporting, role in Pakistan's political system. Scholars have argued that the power of Islamist parties primarily stems from their ability to bring people out onto the street to protest and lobby for specific policies (Butt 2016). This is no doubt true. Protests have helped advance Islamist agendas on issues central to Pakistan's national and religious identity as well as on matters related to foreign policy. For example, since 1953 protestors have demanded, and state authorities have largely acceded to, a steady erosion of Ahmadi rights, including adding a 1974 constitutional provision that Ahmadis are non-Muslim (S. Saeed 2007).

Notwithstanding their key lobbying role, however, Islamist parties have also played an important role in electoral politics. During the 2002–8 period under Musharraf, a coalition of religious parties that called themselves the Muttahida Majlis-e-Amal (MMA) was elected into power in KP (White 2008). The coalition consisted of six parties belonging to various subsects of Sunni Islam, including the two largest parties: Jamaat-e-Islami and Jamiat-e-Ulema Islam (Fazlur Rehman faction). After the 2013 elections, the PTI also formed a coalition with the Jamaat-e-Islami in KP, which involved giving the religious party control over three provincial ministries. The 2018 elections also saw a large number of electoral candidates fielded by two new religious contenders: the Tehreek-e-Labbaik Pakistan Party (TLP) and the Milli Muslim League (MML). Despite only officially forming in November 2017, the Barelvi TLP in particular surprised analysts and observers by receiving the fifth-highest vote total in the country.

Such sectarian parties affiliated with violent movements or those that incite hatred and intolerance are becoming increasingly important as electoral alternatives and as crucial allies of mainstream political parties (N. Siddiqui 2017). This troubling trend is indicative of two related phenomena. First, it suggests that the nature of the local elite is changing and weakly organized parties that once relied on the area's largest feudal landlord for gathering votes must now turn to this religious—and often violent—local power broker. Second, the nature of Islamist parties itself is evolving, away from mainstream religious parties that have ultimately chosen to abide by the democratic process to actors who serve to challenge it even while contesting elections. In chapter 6 Johann Chacko examines the range of parties that fall under the Islamic category, assessing both their role in government as coalition partners and their influence as outside pressure groups. Chacko asks us to pay particular attention to the larger networks of which these parties are part, arguing that their behavior is influenced by both electoral and nonelectoral considerations.

Function: What Roles Do Pakistan's Political Parties Serve?

What roles do political parties in Pakistan play within the political system? Do they aggregate and represent voter interests? If so, in what ways are they able to reflect the interests of voters belonging to different ethnic, sectarian, and class backgrounds? How do the internal organization of parties and their strategies for recruitment and selection of candidates affect their policies? Once elected, how do political parties function on the floor of the Parliament? What roles do parties play outside of the legislative process, particularly while in opposition?

These questions motivate the second section of this book and bring to the forefront three key relationships: between party representatives and their voters or constituents, between party leadership and a slew of party-related workers (including electoral candidates, local-level politicians, and party workers), and among different political parties themselves. Each chapter in this section unpacks one of these key relationships, as outlined below.

Party-Voter Linkages

The precise nature of the relationship between political parties and voters is a question of concern in many democratizing countries. In particular there is still insufficient evidence to explain what factors determine how and why voters vote the way they do. Because free and fair elections often have been interspersed with periods of military rule in hybrid regimes and developing democracies, explanations of voting behavior in the United States or

Western Europe do not travel well. Party labels are usually too new or inconsistently expressed in order to function as useful heuristics for voters, and their efficacy is sometimes limited through frequent party-switching or party fracturing.

Despite these challenges, however, work in various developing contexts finds that partisan cues remain influential (Merolla, Stephenson, and Zechmeister 2008; Brader and Tucker 2012), with partisanship affecting attitudes toward specific policy choices in Brazil (Samuels and Zucco 2014) and electoral decision-making in Uganda (Conroy-Krutz, Moehler, and Aguilar 2015). In Pakistan, too, survey work has demonstrated that partisanship does matter, particularly to specific subsets of the populace. For example, Siddiqui (2018) finds that partisan cueing of specific conspiracy theories affects whether citizens believe in them. Empirical work in the three most-populated provinces in the country (Punjab, Sindh, and KP) has shown that partisan affiliation remains one of the most important candidate attributes for voters, particularly in urban locales (N. Siddiqui 2017; Clary and Siddiqui 2017a).

In recent years, changing technologies and media landscapes have provided new opportunities to impact political mobilization in Pakistan—a fact to which political parties are slowly catching on. For example, Altaf Hussain made use of satellite TV to address large gatherings in Karachi throughout the 1990s and after. More recently, social media has played an influential role in helping generate and maintain partisan links. The PTI was an early mover on this front, when it turned to Twitter and Facebook in order to mobilize the coveted youth vote. In their study of the use of Twitter in the 2013 elections, Ahmed and Skoric (2014, 2242) found, for example, that the "PTI's Twitter usage was the most distinctive as it involved greater interaction with the public, more campaign updates and greater mobilization of citizens to vote." Learning from PTI's success, other parties sought to emulate these strategies in advance of the 2018 elections—strategies that were aided by the introduction of 3G and 4G mobile broadband internet in Pakistan. Some religious political parties, such as the TLP, have also turned to these platforms to spread their ideologies, including incitement to hatred and violence.

The manner in which partisan ties are generated, however, remains an open question. Early research on Pakistani voting behaviors downplayed the role of the individual voter. Alavi (1971) outlines three sets of structured relationships present in Punjabi villages that provide a framework for social and political interactions: traditional social institutions (like *biraderi,* or kinship ties), interpersonal relationships inherent to economic structure, and local government and administration (112). He explains, "Political parties . . . do not operate at the village level" (111) and are essentially "caucuses of influential persons" (120). Inayatullah (1963, 50) similarly writes that the voter in rural Punjab "is an inalienable part of multiple groups which completely overshadow his individuality" and "the family particularly, and the *biraderi* generally are the basic units which make political decisions."

A second wave of research on Pakistani—largely, Punjabi—voting dynamics argues instead that this early literature overemphasized the role of kinship and other social institutions and unfairly discounted the part played by the rational voter. No doubt this research was influenced by a changing and urbanizing Pakistan. Wilder (1999), for example, finds that a party's effectiveness in distributing patronage and maintaining clientelistic channels is a key factor in decision-making in rural areas and that party label and party leader identification are increasingly relevant to voting behavior, particularly in urban Punjab.

More recent research has served to further unpack the precise roles played by the relationship between economic dependence, kinship solidarity, and party label (Javid 2011; Khan Mohmand 2019). Some questions still remain, however. To what extent do policy and ideological positions matter to voters? How are linkages between parties and voters formed and maintained in the years between elections? What is the role of women as voters and constituents? The chapters in this section seek to fill many of these gaps.

In chapter 7 Asad Liaqat, Ali Cheema, and Shandana Khan Mohmand address outstanding questions related to the various forms that party-voter linkages take in Pakistan—particularly in urban areas, a largely ignored context—and examine particularly how parties liaise with constituents and voters outside of election time, including the manner in which voters contact party workers or local politicians to solve day-to-day problems. Their chapter provides a description of political machines in urban Punjab and develops a typology of linkages between citizens and local politicians. In doing so they provide valuable insights on how local politicians access information about voters and how the structures of machines allow for the transmission of citizen voice.

Within-Party Actors

Numerous actors make up the party system in Pakistan. First, parties often rely on brokers to mediate between themselves and their constituents. These brokers can be internal to the party or external to it and can take on numerous forms, in part depending on the rural or urban nature of the constituency. Brokers are particularly essential for parties that are engaged in clientelistic exchange, defined as "material benefits only on the condition that the recipient returns the favor with a vote or other forms of political support" (Stokes et al. 2013, 13).

Second, within each political party itself there are party leaders and party workers. Party workers can be divided into two categories; Mufti (2011, 16) refers to these as constituency politicians, on the one hand, and party loyalists on the other. Party loyalists normally attach themselves to a single political party and enter politics to serve "the interests of the political party they join." They must work hard to rise up in the ranks and must demonstrate their loyalty to the party leadership in order to be given a party ticket to contest elections. A constituency politician (also referred to as an electable) is an "autonomous, free-wheeling agent who needs a party only to augment his or her personal vote in a constituency to win an election" (230).

Either party loyalists or constituency politicians may contest elections, and the relative emphasis on each type of party worker is often indicative of the party's organizational strength. Well-organized parties with greater presence at the local level can rely less on constituency politicians to win elections on their behalf. Because a party's candidate constitutes the public face of the party in elections, relying on party loyalists limits principal–agent problems insofar as party loyalists are more likely to act in accordance with the leadership's commands (N. Siddiqui 2017). Not only do the selected candidates articulate and interpret the party's manifesto and past record of achievement, they also determine the reach of the political party on the ground. In a parliamentary political system like Pakistan's, successful candidates constitute the party in public office and form the pool of individuals from which important public offices are nominated.

Advancement in a candidate's political career often hinges on contesting elections on the "right" party ticket. For the party, winning a seat in Parliament depends on nominating a candidate who can augment the party's vote share among the constituency. Of course, candidates can choose not to join any party ticket, contesting as independents instead. The presence of independents raises questions about the relevance of political parties and party labels. Their role has waxed and waned over the years, across election cycles, and within types of elections (local vs. national). Using survey data from local elections in Sargodha district in Punjab, Liaqat et al. (2019) found that an independent candidate was able to contest in 84 percent of union council elections and that independents won 49 percent of the seats where at least one independent was contesting.[5] This was the first time that party-based local elections were held under a democratically elected government in Punjab. Yet opposition parties largely failed to field candidates, and independents emerged to fill the gap. The researchers concluded that the outsize role of independents "represents a corrosion of party-based accountability, weakens the relationship between local and national democracy, and reduces political ownership of the system among opposition parties."[6] Indeed, local politicians are critical insofar as they allow the needs of ordinary citizens to be represented to their governments. However, the authors also note that "the majority of candidates who ran as independents were jockeying vigorously for endorsement by the ruling party prior to the allocation of tickets," which suggests that party endorsement remains a coveted prize.

In chapter 8 Hassan Javid and Mariam Mufti ask how relevant the political party is to the political process. They find that parties that rely on electoral candidates with independent sources of power and personal resources are unable to elicit loyalty from them. This explains the rampant party-switching observed in Pakistan. While political parties use the promise of patronage, prestigious political appointments, and other inducements to retain their candidates, two out of every five candidates changed their party affiliation in the run-up to the 2013 election (Zhirnov and Mufti 2019). As an electoral strategy, this paid off for the PTI in 2018; the party won 43 percent of the seats in Punjab, of which nearly 70 percent were won by electables who had defected from other political parties.

What role do women play in political parties in Pakistan? Sarah Khan turns the lens to this important and oft-ignored group. Chapter 9 provides an overview of women's systematic marginalization from contemporary party politics in the country. It draws attention to women's exclusion from party leadership structures, parties' reluctance to award tickets to women on competitive seats, and women's underrepresentation in the lower party ranks of workers. The chapter focuses on four main channels of women's entry into electoral politics—parties, electoral institutions, families, and voters—and how the features of each channel perpetuate the exclusion of women. The chapter also considers the effectiveness of institutional solutions of mandating women's presence through a historical guarantee of reserved seats and party candidate quotas more recently. While these solutions do well at achieving numerical targets, they do little to change party incentives for greater inclusion beyond minimums.

Relations among Parties

What is the role of a political party once it is elected to government? How do parties make policy? Sameen Mohsin Ali's chapter 10 examines the governance role of political parties after they have won an election. In particular, it sheds light on the politicization of bureaucratic appointments by party leaders from the PML-Q, the PPP, and the PML-N to achieve their governance agenda: delegation, the pursuit of personal gain, and the pursuit of service delivery. Ali's chapter highlights an important consequence of weak political parties whose survival hinges on the politicization of bureaucratic appointments for the provision of targeted goods to voters.

How do political parties act when they are in opposition? Opposition parties have historically been accused of hindering democracy in Pakistan by engaging in adversarial politics instead of posing credible electoral alternatives. In chapter 11 Sahar Shafqat examines the strategies used by parties in opposition under both authoritarian and democratic settings. Opposition parties in Pakistan have often turned to extra-parliamentary tactics such as street agitation, sit-ins, and permanent campaigning outside of Parliament. Shafqat argues that such tactics are the result of incentives created by the uncertain environment in which parties find themselves, which provide strong motivation to undermine parliamentary processes. However, depending on the regime in which the opposition party is operating, these strategies may both undermine and reinforce the democratic process.

Survival: How Do Pakistan's Political Parties Interact with Other National and International Actors?

Political parties do not exist in a vacuum. They are compelled to interact with other state and nonstate institutions and contend with various societal dynamics. In a context such as Pakistan's, the role of these institutions often comes in conflict with those of political parties. Foreign policy and national security concerns play central roles in the Pakistani political imagination, particularly vis-à-vis India, and have been routinely invoked to justify large defense budgets and the military's encroachment into economic matters as well as the subordinate role of civilian institutions more generally (Fair 2014; Cohen 2004). This context raises a number of questions. First, what explains the resilience and the relatively unrestrained operation of political parties in the face of military-led regimes, which have historically repressed political parties, persecuted party leaders, and manipulated the electoral process? Second, how much space is afforded to political parties to act on policy while in government or in opposition? Finally, how do political parties operate at the international level?

In chapter 12 Ayesha Siddiqa addresses one of the central questions motivating this edited volume: What is the relationship between political parties in Pakistan and the military? How do parties accommodate this powerful institution? How—and when—do they challenge it? Political parties have alternatively given way to the military and chosen to take it on. In the tumultuous decade of the 1990s the military intervened numerous times to prevent the completion of any democratically elected government. The military is also thought to have played a key role in the protests led by the PTI against the PML-N after the 2013 elections and in tilting the playing field away from the PML-N in 2018.[7] Much evidence exists to suggest that the military has supported the entry of right-wing religious parties into the electoral scene over the years (Haqqani 2005). Siddiqa's chapter provides critical, historically grounded details regarding the relationship between the military and the PPP, the PML-N, the MQM, and religious parties. She argues that ultimately Pakistan's military chooses to retain its role as arbiter of politics rather than assuming the role of direct ruler.

The Pakistani courts have also played a critical role in negotiating the political space available to parties to operate and organize during periods of transition both to and from democracy. Yasser Kureshi addresses two questions about the judiciary in chapter 13. First, how has the Pakistani superior judiciary determined the rules of competition between Pakistan's political parties, negotiated the balance of power between the political parties and the military, and arbitrated critical political disputes that have shaped the trajectory of Pakistan's political parties? Second, what strategies have political parties used to shape the courts' appointment and decision-making processes in order to entrench an institutional bias and ensure favorable outcomes? Kureshi finds that while an independent judiciary can facilitate democratic transitions, it can also undermine democratic consolidation in its own pursuit of judicial supremacy.

Christopher Clary in chapter 14 studies the extent to which political parties have been able to impact foreign policy, which in Pakistan is usually considered as falling within the military's domain. He finds that even though parties include mention of foreign policy in their manifestos and have on occasion been able to pursue specific global policies, in large part their role in navigating foreign relations has been limited. Clary demonstrates that this is partly a result of voter preferences; he cites survey data which demonstrates that even though Pakistani voters have strong opinions about the country's relations with its erstwhile enemy, India, they rarely vote according to a candidate's foreign policy positions. This, coupled with imbalanced civil-military relations, has the effect of largely homogenizing party positions on most foreign policy issues in Pakistan. Nonetheless, some important variation remains, particularly regionally, with nationalist parties in Balochistan and even Sindh being quite vocal in their opposition to, for example, the China-Pakistan Economic Corridor.

The volume ends with a review of the key arguments presented in the chapters. Mohammad Waseem argues that the very survival of Pakistan's political parties in the face of supra-parliamentary forces is an important fact to consider, and it must be analyzed together with the role of the establishment or the military-bureaucracy nexus. While there is no "democracy without parties," Pakistan is, in essence, an establishmentarian democracy in which the establishment has defined the goals and means of the country's political parties. Yet the organizational and ideological orientations of political parties, as well as the nature of their linkages with both voters and candidates, are critical in their own right, determining both the functioning of democracy in Pakistan today and its prospects for sustained success in the future.

Methodological Diversity

Carrying out research in Pakistan comes with numerous challenges. To begin with, the country is considered data-scarce. While this categorization is being challenged with an increasing number of surveys being carried out in the country and the digitization of important records, scholars of Pakistan nonetheless face an uphill battle in collecting data to establish important empirical relationships. Second, not unlike other transitional democracies, many political processes are shrouded in secrecy, or at least lacking the level of transparency one might expect to find in established democracies.

Conducting research on candidate-selection—an important party prerogative prior to an election—or the dynamics of using violence as an electoral or party strategy, or on allegations of party corruption, are just a few examples of difficult research agendas that social scientists have attempted to study in Pakistan. Qualitative researchers must seek not only to establish trust with the various actors involved but also triangulate across a number of sources, all the while attempting to set aside their own normative views.

This book draws on multidisciplinary approaches and a number of different field-based research methodologies, including semistructured interviews, surveys, macro- and microlevel data, and ethnography. In particular, the researchers in this volume demonstrate that carrying out high-quality empirical work in a country in which data is not always easy to come by is indeed possible. The chapters highlight the various ways in which multimethod research can be utilized to address specific questions. By putting this collection of essays together, we hope to allay some of these methodological concerns and seek to show how comprehensive work on Pakistan can be achieved.

Conclusion: Charting the Path Forward

The world watches political developments in Pakistan attentively. Pakistan is a critical geostrategic flashpoint, in part because of its antagonistic relationship with India over the disputed territory of Kashmir but also because of its location—as a neighbor to Afghanistan, Iran, India, and China—which has made it an indispensable ally of the United States in the War on Terror. Furthermore, Pakistan's status as a nuclear power with an unstable government confronted by the rising tide of religious extremism has proved to be a matter of grave concern for scholars and policymakers alike.

This book is one step forward in learning more about the range of political actors involved in the governance of Pakistan. But while Pakistan is a "hard country" (Lieven 2011) that needs to be understood on its own terms, it is also important for what it can tell us about other hybrid regimes more broadly. Until very recently the study of hybrid regimes had been largely neglected and deemed difficult to examine. Because institutions in hybrid regimes tend to be ambiguous, they do not function or produce the outcomes one might expect of similar institutions in Western Europe, making neat and parsimonious comparative frameworks impossible. This book shows that studying the role of political parties in hybrid democracies, even data-scarce ones such as Pakistan, is not only possible but incredibly valuable.

Notes

1. See Ben Farmer, "Pakistan Election 2018: Imran Khan Declares Victory as Rivals Decry 'Rigging,'" *London Telegraph,* July 26, 2018; and Mehreen Zahra-Malik,

"Arrests and Intimidation Fuel Fears of 'Dirty' Election in Pakistan," *Guardian*, July 21, 2018.
2. There were 49 parties registered in 2008 and 216 registered in 2013 (Waseem 2016).
3. Niloufer Siddiqui interview of PPP leader, Islamabad, June 2015.
4. For more on the organizational structures of political parties across Pakistan, see Waseem and Mufti 2012.
5. Asad Liaqat, Michael Callen, Ali Cheema, Adnan Khan, Farooq Naseer, and Jacob N. Shapiro, "The Role of Election Competition in Strengthening Pakistan's Fledgling Local Democracy," *South Asia* (London School of Economics blog), accessed March 22, 2018, http://blogs.lse.ac.uk/southasia/2017/05/02/the-role-of-election-competition-in-strengthening-pakistans-fledgling-local-democracy/.
6. Liaqat et al., "Role of Election Competition."
7. Maria Golovnina and Mehreen Zahra-Malik, "Pakistan's Powerful Army Steps In to Resolve Political Crisis," Reuters, August 28, 2014.

Part I

The Form of Pakistan's Party System

1

The Formation, Development, and Decay of the Pakistan Muslim League-Nawaz

Saeed Shafqat

Since its independence in 1947 Pakistan has oscillated between military hegemonic and political party–led civilian governments. These oscillations have entrenched the military in the country's sociocultural life as well as its political and economic institutions. Nonetheless, the people of Pakistan continue to show a general preference for democracy, and political parties retain a popular support base (Shafqat 1998, 2002). Local and global conditions, such as the emergence of electronic media, the rise of social media, and a pro-democracy global environment, also favor a continuation of democracy and party governance. Yet political parties and their leadership—stymied by years of intervention by the military—have been unable to adequately build up the party system. Why has the party system remained fragile while military entrenchment has expanded? And why has the political leadership found it difficult to build consensus on sustaining democracy? This chapter will address these critical questions using the case of the Pakistan Muslim League-Nawaz (PML-N)—a party initially supported by the military but one that has found itself in recent years increasingly at odds with its previous benefactors.

Party development in Pakistan has been hampered by multiple key factors. Dynastic and oligarchic leadership styles have created parties that are often led by founding families, with succession passing on to the leader's wife, children, or siblings. Within each party there are also subsets of dynastic leaders and their extended families who maintain control over local-level electoral constituencies. As a result, the political party is invariably used as an instrument to acquire power, perpetuate personal rule, and extend patronage. Prolonged military rule and the resulting ordinances and acts have further restricted the activity and character of political parties, placing limits on their freedom of expression and association.[1] The evolution and development of party-building has also been shaped by the historical legacy of the Pakistan Movement (1937–47). Many political parties in the country originated from political movements and forms of social protest. This is not unlike parties in many other developing countries that evolved from nationalist movements against colonial rule. Indeed, both the Indian National Congress (1885) and the Muslim League (1906) emerged through this process. The formation of factions has also been influential in party development and continues to play a critical role in party politics in South Asia. Following Muhammad Ali Jinnah's death in 1948, factionalism crept into the Muslim League and still today hampers and shapes its evolution as a political party (Afzal 1986).

This chapter seeks to explain how, in the post-1971 period, the Muslim League went through a process of factionalism, splintering, and reunification to result in the eventual emergence of the PML-N, one of the country's most prominent political parties. The formation and development of the PML-N, as well as the associated rise of Nawaz Sharif as its leader, is a story of the changing dynamics of civil-military relations in Pakistan.

The chapter proceeds as follows. First, I begin with a description of the early days of the Muslim League and its various factions as each sought to carve out a political space for itself against a dominant Pakistan People's Party (PPP). Then I explain how the Muslim League was able to solidify control in Punjab province, in no small part due to the support of Muhammad Zia-ul-Haq's military regime. Next I turn to the manner in which Sharif established control over the party, carving out an autonomous space for himself and bringing him into conflict with his previous benefactors. I conclude with an analysis of the PML-N's most recent time in office (2013–18) and the sustained protests it faced from opposition parties, and I offer future scenarios for the party.

The Muslim League and the Pakistan People's Party: The 1970 National Elections

The fragility of party politics in Pakistan can be traced back to the predatory and preemptive tendencies that the country's military began to show in the early 1950s. The political leadership's inability to generate a consensus on the constitution and its generally poor governance at the time provided the military the pretext to dismantle the fledgling parliamentary system in 1958. The military hegemonic system produced a decade of political stability coupled with unequal economic growth. Gen. Mohammad Ayub Khan's actions during the 1958 military intervention had lasting effects on Pakistan's democratic development: they laid the foundations for a "superordinate-subordinate" relationship for the military with all other institutions in the country—namely, the bureaucracy, the judiciary, Parliament, financial-economic bodies, and religious institutions—and resulted in the creation and expansion of a new class of political elites: business elites, judicial elites, and even religious elites. A primary focus here is on the manner in which the military established a patron-client relationship with the political elite, thus perpetuating the superordinate-subordinate dynamic that remains ingrained in the minds and psyches of the political class today. While at times the political elite have rebelled against this relationship, they have ultimately been unable to liberate themselves from this traumatic birth shock experience.

Rising inequality under Ayub's regime led to a politics of protest, an erosion of political stability, and increasing demands for restoration of democracy (Ziring 1971; Shafqat 1998). Against this backdrop the 1970 national elections, along with the breakup of Pakistan in 1971, served as the catalyst for the development of the party system and a movement to curb the military's hegemony. The 1970 elections brought the PPP to power in the National Assembly, with 85 seats out of a total of 144. Meanwhile, the Muslim League gained a total of 18 seats divided among its three factions: the Muslim League (Qayyum), which had 9 seats; the Council Muslim League, with 7 seats; and the Convention Muslim League, 2 seats. Three religious parties— the Jamiat Ulema-e-Islam (JUI), the Jamiat Ulema-e-Pakistan (JUP), and the Jamaat-e-Islami (JI)—together held 18 seats.

The constellation of social forces and political groupings that constituted the various Muslim League factions in 1970 had four visible tendencies. First, the parties were effectively just groupings of those who supported a strong center: landed elites, urban professionals (including lawyers), and businesses. Second, the parties were motivated by a desire to acquire and stay in power. Third, they sought to align themselves with the religious right. Fourth, they unabashedly sought patronage and collaboration with the military. These four features allowed the Muslim League to remain a potential "king's party," that is, a party whose leadership or segments of it could be enticed by the military to play second fiddle in sharing power.

In pursuit of these goals, in the North-West Frontier Province (today, Khyber Pakhtunkhwa province, or KP) the Muslim League (Qayyum) supported the JUI coalition government, while at the center Khan Abdul Qayyum Khan joined the PPP government as federal minister of interior. In March 1972 Mumtaz Daultana, head of the Council Muslim League, accepted the position of ambassador to the United Kingdom, thus causing a further split within the party. However, these inter–Muslim League realignments, along with the reform of the civil services and land ownership regulations, as well as the prospects of the PPP formulating a new constitution, caused alarm among the political parties and prompted the three Muslim Leagues to unite; in October 1972 they merged into one party named the United Muslim League (UML). Pir Sahib Pagaro became the chairman and Malik Qasim Khan was named general secretary of the newly formed UML. It is pertinent to note here that the Muslim League (Qayyum) remained a part of the PPP government from 1972 to 1977, even though it also officially joined the UML (Ponomarev 1986).

The PPP's emergence as a populist movement and the leadership of Zulifkar Ali Bhutto laid the foundations of party-led civilian rule in Pakistan. Though the military and religious, business, and trader-merchant groups all grudgingly accepted the ascendency of the PPP, they were also quick to devise ways to resist its control (Shafqat 1997, 79–114). Meanwhile, the PPP's path of adopting an independent foreign policy approach while also pursuing reformist policies, using socialist rhetoric, and attempting to establish a dominant party system rather than encouraging multiparty accommodation at the domestic level, proved injurious for democratic consolidation. The PPP made a foreign policy choice to move away from alignment toward nonalignment with the United States. Bhutto was quick to disassociate Pakistan from CENTO (Central Treaty Organization) and SEATO (Southeast Asian Treaty Organization) pacts, to improve relations with the Soviet Union, and to seek peace with India—all threatening moves for the military. The muffling of the press and the judiciary by Bhutto's regime and the regime's efforts to establish a dominant party system alienated the opposition political parties further (see chapter 2 in this volume for more on Bhutto and the PPP). This made it difficult to establish practices of parliamentary politics, and the opposition parties resorted to extra-constitutional means, including calling for street protests and agitations. In January 1977, as Bhutto announced the holding of elections, the opposition declared the formation of the Pakistan National Alliance (PNA), a coalition of nine political parties (Richter 1979). The PNA was a conglomeration of conservative social groups and religious political parties. From the outset the PNA questioned the legitimacy of the electoral process. It demanded the removal of the PPP government, arguing that fair elections could not be held under its administration, and called for the enforcement of *Nizam-e-Mustafa* (sharia law and Islamization). Following the 1977 elections, which the PPP overwhelmingly won, the PNA refused to accept the results and asserted that the elections had been rigged. It launched a movement against the government, seeking to create disorder through protest and to encourage and invite the military to dislodge the government. Bhutto, instead of urgently treating this as a political issue and seeking resolution through consultation and engagement, treated it instead as a law-and-order problem (see Jones 2003 for an authoritative account of this period).

The adversarial relations among political parties, the parties' inability to develop a consensus on the nature and direction of the party system, and opposition parties' attempts to dislodge the dominant party system that Bhutto ventured to establish together provided the pretext for the military to intervene and remove the civilian regime. In July 1977 the PPP regime was dislodged by the military under Zia-ul-Haq (Shafqat 1997, 189–92). The new military regime was quick to champion the idea of Pakistan as an "ideological state" (embracing the PNA's demand for enforcing Nizam-e-Mustafa) and open up avenues of participation for religious groups in the political process. In subsequent years these factors became crucial in shaping the electoral process, party politics, and, in particular, the development of the PML-N.

These internal convulsions were further augmented by two external developments: the Soviet intervention in Afghanistan (1979) and the Khomeini revolution in Iran (1979). Both had a deep impact on Pakistan as the military regime gained greater legitimacy and space to maneuver within civilian politics. The military energized Islamic groups, contributing to a rise in religious militancy. The American decision to wage a "holy war" against the "Soviet infidels" gave rise to a wave of religiosity across the region (see Rubin 1995 for more on this time period). Within a span of less than a year Pakistan transformed from potentially being a progressive, civilian-dominant party regime into a military hegemonic and militant Islamic state (Shafqat 1997). Religion acquired new meaning in the policy arena and led to the making of political Islam, with extremism, militancy, and radicalism emerging as its various facets (Shafqat 2002).

Democracy Restored and Dislodged: Instituting the Muslim League in Punjab (1985–88)

The 1980s were a period of global economic transition during which many developed economies deconstructed the welfare states they had so assiduously built after the Second World War and, in their place, pursued open–market approaches to economic growth, including privatization, deregulation, and decentralization. The military regime in Pakistan embraced privatization and deregulation that did consequently lead to economic growth (Burki 1992). However, the regime's political repression and intolerance for dissent, for freedom of the press, and for political association ignited the Movement for the Restoration of Democracy (MRD). The MRD was formed in 1980 but didn't gain momentum until 1983–85, when protests spread across the nation with demands for the removal of martial law, restoration of the 1973 Constitution, revival of political parties, and the holding of elections.

In 1985 Zia-ul-Haq conceded to nonparty elections on the condition that all acts, ordinances, and orders passed by him as chief martial law administrator would not be challenged or altered in any court of law. On March 2, 1985, when he introduced the Revival of Constitution Order, 67 out of 280 articles of the 1973 Constitution were amended or drastically altered. Two articles were inserted into the constitution that had important consequences for Pakistan's politics: Article 41 Section 7 ensured that someone could simultaneously hold the offices of president and chief of Army Staff, and Article 58 Section 2b empowered the president to dissolve the National Assembly if, in his or her opinion, "a situation has arisen in which the Government of the Federation cannot be carried on in accordance with the provisions of the constitution and an appeal to the electorate is necessary." These insertions were accepted and passed by the Parliament and are referred to as the 8th Amendment. Although the elections were held on a nonparty basis, once the Parliament met, the Muslim League chose, with the blessing of the military regime, Muhammad Khan Junejo, a disciple of Pir Pagaro, as its new leader in Parliament.[2] Junejo was then elected as prime minister of Pakistan.

An astute politician from Sindh, Junejo conveyed an impression of docility and being amicable enough to share power with the military. For the Muslim League it was a momentous occasion as it both led to the party's revival and allowed the party to claim that it had contributed to the restoration of democracy in the country. However, it soon became clear that the military under Zia had intended to merely share power and not transfer power to the elected civilian government. As Junejo began to assert his influence on policy matters pertaining to domestic and foreign issues, the military became alarmed and disconcerted. Its expectation was that the prime minister would not challenge the military's role in governance or policymaking. When Junejo removed some cabinet ministers perceived to be Zia's lackeys and changed the chief of the Intelligence Bureau, alarm bells rang. Additionally, in 1986, to the further discomfort of the military, the civilian regime allowed the return of Benazir Bhutto to Pakistan from self-imposed exile. In March 1988 Junejo called the All Parties Conference on Afghanistan, and in April 1988 Zain Noorani, minister of state foreign affairs, signed the Geneva Peace Accord, which sought formal settlement of the situation in Afghanistan. Zia disapproved of both of these acts, believing they were done in haste by the civilian government and that America had betrayed both Pakistan and Zia during the Afghanistan peace process. This deepened the distrust and hostility between the civilian and military leadership, and on May 28, 1988, Zia dislodged the very Muslim League government he had installed using the presidential powers established under the 8th Amendment. However, the military showed enormous political craftsmanship by dissolving the assemblies while choosing to retain Nawaz Sharif as the chief minister of Punjab (Shafqat 1997, 213–19). This decision eventually gave birth to the PML-N.

Nawaz Sharif as the Face of the Muslim League in Punjab

Under General Zia (1977–88) the military embarked on a three-pronged strategy to regulate domestic politics (see chapter 12 for more on the role of the military in the country's politics). First, it provided patronage to the political leaders and political parties that were willing to accept military hegemony and confronted any who opposed it. This tactic was initiated under General Ayub Khan and has been used by subsequent military regimes. Second, through political and social processes it institutionalized and legitimized the role of Islam as state religion. The PNA movement and its ideological rhetoric of the enforcement of sharia served as important tools to drum up support for Islamization. Third, it wrestled control of Punjab away from the PPP by undermining its support base through coercion, patronage, and, most important, by propping up a new and alternative leadership. The military's privatization and deregulation policies further galvanized business groups, making the rise of the middle class noticeable. These considerations led to careful selection of Nawaz Sharif as a fresh voice and leader of Punjab. Under Zia the military exercised and pursued a deliberate policy of providing patronage to any politicians who would help it maintain its hegemony. Hussain (2007, 25) describes the role of the military in Sharif's political genesis: "His political career owed much to his father's close links with General Ghulam Jilani. The former ISI chief, who was appointed by Zia as governor of Pakistan's most powerful Punjab province as a reward for his role in the 1977 coup, groomed Sharif as the alternative leader to Benazir."

Nawaz Sharif, a novice in politics, had been inducted as finance minister in the Punjab cabinet in 1984, seemingly appearing from nowhere. His careful grooming and image-building indicated that the tradition of propping up a feudal (landed) leader was undergoing a transformation and the emerging business groups and trader-merchant classes were being prepared for socioeconomic change. This laid the foundation for Sharif, the scion of a Lahore-based Kashmiri business family, to become political leader of Punjab.

Sharif echoed the skepticism and doubt that General Zia had regarding Junejo. After Zia's death in 1988 Sharif vigorously opposed Junejo's ability to take on Benazir Bhutto in elections. When Fida Mohammad Khan took control of half of the split PML, Sharif became secretary general, and this faction was recognized as "the legacy of Zia-ul-Haq" (S. Aziz 2009, 92). Because Sharif was also the chief minister of Punjab, a position demanding political grit and tenacity, he was able to acquire effective control over Punjab's bureaucracy. Under his leadership the PML-N transitioned into a political party that was determined to stay in power by developing loyalties and personal affiliations and to be guided by the military rather than through a restoration of democracy, representative government, or a certain programmatic agenda.

Following Zia's death the military was swift in preparing itself for transition to democracy and allowing political parties to participate in elections while still seeking to steer the election process. Chairman of the Senate Ghulam Ishaq Khan, a seasoned and military-trusted bureaucrat, was chosen as president. Gen. Mirza Aslam Beg became the chief of Army Staff, while Punjab remained under the grip of Sharif. Yet the military was averse to having completely free elections that could give unfettered power to the PPP, which was widely expected to sweep the national elections. Therefore—and now it is public knowledge—the Inter-Services Intelligence (ISI) helped create the Islami Jamhoori Ittehad (IJI), a coalition of political parties including the PML-N, rightist political parties, and religious groups, as the countervailing force to the PPP (Jaffrelot 2015, 241–42). Even though the PPP acquired power initially (from December 1988 to August 1990), the coalition proved to be a successful strategy and ultimately paid dividends. Punjab, a bastion of the PPP in the 1970s, was wrested away from the party, and the IJI, led by the PML-N, became the opposition ground for the incoming PPP government. Partly through its own incompetence, partly through the military's meddling, and partly through the confrontational politics of the PML-N, the PPP was booted out and fresh elections were called in 1990 that brought the PML-N to power.

The Rise of the PML-N and Nawaz Sharif

As noted earlier, the making of Nawaz Sharif and the rise of the PML-N were well-crafted strategies that began in the 1980s and allowed Sharif and his family to build a strong support base and business empire in Punjab. Yet it also merits attention that once he entered national politics in the post-1988 phase, Sharif began to show signs of autonomy and self-confidence and devoted his time to reaching out to like-minded politicians within Punjab and across the country. These alliances were driven by anti-Bhutto sentiment, which allowed Sharif to win over political leaders who were antagonistic toward the PPP. At the same time, Sharif was skillful in recruiting party loyalists and mustering the support of business houses, trader merchants, corporate lawyers, media houses, journalists, and a segment of land-owning elites.[3] However, the greatest strength of the PML-N under Nawaz Sharif and subsequently his brother, Shahbaz Sharif, has been its nuanced control over the bureaucracy (see chapter 10 for more on parties and the bureaucracy).

During his first tenure as prime minister (1990–93), Nawaz Sharif's focus was on policies of deregulation, of opening up the economy, and facilitating private investment. In this pursuit Sartaj Aziz, a competent economist and seasoned international bureaucrat who had personal connections with Pres. Ghulam Ishaq Khan, ably assisted Sharif and played the role of messenger between Khan and Sharif. However, as Sharif sought greater autonomy from his benefactors, including the president, tension increased between Aziz and Khan, weakening the former's mediating role (S. Aziz 2009, 132–37).

As a businessman Sharif's father had learned that without a cooperative bureaucracy, conducting business in Pakistan is cumbersome. Bureaucratic red tape and excessive public control can deny financial resources and access to foreign exchange. Therefore, taming the bureaucracy through concessions such as favorable postings and transfers and building loyalty by rewarding those who comply are necessary tactics for garnering support. The early 1990s saw an emphasis on infrastructure development to complement deregulation and foreign investment (119–23)—a policy that resurfaced each time Sharif took office. The Pakistani economy did flourish as a result. Nontraditional exports grew, as did investments in the manufacturing sector, while needed infrastructural developments in areas such as telecommunications, electricity, ports and shipping, and roads complemented the industrialization policies (121). In terms of macroeconomic results, gross investment increased by 70 percent during the period 1990–93, while gross domestic savings increased by 1.7 percent between 1988 and 1993. Additionally, exports grew by 14 percent annually during these three years. Yet these positive changes came along with serious challenges in terms of fiscal deficit and rising inflation. The Pressler Amendment, which imposed sanctions on Pakistan due to its nuclear program, also added an unexpected strain to public resources, and US foreign assistance declined as a result (126–27).[4]

Despite heading the IJI coalition government, Sharif showed a "go-it-alone" attitude by largely ignoring his coalition partners and pursuing megaprojects and bypassing normal bureaucratic institutional processes. This attitude, combined with hasty privatization and ineptitude in sustaining political coalitions, led opposition political parties, the military, and Khan, the sitting president, to believe that Sharif was being pushy and assertive while lacking sufficient political support. This brought to surface the divergence of political styles and economic management between the president and the prime minister. Sharif desired unfettered privatization and quick approval, but Khan demanded that all projects be approved through the appropriate institutions and bodies. Sharif also had a penchant for megaprojects and believed in their political influence, while Khan gave preference to fiscal stability. Finally, differences in approach led to Khan's expectation that the prime minister's office should heed the president's advice, something for which Sharif had no patience (130–31). Khan was also offended by Sharif's decision not to support his reelection and his recommendation that other cabinet members do the same. A series of failed attempts to reconcile the two culminated in Khan demanding certain steps be taken on national and international matters, about which Sharif was asked to report back.[5] This was something Sharif would not agree to, especially given that earlier (in February 1993) he had announced his aim of repealing Article 58 Section 2b of the constitution in order to curb the president's ability to dissolve the National Assembly. Without any substantial consultation or consensus-building with opposition political parties, on April 17, 1993, Sharif declared in a speech to the National Assembly that he would not be dictated to; it was a defining moment for Sharif and marked his emergence as a defiant, determined, and confrontational leader who was conscious of his popular appeal. On April 19 Khan dissolved the National Assembly and dismissed Sharif. A caretaker government took over.

This tussle acquired overtones of personal animosity when Sharif's supporters took the case to the Supreme Court. The Supreme Court was quick to declare the president's decision unwarranted and unconstitutional, and it restored the prime minister. However, the win was short-lived and Sharif eventually had to resign, owing to the hostility he received from the provincial governments. Overambition and a lack of political acumen led Sharif to dissolve the provincial assembly, hoping to replace it with the governor of his choice, Mian Azhar (138). To avoid any further political chaos the military intervened and asked both Sharif and Khan to step down, giving way once again to a caretaker government (Jaffrelot 2004, 248–50).

Moeenuiddin Qureshi, a technocrat from the World Bank, was installed as the caretaker prime minister, and elections were held in October 1993. The PPP won the elections and Benazir Bhutto formed the government. However, in Punjab province Sharif remained a potent force and the PML-N was able to establish itself as a party with a reasonably large national base. Sharif emerged as a popular leader and secured a significant number of seats both in the National and Punjab assemblies (Jaffrelot 2015, 145–46). By retaining control of Punjab and by confronting the Bhutto government at the national level, Sharif made a successful transition from provincial to national leader. By 1993 he had liberated himself from the shackles of the IJI and expanded the PML-N's network across the country. In 1996, when the president once again used Article 58 Section 2b to dismiss the second Bhutto government under charges of corruption and mismanagement, Sharif was eager to contest elections and retake the government at the national level.

The PML-N and the Musharraf Regime

The 1997 elections were won by the PML-N with an overwhelming majority (137 seats). Sharif was elected prime minister for a second time, with a vote of confidence given by 177 members in a house of 207. In addition to forming the government at the center, the PML-N was also able to form governments in all four provinces. In the National Assembly the PPP won only 18 seats and the Muttahida Qaumi Movement took only 12 seats; thus, the parliamentary opposition was marginalized to such a degree that in Sharif's view it did not deserve any consultation. The electoral outcome transformed Sharif: the exuberance, self-confidence, and popularity manifested through this "heavy mandate" appeared to go to his head. He once again embarked on a go-it-alone policy. Showing little signs of learning from his first experience as prime minister, Sharif persisted with mega-infrastructure projects (for instance, the M1 motorway), he flouted rule-based economic and political decision-making, and he showed little interest in or respect for consultation with opposition parties or even coalition partners in the smaller provinces. Sartaj Aziz (2009, 161) has aptly remarked, "This crushing weight of a mandate and exhilaration of popular support created an overwhelming instability which led to a series of actions and reactions culminating in the calamity of October 1999, the effects of which will be with us for a long time."

Five actions and reactions led to this "calamity of October 1999" wherein Sharif was ousted by Gen. Pervez Musharraf in a bloodless coup d'etat. First, emboldened by his heavy mandate, Sharif moved stridently to take away the powers of the president under Article 58 Section 2b. Sharif showed considerable political skill when he managed to receive formal approval from both the National Assembly and the Senate to pass the 13th Amendment, which stripped from the president the power to dissolve the Parliament. Pres. Farooq Leghari, who had earlier dismissed the Bhutto government and expected to be taken into confidence, was dismayed and alienated by this action.

Second, having successfully built a loyalist group of bureaucrats in Punjab, Sharif ventured to apply similar tactics to tame the superior judiciary. But the gamble triggered a crisis when the government and the opposition could not agree on the process for the appointment of the chief justice of Pakistan (see chapter 13 for more on the relationship between parties and the judiciary). The prime minister then chose to dismiss Chief Justice Sajjad Ali Shah and replaced him with Justice Saeed-uz-Zaman Siddiqui. Sharif's supporters stormed the Supreme Court in December 1997 and created an ugly situation whereby the dismissed chief justice wrote letters to the president and the army chief requesting intervention, eventually leading to the suspension of the 13th Amendment and reempowering the president to dissolve the Parliament.[6] However, in December 1997 Sharif surprised his cabinet colleagues and the nation by somehow getting Rafiq Tarar, a family loyalist, elected president of Pakistan.

Third, having tamed the bureaucracy and judiciary and successfully installed a loyalist in the presidency, Sharif began to contemplate taking on the military. In May 1998, as India conducted successful nuclear tests and emerged as a nuclear power, the Pakistan military put pressure on the PML-N leadership and opposition parties to act in concert and respond. Pakistan subsequently conducted its own nuclear tests in late May 1998. This further emboldened Sharif. Gen. Jehangir Karamat, who held the dual appointment of chairman Joint Chief of Staff and chief of Army Staff (COAS), was widely reputed to be a professional soldier and demonstrated an apolitical attitude. He was appointed in 1995 by then–prime minister Benazir Bhutto. Karamat, while addressing the officers of the Naval War College in Lahore in October 1998, remarked that given the law-and-order situation in the country and the challenges of regional strategic environment, the Defense Cabinet Committee should be replaced by the National Security Council (NSC) and comprised of "civil and military experts" (Shafqat 2009, 298; S. Aziz 2009, 200–202). The prime minister took the position that the army chief was undermining the civilian government and asked for Karamat's resignation. The army chief complied and resigned in October 1998; in his place Gen. Pervez Musharraf was appointed as the new army chief. Both within the armed forces and at the popular level, this decision was not well received (Jaffrelot 2015) as it conveyed that Sharif had overpowered the military.

Fourth, without building sufficient consensus among the political parties or consulting with the military, Sharif made efforts to improve relations with India. In early 1999 he invited India's prime minister, Atal Bihari Vajpayee, to visit Pakistan. Religious political parties subsequently launched street protests while the other major political parties watched from the sidelines and the disconcerted military believed that India was secretly involved in the Kargil operations (Shafqat 2009). Finally, the divergence of approaches on relations with India, with the Taliban, and with the United States further aggravated civil-military relations and ruptured the trust between the two.

In early October 1999, while the COAS was on a visit to Sri Lanka, Sharif, showing little respect and understanding about the organization and culture of the military, tried to dismiss him and install the ISI chief in his place. The corps commanders banded together and supported Musharraf to dislodge Sharif and the Parliament.

In short, having won the heavy mandate, the PML-N neither facilitated the strengthening of the party system nor pursued politics of accommodation to build consensus among the political parties. This led to adversarial relations between the military and the PML-N and ultimately further discredited and weakened the party system. More important, it undermined the legitimacy of the electoral process, disrupted the development of democratic norms and values, halted and reversed Pakistan's transition to democracy, and reestablished the military's hegemonic system. Zahid Hussain (2007, 31) has perceptively observed, "Sharif had a total disregard for institutions—he neither understood nor respected nor learnt to live with the institutions of a modern state and followed a patrimonial style of government."

Return of the "Pink Panther": The PML-N's Resounding Victory

In 2013 Sharif won his third term in office. Earlier, in 2008, the PPP had come to power through elections, marking the end of the Musharraf era (1999–2007). The PPP's rule (2008–13) was characterized by misgovernance and rampant corruption, frequent electric power losses, uncontrolled unemployment, and a security crisis. The 2013 elections were historic given that they marked Pakistan's first-ever democratic transition since gaining independence in 1947. The PML-N won 165 out of 342 seats, giving it a decisive win in the National Assembly and a majority in Punjab. A high voter turnout (55–60 percent), despite an environment of threat created by the presence of the Pakistani Taliban, was seen as an important indicator of public trust in the electoral process (Shah and Arif 2015). Analysts from across the world commented on Sharif's political tenacity and perseverance, saying he had "established himself as the most successful politician in Pakistan's history."[7]

Although Nawaz Sharif was ousted by the military in a coup in 1999 because of a reputation he had developed for being corrupt and power hungry, the PML-N bounced back, owing greatly to the fact that the PML-N under Shahbaz Sharif had remained in power in Punjab (2008–13); many hoped this would allow Nawaz Sharif to deliver on his promise of reviving the economy.[8] Large-scale and flashy infrastructure projects, coupled with the Sharifs' "conservative values and Punjabi identity," further allowed the party to win votes in the province.[9] More important, Sharif was also able to engage and captivate small business owners and the religious middle-income public in a province that makes up a substantial majority of the country's population.[10]

Upon assuming the role of prime minister, Sharif faced two main challenges that tested his political acumen in a rapidly changing world order. On the external front, managing relations with Afghanistan, India, and the United States was inherited as a top priority (see chapter 14 for more on parties and foreign policy). Internally, handling a military that was both deeply entrenched in the economic and strategic domains of policymaking and suspicious of Sharif's intents remained crucial. Under the previous PPP government (2008–13), a nuanced and precarious balance had existed in civil-military relations. The military guardedly broached the PML-N victory and Sharif's rise, while Sharif was skeptical about the military's designs, given his previous experience. In other words, suspicion of the "other" was mutual.

Sharif was equally inept in managing relations with opposition political parties. During his third time in office he continued to pay little attention to engaging with the opposition or routinizing parliamentary practices. He remained obsessed with personalized decision-making and personal loyalty. Sartaj Aziz (2009, 111) again provides incisive insight on Sharif by reminding us that invariably his motive was "to strengthen his personal power base rather than strengthen the institutions that are the main pillars of a viable democratic process." In August 2014 simultaneous mass protests broke out, led by Imran Khan, the leader of Pakistan Tehreek-e-Insaf (PTI), and cleric-politician Tahir-ul-Qadri. Hundreds of thousands of protestors held sit-ins in Islamabad and had many anticipating a military intervention (see chapter 11 for more on these protests). The PTI claimed the 2013 elections were rigged by the PML-N, while Tahir-ul-Qadri campaigned for constitutional reforms—and both demanded that Nawaz Sharif resign.[11] The army was called in briefly to provide added security but otherwise remained silent in what was perceived by some as a novel incidence of respect for civilian leadership and support for democracy. Whether the intelligence agencies were really in direct conversation with these protesters, as many have alleged, is another debate. Sharif survived the political crisis, even if only temporarily, owing to the split in public opinion that emerged. Some believed that it was premature to demand his resignation and that the number of protestors was too small to bring about transformative change.[12] Opposition parties such as the PPP and the Awami National Party (ANP) also showed restraint in backing Imran Khan and Tahir-ul-Qadri, warning against reaching a point where the armed forces would have to come in (Shah and Arif 2015). Others felt Sharif's resignation was fundamental in promoting democratic values such as accountability and free and fair elections. Ridding the country of a corrupt leader would help in maturing institutions of governance and in keeping even the highest ranks of leadership in check. Despite the sit-ins not being able to achieve their ultimate goal (Sharif's resignation), they nonetheless were able to dent Sharif's administration. The government was compelled to call the military to restore law and order. Zahid Hussain aptly observed at the time, "The government . . . called in the army, which is proof of its failure. This is what PTI and Qadri wanted."[13] This incident thus marked the beginning of what was to be the most testing period of Sharif's political career. The first tile of this domino effect had been toppled and Sharif's premiership was now headed into even darker terrain, with his party experiencing political volatility like never before.

The Panama Papers: The Beginning of the End

The PML-N's political crisis escalated on April 4, 2016, when the Panama Papers leak revealed that Nawaz Sharif and his family members were included in a list of world leaders and high-profile industrialists who had links to offshore companies. The revelation that eight such companies were held by his three children led to widespread controversy over their use for money laundering and/or tax evasion. By November of the same year, under great pressure from the opposition and catalyzed by fervent campaigns by Imran Khan, the Supreme Court set up a judicial commission to examine the charges. A split-decision resulted, with two of the five judges from the apex court recommending Sharif's disqualification. By April 2017, however, the Supreme Court had introduced a six-member joint investigation team (JIT) to inquire further into the matter. Two members of the team were associated with Pakistan's intelligence agencies, indicating for some the military's evident supervision of the entire matter.[14]

Weeks of judicial questioning by the Supreme Court followed; Sharif's children maintained their innocence and the PML-N argued that the JIT was purposefully "sensationalizing" the case.[15] On June 15 Sharif became the first prime minister to be interrogated by a judicial committee while in office. Claiming that the investigation was unfair and demanded accountability from an unrealistic timeline, Sharif responded: "The process of my accountability stretches from before my birth and extends to my future generations. Has any other family in the country faced such ruthless accountability?"[16]

When Sharif's daughter, Maryam Nawaz, was summoned to court for questioning five days before the JIT's final report was submitted, her statement to the press left many feeling as if she were next in line to take on the PML-N's leadership. She upheld her father's commitment to democracy and argued that he was the only politician who had been brave enough to fight for the civilian government's power. This statement came among various headlines noting the Pakistani military was once again emerging from the imbroglio as *the* undeterred institution of power, only changing its mode of influence from carrying out a direct military coup to a soft coup or judicial coup.[17]

Regardless of the PML-N's perseverance in fighting back, the reality is that much of Nawaz Sharif's political hold had loosened by this time. The media was quick to reject his ability to bounce back and began debates on who was likely to take over in this "game of thrones in Pakistan's dynastic politics."[18] The allegations of corruption, which Sharif had intermittently been facing since the 1980s, seemed like a slight hiccup that he would easily be able to manage again. Yet his third stint in power was riddled with both external pressures and internal turmoil, the latter snowballing into his final decline. On July 28, 2017, the Supreme Court disqualified Sharif from political office for life and on February 21, 2018, it ruled that he could no longer be the head of a political party. Despite this, Sharif continued his campaign of criticizing the Supreme Court judgment and insinuating that unconstitutional forms of governance had spearheaded his removal. These efforts were ultimately lost when on July 10, 2018, Sharif and his daughter were sentenced to ten years in jail on corruption charges.

The Future of the PML-N

As Pakistan approached the July 2018 general elections, the PML-N's dwindling power became apparent. Legal cases of corruption and misgovernance, defections from the party, and dynastic power struggles for control over the party between the two Sharif brothers dominated the weeks leading to election day. As discussed earlier, the PML-N underestimated the popular appeal of Imran Khan and the support base of the PTI. It projected their campaign against corruption and their protests against the government as being prompted by the military. A segment of the media and policy analysts reinforced these claims. The PML-N's confrontational posture against the military proved to be ill-timed and imprudent, costing the party severely.

The greatest failure of Nawaz Sharif was his lack of interest in building parliamentary consensus with opposition and coalition parties in order to establish the supremacy of the Parliament and party system as the alternative to military hegemony. His prolonged absence from Parliament reinforced his image as a "sultanic" leader who was undemocratic and remote, which further estranged his supporters. The PML-N's electioneering was that of a wounded lion: rancorous, incensed, and adversarial toward the military. The election results clearly show that these factors, in addition to Imran Khan's popularity, affected the PML-N's strength. The PTI, with 158 seats in the National Assembly (house of 270), emerged as the largest party, and the PML-N was trounced, securing only 82 seats (a loss of more than 50 percent as compared to the 2013 elections). In the Punjab Assembly, which has traditionally been the foundation of the PML-N's support base, the party won 164 seats, while the PTI won 179 seats.

If denied power in Punjab, what is the future of the PML-N? Embattled and bruised, will the party sustain itself until the next elections in 2023? There are at least five possible scenarios to consider. First, the party could decay and further factionalize. Nawaz Sharif has lost his personal repute and the moral authority to hold the party together, while his brother, Shahbaz, and daughter, Maryam, have roused little confidence. However, despite his absence, the party has managed to maintain some form of unity. This is partly because many defections from the party had occurred before the elections and partly because, after the formation of government, the PTI made little effort to win over PML-N party dissidents. Equally important, the prospect of corruption charges being pursued by the National Accountability Bureau has created comradery among key party leaders. At this point the intelligence agencies have shown little interest in causing disruption within the PML-N.

A second possible scenario would be determined as a result of the courts' decision in March 2018 to give relief to Sharif for six weeks, based on his ill health. The relief led to considerable speculation in the media that Sharif was seeking a deal with the military to move abroad. In such an eventuality, the PML-N would undoubtedly fragment and would seal the fate of Sharif as the leader of the party.

A third possible scenario for the future of the PML-N is largely based on the performance of the PTI. In its first year in government the PTI has failed to show a sense of direction or clarity of purpose in pursuing its agenda and development of goals. Failure to perform by the PTI government could potentially embolden the military to replace the democratic administration with a technocratic government. Given the 18th Amendment, which has considerably empowered the provincial governments and eliminated the president's power to dismiss the parliaments, this nonetheless remains a remote possibility.

Fourth, if Sharif is able to learn from his previous experiences and show a sense of purpose and political acumen in winning the confidence of opposition parties—abandoning his go-it-alone attitude—the PML-N could reemerge as a resilient democratic force. This could rejuvenate the party system and consolidate democracy in Pakistan. This is possible if he is acquitted from the various criminal cases against him or moves abroad and shows courage and determination to maintain control over the party.

Finally, economic and social discontent caused by incoherent policies and poor performance under the PTI government could spark mass protests in the urban centers. This could either reshape the democratic process in the country or deepen political chaos that develops into a sensitive law-and-order situation, ultimately prompting military intervention. Indeed, while Pakistan does have a credible record of pro-democracy protests and mass movements, not all these movements have been successful and some have instead resulted in regime change. The 1967–69 student movement developed into a mass movement vigorously led by Zulfikar Ali Bhutto; it did eventually bring about substantive structural reform (accompanied by the breakup of Pakistan). A second significant movement was the 1977 Pakistan National Alliance (PNA) Movement, which triggered military intervention and led to the overthrow of a civilian government that was showing signs of authoritarianism. A third movement, the Movement for the Restoration of Democracy (MRD), was a popular pro-democracy movement that the military regime of General Zia skillfully restricted to parts of Sindh and Balochistan, at least initially. The movement reached its peak in 1984 and eventually forced Zia to concede by holding general elections in 1985 on a nonparty basis. In 2007 the Lawyers' Movement forced President Musharraf to resign and restored the chief justice. Most of these mass movements originated in the urban centers and remained an urban phenomenon; Lahore, Karachi, and Rawalpindi were the core cities and the nucleus of the movements.

In the launch, sustenance, and success of a mass movement, leadership, timing, and the presence of a core area/city all play a critical role. The PML-N's reputation is badly bruised because of corruption cases and allegations, and it therefore seems to have little ability to lead a mass movement. The case of the PPP under Asif Zardari is no different. Thus the chance of any mass movement led by a Nawaz-Zardari coalition remains limited, although both are capable of manipulating popular discontent or a situation of economic crisis. At this point any prospect of a younger generation of nondynastic leaders being able to assume PML-N party leadership and accelerating protests and mass movement appear slim. If that happens, however, Pakistan could see the rise of a plausible pro-democracy movement.

Despite the restoration and continuation of democratic changeovers since 2008, and given these possible scenarios, the future of the PML-N specifically and the party system and parliamentary democracy more broadly remain perilous in Pakistan.

Notes

1. See Political Parties Order 2002 Chief Executive's Order No. 18, June 28, 2002.
2. Although elections were held on a nonparty basis, once the Parliament became functional, the Muslim League was quickly revived with the military's blessings.
3. For a sympathetic view of Nawaz Sharif as an opposition leader and an effective chief minister, see Qureshi (1995, 29–35).
4. The Pressler Amendment passed by the US Congress in 1985 bans most economic and military assistance to Pakistan unless the president certifies that Pakistan does not possess nuclear weapons.
5. Sartaj Aziz provides considerable detail on how the diverging styles and goals of the president and prime minister sowed the seeds of parting of ways.
6. For a detailed personal account on the judicial crisis, see Aziz (2009, 172–81).
7. Owen Bennett-Jones, "Pakistan Election: Why Voters Backed Nawaz Sharif," *BBC News,* May 13, 2013.
8. Bennet-Jones, "Pakistan Election."
9. Bennet-Jones, "Pakistan Election."
10. According to the 2017 census of Pakistan, Punjab has a population of 110 million, out of a total of 207 million in Pakistan.
11. Tim Craig and Shaiq Hussain, "Protestors March toward Pakistan's Parliament in Sign of Deepening Crisis," *Washington Post,* August 19, 2014.
12. Craig and Hussain, "Protestors."
13. Craig and Hussain, "Protestors."
14. Raza Rumi, "Opinion: A 'Judicial Coup' against Pakistani PM Sharif," Deutsche Welle, July 28, 2017.
15. Raza Rumi, "A Timeline of the Panamagate JIT's 60-Day Investigation," *Dawn,* May 17, 2017.
16. Rumi, "Timeline."
17. Rumi, "Opinion: A 'Judicial Coup.'"
18. Raza Rumi, "A Game of Thrones in Pakistan's Dynastic Politics," *The News,* July 31, 2017.

2

Pakistan People's Party
From Populism to Patronage

Philip E. Jones

In the forty-three years between 1970 and 2013 the Pakistan People's Party (PPP) went from being a national party that was able to form the national government after the secession of Bangladesh, to a regional political party dominant only in Sindh (Karachi and Hyderabad excepted) and locked out of Balochistan and almost completely from Punjab and Khyber Pakhtunkhwa (KP, previously the North-West Frontier Province). The decline of the PPP, one of Pakistan's most secular and progressive political parties, has many causes, including both missteps by party leaders and the party's inability to counter the powerful social and political forces arrayed against it. This chapter examines the PPP's decline and suggests some implications for the future of Pakistan. At the same time, this study of the PPP can shed light on the role of political parties in Pakistan more broadly. It is, after all, the primary objective of political parties to achieve political power, to govern, to make policy, to rule, to control, and to preserve the state, whether in the interests of socioeconomic groups or coalitions of these, or oligarchies, or dictators, or demagogues, or in the service of some universal ideology or religion. "'Parties,'" as Max Weber noted, "live in a house of 'power,' . . . their leaders normally deal with the conquest of a community" (Gerth and Mills 1947, 194). In modern political systems, among all the institutions that function within a government or have an outside interest in the policies a government implements, only political parties have as their singular aim the capacity to rule the state.

With this in mind, the most interesting question to ask is, How close have political parties in Pakistan come to actual unimpeded control of the national government? The recent record shows that democratic processes such as elections have not normally determined who controls the state and that political parties that win elections serve, at best and on good behavior, as junior partners to a more powerful military-bureaucratic establishment. However, in two circumstances a political party can be said to have governed the country. The first occurred immediately after independence, when the Muslim League founded Pakistan and brought the state into existence; the second came after the catastrophic loss of East Pakistan, when the PPP held uncontested governing authority for half a decade. Nonetheless, apart from these exceptions, in one form or another the military-bureaucratic establishment has provided political guardianship to the state, whether overtly in military takeovers or behind the scenes in removing parties from government.

This chapter contains a review of the evolution of the PPP as a case study in how parties in Pakistan have been shaped by a political system dominated by a powerful, authoritarian military-bureaucratic establishment that sees uncontrolled democratic institutions as a threat to Pakistan's survival as a national security state. The decline of the PPP, from a governing power to a "has-been," was the result in part from mistakes made by its founding chairman, Zulfikar Ali Bhutto, but also as a result of the determination of the establishment, then under Gen. Muhammad Zia ul-Haq, to crush the political charisma of the Bhutto family. The military-administrative establishment has been the consistent winner in the underlying struggle to determine who will control the state, in part because it too is a rising force in the political system, shaping its tools and honing its capabilities to manage the political parties, engineer elections, shape the media, and control any other manifestations of a free democratic order.

Background: Political Parties and the Administrative State

The dominance of the military-bureaucratic state was established at the advent of the Pakistani state. The situations faced by each of the two successor states of the British Indian Empire were very different. In India, a well-organized, well-led, and massively popular Congress Party took over a pre-existing state, its capital, its governmental institutions, and its armed forces. Under Prime Minister Jawaharlal Nehru the Congress Party reformed the powerful Indian Civil Service, established the principle that elected governments would rule, and set the country on the path of parliamentary democracy. By comparison, in Pakistan there was no state to take over and it had to be created from the assets at hand: the highly regarded Punjab Civil Service (minus its large Hindu cadre), bureaucrats from Sindh and the North-West Frontier Province, and a smattering of senior officials with experience in the Indian civil and political services and the various ministries of the vice-regal system. Mohammed Ali Jinnah knew the Muslim League could not carry the new state by itself. It had succeeded as a political movement but, lacking a party-type organization, was still a loosely structured body linking together disparate groups from around India that were united by the appeal of Pakistan but with varying regional cultures, languages, economic interests, ambitions, and political capabilities. For Jinnah, who faced the cataclysm of Partition and the absence of central institutions, the first requisite was law and order, without which the new state could not be built. He knew the institutional levers of power resided in the Government of India Act of 1935. Hence, he took over as governor general. We do not know what kind of constitution Jinnah would have promoted, for he died almost within a year of Pakistan's founding. Nonetheless, by retaining the imperial framework Pakistan was, from the very beginning, a direct descendant of the vice-regal state (see Braibanti 1966; Goodnow 1964; Habib 1973).

The circumstances of independence and Partition also ensured that the military had to develop a guardianship role in Pakistan's political arena and control its strategic, military, and foreign policy objectives. Within weeks of gaining independence, Pakistan was at war in Kashmir. This illuminated the larger strategic issue for the national leadership and the Pakistan military. Given its far greater size, manpower, resources, and fundamental hostility to Pakistan, India was considered a permanent existential threat to the new nation, and the Pakistan Army was the instrument that could ensure the survival of the state. This perception of reality was hammered into an unchanging strategic doctrine that has profoundly shaped the history and political institutions of the country. In order to survive Pakistan needed both a secure source of modern weapons and a protecting power, needs that were soon met by its growing alliance with the United States. Internally, as a garrison state the military needed to ally with the superior administrative services in order to command resources for war, ensure control over a large share of the national budget, pursue administrative centralization, and press for rapid economic development. The generals understood mission-oriented organization, rational and coherent decision-making, and meritocracy. They did not like the kinds of political factionalism, parochialism, social and religious movements, corruption, or separatist provincial politics emerging in either the central or the provincial League governments. These they considered threats to the existence of the state.

The military-bureaucratic establishment tackled these issues via the military takeover of October 8, 1958. Gen. Mohammad Ayub Khan (later president and field marshal) ruled Pakistan until March 26, 1969. During that period Ayub Khan forged a military-administrative alliance, attempted a wholesale reordering of Pakistan's governance, and pushed economic development as the highest priority. Apart from the latter initiative, much of Ayub's makeover failed. Certainly his attempt to depoliticize governance by imposing a retrogressive constitution, a presidential system based on indirect elections by 80,000 Basic Democrats, and the control of political parties did not succeed (Ziring 1971). However, the Ayub regime did succeed grandly in economic development. The regime made a major commitment to modernization, particularly in agriculture, but left industrial development to the private sector. The results were impressive. Overall, Pakistan's GDP, which had grown by only 2.7 percent between 1949 and 1959, jumped to 6.6 percent between 1959 and 1965 and 7.2 percent between 1965 and 1970 (Burki 1988, 44). Industrial production jumped by 160 percent from 1960 to 1968 (44). These were the dream years for development technocrats and economists: it was all scientific, planned, algorithmic, refereed, geared to verifiable results, and unencumbered by the inchoate, emotional, amoral world of politics and political parties.

The Emergence of Zulfikar Ali Bhutto

Zulfikar Ali Bhutto was a mere thirty years old when he ascended to the national stage by joining the first cabinet of Ayub Khan. Within five years he became well-known at home and abroad, in the corridors of power, and in diplomatic salons from Islamabad to New York, London, Moscow, even Beijing. The scion of a major landed clan in Sindh, Bhutto was wealthy, well-educated (Berkeley and Oxford), articulate, somewhat arrogant in the feudal way, always dapper, and politically ambitious (Wolpert 1993, 3–5). Bhutto held a number of portfolios before achieving his stated goal of taking over the Foreign Ministry in December 1963. Clearly of a younger post-Partition generation, Bhutto stood out in the pro-American Ayub government for his assertion that postcolonial states had yet to achieve sovereign equality in a world where great powers—read the United States—pursued neocolonial, interventionist, even punitive policies that robbed new states of the capacity to serve their own people (Z. A. Bhutto 1969). Bhutto was a strong nationalist and proponent of Kashmiri self-determination. He worked to advance relations with Beijing, declaring "unconditional friendship" with China, which gave him a China connection that he later used politically.

Bhutto stayed in the first four of Ayub's five cabinets until he broke with his mentor over the results of the Indo-Pakistani War of 1965, specifically the Tashkent Declaration of 1966 that ended it. This war over Kashmir lasted from September 6 until a ceasefire, facilitated by the United Nations, took hold on September 23. Mediated by the Soviet Union at Tashkent in early January 1966, the war was settled by restoration of the *status quo ante bellum* as set down in the Tashkent Declaration. Although Ayub and the generals knew they lacked the means to continue fighting and needed to negotiate, Bhutto argued Pakistan could continue fighting by accepting proffered Chinese military aid and adopting unconventional warfare methods (Jones 2003, 83). He opposed the Tashkent Declaration, and later, when he was out of the government and in opposition, on numerous occasions hinted that shameful and invidious concessions to India had been made at Tashkent, although he never made an explicit claim or gave details. As a result of his opposition to

Tashkent, Bhutto became a potential threat to Ayub and was dropped from the cabinet in February 1966.

Bhutto: Founding the Pakistan People's Party

Bhutto came out of the Indo–Pakistani War of 1965 a hero to a generation of Pakistani youth. They had been electrified by his speeches at the United Nations during the Security Council's deliberations on the war. They thought Bhutto was the true champion of Pakistan and that President Ayub had knuckled under to superpower pressure. Everywhere he went Bhutto was mobbed by crowds of students, journalists, lawyers, various professionals, and even some civil servants. And everywhere Bhutto highlighted his opposition to the highly sensitive, already politicized Tashkent Declaration. Because he believed they had been fed a propaganda line that Pakistan had won the war and because the war itself had aroused intense nationalism across the country, the declaration shocked Pakistan's populace, who began to demand an explanation for the failure to consolidate the gains claimed by Islamabad (Jones 2003).

Bhutto adroitly used the political consequences of the 1965 war to found his own independent political career. The Pakistan People's Party was established at Lahore on December 1, 1967. The main organizer of the founding event and author of the party's foundation documents, including the party's detailed organizational structure, was J. A. Rahim, a former Indian Civil Service officer, retired ambassador, and avowed Marxist with connections to British leftist circles. Not surprisingly, the foundation documents reflected Rahim's socialist views. These views were not alien to Bhutto, who had contacts in the same British left-labor and university circles. His identification with the postcolonial left in the developing world and his expressed pro-China sympathies put him in the international progressive tradition.

Having spent nine years as a cabinet minister in the Ayub regime, however, it is doubtful that Bhutto could have suddenly emerged as a hard-left ideologue bent on building a highly structured political party. In essence Bhutto was a nationalist who saw himself as the ideal successor to Mohammad Jinnah, the *Quaid-i-Azam* (great leader). It made sense to Bhutto that his student supporters and party followers started calling him the *Quaid-i-Awam* (leader of the people). His ultimate objective was to lead and to gain power. He wanted to exploit his rising popularity, the vulnerability of the Ayub regime, and his emerging stature as the main leader of opposition. In founding the PPP his aim was less to establish a political party than it was a political movement powered by a left-populist program: *roti, kapra, aur makan* (bread, clothing, and house) for all. He aimed to follow Jinnah's electoral strategy and pull together a diverse coalition of social groups that could win elections. For this he needed freedom to act and negotiate without the niggling demands of a controlling party organization. In the end tactical realities and practical necessities were more important than organization or ideology. Like Jinnah, he wanted to stand above the rest. As a common observation at the time put it, "Bhutto is the People's Party; the People's Party is Bhutto" (Jones 2003, 148).

The Fall of Ayub Khan and the 1970 Elections

The mass movement to end the regime of Ayub Khan began on November 7, 1968, and lasted for 138 days until March 25, 1969, when Ayub Khan stepped down and handed over power to Gen. Agha Muhammad Yahya Khan, commander in chief of the Pakistan Army. One of the longest-running popular uprisings in recent South Asian history, it was a country-wide, largely urban movement that brought into the political arena people and groups from all levels of society, especially in Karachi, Punjab, and East Pakistan. Before it was over, an estimated 250 people lay dead, some 1,000 were badly injured, and thousands were incarcerated (though no accurate numbers exist).

The People's Party movement, where it was most intense, as in Punjab, was the breakthrough of the common man into the political arena and signaled a new age of participatory politics in Pakistan (Jones 2003). The strictures imposed on normal politics by Ayub's system could not contain the pressures building up in Pakistani society. The political parties and groups pushed out of the political arena by Ayub in 1958, combined with many new special interest organizations spawned by the previous decade of development, gave the movement unstoppable force and momentum. The movement turned violent in March when workers shut down or burned factories, disrupted railways, and torched government buildings. More police were sent in and additional protesters died. Eventually police morale broke down and the army was called out in Lahore and elsewhere. This was the beginning of the end, because the army does not like to shoot its own citizens. With reports coming in from IV Corps Command in Lahore that soldiers were putting down their weapons, it was clear to the military top brass that Ayub had to go and with him the apotheosis of the administrative state (see chapter 12 for more on the military and its history in Pakistan).

The new chief martial law administrator, Yahya Khan, accepted Bhutto's demand for national and provincial elections based on universal adult suffrage. Held on December 7, 1970, the elections were the first such elections in the country's history and may well have been the freest and fairest, since every subsequent election has, to a greater or lesser degree, been affected by regime pressure tactics. The energy of the PPP's grassroots movement against Ayub poured into the election campaign. Prominent individuals and important organized interest groups (including engineers, teachers, government staff unions, and labor unions) declared support for the PPP, setting off a bandwagon effect. Literally thousands of self-organized local groups sprang up all over Karachi and Punjab, called themselves local party units, and then bid for recognition from one of the provincial or city factions. Most of these were common people and newcomers to politics, but in Sindh many powerful landed notables were organizing PPP units, recruiting their tenants and old vote banks, and contacting Bhutto for ready acceptance into the party organization. Bhutto, with his iconic Mao cap, was a charismatic speaker who aimed his message at the urban poor, the rural tenant farmworker displaced by mechanization, the man at the bottom of society, the *rickshaw wala*, the brickmaker, the *rehri wala* pushing his handcart and selling vegetables or trinkets by the road, the mechanic, the household servant. To these Bhutto gave a sense of humanity and dignity—and they repaid with their loyalty in 1970 and still constitute an essential part of the PPP vote bank.

The election was an unexpected but astounding success for the PPP, which won 62 of 82 National Assembly seats from Punjab and 18 of 27 in Sindh. Most of the latter were rural Sindh seats. In Karachi, independents and religious parties won most of the seats. The PPP win in Punjab's cities and towns was particularly strong, but it also won in the canal colonies and many of the small-to-middling peasant constituencies in the rain-dependent eastern subregion. This election in Punjab, like that of 1946, was a victory of party over traditional parochial loyalties that resulted from the arrival of participatory politics in the mass movement against the Ayub Khan regime (Jones 2003, 312). Parochial identities played a role in later elections, but the qualitative relationship between ruler and the ruled changed in 1970. No longer could the big landlord, the clan leader, or the urban trade union chief count on the automatic support of his vote bank. Now he had to listen to voters' demands and produce real results.

If the military-bureaucratic oligarchy was surprised by the PPP victory, it was more shocked by the Awami League sweep in East Pakistan. That election, together with the long-developing crisis between the two wings as well as the Yahya Khan regime's decision to crush the Awami League's evident move toward secession, propelled the country into a disastrous civil war and the emergence of independent Bangladesh. This larger topic would take us far afield from the current discussion, but suffice it to say the main result in the West was to hoist the PPP into power. Given his long cabinet-level government experience and the fact that the PPP held 82 of 136 seats in the National Assembly of what remained of Pakistan, no other individual besides Bhutto had the credibility to take over.

Bhutto in Power

Future historians may disagree that Bhutto's greatest service was to preserve the remaining half of Pakistan as a viable state, to rebuild the people's morale, and to give the country a new direction. With the fall of Ayub Khan and the humiliation of the surrender in Dhaka, the military-bureaucratic oligarchy was in retreat, leaving the field open to Bhutto and the PPP. From 1972 to 1977 Bhutto was the sovereign governing authority in Pakistan, based on his party's electoral victory and the East Pakistan catastrophe. He negotiated at Simla a better deal than Indian prime minister Indira Gandhi and got military and civilian POWs returned. He fired many of the most senior officers of the army but otherwise protected the military by not releasing the *Hamadoor Rehman Commission Report* on the army's failure in East Pakistan and made no move for radical reform there—although he wanted to find institutional ways to keep the generals away from politics.

Domestically Bhutto pushed through a new constitution, reestablishing a parliamentary system that has lasted to this day, despite some back-and-forth amendment politics. He persuaded the crowned heads and presidents of Muslim states to come to Lahore for an Islamic summit, which gave him cover to free Mujibur Rahman, the arrested leader of the Awami League, and send him back to Dhaka. He initiated Pakistan's nuclear weapons, missile, and space programs, exited the US-backed Central Treaty Organization, and forged stronger ties with China. Bhutto did not forget his party constituencies: despite bureaucratic foot-dragging and some circumventing, he distributed land among landless farmers, invested in schools and health facilities in urban slums and remote villages, initiated housing and infrastructure schemes, and funded institutions of research and learning. Inevitably, politics and bureaucratic inefficiencies plagued some of these initiatives. The almost wholesale nationalization of industry did not work well and created a bitter enemy for Bhutto among the industrialist, commercial, and business classes. Wealth poured out of Pakistan to be invested elsewhere, while foreign investment declined. Overall economic growth under the PPP government slid to a third of what it had been under Ayub. In the year before the 1977 election annual GDP growth had sunk to 0.83 percent (Burki 1988, 44, 177).

Despite its success in the 1970 elections, the PPP did not fare well after Bhutto's assumption of power. Lacking adequate organizational structure, it was a weak reed on which to lean once the party came to power. Needing the competence of the bureaucracy, Bhutto reopened the door to the return of the administrative establishment, an arena he understood intimately. Once in power, the chairman largely ignored the question of party organization. Indeed, the assumption of power marked the decline of the PPP as an organization. Bhutto took an authoritarian and at times angry approach to both party and governmental matters. One by one, most of the old guard departed: driven out, humiliated, and some, like co-chairman Rahim, beaten up. As many of the original leaders were pushed out of the PPP, the big landlords began to come in: the Legharis and Khosas of Dera Ghazi Khan; the Pirachas, Tiwanas, Bandials, and Qureshis of Sargodha; various members of the Bukhari Sayyid lineages (Pir Mahal, Kuranga, and Shah Jiwana); the Daultanas, Khakwanis, Gilanis, and Qureshis of Multan; the Kharrals of Faisalabad; the Pirs of Makhad, Manki Sharif, and Taunsa Sharif; the Tammans and Jodhra Rajputs of Attock; and others. In addition, a number of retired civil service moguls began to join the PPP, including Aziz Ahmad and Malik Khuda Bakhsh Bucha. After the shock of 1970 the landed notables and some chiefly families sought to reinsure their access to land, power, prestige, pelf, and patronage.

Always avid for more and better information—intelligence—Bhutto markedly enhanced the resources, authority, and domestic role of the "agencies," particularly the Inter-Services Intelligence (ISI) and the Intelligence Bureau. According to Brig. (Ret.) Syed A. I. Tirmazi, the head of ISI counterintelligence, ISI was Bhutto's chief source of information during the 1977 elections, and the government's white paper on the time is full of references to ISI activities and reports, all indicating a remarkably expanded domestic role in providing the prime minister with a full range of domestic intelligence on enemies and friends (Tirmazi 1995). If there is a "deep state" in Pakistan, we may fairly mark its origins to the country's first democratically elected leader.

A darker side of Z. A. Bhutto emerged within months of taking power. There were many instances of temper and orders from the prime minister that led to violence and even alleged murder. These included crushing striking police and workers, putting down a Sindhi language movement, using helicopter gunships to strafe the summer encampment of the Marri Baloch Tribe, and trashing various opposition meetings. Some of this was done by the new Federal Security Force (FSF) set up to deal with domestic disturbances in lieu of bringing in the army to aid the civil power. This force was recruited from retired and cashiered policemen and had its quotient of thugs and men whose notion of policing started and ended with the iron-tipped *danda* (bamboo staff for interrogations and crowd control), which today has upgraded to the AK-47. Starting in 1973 the prime minister began to use the FSF as his personal militia. The most fateful event involving the FSF occurred on November 11, 1974, when Nawab Mohammad Ahmed Khan Kasuri was shot to death while traveling with his son in Lahore. The real target was Nawab's son, Sahibzada Ahmed Raza Khan Kasuri, a member of the National Assembly and one of the earliest student supporters of Bhutto and the PPP. Raza Kasuri had fallen out with Bhutto early on and had joined the opposition benches from whence he asked questions designed to acutely embarrass the prime minister. It was this case for which Bhutto was tried for capital murder and hanged in 1979.

The wholesale arrival of the landed notables and chiefly families in the PPP, plus senior former bureaucrats, as well as Bhutto's daily dependence on the prime minister's secretariat and its corps of officers on special duty, signaled the restoration of the administrative state and, in time, turned the party into a shadow of its former self: useful for window dressing but without substance. Nowhere was this more evident than in Bhutto's preparations for the 1977 elections (Government of Pakistan 1979). In the run-up to the election, Bhutto's effort to ensure the PPP's victory was implemented by a special cell in the Prime Minister's Secretariat, which was composed of senior civil servants, officers on special duty, and elite late arrivals to the PPP. The election arrangements were organized through the bureaucracy down to the tehsil level and below. There is no evidence of a major campaign drive by the PPP, although some PPP candidates individually pursued violent and intimidating agendas. As is evident from the documentation in the white paper on the general elections that was published by the government, the scope of the arrangements and Bhutto's personal involvement were intensive (Government of Pakistan 1978). Bhutto mobilized the resources of the government—officialdom, vehicles, money, manpower—to assure a PPP win.

The election campaign increasingly became a free-for-all after nine opposition parties combined under the banner of the Pakistan National Alliance (PNA) to run a single candidate against the PPP in 169 National Assembly constituencies. In Pakistan's single-member, first-past-the-post constituency system this development clearly threatened Bhutto's demand for a two-thirds majority, or possibly even an electoral majority. The second development was the leadership of the PNA by the highly respected Maulana Mufti Mahmood and the fact that the religious parties in the PNA, particularly the Jamaat-i-Islami (JI), chanted the slogan "*Nizam-i-Mustafa*" (Islamic governance). This raised the stakes by introducing the volatile subject of religion and put Bhutto on the spot for his lifestyle. Threatened with failure, Bhutto's bureaucratic election machine went into overdrive and the election campaign descended into mayhem: violent attacks on opposition rallies, kidnappings, some murders, candidates bribed or otherwise forced to withdraw. Bhutto was the only candidate from his Larkana constituency. Of course, Bhutto knew all about this from the twice-daily situation reports provided by the ISI (Tirmazi 1995, 54).

The National Assembly election went ahead on March 7, 1977, followed by provincial assembly elections three days later. Amid reports of ballot stuffing and ballot box stealing, polling places being closed to opposition supporters, and other nefarious tactics, the PPP "won" four-fifths of the National Assembly seats. Astonished like most others, the PNA demanded a reelection, announced a boycott of the provincial assembly elections, and made no attempt to stifle violent protests in the streets being led by the JI's student group, the Islami Jamiat-ul-Tuleba (IJT). The situation evolved into more violence and a further breakdown in law and order in Karachi, Quetta, Peshawar, and urban Punjab. The ISI provided a list of thirty-three constituencies where PNA candidates were clearly robbed of victory and suggested

Bhutto hold reelections in these (Tirmazi 1995, 58). But Bhutto refused—although it probably would have brought the seat totals closer to what most analysts agree would have been a fair result. With desultory negotiations going nowhere, the PNA protests turned into a mass movement, the army was called out, three brigadiers in Lahore asked to be relieved of civil affairs duties, and the chief of the army staff, General Zia-ul-Haq, declared martial law and took over the country. Beaten at his own game, Bhutto was detained and then jailed on murder charges.

How do we evaluate Bhutto from this distance? Certainly his failure to build up the PPP was a factor. A strong party would have reduced his dependence on the bureaucracy in the 1977 elections. Perhaps Bhutto believed he could turn the party around as needed, but in such matters timing is everything. His dependence on the bureaucracy was risky. Their loyalties are institutional, not personal. The darker side will always be troubling in evaluating Bhutto. For Westerners, world-class diplomats, tough journalists, and graduate students, Bhutto always impressed. But once out from under the relatively benign leadership of Ayub Khan, Bhutto's vaulting ambition for power became more evident—not that this in itself was an issue, because power is what politicians aim for. It was more a matter of how it was done. Bhutto always reached for the tools that would get him ahead, but he had no loyalty to people or institutions. As he told this writer, he believed he could always orchestrate power (Jones 2003, 148), forgetting that great leadership requires a rational balancing between opposing forces, not a search for control by fear or manipulation. In the end Bhutto's determination to maintain power led him to overreach. The creation of the FSF was a mistake, as was his appointment of General Zia-ul-Haq as the chief of army staff after Gen. Tikka Khan. Zia was in every way the opposite of Bhutto: a military man who stayed long enough to achieve the rank of corps commander (over more senior generals), pious and conservative in religious belief, (very) shrewd, narrowly educated, and of middle-class (or lower) origins. Bhutto reportedly threatened Zia when they met after the coup and was openly threatening to the judge overseeing his case in the Lahore High Court. Probably aware of the potential for Bhutto's charisma to control the outcome of what many regard as a flawed judicial process, General Zia hounded Bhutto to the gallows.

The PPP under Benazir Bhutto

The PPP survived the death of its founder, principally through the political career of Benazir Bhutto, his first daughter and eldest child whom he had been grooming for leadership. Upon the execution of Z. A. Bhutto on April 4, 1979, the leadership of the party fell to the Bhutto women, especially Benazir. For the next decade the party and its leadership were in the political wilderness. General Zia-ul-Haq's treatment of the Bhutto women was cavalier and cruel. Benazir spent most of the seven years following her father's execution incarcerated, including months in Class C solitary confinement, before pressure from friends in the United States and United Kingdom won her exile to Britain. Meanwhile, two developments profoundly changed the domestic and external environments for Pakistan. The first of these was the Islamization Program of President Zia, which was designed to remake Pakistani society in an Islamist mold, to do away with parliamentary democracy, and to eliminate party politics. Zia's political sympathies clearly lay with the JI, and its fingerprints were all over Zia's programs and policies. A cadre-based, highly disciplined vanguard party—without doubt the best-organized party in Pakistan—the JI does not seek power through elections but rather by recruiting internally and controlling policy from the inside (Nasr 1994). Zia, who arose from the same social milieu as much of JI's leadership, appears to have been its ideal patron. He was related to the then-*amir* (president) of the JI, Maulana Tufail Muhammad; both were from the same *biraderi* of Jullunduri Arains (traditionally market gardeners). How this was accomplished requires further research, but there is no secret that Zia pushed out army officers who were too progressive, replaced liberal professors in the universities with members of JI, and promoted both Islamists and orthodox conservatives in the army, the ISI, the bureaucracy, and the judiciary.

The second development was the wholesale change in the regional security environment within which Pakistan had to operate: the fall of the shah of Iran in February 1979, the Soviet invasion of Afghanistan in December 1979, and Washington's search for a regional policy to counter Moscow's southward moves while still opposing the looming nuclearization of the subcontinent—a rather difficult balance to straddle. The arrival of Soviet forces on Pakistan's lightly administered and restless frontier had potentially fateful consequences for the country, but Zia handled the situation, involving both superpowers, adroitly. These external developments ensured that the next decade saw the hand of the military-bureaucratic oligarchy lie heavily within political society.

In September 1981, prior to their incarceration, the Bhutto women organized a mass movement led by eight political parties and the PPP, called the Movement for the Restoration of Democracy (MRD). Although the MRD survived as a paper organization until 1988, it never amounted to much, and Benazir Bhutto cut ties with it before the 1988 election. Any chance that the Bhutto women could reenergize popular politics was postponed for years when Benazir Bhutto's brothers, Murtaza and Shahnawaz, organized a half-baked terrorist group, Al-Zulfikar, to attack Pakistan's military leaders. Based in Kabul and linked to KHAD (Khadamat-e Aetela'at-e Dawlati), the Afghan intelligence agency, the group hijacked a Pakistan International Airlines aircraft flying from Peshawar to Dubai and took it to Kabul, where the brothers met it and executed one traveler, a Pakistani Foreign Service officer who had been flying to Pakistan to bury his father (Anwar 1997, 106). After this Benazir, who had opposed the formation of Al-Zulfikar, was re-arrested and placed in solitary confinement.[1]

Following an interlude in the West, where Benazir Bhutto made many contacts and organized a skeletal PPP central committee in London, she returned to Pakistan in April 1986 to massive welcoming crowds. Martial law had been withdrawn the previous December, and Zia had called for nonparty elections. After Zia's death in the still unsolved plane crash in August, the Supreme Court agreed the elections could be held on a party basis. Despite opposition from Ghulam Mustafa Jatoi and other members of the senior old guard of the party, Benazir Bhutto established her precedence and led the PPP to a victory of sorts in the 1988 elections, taking 93 of 206 seats—or actually 122 seats, after the women's, tribal, and minority seats were declared. It is possible the PPP would have won a majority had the ISI not engaged in rigging on behalf of the Islami Jamhoori Ittehad (IJI), a coalition of religious and conservative groups it had pulled together under newcomer Mian Nawaz Sharif. By aligning with the Mohajir Qaumi Mahaz (MQM, today the Muttahida Qaumi Movement) to win 13 Karachi seats, Benazir Bhutto gained a majority and became the first woman leader of any Muslim state. She was also pregnant. In an arranged marriage the year before she had wed Asif Ali Zardari, a Sindhi businessman with middling landed antecedents and a polo team. Their first child was named Bilawal Bhutto-Zardari.

Benazir's Bhutto's first term as prime minister was not a success. She was opposed at every turn by conservative men in the military-bureaucratic oligarchy who disliked the idea of a female prime minister. With her Western education, lifestyle, and progressive, nonideological perspectives on religion, Benazir Bhutto was anathema to the JI-connected and Zia-era bureaucrats and military officers. She blamed the "Zia bureaucracy" for her political difficulties and charged the ISI-JI cell with holding a grip on political power, unwilling to relinquish the control it had gained under Zia (B. Bhutto 2008, 195–205). The prime minister's relations with Pres. Ghulam Ishaq Khan, an old school bureaucrat, and Gen. Mirza Aslam Beg, the army chief, were contentious. Both men were part of Operation Midnight Jackal, a plot to overturn her government through a vote of no-confidence by bribing enough PPP parliamentarians, that was put together by Lt. Gen. Hamid Gul along with director general/ISI and former ISI officer Brig. Imtiaz Ahmed and others.[2] Benazir Bhutto claimed Osama bin Laden had provided the funds to make the plot work (201). The vote failed and she was able to move against Gul and Ahmad—although the latter was later rehabilitated by Nawaz Sharif. In other areas she made gains for women's rights, freed up the environment for NGOs, and negotiated an agreement with Indian prime minister Rajiv Gandhi that neither state would attack the other's nuclear facilities. She also visited the Siachen Glacier area to meet Pakistani troops fighting in the world's highest battlefield, the first Pakistani head of government to visit an active battlefield, and sought to strengthen the PPP organization by holding internal party elections, although these were marred by accusations of rigging in Punjab.

On August 6, 1990, using the 8th Amendment as a pretext, Pres. Ghulam Ishaq Khan dismissed her government for corruption and maladministration. Elections were held in November, putting the IJI of Nawaz Sharif into office. This election is widely believed to have been thoroughly rigged by the ISI. In turn, the Sharif ministry was dismissed in April 1993 for corruption and maladministration. This was the period of dysfunctional trilateral government (army-bureaucracy-party) manipulated by the military-bureaucratic establishment (see Nasr 1992). Bhutto and Sharif later traded roles as prime minister, although they also combined to vote President Ishaq out of office after the PPP won a plurality in the 1993 elections and they cooperated to bring in Sardar Farooq Leghari as president. With 86 PPP seats to 73 for the Pakistan Muslim League-Nawaz (PML-N), the PPP vote was strongest in Sindh and rural Punjab, and less so in industrial and urban Punjab.

Benazir Bhutto's second tenure was more successful. She had good relations with the army. Most of the military officers she picked for senior posts, including for the first time some from among the air force and the navy, had experience in UK or US staff colleges and thereby—presumably—a broader view of the world. She backed continuing efforts to achieve a nuclear weapons capability, all while giving way to the army's dominance on foreign and security policy. Confronting the army on these issues was a battle she knew she could not win. She kept a previous promise to reverse her father's nationalization of industry but had to fight senior party members who had benefited from posts in the state-owned industries. She moved to advance the PPP's populist programs, including getting the World Bank to initiate its multiyear Social Action Program in health and education. During her second tenure she showed maturity and a capacity to govern that, if continued and deepened, might in time have given her command of the state and put the country on something like the moderate secular path Jinnah had envisioned.

However, accusations of corruption began to emerge and envelop her government; these centered on the activities of her husband, Zardari. Initially it was said he would have no role in politics or governance. Then he began attending cabinet meetings, and whispers of kickbacks on government contracts arose, and finally people started calling him "Mr. Ten Percent" (Lamb 1991, 178). With this unfolding during her first ministry, in her second she made Zardari her minister of investments, undoubtedly a maladroit move, and allegations began to pile up.[3] Pres. Farooq Leghari dismissed her government for corruption on November 4, 1996. In her last book, published after her assassination, Benazir Bhutto labeled all these charges and court cases as politically motivated (B. Bhutto 2008, 224–30). The *New York Times* published a major article detailing Zardari's "vast corruption and misuse of public funds." Included were allegations of a $200 million kickback on a $4 billion contract with French military contractor Dassault and two payments of $5 million from a gold bullion dealer who held a monopoly on gold imports. Foreign and Pakistani investigators concluded that Zardari (and Bhutto) allegedly had accrued some $1.5 billion in illicit profits through kickbacks in virtually every sphere of government activity.[4] Zardari was indicted by both the Swiss and Pakistani governments for money laundering. In April 1999 Zardari and Bhutto were convicted for receiving indemnities from a Swiss goods inspection company that had been contracted by the Bhutto government to end corruption in the collection of customs duties.[5] Additional charges and convictions came and, later, information that emerged from the Panama Papers stymied the Bhutto-Zardaris—and the family of Nawaz Sharif.

Charges of corruption all but wrecked the most promising part of Benazir Bhutto's career. In the 1997 elections the PPP gained only 18 National Assembly seats, all in Sindh, while the PML-N gained its largest victory. The second PML-N ministry lasted until the December 1999 military coup by Gen. Pervez Musharraf, author of the Kargil Incident and the war crisis it engendered between the two nuclear-armed neighbors. For Bhutto and Zardari the Musharraf years were ones of court cases, imprisonment, and exile. Bhutto was sheltered from much of this in self-imposed exile in the West, while Zardari spent years in prison. In a world that had changed massively with the rise of the Taliban, Al-Qaeda, a plethora of radicalized religious groups, and the events of September 11, 2001, Bhutto attempted her second return to the political arena. During the tumultuous welcome for her in Karachi on October 18, 2007, bomb attacks on her convoy that aimed to kill her—killing at least 179 supporters and injuring hundreds more—made it clear there were powerful political and religious forces maneuvering to remove her permanently. This they accomplished on December 27, 2007, at Liaquat Bagh in Rawalpindi. Benazir Bhutto was told by both the Musharraf government and a foreign Muslim government that four suicide squads would attempt to kill her upon her return to Pakistan. Baitullah Mehsud, head of the Tehreek-e-Taliban-e-Pakistan (TTP), was reportedly the leader of the plot (B. Bhutto 2008, 218). After her assassination Pakistan president Musharraf blamed Baitullah Mehsud for her death, as did US CIA director Michael Hayden.[6]

Benazir Bhutto's death opened the way for her husband to become president of Pakistan. In her political will she had designated Zardari as her political successor (Munoz 2010, 78). Following the assassination, the election of 2008 gave the PPP a 91-seat plurality and enabled the party to form a coalition government. Zardari was elected president after he and Nawaz Sharif cooperated to force President Musharraf from office under the threat of impeachment. Pushing aside the PPP's popular choice for prime minister,

Makhdoom Amin Fahim, Zardari chose Yousaf Raza Gilani as prime minister, whose footing in southern Punjab gave the PPP some much-needed presence in the province. The PPP government brought stability to a judiciary that had been treated harshly in its conflicts with Musharraf. As a businessman who had made a business of politics, Zardari was not a "people's president"; rather, he operated more comfortably in the realm of elite politics and backdoor deals, appointing cabinet ministers for loyalty rather than competence. He was severely criticized at home and abroad for failing to return to Pakistan after the July 2010 floods put one-fifth of the country under water, pushed 22 million people from their villages, and destroyed immense infrastructure. Yet, in a major constitutional development, in 2010 Zardari signed the 18th Amendment bill passed unanimously by Parliament, which turned the presidency into a ceremonial office without the power to dissolve Parliament or remove the prime minister. Perhaps Zardari's greatest contribution is simply to survive: he has so far survived conviction in the six remaining cases against him when he assumed the presidency, where he had constitutional immunity from prosecution. Remarkably, his presidency was the first in Pakistan's history to last a full term.

The 2018 national elections tested the current condition of the Pakistan People's Party as the party's leadership was devolved to twenty-nine-year-old Bilawal Bhutto-Zardari. Educated at Oxford, Bilawal signaled his intention to assume the mantle left by his mother when he organized the Mohenjo Daro Cultural Festival in January 2014, a glitzy song and dance festival that mixed modern and traditional themes and showcased the rich cultural history of Sindh. This was followed in October by a mass meeting in Karachi that attracted at least one hundred thousand people, mostly from rural Sindh. Bilawal, who has the looks of both his grandfather and mother, is trying to reincarnate the PPP progressive movement by connecting to the party's base, by adopting the rhetorical mannerisms of Z. A. Bhutto, by stressing the programs and martyrdom of Benazir Bhutto, and by appealing to youth. His election manifesto expanded the promise of the PPP from *roti, kapra, aur makaan* to include *ilm, sehat, aur sab ko kaam* (bread, clothing, and shelter; education, health, and jobs for all). However, it was difficult for the Bilawal Bhutto–led PPP to break into the public mind as the party of the future. Unlike in 1970, the PPP was not riding a popular wave to power: it was dealing with the widespread disappointment of the Zardari presidency.

To revive the flagging fortunes of the PPP and prevent the party from becoming restricted to Sindh, Bilawal Bhutto attempted to rebuild the party in the dominant Punjab province, where electoral support is a sine qua non for national power. In 2013 the PPP swept the National Assembly constituencies in rural Sindh and the province's towns and lesser cities but won none in Punjab, a provincial polarization that is worrisome for national unity. In Sindh the main challenge came from Imran Khan, who promised to defeat the "PPP pharaoh"—Asif Ali Zardari—by running a number of serious candidates in the province, including in Larkana, the home ground of the Bhuttos. Hence Bilawal Bhutto also had to firm up the Sindh PPP, which experienced the defection of several senior officeholders and former provincial and national ministers to the Pakistan Tehreek-e-Insaf (PTI) in 2017 and 2018. Although the PML-N is the old enemy of the PPP, today the PTI is its primary challenger. The PTI has won the support of middle- and upper-class youth for its tough stand against corruption and is likely the preferred party of the military-administrative establishment.[7]

The 2018 Elections

In 2018 the PPP suffered its worst defeat since 1997, when the popularity of the party collapsed under a welter of charges of corruption and incompetence. In 1997 in the National Assembly it won only 18 of 207 general seats (8.7 percent); in 2018 it gained 43 of 272 general seats (15.8 percent). This was a far cry from its best elections: in 1970, its maiden effort under Zulfikar Ali Bhutto, it won 59.4 percent; in 1988, 44.9 percent in Benazir Bhutto's first try; and in 2008, 46.0 percent of the seats after her assassination in 2007. In its early elections the PPP took between 36 and 39 percent of the votes polled, dropping to 22 percent in 1997. This pattern continues to hold for strong and weak elections alike, which suggests that the party's solid vote bank at the national level is around 20 percent and rises higher depending on the circumstances of the election and the provincial distribution of the seats.

The 2018 election was preeminently a contest between the PML-N and the relatively new PTI led by the charismatic former cricket champion Imran Khan. The PPP was not a competitive player at the national level. It was cut out of Khyber Pakhtunkhwa, Balochistan, and Islamabad. In the Federally Administered Tribal Agencies it gained one seat, the Parachinar seat in the Kurram tribal agency, home of the Shi'a Turi Tribe. In Punjab the PPP gained a paltry six seats. One of these was Rawalpindi II, which went to a party influential, Raja Pervaiz Ashraf. Three contiguous seats in southwestern Muzaffargarh district went to members of the Khar clan, one of the founding social groups of the People's Party. In Rahim Yar Khan the PPP took two seats. One of these went to the Jamaldinwali family, an old Darbari political family reaching back to the pre-independence days when Bahawalpur was a princely state.

In Sindh the PPP was on home ground, winning 36 of 61 National Assembly seats and 76 of 126 seats in the Sindh Provincial Assembly, where it formed the government. In largely urban and rural Sindh the PPP dominated on both sides of the Indus River plain. Both PPP chiefs won from their home constituencies, Bilawal Bhutto-Zardari from Larkana I and Asif Ali Zardari from old Nawabshah I, renamed Shaheed Benazirabad I. The party lost Jacobabad and Ghotki II to members of the Maher Tribe and the Mirpurkhas I seat to an independent. However, the PPP's major loss came in Karachi, where it won only 1 of 20 seats, with the bulk going to the PTI. The PPP even lost the Lyari seat (NA-246, Karachi South I), its historic base in Karachi, where Bilawal Bhutto-Zardari lost to the PTI candidate.

The strength of the PPP in Sindh is based on a degree of soft Sindhi nationalism, which is moderate in comparison to a plethora of small, militant Sindhi nationalist and separatist movements in the province. Both Zulfikar and Benazir Bhutto are seen as martyrs who upheld the essentially secular, nationalist, and populist politics that characterized the independence-period Muslim League. The present scion of the party, Bhutto-Zardari, has yet to demonstrate the political capacity and intellectual power of his forebears, particularly Z. A. Bhutto. The party also continues to suffer from the bad reputation and suspicious business dealings of his father, who is something of an albatross around the neck of the PPP. The two co-leaders have not advanced even a modicum of party organization they inherited, one of the PPP's repeated weaknesses.

Bhutto-Zardari's electoral efforts also did not inspire. Certainly his championing of a new province of South Punjab, or Seraikistan, did not resonate in Multan, in the trans-Indus districts, or in the old state of Bahawalpur, except perhaps among the Jamaldinwali Makhdooms. In any event, the 2018 election was not a congenial one for the PPP. The army, which has no love for the Bhuttos, was up to its old game of wrangling the election in support of its preferred candidate, Imran Khan and his PTI. Acting through its own instruments, mainly the ISI, the powerful military establishment mounted a barely hidden campaign against the then-government and party of Prime Minister Nawaz Sharif. The campaign went after critics of the Pakistan Army in the news media and social networks. Journalists were intimidated, abducted, and roughed up. The crackdown on dissent included the abduction and beating of Ms. Gul Bukhari, a prominent columnist and critic of the army, as well as an attempt to block the circulation of *Dawn*, the country's largest English-language newspaper.[8] Perhaps it was a good time for the PPP to stay out of the line of fire and keep its head down.

Conclusion: From Populism to Patronage

Its strong base in Sindh combined with pockets in Punjab, where support could be revived, means the PPP remains a factor in Pakistan's politics. Its vote banks still retain millions of loyal supporters, a generation that came of age in politics during the anti-Ayub movement and the 1970 elections. It is the only party that has spoken for the peasantry in rural Sindh and Punjab, although this combined potential vote bank is now dominated by the landed elites and village chiefs and by brokers and thugs who sell votes to party patrons. "Bhuttoism," the mix of mass movement politics, left-socialist ideology, and party-dominant government, has little appeal for Pakistan's millennials. The shift from ideology to pragmatism was visible under Benazir Bhutto, while President Asif Ali Zardari clearly preferred to engage in elite patronage politics. Nonetheless, the PPP still has the Bhutto dynasty as its focal point of leadership, which frustrates some of the old guard who have defected to other parties and leaders but seems necessary in Pakistan's political culture, where personalized leadership is the norm. The PPP organization has developed with experience in government at the national, provincial, and local levels, plus it has experience in organizing electoral campaigns and mass meetings. The party maintains a national level organization in its executive committee, at the provincial level in Sindh, and down to the district level. Punjab also has a provincial PPP organization—although its head defected to the PTI in 2017—but fewer organizations at the district level. Further, while the original primarily ideological factions in the PPP seem to have retained a shadowy existence, they have been superseded by patron-client networks (a dynamic that would benefit from further research).

What seems most striking about this review of the Pakistan People's Party is the persistence of the national security framework within which all political parties have had to operate since the country's independence. The military-administrative establishment does not want to see another "breakthrough" by a political party as occurred with Bhutto's PPP in 1969. Working through the "security agencies" and now the courts, it has become adept at engineering elections and managing party governments. It is hard to see any change in this dynamic. For the near term, Bilawal Bhutto-Zardari's PPP seems fated to be a regional party, pursuing Sindhi interests in areas like water distribution, jobs, and culture. It will be threatened by terrorism and the hatred engendered by radical religious groups, so much so that Bhutto-Zardari's personal security must remain a constant priority.

Notes

1. Nadeem F. Paracha, "Al-Zulfikar: The Unsaid History," *Dawn*, April 9, 2010.
2. Idrees Bakhtiar and Zafar Abbas, "The Day of the Jackal," *Herald*, August 1994.
3. "Take the Money and Run," *Newsline*, August 1990.
4. John F. Burns, "House of Graft: Tracing the Bhutto Millions," *New York Times*, January 9, 1998.
5. Celia W. Dugger, "Pakistan Sentences Bhutto to 5 Years for Corruption," *New York Times*, April 16, 1999.
6. "CIA Boss Names Bhutto 'Killers,'" BBC News, January 18, 2008.
7. "Bilawal Too Young to Understand Politics: Imran Khan," *Dawn*, November 13, 2015.
8. Mubasher Bukhari and Drazen Jorgic, "Pakistani Journalist Critic of Military Freed after Abduction," Reuters, June 5, 2018; and "Move to Stifle Press Freedom Slammed," *Dawn*, June 7, 2018.

3

Pakistan Tehreek-e-Insaf
From a Movement to a Catch-All Party

Tabinda M. Khan

The Pakistan Tehreek-e-Insaf (PTI) emerged as the largest party in Parliament in the 2018 general elections, enabling it to lead a coalition government. It was a remarkable victory for a party that had had almost no electoral success prior to 2013. This chapter seeks to explain how the PTI transformed itself from a grassroots movement into a catch-all party, forcing it to sacrifice some of its founding ethos in exchange for electoral success and political power. In the lead up to the 2013 elections, and again before 2018, the PTI promised a *naya* (new) Pakistan and a new style of politics in a country that, it argued, had long been saddled with dynastic and corrupt civilian leaders. It accused the Pakistan People's Party (PPP) and the Pakistan Muslim League-Nawaz (PML-N)—both of which were signatories to the Charter of Democracy—of having a *muq muqa* (nefarious deal, in Punjabi slang) whereby they acted as "friendly opposition" to one another and took turns in government in exchange for turning a blind eye to each other's corruption.[1] Cricketer-turned-politician and PTI chairman Imran Khan condemned the PPP's Asif Ali Zardari and the PML-N's Nawaz Sharif as corrupt dynastic rulers and presented himself as an honest leader—not a "politician" (which he treated as a bad word)—who could build a new party that would transform Pakistan.[2] From its inception the PTI was different from the PPP and PML-N: it had a core of urban upper-middle and middle-class activists, it relied on text messages (or SMS) and social media to recruit members, it used its website and Facebook pages to disseminate its message, and it relied on the Pakistani diaspora to raise funds. In 2012 Khan promised that the PTI would be the first national-level party to hold intraparty elections, although it is worth noting that other religious parties, like Jamaat-e-Islami (JI), and regional political parties, like the Awami National Party (ANP) and

Muttahida Qaumi Movement (MQM), have also consistently held intraparty elections.

Along with these new forms of recruitment and organization, the PTI introduced an agenda for institutional reform. It spoke of the need for the rule of law in the place of privilege and preferential treatment for elites, for spending on health and education rather than on large infrastructure projects in big cities, for transparency and accountability instead of nepotism and corruption, for depoliticizing the bureaucracy instead of running institutions on political whims, and for instituting democracy and meritocracy within political parties instead of allowing certain families to monopolize decision-making and control (Pakistan Tehreek-e-Insaf 2013).

The dream for the kind of new Pakistan that PTI promised before the 2013 elections won it government control in Khyber Pakhtunkhwa (KP) but not in other provinces or in the center. As a result, Khan and his closest advisers became convinced that the only way to attain power at the center was to attract as many "electables," or local notables, as possible.[3] The tension between PTI's "old guard," which consisted of urban middle-class professionals and businesspeople, and the "new entrants," who were often professional politicians from the industrial and landholding elites, was already apparent in 2012, but, at that time, Khan successfully mediated between them and tried to balance their demands. However, from 2014 onward, when the PTI led a series of *dharnas* (sit-ins) to oust Prime Minister Nawaz Sharif, funding from big donors among the new entrants increased, expatriate funding declined, and intraparty democratic institutions were progressively dismantled, all of which tilted the balance of power disproportionately toward professional politicians. The question that I will explore is whether the PTI had the potential to become a genuine alternative to the established political parties (especially the PPP and the PML-N) or if it was bound to transform into a traditional political party in order to become electorally relevant. What external and internal factors led it down the latter path?

I argue here that in its original form the PTI most closely resembled the mass-party model, but the PTI's party leadership came to believe that its electoral fortunes in Pakistan lay in transforming itself into a catch-all party that could appeal to a broader group of people by diluting its ideological and organizational appeal (see Krouwel 2006). Otto Kirchheimer's (1966) concept of a "catch-all" people's party replaced the "mass integration party" that had emerged earlier in a period of sharp class distinctions and denominational structures. The catch-all party abandoned "attempts at the intellectual and moral encadrement of the masses" in exchange for "a wider audience and more immediate electoral success." This kind of organization had five features: a "drastic reduction of the party's ideological baggage"; a "further strengthening of the top leadership groups"; a "downgrading of the role of the individual party member"; a "de-emphasis of the *class gardee*, [and] specific social-class, or denominational clientele, in favor of recruiting voters from the population at large"; and a process of "securing access to a variety of interest groups" (cited in Mair 1997, 37). In Peter Mair's words, a catch-all party "severs its specific organizational links" with society, operates "at one remove from its constituency," shifts from a "bottom-up" to a "top-down" party, and "chooses to compete on the market rather than attempting to narrow that market" (38). In 2019 the PTI can be classified, in terms of ideology and organization, as a catch-all party, but it began as a bottom-up social movement.

From its founding in 1996 until 2011 the PTI witnessed steady but slow growth and did not yet have a mass support base, constituency offices, or a nationwide network. It was only after PTI's political rally in Lahore in October 2011, which was attended by an estimated one hundred thousand supporters, that observers began to see it as a viable political party. After this rally a variety of social groups—urban professionals, students, and political workers and leaders from other parties—were attracted to the PTI. This momentum led to the PTI winning 59 seats in KP and forming the provincial government in 2013. At the national level the PTI became part of the opposition, winning the third-highest number of seats. However, as the PTI gained prominence as a viable third party in Pakistan's party system, it also gradually transformed into a "top-down" party controlled by leaders and not ordinary members. In trying to make itself as electorally marketable as possible, the PTI compromised on its identity as a party that was not made up of dynastic politicians and opened its doors to "electable" candidates belonging to established political families (see chapter 8 in this volume). Today the PTI's old workers and outsiders alike criticize the party of indiscriminately welcoming *lotas* (turncoats) from other parties.

The research for this chapter is based on ethnographic fieldwork, review of primary documents, interviews with PTI leaders in March 2018, and study of secondary sources. From 2012 to 2016 I was an official member of the PTI and left when the party's election commissioner, Tasneem Noorani, resigned and the chances for intraparty elections and party reform through that route appeared slim. Therefore I have been both an "insider" within and an outsider of the PTI, straddling two perspectives. In 2012 I joined the PTI as a volunteer for the Women's Wing in Lahore Cantonment, I contested (and won) the joint secretary position for Lahore Cantonment in the intraparty elections of March 2013, and I was part of the team that ran the volunteer office for Hamid Khan, one of Pakistan's preeminent lawyers and a founding member of the PTI. This prolonged exposure to internal party matters gave me access to people, documents, and events greater than a researcher studying the question solely as an "outsider" would have had, but it also means that I was embedded in a particular group of associates within the party and may, in drawing some conclusions, share their biases. Most PTI associates, including myself, were affiliated with the old guard and also called themselves the *nazryati* (ideological) workers. For the past two years I have not had any formal association with the party and have had the opportunity to reflect critically on what the party's existence has meant for Pakistan's politics, although I am by no means certain of its legacy. The PTI is very much a work in progress.

This chapter is divided into four parts and chronologically traces the PTI's evolution as a party. The first part discusses the years from the party's founding in 1996 until the 2002 elections, when it was able to win only Imran Khan's National Assembly seat. The second part discusses its growth from 2002 until the historic October 2011 *jalsa* (rally). The third examines the struggle between the old guard and new entrants from 2012 until 2018 and explains how this struggle transformed the PTI ideologically and organizationally. The fourth part reflects on the PTI phenomenon, though it must be said that we are still too close to these historical events and can, at best, offer only a tentative analysis.

The Personality of Imran Khan and the PTI's Early Years: 1996–2002

On the morning of April 25, 1996, at the home of Dr. Nausherwan Burki, the head of Shaukat Khanum Memorial Hospital (SKMH), Imran Khan discussed the idea to form the PTI with Pervez Hasan (a lawyer also on the board of SKMH), Naeemul Haq (Khan's former bank manager and close friend), Abdul Hafeez Khan (a Pakistani expatriate businessman from Canada), and Ahsan Rashid (the former head of an oil company and leading SKMH fundraiser in Saudi Arabia).[4] Later that evening Khan's friend, Qamar Bobby, approached Hamid Khan, a constitutional lawyer, and asked him to join the party. In their first conversation about the party, Hamid Khan asked Khan, "Are you *sure* you want to start a political party?"[5] Khan responded that he was sure he did because the government had left him with no other option. He wanted to expand his philanthropic efforts to the education sector, but Benazir Bhutto's government viewed him as a threat and would not let him enter government schools, let alone contribute financially. A commitment to philanthropy and frustration with government corruption is what united the founding members of the PTI; a critique of traditional politicians became the hallmark of the PTI's appeal. However, it is also true that the party remained largely synonymous with the person of Imran Khan during this early period.[6]

When the party was founded Khan instructed leaders to keep the fundraising activities of SKMH separate from the PTI because "charity should not be mixed with politics."[7] However, most of the PTI's founding members were committed donors and fundraisers for SKMH. The hospital facilitated Khan's transition from philanthropist to politician. Due to its roots in philanthropy, the party's early rhetoric and activities bore not only the marks of upper-class noblesse oblige—particularly the outlook of Lahore's elite—but also were centered on caregiving, fundraising, and volunteerism, all activities typically associated with women. Among the party's earliest members were Fauzia Kasuri (a leading SKMH fundraiser in the United States, whose family is well known for its business and political accomplishments), Saloni Bokhari (a Lahori businesswoman and SKMH donor), and Sadiqa Sahibzad (Hamid Khan's sister-in-law and a committed philanthropist). A speaker at a PTI Women's Wing meeting in March 2018 chaired by Imran Khan said with pride that the PTI women volunteers were from "good families," from the kinds of families whose women had never stepped onto the street or joined political movements.[8] By building a hospital in memory of his mother, whom he repeatedly credited with his success, Khan suggested that sensitivity and love—virtues that one does not immediately associate with the machismo surrounding cricketers—could be the basis for collective action. It was this philanthropic message that attracted the PTI's party activists during its first fifteen years. Many of the most committed workers in these early years were upper- or upper-middle-class women because PTI's normative commitments, as well as party culture, were spaces where women from the *shareef* (respectable) classes could feel comfortable.

However, while the PTI appeared progressive on some policy issues, it maintained conservative policy stances on others. Indeed, the PTI remained fairly fluid in its early years, led mostly by the force of Khan's personality; its ideology was being heavily shaped by evolutions in Khan's own thinking. While the party put women at the forefront of party organization and mass rallies, Khan also propagated an Islamist narrative and justified the Taliban as "freedom fighters," which led his worst critics to label him "Taliban Khan" from the Musharraf era onward.[9] Many of Khan's critics allege that the PTI was always an establishment party created by Pakistan's powerful intelligence agency, the Inter-Services Intelligence (ISI), to bolster its national security narrative by legitimizing jihadi groups and that the party has mainstreamed extremism.[10] Analyst Babar Sattar writes that although Khan has been "urban Pakistan's great hope since 2011 as an alternative to the horrid status quo," he seems "plain wrong on the existential issue of our times: the threat of religious extremism and militancy, its causes and solutions."[11]

It is more likely that Khan's personal journey of self-discovery informs his views on Islamist groups. In several early interviews he spoke of his disgust with "brown sahibs" who blindly aped the West and were ignorant of their Islamic heritage and devoid of national pride and self-respect; a 1996 profile noted the irony in Imran's hatred for "brown sahibs" because he, his friends, and his family all fit this description.[12] These views have undoubtedly won him sympathy among Islamist parties and jihadi sympathizers, but his severe criticism of the military regime during Musharraf's tenure, his opposition to the Pakistan military's cooperation with the US War on Terror, and his participation in the Waziristan march to oppose drone strikes in 2012 also did not endear him to the military establishment.[13]

A senior PTI leader with knowledge of Khan's early thought processes describes Khan as a "man of action" who lacks the intellectual sophistication needed to understand the dynamics of military authoritarianism in Pakistan.[14] It is true that the narrative Khan adopted for *naya* Pakistan was remarkably similar to the one that military rulers had long been peddling; in this story, corruption and politics are synonymous and Khan was the solution because he was "not a politician" and somehow "beyond politics." Khan and many of the PTI's early founders and activists were "drawing room politicians"—professionals, businessmen, retired government servants, and army officers—who discussed the country's fate over tea and biscuits.[15] They had never experienced political violence or persecution as leftists had throughout Pakistan's history or as workers from the PPP, the PML-N, or the MQM had when their opponents were in power. From where Khan and his allies were sitting, politicians and politics *were* the problem and the military had saved Pakistan whenever politicians had faltered in the past. Moreover, the PTI's founding group was connected to high-ranking military officials and politicians aligned with the Musharraf regime through family ties and long-standing friendships. They did not see the military as an "external" force, as politicians from Sindh and Balochistan saw them.[16] Due to these links, a convergence in their paths and interests was a possibility but neither evident nor predetermined in the PTI's early days.

From 1996 until 2002 the party did not have a sufficiently large cohort of activists to make democratic contestation within the party competitive or meaningful. Members of the PTI's old guard remember the days when no one was willing to assume the highest offices in the party.[17] As many people left the party as joined the party; members of the old guard who stayed believed that Khan, despite his limitations, had the ability to communicate with people and draw a crowd. Without his charisma they had just ideas and activists, which could not translate into mass mobilization let alone electoral success. But despite Khan's charisma, the PTI performed dismally in the 1996 and 2002 elections. The PTI went into the 1996 elections without any preparation and managed to win only Khan's seat from Mianwali, which the PTI did again in 2002. The electronic media had not yet been liberalized, which made it difficult for a new party to communicate with the masses and build its brand.

Before 2011, constitutional lawyer Hamid Khan, who had been an activist since the Ayub Khan period and describes himself as a social democrat, was the foremost intellectual influence on the PTI and therefore, in the party's official documents and constitution, a commitment to social democracy, constitutionalism, and the rule of law is evident. The preamble from the 1996 Constitution, which was repeated in the 1999 and 2012 drafts, expresses a commitment to a democratic social welfare state as well as political decentralization, a taming of the repressive colonial state, and the importance of the rule of law (Pakistan Tehreek-e-Insaf 2012). The party sees itself pitched against a ruling elite of "inept, corrupt and selfish politicians, feudals, civil and military bureaucrats with vested interests" who have "plundered" the country and brought it to "the brink of disaster" (2). The document displays a tension between the conception of the PTI as a social movement, whose goal is completing the work of the Pakistan Movement initiated by Muhammad Ali Jinnah, and the PTI as a political party—a tension that can be traced throughout its history. In a March 2018 address to the PTI Women's Wing in Lahore, Khan emphasized that the PTI was not just a party but a *tehreek* (movement) and, like other great movements such as the movement for independence from the British, it could take decades for the struggle to materialize.[18]

On the Road to *Naya* Pakistan: 2002–11

The PTI's efforts from 2002 to 2011 were focused on building a grassroots organization that could mobilize its supporters in the educated middle class, particularly in affluent urban localities; the goal was not centered on *biraderi* (kinship) or building landholder-peasant networks used by traditional parties to mobilize the vote in lower-middle and working-class rural and urban areas. The party was poised for a better performance in the 2008 elections but boycotted them because General Musharraf had refused to step down as president.

The PTI's growth in the 2002–11 period was substantively different from 1996 to 2002. First, General Musharraf liberalized electronic media in 2002 in a bid to sell himself as a liberal and enlightened ruler. With Benazir Bhutto and Nawaz Sharif in exile, Khan received attention on the political talk-show circuit far in excess of the PTI's actual electoral strength. From 2002 to 2008 Khan started appearing on talk shows regularly; he was still not taken seriously as a political contender but was entertained as an independent-minded critic. Following Bhutto's assassination and Zardari's assumption of the presidency, Khan developed a political niche anchored in the vilification of Zardari and Sharif, both of whom he accused of looting the national exchequer to amass fortunes abroad. Second, the activation of the urban middle class during the 2007–9 Lawyers' Movement and the pro-democracy movement that followed Musharraf's Emergency, Benazir's Bhutto's death, and the disillusionment of PPP workers with Zardari's leadership and the collapse of Musharraf's Pakistan Muslim League-Quaid (PML-Q) party, together gave the PTI a steady stream of workers and leaders looking for a new political home. PTI workers, especially students from its student wing, the Insaf Students Federation (ISF), regularly attended Lawyers' Movement rallies carrying PTI flags, which increased the party's visibility. These movements also drew participation from the urban middle class, which realized its own political power with the help of Urdu news channels and civil society associations. New urban middle-class activists, who had never before voted and who had always seen politics as a dangerous and futile endeavor, began to see a role for themselves in the political process and began to see the PTI as a possible platform for political action (Shafqat 2018).[19]

However, the stream of new entrants into the party was accompanied by the simultaneous entry of professional politicians, from both right- and left-wing parties, which increased the PTI's ability to function as a catch-all party. PTI senior leaders claim that the policy of recruiting electables was always in place in the party, even before the October 2011 jalsa; the only difference was that few professional politicians were interested in joining the party until it seemed like a viable electoral option (see Mufti 2016a). It was around 2007 that some prominent Jamaat-e-Islami leaders joined the PTI. There was also a slow trickle of student activists from the JI student wing, Islami Jamiat-ul-Tuleba, into the PTI. Between 2008 and 2011 two other streams of political activists—leaders and workers—flowed into the PTI. First, former members of the PML-Q, a party created by Musharraf out of the PML-N, were desperate to find a new political platform after Sharif returned and they found that they were no longer welcome in the PML-N. Second, PPP workers in Punjab disillusioned by Zardari's leadership of the party after Bhutto's death were looking for a new home as well. Workers from both the PML-Q and the PPP slowly flowed into the PTI, and high-profile leaders followed. Jahangir Tareen and Aleem Khan, former ministers in Musharraf's regime, joined the PTI in 2011 before the October jalsa, and Shah Mehmood Qureshi, the former foreign minister of the PPP, joined in 2012. Another more surprising entry in 2012 was that of the veteran PML-N leader Javed Hashmi, who said he was disappointed with Sharif's dynastic politics and wanted to support an internally democratic party that prioritized the youth.[20]

During the lead-up to the October 2011 jalsa, then, the PTI was a bottom-up movement driven by activists and politicians in search of a third option. Its organization was somewhat removed from constituency-level networks and concerns, in the manner of Kirchheimer's catch-all party. Instead, the PTI attempted to mobilize constituencies that had been disengaged from the political process in line with the mass party model (see Krouwel 2006). This was done in three ways. First, expatriates in the United States and United Kingdom used the PTI's website to raise funds from among the Pakistani diaspora. Their efforts were reinforced by veteran SKMH fundraisers like Fauzia Kasuri, which meant that PTI local associations did not have to rely on locally generated funding. International funding also allowed the PTI to run several smaller social welfare projects, like the *sasta tandoors* (affordable bread ovens) that distributed bread in low-income communities; these were funded through monthly contributions from Pakistani expatriates (as little as US$20) transferred through the PTI website. Second, it was possible to become a party member by visiting a city office and filling out a membership booklet or by registering one's ID card with the party database through an SMS. This meant that the process of recruiting and organizing members was blind to biraderi and other networks important in traditional constituency politics. Third, the PTI built its structure using the latest communication technologies, which made it especially popular among younger voters and exponentially expanded its reach but also meant that its organization was removed from constituency concerns. It used SMSALL.PK, a platform to recruit members and communicate with them. By 2013 the PTI was estimated to have 10 million members worldwide.[21] The Lawyers' Movement of 2007–9 was the first movement in which cell phones, particularly text messages, were used to mobilize protests, and they became central to the PTI's recruitment and communication strategy. It still used paper membership booklets for campaigns but also pioneered linking SMSs to a party database, where the names, phone numbers, and ID card numbers of members could be stored; this data, in turn, was used for intraparty voting.

These new organizational strategies, combined with strategic investments by donors, led to the success of the October 2011 rally in Minar-e-Pakistan Lahore and created a cultural and organizational template for a new kind of rally in Pakistan that was used in all of the PTI's protests after 2013. At that rally organizers hailed from posh localities in Lahore, from the ISF, and from the PTI's Lahore party organization. Its environment was appreciated for its "family atmosphere": a separate enclosure was created for women, and activists created human chains to control the crowd and safely escort women participants into the safety of the enclosure. Another departure from the norm was that many of these women and young people were from the upper and upper-middle classes, whom the PTI's critics disparaged as the "mummy daddy" (or "burger") crowd, which in local slang are derogatory terms used to mock entitlement and privilege. Moreover, by choosing for its venue Minar-e-Pakistan, the symbol of Pakistan's independence, the PTI proclaimed that its goal was nothing short of national rebirth: the creation of a new Pakistan. The aesthetic adopted at that rally became a staple of PTI rallies. Speeches by Imran Khan and other PTI leaders, whom no one yet knew, were interspersed with patriotic songs and party anthems sung by Pakistan's leading musicians. The rally was a political carnival, part protest and part music concert simultaneously displaying patriotism and self-righteousness, service and privilege, zeal and seriousness—in short, the conflicting poles of Khan's own personality—which explains why at a later date it could so easily be channeled into protests to overthrow an incumbent prime minister.

Struggle between Old and New Members: 2012–18

The entry of professional politicians from the PML-Q, the PPP, and the PML-N into the PTI that began in late 2011 and intensified in 2018 after Nawaz Sharif's disqualification from political office strained and ultimately unraveled the PTI's nascent internal democracy and fundraising structure and reduced the momentum of its membership campaign. The struggle between old and new leaders in the PTI was already evident in 2012, but at that time Imran Khan—who still listened to the counsel of constitutionalists like Wajihuddin Ahmed and Hamid Khan and old comrades like Ahsan Rashid (president PTI Punjab) and to the PTI's Youth Wing and ISF—agreed that the way to resolve this conflict was through intraparty elections (IPE). The first IPE was held in March 2013; members who had registered via SMS could choose a candidate either through SMS or at polling booths in their neighborhoods. PTI workers elected at the union council level elected the workers for the town (constituency) and district (city) bodies, which in turn elected the provincial and central councils. Hamid Khan was the election commissioner, and the PTI's lawyers' wing provided personnel for the election. In the short term the election increased factional conflict and undermined the unity of the PTI's constituency campaigns in the 2013 general elections. In the long term, and particularly after the 2014 dharna, the former PML-Q leaders Jahangir Tareen, who became general secretary, and Aleem Khan, who became president of Lahore, gained more influence in Imran Khan's inner circle, and the old guard was sidelined.

Reports released by the Tasneem Noorani Commission and Justice (Ret.) Wajihuddin Ahmed Election Tribunal confirmed manipulation of the IPEs (Ahmed and Skoric 2014).[22] Due to this manipulation, many party positions and party tickets were given to new entrants rather than original party members, and most decisions about party positions were made in a very centralized manner by the top leadership of the party (see Mufti 2016b). Wajihuddin presented his report in October 2014 and ordered the expulsion of Jahangir Tareen, Aleem Khan, Pervez Khattak, and Nadir Leghari from the PTI because they had rigged the IPEs and unlawfully occupied key party positions.[23] Wajihuddin and the PTI's grassroots workers pressured Khan to take action against these leaders, but he told a workers' convention in 2015 that just as a CEO knew best about the team he needed, so too did a political leader. He said he believed in the capability of the four accused men and would never desert them. This was a "my way or the highway" message to workers, and it was from this point, in 2015, that they began to leave the PTI's grassroots structure in droves.

There was also a steady attrition of veteran leaders from the PTI. Javed Hashmi was the first high-profile leader to leave (in September 2014) after accusing Khan of colluding with Tahir-ul-Qadri, the leader of the Pakistan Awami Tehreek (PAT), and elements from the military establishment to overthrow Sharif through a judicial coup.[24] Wajihuddin was the second to leave in 2015; he eventually established his own party, the Aam Log Ittehad (Common People's Union).[25] Khan refused to let the PTI's election commissioner, Tasneem Noorani, hold elections for the national team, insisting that the election be for the chairman, who would then have the right to nominate his team at the center. Noorani resigned in 2016.[26]

After the PTI's performance in 2013, when it won only 28 National Assembly seats, Khan had grown convinced that the strategies of traditional political parties—including the recruitment of moneyed electables, reliance on large donors, and centralized top-down decision-making and election management—were necessary to win elections, and he put the party's institutionalization on the back burner.[27] Because the party's organization had been dissolved in 2016 in preparation for the IPEs (which were not held), there were no longer elected intermediate bodies to represent the interests of PTI workers; the national Central Executive Committee was appointed by Khan and his associates, and the lower organizations were appointed by their selected delegates.

The lack of conflict-resolution mechanisms led to further defections by leaders and workers who identified with the "old" PTI. In July 2017 Naz Baloch left for the PPP, saying that in the PTI only men had decision-making power, while women were sidelined and youth were confined to social media. She believed that this was the reason why "disappointed ideological party workers" were "quitting the party and joining other parties."[28] A month later Ayesha Gulalai, a PTI member of the National Assembly, stated that Khan and the men in his circle "dishonor respectable women" and disrespected workers in general: "You [Khan] sit in Bani Gala, but your workers are beaten, they are teargassed and shelled and killed, and then you call them 'small workers.'"[29] Once Khan closed all outlets for internal grievance expression and redress in an attempt for centralized control by an almost entirely male leadership, many leaders and workers unhappy with party decisions felt there was no choice but to go public with their criticisms and leave the "party.

Only in 2017, when the Election Commission of Pakistan (ECP) required parties to hold intraparty elections, did Khan and his national team hold an election between the incumbents and a team of unknowns. The voter turnout was only 10.4 percent; grassroots workers showed little interest, and within the party it was viewed as a sham exercise to fulfill ECP requirements.[30] As Khan and his kitchen cabinet plus a handpicked central executive committee determined candidate selection for the 2018 elections—rather than the selection being done by a body regarded as representative of worker interests—protests against their decisions were to be expected.[31]

In the run-up to the 2018 elections, the PTI was accused of facilitating a "judicial coup" against Prime Minister Sharif because it had petitioned the Supreme Court to disqualify him from political office on the basis of his "dishonesty."[32] It was also accused of failing to defend the freedom of media houses like GEO and Dawn, which were critical of the military's political interference and supported Sharif's struggle for civilian supremacy.[33] It is indisputable that since 2014 the PTI has been largely controlled by traditional politicians, several of whom served in General Musharraf's regime or are known to have close ties to the military establishment, and also that it has sided with the judiciary and military against the free press and the ruling party. Moreover, it has also used the "religion card" against the ruling party, much as Sharif had used it against Benazir Bhutto when he was the favored child of the military establishment in the 1980s and early 1990s.[34]

In 2018 Fauzia Kasuri wrote an opinion piece boldly criticizing the party's deviation from its original ideology.[35] Kasuri blamed the party for converting its youth into a "lynch mob" against anyone who disagreed with "the supreme leader" or his "sacred cows." After two decades of working for the party, these were her parting words:

> We had set out to build an institution, but sadly, what we have now is a cult of personality. It is extremely unfortunate that the aspirations of millions of Pakistanis have been reduced to rubble. Even if by some major miracle we win, what locus standi would we have to claim the moral high ground that enabled our meteoric rise in 2011? All that is left, really, is the mirage of the PTI's coronation by the "men behind the curtains." Given our track record, it is more likely that they will take center stage themselves.[36]

The 2018 Elections and Their Aftermath

In the July 2018 elections the PTI's National Assembly seats increased fivefold, from 31 to 157, yet the (army-engineered) lack of a "level playing field" before the elections and its alliance with right-wing religious parties and electables have mired it in a crisis of legitimacy and administrative chaos.[37] Opposition parties and most analysts interpreted the PTI's victory as a victory for the military establishment,[38] while some are more sympathetic to the PTI.[39]

While the PTI was able to deploy some new organizing strategies that could have accounted for better electoral performance, it continued to be plagued by factionalism, which led to administrative chaos once it was in power.[40] For instance, Khan appointed Sardar Buzdar, an independent formerly aligned with the PML-N, as the chief minister of Punjab, but it was reported that there were actually four de facto chief ministers. Tasneem Noorani complained of confusion and paralysis among the bureaucracy: "Under Shahbaz Sharif, they knew who to take orders from, or who to advise to amend his orders. Now, however, orders in Punjab are coming from four different directions."[41] "Who rules the Punjab?" became a common question.[42] Political analyst Hafeezullah Niazi once mused, "Nobody is running Punjab; it's a rudderless ship without any direction."[43]

The PTI's election rhetoric spoke of a "new Pakistan," but its election strategy was to ally with established power centers—the military, business, politicians, and right-wing religious groups—and, once in power, it caved to pressure from one lobby after another. After the turnover of its original members, most of the PTI's cabinet consisted of former PML-Q and PPP ministers. Among its embarrassments were a Punjab bill that increased legislators' salaries, made concessions to sugar mills, stalled police reforms in Punjab, and failed to give safe passage to Aasia Bibi—a woman convicted of blasphemy and sentenced to death—due to protests by Tehreek-e-Labaik Pakistan, whose narrative the PTI had supported during the elections.[44] At various points the PTI did take "U-turns" to reverse some of these changes, but these concessions and reversals only increased instability.[45] Finally, though Khan had once promised a civilian audit of the military's budget and an end to extra-judicial disappearances, under his government the military budget has increased, the higher education budget has been slashed, and he has had to walk back his statements in support of the Pashtun Tahaffuz Movement, a social movement for Pashtun human rights that advocates against forced disappearances.[46]

Conclusion

Because most prominent ministers serving in the PTI's cabinet come from the PPP or the PML-Q governments, the party has neither developed its own leadership nor been able to promote them over politicians from established parties. It appears that the party's shift to a catch-all model, and the enabling environment created by the army, led to the electoral success its leaders hoped for and made it possible for the party to come to power. However, it is important to remember that genuine grievances drew people to a new political platform and internal and external pressures transformed the PTI from a bottom-up social movement to a top-down catch-all party that disenfranchises ordinary members and tailors its ideology to fit the electoral market—which in the case of Pakistan can mean pandering to religious prejudices and hatred. Catch-all parties were probably not detrimental to the health of West European democracies, from which this term originates, but given the dynamics of military authoritarianism in Pakistan, a party that has a diffuse central guiding principle and is detached from localized concerns and networks can be co-opted into protecting military prerogatives by bullying dissidents and labeling them as unpatriotic and anti-state traitors. Top-down political structures are dangerous in Pakistan because they are so easily co-opted. It is this feature of the PTI's organization that, for the time being, has precluded it from becoming a genuine alternative to established parties—which it certainly had the potential to become—and has instead rendered it a party that is simply more of the same.

Notes

1. The Charter of Democracy was signed by party leaders Benazir Bhutto and Nawaz Sharif in 2006. Both parties made a commitment to refrain from supporting military intervention in Pakistan's politics and remove all clauses from the constitution that had been introduced by Musharraf while he was Pakistan's president and chief of the army staff from 1999 to 2008.
2. Madiha Tahir, "I'll Be Your Mirror: What Pakistan Sees in Imran Khan," *Caravan*, January 1, 2012.
3. Fahd Hussain, "The Great Leap Forward: Imran Khan's Soaring Popularity," *Newsline*, November 2011.
4. SKMH, a cancer hospital built in 1994 by Imran Khan, aimed to make cancer treatment accessible and affordable to people of all backgrounds. It is the largest cancer hospital in Pakistan, with plans for expansion. Khan named it in memory of his mother, who lost her life to cancer.
5. Author interview of Hamid Khan, Lahore, March 21, 2018. Most of the information about the PTI's founding was provided by Hamid Khan in conversation with the author.
6. Tahir, "I'll Be Your Mirror."
7. Author interview of Hamid Khan.
8. Women's Wing meeting with Chairman Imran Khan, Lahore, March 17, 2018.
9. See "Imran Khan Calls Pakistan's Taliban a 'Terrorist' Group," Al Jazeera, July 30, 2016; Dawn, "PTI Chief Urges Government to Allow Opening of Pakistani Taliban Office," *Dawn*, September 25, 2013; Farhat Taj, "Deconstructing Imran Khan's Taliban Narrative," *Daily Times*, November 11, 2011. In 2016 Imran Khan conceded that any group that killed innocents, including the Taliban, were terrorists.
10. Hussain, "Great Leap Forward"; Tahir, "I'll Be Your Mirror."
11. Babar Sattar, "Mainstreaming the Taliban?," *The News*, June 25, 2016.
12. "Brown sahib" is a derogatory term used to describe natives of South Asia who mimic Western values, lifestyles, and judgments and who display an inferiority complex vis-à-vis the West, which leads them to judge their culture negatively and to internalize and propagate colonial biases. See Tim McGirk, "Profile: Imran Khan, Mogul on the Stump," *Independent*, April 21, 1996.
13. Sidrah Moiz Khan and Zulfiqar Ali, "Imran Khan Leads PTI 'Peace March' to South Waziristan," *Express Tribune*, October 6, 2012.

14. Author interview, Lahore, March 2018. Name withheld to protect anonymity.

15. This is the author's assessment of the sociological characteristics and political background of the core national-level leadership in Lahore based on attending countless party meetings from 2012 to 2016. A more systematic study and profiling of the entire leadership is needed, so this should be taken as a preliminary assessment based on participant observation.

16. For instance, PTI's general secretary for many years after the 2002 elections was Air Marshal (Ret.) Shahid Zulfiqar. Chief of Army Staff Raheel Sharif was a family friend of the former PTI Punjab president Ahsan Rasheed, who called him by his nickname, Bobby.

17. Author interview of Shahid Zulfiqar Ali, Lahore, March 24, 2018.

18. Women's Wing meeting with Chairman Imran Khan, Lahore, March 17, 2018.

19. See, for example, Daud Munir, "Struggling for the Rule of Law: The Pakistani Lawyers' Movement," *Middle East Report* 251 (2009): 37–41; Ayesha Siddiqa, "Looking Back at the Lawyers' Movement," *Friday Times*, March 24, 2012.

20. Author interview of Hamid Khan.

21. Peter Osborne, "The Men behind Imran Khan's Bid to Lead Pakistan," *Telegraph*, April 19, 2013.

22. Tasneem Noorani, *Tasneem Noorani Review Commission Final Report*, 2014, https:// pkpolitics.com/wp-content/uploads/2014/11/PTI-party-election-review-re port.pdf.

23. This information was gleaned from correspondence between Justice Wajihuddin Ahmed and Imran Khan, which the former shared with the author.

24. Tahir-ul-Qadri is a Canada-based cleric who founded the Pakistan Awami Tehreek (PAT) in 1989. The PAT, an Islamist organization that has occasionally participated in elections, is based in the Barelvi tradition. Qadri has had shifting alliances with Sharif's PML-N, with Musharraf and, most recently, with Khan's PTI. The PAT led the Long March in 2014, which culminated in a dharna that was joined by the PTI in demanding the resignation of the PML-N government. "'Election in September, CJ Will Favour Us and Govt Will Fall,' Hashmi quotes Imran," *Express Tribune,* September 1, 2014.

25. Kashif Hussain, "Syed Wajihuddin Forms Aam Log Ittehad Party," *Daily Times*, December 8, 2016.

26. Qamar Zaman, "Intra-Party Polls: PTI Chief Election Commissioner Tasneem Noorani Resigns," *Express Tribune*, March 26, 2016.

27. Express Tribune, "PTI Received Second Most Votes in General Election," *Express Tribune*, May 27, 2013.

28. "Naz Baloch Quits PTI, Joins PPP," *Dawn*, July 17, 2017.

29. "MNA Ayesha Gulalai Quits PTI Amid Scathing Allegations against Imran Khan," *Dawn*, August 1, 2017.

30. "Imran Khan's Panel Wins PTI Intra-Party Polls Which Had Only 10.4 Percent Turnout," *Express Tribune*, June 13, 2017.

31. Zohaib Ahmed Majeed, "PTI Workers Stage Sit-In outside Banigala as Khan Gets a Taste of His Own Medicine," *Dawn*, June 19, 2018.

32. Aqil Shah, "Pakistan's Court Sets a Dangerous Precedent," *New York Times*, July 28, 2017.

33. "Dawn Leaks: Nation Needs to Know What Has Been 'Settled,' Says Imran Khan," *Express Tribune*, May 10, 2017; "Panamagate Probe: PTI Announces Jang-Geo Boycott over 'Biased Coverage,'" *Express Tribune*, June 17, 2017.

34. In campaign speeches for the 2018 elections, for example, the PTI repeatedly accused the PML-N of changing the words of an oath for candidates by which they declare Ahmadis to be non-Muslim at the behest of foreign powers. In doing so they sided with groups that were protesting against the PML-N and demanding the resignation of the law minister who oversaw this change.

35. Fauzia Kasuri, "PTI's Inconvenient Truth," *Express Tribune*, March 27, 2018.

36. Kasuri, "PTI's Inconvenient Truth."

37. Saad Sayeed and Drazen Jorgic, "How a Phone App and a Database Served Up Imran Khan's Pakistan Poll Win," Reuters, August 4, 2018; "Imran Khan Calls Pakistan's Taliban a 'Terrorist' Group," Al Jazeera, July 30, 2016.

38. C. Christine Fair, "Pakistan's Sham Election: How the Army Chose Imran Khan," *Foreign Affairs*, July 27, 2018; Christophe Jaffrelot, "Imran Khan, the Army's Choice," *The Nation*, September 4, 2018.

39. Madiha Afzal, "Did Pakistan's Imran Khan Win a 'Dirty' Election or a Real Mandate?," July 27, 2018, https://www.brookings.edu/blog/order-from-chaos/2018/07/27/did-pakistans-imran-khan-win-a-dirty-election-or-a-real-mandate/.

40. Sayeed and Jorgic, "How a Phone App."

41. Tasneem Noorani, "Grass-Roots Reforms," *Dawn*, February 19, 2019.

42. K. K. Shahid, "Who Rules the Punjab?," *Newsline*, December 2018.

43. Cited in Mehmal Sarfaraz, "When Imran Khan Bowled the Buzdar Bouncer," *The Hindu*, February 16, 2019.

44. See "Government to Review the Bill Raising Salaries of Lawmakers, Says CM Buzdar," *Frontier Post*, March 21, 2019; "PM Imran 'Extremely Disappointed' over Punjab Ministers' Salary Raise," *The News*, March 14, 2019; "Budget Cut Affecting Higher Education," *The News*, April 15, 2019; Shahbaz Rana, "Giving in to Pressure, Govt Allows 1.1m-Ton Sugar Export," *Express Tribune*, December 5, 2018; Tasneem Noorani, "Good Governance: In Which Direction Is the PM Headed?," *Dawn*, October 20, 2018; Madiha Afzal, "Imran Khan and Pakistan's Hardliners," *Brookings Institution blog*, November 7, 2018, https://www.brookings.edu/blog/order-from-chaos/2018/11/07/imran-khan-and-pakistans-hardliners/.

45. Umair Javed, "Contradictory Pulls," *Dawn*, April 22, 2019.

46. Syed Irfan Raza, "No Axe to Fall on Defence Budget, Decides Cabinet," *Dawn*, February 8, 2019; "Budget Cut Affecting Higher Education"; Dilawar Khan Wazir, "Foreign-Funded Elements behind FATA Unrest," *Dawn*, April 25, 2019. Ahmed tweeted, "*Imran Khan Sahib qadam barhain, DG-ISPR Sahib aap ke saath hain*" (Mr. Imran Khan take the step, the director general of Inter-Services Public Relations stands with you), @Guffi1998, April 30, 2019.

4

What Remains of the Muttahida Qaumi Movement

Tahir Naqvi

The Muttahida Qaumi Movement (United Nationalist Movement, MQM) is an ethnonationalist movement and party primarily based in the cities of the southern Pakistani province of Sindh. Its rapid and militant ascent—from student group to movement to Pakistan's third-largest political party—had by 1989 unfolded into a conjuncture of cold war geopolitics, military–civil "transition," and growing ethnic and sectarian tensions at the urban, provincial, and national levels. The MQM was formally launched in 1986 in the wake of ethnic riots between Karachi's Muhajir and Pathan communities; in response the movement positioned itself as *the* representative of the province's urban Muhajir majority—at the height of Pakistan's third military dictatorship. *Muhajir* (literally translated as "migrant") is the name given to the section of Pakistan's Partition-era migrant population that originated in northern and central India, or what is often referred to as the "minority Muslim provinces" of India.[1] Like the vast majority of post-Partition migrants who hailed from (what is now Indian) Punjab, Muhajirs came as part of a mass-migratory flow of Muslims from India into the eastern and western wings of Pakistan. In contrast to Muslims arriving from (Indian) Punjab, Muhajirs from the minority-Muslim provinces were not designated as affectees of communal genocide by the postcolonial state, such that their migration to Pakistan—the first Muslim nation-state of the modern era—continues to be viewed as largely voluntary and ideologically motivated in nature (Talbot 1996; Naqvi 2007).

From its arrival on the national stage in the mid-1980s until 1997 the MQM was known as the Muhajir Qaumi Movement, which signaled, among other things, its exclusive focus on the subnational recognition of, and rights for, Muhajirs. When Pakistan returned to party-based democracy in 1988 after the end of the military dictatorship of Muhammad Zia-ul-Haq, the MQM began a tentative but significant shift toward a more universal (pan-ethnic) political platform that reflected the emerging possibilities of party-based electoral mobilization. This new orientation was reflected in the 1997 renaming of the movement as the Muttahida Qaumi Movement. The MQM party leadership, unusual in Pakistani politics due to its lower-middle-class background, often refers to the period of Muhajir nationalism as a "beginning" (*shurooaat*).

At the time of writing, the MQM has splintered into a number of competing factions. In 2015 its top domestic leaders severed ties with Altaf Hussain, one of the party's founding leaders who has lived in self-imposed exile in London since 1991. The explicit reason given for the split was that Hussain had crossed a line by making certain "anti-Pakistan" remarks in an August 2016 speech to supporters.[2] Hussain's remaining defenders are activists like himself who live in similar self-imposed exile outside of Pakistan. The domestic faction of the MQM now calls itself the MQM-Pakistan (MQM-P) and maintains an electoral profile at the local, provincial, and national levels. Another offshoot, the Pak Sarzameen Party (PSP), led by Mustafa Kamal, a former MQM party member and former mayor of Karachi, was launched in 2014, and rumors are mounting of other breakaway parties in the future. Indeed, the 2018 general election saw the party's electoral fortunes decline: the party won only six seats at the national level (and the PSP won none). While this number was sufficient for the party to be included in the governing coalition led by the Pakistan Tehreek-e-Insaf (PTI), it signaled a sharp reversal of fortunes from the nineteen seats it had gained in 2013.

Given the receding sense that Karachi is a city whose ethnic factions are at war with one another and therefore require protection, is there an *enduring* political and ideological narrative that the MQM's various factions can continue to draw on and revise? This is an especially urgent question since recent actions on the ground in Pakistan suggest that many of the MQM's activists have unlinked themselves from its leader, who cuts a King Lear–like figure in sharp relief. Furthermore, as the recent struggles between the MQM-P's central coordinating committee and the party's current convener, Farooq Sattar, suggest, the domestic factions of the MQM do not seek to create a new spiritual-political leader. However, the decline of Altaf Hussain has prompted a refreshing level of internal debate within the emergent MQM-P. The question has nevertheless arisen: What, if anything, of the MQM will remain beyond the instrumentalities of political power?

To answer this question, I examine the historical, ethical, and affective dimensions of the Muhajir narrative of sacrifice (*kurbaani*) and its resultant impact on the nature of its political representation. The assertion that Muhajirs sacrificed by participating in the movement for independence and then by leaving their ancestral homes in India to settle in Pakistan "for the sake of Islam" is a complex claim for recognition. It is a claim that historically precedes the formation of the MQM yet figures prominently within the movement's ethnopolitical discourse. I contend that while the Muhajir conception of sacrifice displays features of a postcolonial nationalist discourse, it is one that cannot be examined through the usual "critique of essentialism" that would seek to deconstruct the mythical representation of a pure (sovereign) identity. While at one level the narrative of Muhajir sacrifice is essentialist, I argue that this essentialism is not focused on either implicitly or explicitly securing a sovereign (or self-actualizing) Muhajir *identity*.

This framing of Muhajir difference is expanded later, but at this stage it is important to explicate some underlying assumptions: (1) the categorical newness of Muhajirs (as the product of Pakistan's independence they are not marked *as such* within the colonial archive); (2) the status of Muhajirs as a historical community born through mass migration and settlement (primarily) in urban Sindh; and (3) the relationship of both the category and the community to the process of postcolonial nation-state formation. The problematic of sacrifice therefore reflects a central tension that has existed since the inception of Pakistan: between the universalizing ideal of Muslim nationalism and the actuality of multiethnic difference. As I show, this is a movement of skepticism and agency—of questioning—that MQM activists enact through an essentialist construction of action (*amal*). By deconstructing the MQM's narrative of Muhajir sacrifice, my aim here is to examine historically given facets of the Muhajir political imaginary that will endure after the demise of the MQM as we have come to know it.

This chapter proceeds as follows. First I provide a brief account of the MQM's origin and history while noting its current challenges. Next is an exploration of facets of the MQM's ideological discourse of nationalism, which is deeply rooted in the historical claim of sacrifice. The conclusion suggests that while the MQM may not continue to exist in its current iteration, its *appeal* will endure precisely because of the discursive foundations laid by its leaders.

MQM: The End?

The histories and ethnographies of the MQM have devised many different strategies to capture the dynamic relationship between the movement's internal political organization and its far-reaching effects on politics and everyday life in Sindh. The influential full-length studies by Verkaaik (2004) and Khan (2010) focus on the MQM's early discourse of Muhajir exclusivism and its ethos of urban militancy and martyrdom. My own work, which is based on fieldwork conducted in Karachi between 2002 and 2004 among MQM activists and citizens at large, reflects a period when the movement was no longer engaged in the same kind of pitched territorial battles for survival against state agencies and their proxies. Rather, the MQM at this time was involved in rebuilding its political organization, in part by continuing efforts it began in the early 1990s to remake itself into a pan-ethnic movement.

To write about the MQM requires the ability to distinguish between its phases, changes, and endings, with an eye toward identifying certain durable features of the Muhajir political imaginary. What follows is a linear history of the movement that does not seek to explain the breakup of the movement but instead introduces it to readers who may not be familiar with its emergence and effects on Pakistan's urban and political landscape. It is important, however, to remain conscious of the implicit political evaluations that often get baked into linear historical accounts (maturation, entropy, degradation). A sketch such as this will also have its own points of emphasis: this one is political action and transformation. Crucially, these processes are in no way separate from the conditions of violence within the MQM. Finally, the following brief account is a novel exercise insofar as it experiments with the idea of a *past tense* history of the MQM. Thus, one should not assume that the MQM-P, the branch composed of the domestic leadership of the MQM, is *the* MQM that emerged in the mid-1980s.

The Muhajir Qaumi Movement gained prominence in the mid-1980s against a backdrop of martial rule and urban violence. The most decisive clashes occurred in Karachi, a city whose postcolonial urban landscape had been shaped by mass migration, military and civilian governments, and the illicit productivity of a vast informal sector (Hasan, Younus, and Zaidi 2002).[3] Local practices of vigilance and siege translated the disorder of Muhajir-Pathan riots into a militant style of territorial politics that brought poorer sections of the Urdu-speaking Muhajir community into the movement's fold. These events and the ensuing micropractices joined with the fiery rhetoric of the MQM's founder and leader (*qaid*), Altaf Hussain. He galvanized the Urdu-speaking community to vote self-consciously along ethnic lines in 1987 in "nonparty" municipal council elections that were held at the height of the military dictatorship of Zia-ul-Haq (1978–88).

Pakistan's longest and most influential periods of military rule included the introduction of this system of "nonparty" local government. Under martial rule, the nonparty local council system was allowed to flourish during the wider ban on political parties, whose elite leaders had historically focused their sights on the country's provincial and national legislatures. It is often argued that the absence of formal civilian (party-based) control of the legislature created a political vacuum that was filled by ethnic and sectarian formations, which initially operated outside the parliamentary framework. Capitalizing on its untested and liminal status as an ethnic movement, the MQM was able to appeal directly to the urban electorate in Sindh in ways that the country's existing (but formally banned) parties could not. Thus by 1986 the MQM had managed to gain a political foothold in the major cities of Sindh, where Muhajirs had amassed a majority soon after their arrival as mass-migrants following independence in 1947 (Gayer 2014). Following the country's return to civilian democracy in 1988, the MQM was able to translate the municipal gains it had made in Sindh under martial rule into a sizable ethnic vote bank, making it the second-largest political party in Sindh and the third-largest political party in Pakistan (despite at the time having no popular support outside of Sindh). Crucially, the political rise of the MQM solidified a new narrative for the Muhajirs: once seen as exemplars of Pakistan's Muslim nationalist ideal, they now demanded recognition as a subjugated migrant nation within Pakistan, a stance that was as much at odds with its own past as it was with the country's native ethnonationalist movements whose discursive tactics were readily appropriated by the second-generation leadership of the MQM.[4]

The MQM quickly transformed Karachi's Muhajir-majority neighborhoods into crucibles of ethnic siege, parallel government, and illicit accumulation. As is well known, this included the use of extortion against Muhajir as well as non-Muhajir citizens. By 1992 the army and the civilian government had decided to wage an operation against the MQM on charges of criminality and murder that continued throughout the nineties and left thousands dead. Residents of Karachi and Pakistanis at large view this period as *the* critical threshold of the country's descent into acute forms of weaponized political violence, whose causes and agents have become increasingly heterogeneous and transect ideology, political affiliation, and geopolitical scale (Gayer 2014). Throughout this period the MQM, under its founder-in-exile Altaf Hussain, maintained territorial and electoral political control of the province's major cities of Karachi and Hyderabad.

In July 1997, after years of victimization at the hands of successive civilian governments and the armed forces, the MQM held a festive rally in Karachi to announce its new name: the Muttahida Qaumi Movement, or United Nationalist Movement. Under this new mantle the MQM claimed to represent *all* of Pakistan's ethnic communities (in their diversity) under the banner of its movement and party. Some commentators suggest that this shift to a "united" (*muttahida*) nationalist project was part of an attempt to reenter the political mainstream after years of state persecution and violence. The name change continues to prompt concern among supporters that the interests of and sacrifices made by Urdu-speaking Muhajirs to Pakistan and to the MQM itself have been diluted.[5] The use of the discourse of Muhajir sacrifice in mediating this tension is discussed later.

Such concerns were allayed only in part during the next phase of the MQM's history (1999–2009), which was defined by its reengagement with the same kind of praetorian system of nonparty local council elections, which accounted for its rapid political ascent during Muhammad Zia-ul-Haq's military dictatorship. Under Musharraf's martial rule the structure of elected municipal government was designed to ensure municipal autonomy from provincial control. This advantaged the MQM until the reintroduction of civilian democracy in 2008, which led to a constitutional-political struggle between the MQM and the ruling PPP government in Sindh over the role and powers of municipal government. Throughout this time the MQM continued to recruit non-Muhajirs into the movement.

The 2015 defection of the MQM's senior leadership from Hussain was an unprecedented threshold for the movement. Through past defections and countless struggles with Pakistan's civilian and military governments, the discourse of keeping "blind faith" (*andha ehtamaad*) in Hussain was an enduring political sign that transected both movement and party-based iterations of the MQM. It worked in conjunction and in tension with the MQM's original role as an ethnonationalist movement exclusively committed to the national recognition of the Urdu-speaking migrant population. The creation of the MQM-P and the PSP from the rubble of Hussain's leadership therefore allows for a genuine reckoning.

Clearly much of the political outlook for the MQM hinges on the exigencies of Pakistan's electoral democratic process. The buildup to and aftermath of municipal, provincial, and national elections will provide a clearer picture—not just about *which* Muhajir party will be able to galvanize the Muhajir vote in urban Sindh but whether or not they can retain the original ethnic vote bank.[6] Despite such cleavages, certain dynamic consistencies will continue to define the electoral landscape in urban Sindh. They pertain to the looming macropolitics of numbers (Muhajirs are a declining plurality), to the role of Pakistan's establishment, and to both the real and the perceived capacity of various parties to achieve effective urban service delivery.

Finally, understanding what will endure beyond the MQM is significant for reasons that go beyond the normal routes of political prognostication. For this reason, this discussion does not delve into the nuances of the MQM's current internal crisis (which are simultaneously there for all to see and quite opaque), nor does it outline a set of abstract variables that might determine which faction of the MQM will eventually control urban Sindh. Rather, the purpose here is to reflect on what it is that remains of this nationalist political formation beyond the institutional shell of any particular movement or party. What name and form can we give the set of forces that transects the past and emerging iterations of the MQM?

Sacrifice and the Questioning of National Attachments

Drawing on Islamic and nationalist conceptions of migration and the voices of activists, ideologues, and cultural producers within the MQM, I turn to the various historical and political iterations of the discourse of Muhajir sacrifice, which I argue are politically articulated in the meta-linguistic form of claim: that Muhajirs deserve recognition and belonging in Pakistan on the basis of both their unparalleled support for the movement that led to the creation of Pakistan and their decision to willingly abandon (i.e., sacrifice) their ancestral homes in India "for the sake of Islam."

The narrative subject of sacrifice precedes the MQM and plays a prominent role in its ethnopolitical discourse. Moreover, this discourse of sacrifice privileges action as the source of Muhajir identity and belonging in ways that allow Muhajirs to claim *and* refuse one's attachment to the dominant Muslim national ideal of Pakistan. In this sense the discourse of Muhajir sacrifice organizes incommensurability and affect in the evaluative gap between universality and collective experience—what Judith Butler (2005), in her reading of Adorno's (2000) moral philosophy, describes as a stance of "moral questioning."

The signifier "sacrifice" (*kurbaani*) is used throughout Pakistan to denote the collective and subjective consequences of political participation, to the extent that the "giving of sacrifice" is often used interchangeably with *shirkat* to denote political participation (Verkaaik 2005). The construction of political participation as something requiring the renunciation of individual desires and interests has a particular historical resonance in the modern South Asian context, where the imagination of nation and community has been intertwined with the rise of colonial publics, starting with elite reform movements in the mid-nineteenth century and culminating in the mass-politics of the All-India Muslim League, the party at the forefront of the movement for a Muslim state (Gilmartin 1998; Kelly and Kaplan 2001; Chatterjee 1993; Witsoe 2013). This conjunction and friction between nation and demos has its impetus in modern colonialism's constitutional-political field in which nationalists were required to voice their claims for emancipation in a representative political context. One outcome of this historical entanglement of nation with electorate is the sacralization of participation itself. For example, David Gilmartin (1998, 189) writes that the Muslim League in Punjab distinguished its Islamic and modernist politics of "conscience" (*zamir*) and "faith" (*imandari*) from the workings of Punjab's dominant Union Party, whose leaders are vilified as "intermediaries within the British imperial system." Rooted in colonial-era distinctions between "faith" (*deen*) and the self-interested "world" (*dunya*), the register of sacrifice continues to define political agency as a transcendent practice of participation in, and solidarity with, a movement.[7]

Nationalism, argues Anderson (1991), seeks to elicit "political love" from its adherents, an affect it is able to enlist by the recursive articulation of territory, language, and ethnicity as a natural, ancient, and hence "unchosen" feature of identity (143). The puzzle of nationalist sacrifice—materialized in the willingness of the subject to suffer loss in the name of such an impersonal and recent force as the nation—has prompted scholars of nationalism to consider the discursive and material conditions that shape and sustain affective attachments to the nation (Anderson 1991; Appadurai 1998, 2006).[8] In contrast to the juridical logic of the social contract, which grounds freedom in the mythical staging of individual consensus on the legitimacy of the law, the enlisting and performance of sacrifice works in a space that can be imagined to exist outside the law, such that although the "law can impose risks . . . it cannot demand a sacrifice" (Kahn 2012, 7). This helps account for the discursive and political centrality of sacrifice within nationalism as a manifestation of the kind of "surplus affect" or "political love" that exceeds the framework of democratic legitimation found in republicanism (Appadurai 1998). In such cases the discursive and ethical *autonomy* of sacrifice—its ability to produce its own universe of affective and ethical relations—comes to be subordinated under the bedrock of *identity*. Sacrifice is simply the manifestation of an essential, unchosen political love.

The discourse of Muhajir sacrifice is not a discourse of political love so much as it is a form of what Judith Butler (2005) calls "moral questioning." Butler points to the gap between universal ideals and the experiential actuality of the particular as "the condition for moral questioning" (7). Such a gap and its modes of apprehension and evaluation are historically and culturally situated. Sacrifice is not just the act of renouncing one's self in the name of a higher power, nor is it limited to the memory of such acts in the present. It is also an evaluative stance that makes it possible to reflect on and question one's attachment to the collective, including at those times when "the collective ethos has ceased to hold sway" (Adorno in Butler 2005, 7; see also Zigon 2007).

Mass Migration and the Genesis of Muhajir Sacrifice

In Pakistan the term Muhajir embodies a range of conflicting meanings that reflect the historical role of migration in shaping the territorial, ideological, and material bases of inclusion and exclusion in the nation-state. At the time of independence *all* incoming migrants to Pakistan were classified as Muhajirs in camp records, census reports, and, most notably, the emerging public debate about the material and political effects of mass migration. Migrants from the nonpartitioned minority-Muslim provinces of India were differentiated within this larger grouping as voluntary migrants to Pakistan, which only heightened the difference in their moral standing compared to the vast majority of Muslim refugees from the "agreed" areas of India like Punjab, where the conditions of communal genocide prompted a large-scale *involuntary* transfer of population between India and Pakistan (see Naqvi 2007).

Muslims residing in the "non-agreed" regions of northern and central India were actively discouraged from migrating by the Pakistani state and faced more difficulties accessing rehabilitation benefits upon their arrival. The rationale for their exclusion was biopolitical, however, and not sectarian: the non-agreed regions had endured less violence and, though Muslims from these parts of India were never forcibly turned away from Pakistan, leaders in the provincial and federal governments asserted that the country lacked the spatial and economic "capacity" to manage the complete transfer of India's Muslim population (Zamindar 2007; Naqvi 2012). Thus the moral, ideological, and regional delimitation of the Muhajir subject as someone whose migration amounted to a willing "sacrifice for his faith" (Talbot 1996, 135) originated in attempts by the first federal government, dominated at the time by politicians and bureaucrats from north India who "opted" to live and serve in Pakistan, to counter the use of biopolitical arguments about capacity by provincial governments. While such debates were tied to the material, territorial, and political immediacies of the largest mass migration of modern history, they gave rise to a more enduring practice of invoking Muhajirs as exemplary yet vulnerable subjects who embodied the extra-territorial ideal of Muslim nationalism. By the mid-1950s the biopolitical argument propelling the use of the category Muhajir (as refugees to be spatially and economically integrated into an existing population by a newly constituted federal state) had given way to the institutional, political, and cultural imperatives of nation-state formation—of making a *Muslim* nation-state.

Muhajirs as a Regulative Ideal

To understand the role of sacrifice in organizing the MQM's eventual refusal of the Muslim nationalist ideal, it is worth examining the historical forces that conditioned the representation of Muhajirs as a kind of marked universal: a group whose difference and vulnerability within the post-independence national order of things is paradoxically tied to the idea that it embodies the universal virtues of Muslim nationalism. Mohammad Waseem (2001, 249) notes that prior to the rise of the MQM, Muhajirs were recognized as having an "enhanced commitment to ideological mobilization and a lack of tolerance for provincial and ethnic aspirations." In a similar vein, A. R. Siddiqui (2008, 123) observes how "mohajirs' [*sic*] existential reality embraced all the vital features of Pakistan's art, culture, language, and politics. They could not by any means be dismissed as *just a parochial group* outside the national mainstream" (emphasis added).

By the late 1950s Urdu and north Indian Islamicate culture came to occupy the ideological and discursive center of the post-independence national order. Urdu-speaking migrants mattered within official pedagogies of nation-building as a kind of ethnically unmarked exemplar of the universal confessional ideals of Muslim nationalism. This allowed them to be positioned against Pakistan's *native* ethnolinguistic communities and the politics of provincialism.[9] It is an image that Muhammad Ali Jinnah, the leader of the All India Muslim League and "founder" of Pakistan, substantiated in 1947 when he compared the participation of Muslims in the minority-Muslim provinces of India to a "state of slumber" in the Muslim-majority provinces, which by this time were already slated to make up Pakistan.[10] Siddiqui's (2008) use of the terms "parochial" and "mainstream" does not resolve their meaning so much as assemble them into the form of a *claim* of Muhajir recognition. As the statement makes clear, it is a claim that draws much of its legibility from Pakistani nationalism.

The marginalization of Muhajirs, as neither fully settler nor alien within Pakistan, was framed as a threat to the very universality of Pakistani nationalism by the forces of parochialism. Writing at the height of the Pakistan National Alliance's campaign to oust the democratically elected regime of Zulfikar Ali Bhutto, conservative journalist and a stalwart of the Pakistan Movement Z. A. Suleri argued that the government's increasing tolerance of "provincialism" posed a threat to the ideological and territorial integrity of the Pakistani nation-state.[11] Suleri's commentary, written seven years after the secession of East Pakistan, invokes the familiar idiom of exemplary nationalist sacrifice. Unlike that of Pakistan's native ethnic communities, he argues, the belonging of Muhajirs is secured by their historic participation in the creation of Pakistan. For Suleri, Muhajirs merit a "commandment of distinction" for their participation in the Pakistan Movement and, eventually, for leaving their homes in India. Both acts not only offered "absolute proof" of their loyalty to Pakistan but confirmed the very coherence of Pakistani "national culture" as such. Suleri's staging of Muhajir universality equates the marginalization of the Muhajir community at the hands of provincial forces with the "erasure of Muslim national ideology."

Questioning and Refusal

In light of these historical investments, the onset of Muhajir nationalism in the mid-1980s "represents an immensely interesting case of political mobilisation on the basis of a remarkably successful transformation of political identity" (Verkaaik 2016, 844). Thus the marginalization of the Muhajir bureaucratic elite throughout the 1960s and 1970s revealed the universalizing limits of Muslim nationalism to the second generation (Kennedy 1991; Haq 1995). Shahzeb, a senior MQM activist, elucidates the paradox of Muhajir injury by recalling his childhood: "In school we read about Sindhis and their camels, Pathans and their tribal councils, and the toil of the Punjabi farmer. Only *we* were missing. Where were we? We were in the words every child used to read in the [Urdu] textbook. But this is how it became so easy to pass us by and steal our rights from us."[12]

Shahzeb challenges the universality of Muslim nationalism and acknowledges the complicity of Urdu-speaking Muhajirs in producing its very exclusions. Imran Farooq, the MQM's convener who since 1991 lived in self-imposed exile in London with Altaf Hussain, until his murder in 2010, frames the departure from marked universality as an argument about the *inherent* inoperability of Muslim national attachment:

> Muhajirs never gained an attachment to their land either before or after partition. Muhajirs need to gain an attachment to the land of Sindh. . . . The theories of pan-Islamism we were drawn to during the Raj were like a drug-induced trance. Who could be fooled into thinking that while there are Muslims all over the world, you [can] find a Muslim who says "I belong to the whole world"? There will always be an attachment to the land. This idea that we are only Muslims, and that we can only have one identity, attachment, one link, which is religion, shows the level of our *brainwash.*"[13]

Sacrifice as Ongoing Action

The turn to muttahida nationalism in 1997 spawned an anxiety among members of the Urdu-speaking migrant community that perhaps the MQM had moved beyond their particular needs and interests. Hussain, in an address taken from the 1997 Elan rally, sought to allay such concerns by employing the historical and affective medium of sacrifice:

> *Baniy-e-Pakistan* [Makers of Pakistan], you made sacrifices to make Pakistan; you made Pakistan; you sacrificed with your life. *Baniy-e-Pakistan!* This is what your children have inherited. These black English [*kaala engrehz*, referred to later as the "power mafia"] have reduced the territory of Pakistan [*zamin tang kardiyeh*]; they've cut your rights, they've made you a third- and fourth-class citizen. . . . Your sons started a movement [MQM] against injustice and violence and they were assailed. Not just this, but they were accused of treason [*ghadari*].

As this narrative suggests, one of the most crucial objectives in the wake of the renaming of the MQM was to frame a coherent narrative in which the recent historical commitments of Muhajir nationalism—sacralized here in the figure of the slain MQM activist—could be reconciled with the movement's emerging pluralist orientation. Clearly, this was a balancing act.

In 2012 the MQM released *Jehd-e-Musalsal* (*Ongoing Struggle*) and *Naqeeb-e-Inqilab* (*Author of the Revolution*), two made-for-prime-time television dramas that emphasized the subjective and political continuity between the movement's "Muhajir" and "Muttahida" period. *Jehd-e-Musalsal* provides perhaps the most elaborate framing of the MQM's construction of sacrifice as a stance of questioning Muslim nationalism.

Jehd-e-Musalsal's main protagonist, Khurshid, is a young Muhajir activist whose headlong involvement with the MQM distracts him from his studies, to the disappointment of his widowed mother. Her appeals to Khurshid to study, earn, and marry prompts concern and ambivalence on the part of the boy's paternal grandfather, a lower-middle-class shopkeeper whose political quietism points to his embodiment of the north Indian Islamicate ethos of respectability (*sharafat*) and his personal experiences of loss. While a young man living in pre-Partition India, his own father was killed for his role in the Pakistan Movement. Decades later his son (Khurshid's father) was assassinated in Karachi for his activism with the MQM. As the sole provider, the aging grandfather is invested in Khurshid leading a normal life outside politics (*siasat*).

In a series of poignant scenes the skepticism the grandfather reveals to his Muhajir peers about the MQM unleashes the involuntary memory of his own experience as a boy in India at the height of the struggle for Pakistan (rendered through an "archival" black-and-white filter effect and an emotionally stirring orchestral vamp that conjures Pakistan's national anthem). At one point an associate of the grandfather tries to allay his fears that the boy is wasting his life "cleaning gutters" for the MQM by reminding him of his own activism during the Pakistan Movement following the death of his father: "Your grandson can't help it. . . . It's in his blood. . . . When did our elders think? They just decided. If one thinks then decides can they act? . . . I wish they had thought then, at least we would not be in the position we are today." The story ends neatly: Khurshid receives his grandfather's blessing, agrees to attend university, and embarks on a mission to enlist non-Muhajirs in the MQM, which he continues in the sequel's secular, multiethnic, and progressive university setting.

Like Hussain's comments to his Muhajir supporters at the 1997 rally, *Jehd-e-Musalsal's* multigenerational interplay of skepticism, memory, and sacrifice reveals a dense and uneven rhetorical infrastructure of populist mediation. Its most salient feature, I suggest, is its production of a pre-political subject whose attributes and attachments are defined in relation to an inherited potential for action (*amal*), where action is understood to yield sacrificial loss. In his rumination on action the grandfather's associate makes clear that the capacity for action is neither a static ethnic marker of identity nor a situated calculation of personal or political cost and benefit. Rather, it is understood in both ethical and temporal terms as the revolutionary moment when one decides to leave behind what is familiar (and immanent) for an unfamiliar and transcendent ideal.

The plea by the grandfather's associate—"If one thinks then decides, can they act?"—resonates with the Islamic vitalism of the early twentieth-century thinker Muhammad Iqbal (1992), for whom "the final act is not an intellectual act, but a vital act which deepens the whole being of the ego and sharpens his will into creative assurance that the world is not just something to be seen and known through concepts, but to be made and remade by continuous action." First-generation migrant informants who participated in the Pakistan Movement as young men took pride in relating their lack of familiarity with its specific aims: "There was an emotion" (*aik jazbaa tha*), remarked one elder from Karachi's Bihari migrant community on his experience at the time, "and there was a togetherness" (*aik harmdardi thi*).[14]

At one level the naturalizing construction of an inherited "passion for sacrifice" that informs the "ongoing action of generations" (*naslon ka amali tasalsul*) is not unlike the discourse of native ethnic attachment insofar as MQM activists imagine action (rather than territory or language) as a moral substance that is transmitted through blood ties. Such ties may resonate with the idea of an unchosen or given ethnic attachment and, in a very evident way, may mediate the inclusion of Muhajirs within Pakistan's larger nativist framework of multiethnic recognition that privileges an idiom of "blood and soil" attachment unrecognized within official Pakistani nationalist discourse. Yet, in contrast to the essentialist subject of ethnic nationalism, the logic of sacrifice does not generate stable ontic markers of "the Muhajir people," since what is imagined as unmediated and inherited is the very potential to undo previous forms of self-recognition in the name of a transcendent ideal.

Conclusion

The discourse of Muhajir sacrifice emphasizes its role as an enduring yet historically given cosmology of moral questioning and political action, leading Pakistan's Muhajirs to come to identify themselves as a distinct community. The sacrificial imaginary of action draws on and questions the idea of Pakistan as a Muslim nation. In this sense the MQM acknowledges the "origins" of Muhajir nationhood in Pakistani nationalism (A. Hussain 2011) yet continues to question it on the basis that it is no longer legitimate and actual. Rather than conjuring Muhajirs as a sovereign nation with their own self-actualizing cultural essence, then, the sacrificial logic of alterity reflects the primacy of action, participation, and grievance over any essentialist narrative of identity. This push to unsettle rather than secure attachment is not a contemplative or pacific stance of awareness (Rorty 1989). To endure as a Muhajir, then, is not to affirm the certainty of who you have always been. Rather, it involves being captive to the illusion of difference and the unsettling of that certainty. In this crucial sense, identifying as a Muhajir entails imagining oneself as someone with an ongoing capacity for political action and participation in a larger formation—whether this is as a part of the All India Muslim League, of the MQM, or of the MQM's various emerging factions. This larger *affective* dependence on political action as a source of nationalist identification, embodied in the claim of sacrifice, will continue to define the Muhajir political imaginary irrespective of which political movement or party makes use of it at the rhetorical or ideological level.

Notes

1. The territories constituting Pakistan at the time of independence, which included East Pakistan (now Bangladesh), were known as "majority-Muslim" provinces.
2. See "What Altaf Said," *Dawn,* August 23, 2016.
3. The riots pitted Muslim migrants from northern and central India (Muhajirs) against ethnic Pathans who had been migrating to Karachi from the upcountry province of Khyber Pakhtunkhwa since the early 1960s in search of work in the manufacturing, transport, and construction sectors. This was followed by an infusion of Afghan Pathan refugees during the Afghan-Soviet War and speculation that the Pathan attacks in 1986 against Muhajirs living in Orangi were the result of a rumor, floated by Karachi's Afghan heroin mafia, that a drug raid in the majority Pathan area of Sohrab Goth had been conducted at the request of the Muhajir community as part of a deliberate attempt to "evict Pathans from Karachi" (Hussain 1990, 187).
4. Sindh's overall rural majority continues to favor the Pakistan People's Party. See Philip Jones's chapter in this volume.
5. Anonymous, "MQM by Any Other Name," *Himal: South Asian,* September 1997, accessed on March 30, 2019, http://old.himalmag.com/himal-feed/58/2717 -MQM-by-any-other-name.html.
6. One pattern that developed after the defection of the MQM (Haqiqi) from the original MQM (led by Hussain) in the early 1990s was the latter's tendency to lay its failures at the feet of the defector. The MQM-Altaf accused the MQM-H of being the parent of the MQM's militant culture.
7. The All India Muslim League's version of spiritual politics was not without its detractors in the form of members of India's *ulema,* such as Maulana Husain Ahmad Madani, who asserted in 1945 that "the principles of the League were shut off from the light of the holy Shariat" (Gilmartin 1988, 190).
8. Appadurai suggests that the "largeness, historical diversity, and abstractness of the social relations encompassed (and valorized) by the modern nation-state make it difficult to understand the willingness of modern citizens to kill and to die for it" (Appadurai 1998, 4,446).
9. This outcome, as political historians of Pakistan suggest, was overdetermined and had equally to do with (a) the recognized historical origins of the Pakistan movement in the minority-Muslim provinces of present-day India; (b) the early but short-lived primacy of north Indian migrants in the federal government; and (c) the availability and configuration of Urdu as an extraterritorial "link language" within Pakistan's multiethnic landscape (Ayres 2009, 32; Rahman 1996).
10. Address to the Partition Plan Council, June 1947.
11. Z. A. Suleri, "Muhajir kaa tahriikhi kirdaar aur maujooda farz" [The historic role of the Muhajirs and their present obligations], *Roznaama Jang,* February 20, 1975.
12. Author interview of Shahzeb, July 2003, Karachi.
13. Author interview of Imran Farooq, November 2002, London.
14. Author interview of Imtiaz Sahib, December 2003, Orangi Town.

5

Leftist Parties in Pakistan
Challenges and Limitations

Anushay Malik

Few in Pakistan today remember the movement in the late 1960s against Field Marshal Muhammad Ayub Khan, and fewer still remember that the movement represented, for many who took part in it, a victory for the Left in Pakistan. Raghavan (2013, 15) describes the movement against the wider backdrop of global progressive protests led by students in the 1960s and goes so far as to say that "it was arguably the most successful of all the revolts in that momentous year." The obvious evidence for the "success" of this movement is what happened after it: Ayub Khan stepped down from power and the first national elections were held in Pakistan, ushering in the Pakistan People's Party (PPP) under Zulfikar Ali Bhutto's leadership. The subsequent historical dominance of the PPP in Pakistan's electoral politics meant that the anti-Ayub movement was not seen as a movement of the Left but rather as the moment that brought the PPP into power. In fact, it was the other way around. The movement itself and the way in which it propelled a language of the Left—through its demand for nationalization, land reform, and workers' rights—provided a basis on which the PPP was able to capitalize and come to victory. In doing so the PPP usurped the mandate of the movement and of other left-wing groups that could have used this moment to unite and become a force capable of winning elections (see A. Malik 2018). Indeed, if one were to trace the origins of all leftist groups in Pakistan today, one would find that almost all of these groups cut their political teeth in this anti-Ayub movement. This includes leaders of nongovernment organizations like the Human Rights Commission in Pakistan (HRCP); labor leaders such as Meraj Muhammad Khan, who went on to form his own left-wing party, the Qaumi Mahaz-e-Azadi (National Freedom Front); and some members of the PPP itself, like Aitzaz Ahsan, who later emerged as the leader of the Lawyers' Movement (see chapter 11 in this volume).

In part this historical amnesia arises from realities of the day: the Left in Pakistan has largely failed at influencing national policies, such as on land reform, or in fomenting revolution. Contemporary leftist parties such as the Awami National Party (ANP), the Awami Workers Party (AWP), and the Mazdoor Kissan Party (MKP) have been unable to make a significant impact on Pakistan's electoral politics. However, they have maintained active party organizations and have upheld an anticapitalist and secular discourse that has helped minorities and subaltern groups gain some space within Pakistani politics.

Why did the Left fail to live up to the potential it exhibited in the late 1960s? Some scholars have argued that the Left was dismantled and marginalized within Pakistan (Toor 2011) and that its appeal was diluted by the greater efficacy of patronage politics or "common sense" among the lower classes in the country (Akhtar 2018). However, I focus on the long-term effects of the events of 1969 to 1971, which served to limit the possibility of a strong left emerging in Pakistan. The anti-Ayub movement and the period immediately following the loss of East Pakistan fundamentally changed the nature of left-wing political parties in Pakistan and stunted the growth of a robust left movement, particularly in comparison to what existed in neighboring Bangladesh and India. These challenging years marked a legacy that left-wing political parties were never able to overcome, hampering their development and ability to become electorally significant.

This curtailment of the Left was part of a longer process that started at the very inception of Pakistan. First, the territories that became Pakistan had little to no experience with left movements and had a numerically smaller working class compared to India. This was particularly true of Punjab, where communism never really took root. Second, immediately after Partition the left-wing parties were repressed and persecuted in Pakistan, which meant that these parties were forced to operate underground and adopt alternative platforms. This ultimately weakened their ability to mobilize as left-wing parties in the electoral arena and in the public sphere in general. Third, the anti-Ayub movement represented a moment in time when the fragmented leftist parties came together momentarily but were unable to make any sort of electoral headway. After throwing their weight firmly behind Z. A. Bhutto, who initially took up the mantle of socialism in Pakistan, Bhutto's left-wing supporters were ultimately pushed aside in favor of preserving the elite status quo (see chapter 2 in this volume). Fourth, and finally, the war of liberation in East Pakistan deeply impacted left-wing political parties in the country. Because these parties were in the opposition and often represented regional interests, they were viewed as being antithetical to the territorial integrity of the Pakistani state. The perceived threat of regional interests became that much greater after the loss of East Pakistan in 1971 and led to left-wing parties in Pakistan being attacked—ideologically and literally—not because they were left-wing but because they were perceived as espousing a secessionist ideology. These developments continue to affect Pakistani politics today and are an important part of understanding why leftist parties have been unable to make any electoral headway in the country.

The findings presented here were gleaned from historical sources including newspapers, National Assembly debates, and other archival material. The main challenges faced when accessing such material are the poor condition of documentary records in Pakistan and the arduous process of securing permission to access them. Moreover, the persecution of the Left by the state and its vulnerability to factionalization has led to numerous published and unpublished accounts that are often contradictory. For instance, the development of one of the only national left-wing parties in Pakistan's history, the National Awami Party (NAP), is perhaps one of the most hotly contested debates among those who identify with the Left. There is little consensus on the extent to which the NAP was influenced by Moscow or Beijing, and the dizzying array of splits within the party are not well documented, especially as the leadership and number of factions varied across provinces (Rashiduzzaman 1997, 407–8; F. Ahmed 1972).

This chapter is divided into five sections and proceeds as follows. The first section defines what it means to be a left-wing political party in Pakistan. Second, I examine how the international environment of the Cold War made the Left in Pakistan a target of state repression. The third section traces how the NAP became synonymous with the Left in Pakistan, thus effectively linking the politics of regionalism to the politics of the Left. The fourth focuses on how events from 1969 to 1971 represent a shift in the fortunes of the Pakistani Left, from which it never quite recovered. The fifth looks at how this shift was further compounded by the depoliticization and repression of the 1980s and 1990s. The last section explores contemporary leftist parties and concludes that, despite the Pakistani Left's lack of electoral success, it has still been able to carve a niche—albeit one limited in scope—within Pakistani politics, particularly in providing a voice to the marginalized.

What Is a Left-Wing Party in Pakistan?

Left-wing parties in Pakistan have historically been quite small and at times appeared to have ceased to formally exist altogether, because they were either banned (as in the case of the Communist Party of Pakistan in 1954) or internally factionalized. Tracing the lineages of contemporary left-wing political parties and understanding why they have failed to be electorally significant in Pakistan requires understanding which parties are deemed "leftist" and why these parties have remained so limited in their reach.

A prominent leftist activist in Pakistan has noted that "even informed observers of Pakistan might have little or no knowledge of leftist forces in the country" (Akhtar 2012, 27). For instance, if one were to look at only the 2008 elections, a common misconception is that the PPP was the main left-wing party in Pakistan and it formed the government in coalition with another center-left party, the Awami National Party (ANP). The benefit of using a longer time frame is that one would know that this was the same PPP that dissolved the coalition government of the NAP—ANP's parent party—in North-West Frontier Province (now Khyber Pukhtunkhwa, or KP) in the 1970s. At the time the PPP's political expediency and desire to hold on to power trumped any ideological camaraderie it may have had with the NAP (see chapter 2 for more on the PPP).

It is difficult to apply to Pakistan understandings of the Left that are derived from the primarily Western European context. Typically, "left wing" describes secular political parties or movements that are progressive and ideologically oriented to an anticapitalist agenda (Przeworski 1985). In Europe, left-wing political parties have variously referred to themselves as Marxist or Trotskyist—labels that have typically mirrored divisions in international socialism (K. A. Ali 2015). Opposing to the status quo, highlighting class as the basis of conflict, associating with workers' unions, and being resistant to neoliberal global policies are all characteristics associated with left-wing parties in the European context (Przeworski 1985; Sartori 1990; Adams, Haupt, and Stoll 2009). However, it is important to recognize, as Sartori (1990, 162) does, that the nature of a left-wing party is highly contextual and that lumping parties into one catch-all category of the left is "little more than a weird ideological aggregate." The specificity of what it means to be left wing can be pinned down only within the particular geographical and temporal context in which a party exists. This is precisely what E. P. Thompson (1966, 8–10) argues in a well-known passage of his seminal work, *The Making of the English Working Class*: the "finest meshed sociological net" could not capture a definition of class, because it was contextually contingent and created out of class struggle; "men make their own history." Similarly, Leo Panitch's (1987) review of Przeworski and Sprague's (1986) *Paper Stones* makes an important critique: that linking the development of a left party too closely to the numerical strength of the working class in a particular area obscures the importance of political movements in allowing left-wing parties to shape class struggle. This, it can be argued, is even more true of the Global South, where left-wing political parties have been intrinsically tied not so much to the industrial working class but to anti-imperialist struggles (Akhtar 2015, 105).

If the definition of a left-wing party is one that attempts to challenge the elite status quo and calls for fundamental changes in the class structure, then in Pakistan the elite status quo consists of military control, Punjab's hegemony over other provinces, and the disenfranchisement of workers and peasants in a context of increasing concentration of wealth and privatization of industry (Alavi 1972a; Candland 2007b; Akhtar 2006). However, even if parties adhere to anticapitalist and other leftist principles, they may not all agree on the same course of political action. An important difference among left-wing parties has to do with how they propose to participate politically. Parties such as the ANP and the AWP believe in contesting elections, while others, such as the MKP, believe in bringing about change by fomenting revolution. What, then, do left-wing parties in Pakistan have in common?

A party's self-definition as Marxist is insufficient for the party to be considered left-wing. Rather, the party must also have links with workers and peasants, must espouse an agenda that highlights the importance of class, and must be perceived by others to be leftist. Besides opposing the status quo, it must also advocate for provincial autonomy, given that the Pakistani establishment is intrinsically connected to Punjab's dominance in the country's politics at the expense of the other provinces. Even though Punjab also has subaltern groups operating within it, particularly in the south, Punjab is the seat of power (Samad 1995).

Repression and the Cold War

The first left-wing party in the newly formed Pakistan was a faction of the Communist Party of India (CPI). Examining why it created a Pakistan wing provides important insight into why left-wing parties were seen by the Pakistani establishment as inimical to the fledgling state. In order to justify the creation of Pakistan, members of the CPI drew on discussions taking place within the Soviet Union regarding the rights of nationalities to secede (K. A. Ali 2015). The CPI believed that Muslims were an economically marginalized group within India that had the right to form a separate nation. Since this right was the party's justification for supporting the formation of Pakistan, the party and its leaders had a natural affinity for the more radical nationalists (31–33) and encouraged its members to work with the Muslim League to form the Communist Party of Pakistan (CPP).

Very early on the groups that claimed to be left wing, like G. M. Syed's Sindh Awami Mahaz (Sind National Front) and Bacha Khan's Khudai Khidmatgar (Servants of God), pushed for regional autonomy over and above other ideological goals. Official state documents from this early period reveal that provincialism and communism were seen as two of the major threats faced by the nascent country (A. Malik 2013). Many members of the CPP who had previously been a part of the CPI did not break off their links with Indian communists, which made them subject to state scrutiny. Their links to India were viewed as gravely threatening to the Pakistani state because of how quickly relations between the two countries had deteriorated after Partition.

Other geopolitical factors also played a role. Throughout the 1950s and 1960s the Pakistani state's attempts to protect itself from India meant beefing up its anticommunist credentials in order to win over the United Sates as an international ally. Because India was edging closer to the Soviet Union despite being a member of the nonaligned movement, the politics of the Cold War necessitated that Pakistan cement its relations with the US in the hope of receiving economic and military aid. The search for such alliances was all the more urgent due to border tensions in Kashmir and the negative perceptions of the "other" being engineered by the state on both sides. It is no coincidence that the timing of Pakistan's entry into military pacts with the United States and the ban on the CPP (in 1954) directly overlapped. Prior to the ban CPP chief Sajjad Zahir and other party workers such as Faiz Ahmed Faiz were implicated in the Rawalpindi Conspiracy and charged with conspiring to seize power by conducting a coup (see Dryland 1992).

The severe crackdown on the CPP's public activities and imprisonment of its workers and activists had broader consequences that affected the ability of the Left in Pakistan to fashion itself into effective parties that could win elections. Interviews of leftists at the time and statements by activists themselves have pointed out how left-wing political organizations suffered due to widespread anticommunist sentiments (Keddie 1975; Mahmud 1958). Meanwhile, their competitors benefited from a more open playing field and often utilized the tactics of the Left themselves. For example, the Jamaat-e-Islami (JI) was influenced by the success of the tactics used by the Left to mobilize support during the 1950s and 1960s (Iqtidar 2010).

The CPP expanded its networks among labor unions, journalists, and other intellectuals who together formed its support base. Although these groups did not necessarily see eye to eye, they were united by their broad commitment to progressive politics and the various worker, writer, and student fronts engaged in a range of activities (H. Malik 1967; Toor 2011; Raza 2013; A. Malik 2013). As was the case with Marxist and leftist movements across the world, what it meant to be leftist in Pakistan varied greatly and sometimes involved taking up contradictory positions that the participants themselves found to be perfectly reconcilable (Kalra and Sharma 2013, 4).

Some of these people met in spaces like coffee and tea shops and union and party offices for reading circles, literary activities, and discussions. With the banning of the CPP and the state's commitment to end communism in Pakistan, these spaces also became targets of repression (A. Malik 2013; H. Akhtar 2009; Toor 2011). Organizations loosely affiliated with the CPP had their activities constrained by constant surveillance by the state, which only served to benefit competing organizations that were not affiliated with the Left. For example, the All Pakistan Confederation of Labor became much stronger during this time at the expense of the Pakistan Trade Union Federation, which was affiliated with the CPP and stopped functioning (K. A. Ali 2015, 78–80, 154).

Given the arrests and intimidation to which leftists were subjected from the early years of Pakistan, it is actually quite remarkable that their story did not end there. Indeed, while their activities were constrained, they did not come to a halt. The resilience that they were able to show was in part due to their success in finding alternative platforms and in a sense "hiding" within political parties that were not overtly leftist. For instance, many who had initially joined the Muslim League as part of its progressive faction and continued their alliance with the CPP switched to the Azad Pakistan Party (APP) founded by Mian Iftikharuddin. The APP, a small and geographically narrow party, had limited influence in East Pakistan, home to more than half the country's population, making success at the national level unlikely. Within this context the evolution of the NAP became important.

Regionalism and the Left-Wing National Awami Party

During the 1950s and 1960s the Left was represented by the Pakistan National Party (PNP) in West Pakistan. The PNP, formed in September 1956, was a conglomeration of minor parties including the Khudai Khidmatgar, the Wrore Pukhtun, the Sind Hari Committee, the Ustaman Gul, and the Azad Pakistan Party. In East Pakistan, Maulana Bhashani, a firebrand peasant leader, diverged from his parent party, the Awami League, on matters of foreign policy; he led a significant portion of the Awami League to form a separate faction. On July 25, 1957, the PNP and Bhashani's Awami League merged to form the National Awami Party (NAP). This new party was a loose conglomeration of leftists (including Afzal Bangash, Mian Iftikharudin, Mahmud Ali Kasuri) and autonomists (such as G. M. Syed of Sindh, Bacha Khan in KP, and Mir Ghaus Bukhsh Bizenjo, Khair Bukhsh Marri, and Abdul Samad Achakzai in Balochistan) who were committed to the dissolution of the One Unit policy, regional autonomy, economic reforms, and nonaligned foreign policy (Aziz 1976, 113).

After the 1956 Constitution was announced, elections were promised for February 1959. Had elections been held, the NAP would have emerged as a powerful party in the legislature. However, in 1958 Ayub Khan declared martial law and promptly banned all political parties. The NAP was persecuted more than any other party because of its leftist credentials; activists and workers were unlawfully detained, tortured, and harassed.[1] The NAP was a thorn in the side of the Pakistani establishment because it had demanded the abolition of the One Unit scheme to amalgamate all West Pakistan provinces into one unit in order to undermine the absolute majority of East Pakistan and secure the dominance of Punjab's establishment (Sayeed 1959). The NAP's call for the abolition of One Unit and the concomitant demand for greater regional autonomy was viewed by state officials as a declaration of hostility against the new country. This was asserted repeatedly in official statements. In 1957 Pres. Iskander Mirza declared that provincial autonomy was tantamount to demanding the disintegration of Pakistan.[2]

Under the NAP's umbrella, regional identity and leftist demands came to be mutually intertwined. Most discussions around regionalism have assumed that provincial identity is derived from ethnonationalism and that the baton carriers of this identity—and therefore the leaders of regional political parties—essentially draw their power from their linguistic identity. However, as recent writers looking at the Punjabi context have pointed out, the Left has crucially linked linguistic identity to class identity through their movements. This link is an organic one that derives from extant social inequalities in South Asia that overlap with language hierarchies created during colonialism (where, for instance, Punjabi was the language of the peasants while Urdu, the language of the elite, was seen as the route through which one could gain access to prestigious public-sector jobs) (Kazmi 2017; Kalra and Butt 2013).

At the same time, international politics also affected the NAP's political trajectory. The development of Pakistan's relations with China in the aftermath of India-China border clashes in 1962 and rifts in the international communist movement fueled tensions within the NAP, resulting in a split in the party along pro-China and pro-Soviet lines. Problematically, the pro-China faction in the party, led by Maulana Bhashani, softened its stance toward the Ayub regime because of the latter's pro-China foreign policy, thus further weakening the ability of the Left in Pakistan to work together in the lead-up to the 1970 elections.[3]

The Turning Point: The PPP and Bangladesh

A commonly accepted narrative within Pakistan is that the primary left-wing party in the country is the PPP. However, the PPP's taking up of the mantle of socialism in fact sidelined other smaller left-wing parties and ultimately proved to be a disservice to the leftist cause. The PPP was unique in that it attracted a diverse group of people who were united in their desire to reconstruct the economy and society on socialist lines. On the one hand, the PPP attracted urban intellectuals like Mubashir Hassan and J. A. Rahim, who helped coin the party's motto, "Islam is our faith, democracy is our polity, socialism is our economy, all power to the people" (Pakistan People's Party 1967, 11). On the other hand, it also attracted ideologically antifeudalist and erstwhile members of the Pakistan Muslim League like Sheikh Rashid, who fought for the rights of peasants. Another group from the Muslim League was the "Islamic socialists" (Jones 2003, 124–25) led by the likes of Hanif Ramay and Khurshid Hassan Mir, who agreed with the leftist socialists in principle but also found Quranic support for the nationalization of industries and land reform (222–23). At the helm of the party was Z. A. Bhutto, who astutely understood that the Pakistani populace had nationalistic aspirations but not necessarily revolutionary ones. The party's slogan emerged from an alternative ideology: *roti, kapra, aur makaan* (food, clothing, and shelter), and new mobilizing techniques such as mass-based rallies helped make the party successful. The PPP won the 1970 elections by a landslide in West Pakistan on the basis of a socialist rhetoric, but after forming the government it changed its tune. Very quickly the party moved to exclude the more radical leftist elements, including persecuted laborers who were on strike. These strikers, many of whom had taken control of the factories, were fired on, and several were killed (K. A. Ali 2005; Shaheed 1979, 2007). Eventually disheartened by PPP's brand of politics, Meraj Muhammad Khan, one of the party's founding members, broke away to form the Qaumi Mahaz-e-Azadi.

In East Pakistan the Left was better organized and more militant. The peasant movements of the 1940s and labor strikes during the 1950s provided the Left with an already mobilized support base. The anti-Ayub movement in East Pakistan was more widespread, involving both the rural peasantry and urban intelligentsia in a way that was not replicated in West Pakistan (Shaikh 2010). East Pakistan was the voice of opposition constantly challenging the Punjabi establishment and West Pakistan's exploitation of East Bengal. The rural and urban working classes in East Pakistan hailed Maulana Bhashani as a potent force in mobilizing anti-Ayub protest and posed a threat to the Pakistani state in a way that had never been witnessed. Bhashani's boycott of the 1970 elections paved the way for Mujibur Rehman's Awami League to win a landslide victory. The later secession of East Pakistan also meant that the political presence that could be exerted by the progressives in West Pakistan, already smaller in number, was further diminished.

The separation of Bangladesh resulted in the loss of a large and mobilized section of the Left. It also represented the unequivocal end of the two-nation theory: the theory had to be reimagined and a new history had to be written. Fearful of further secessionist claims, the state dramatically increased its hostility toward regional leaders. During one National Assembly debate Khan Abdul Wali Khan of the NAP suggested that the constitution's outline be debated in public to allow the say of a wider cross section of society. Regardless of the merits or problems of such a suggestion, the hostility he faced speaks volumes about how nationalist leaders were viewed as troublemakers even when they were a part of the National Assembly (National Assembly [Constitution-Making] Debates, December 31, 1972, 21). Instead of equitably allocating resources and devolving power to the provinces, the response to 1971 was to increase the centralized authoritarian tendencies of the state. Shortly after he came to power Bhutto dissolved the assemblies in Sindh and North-West Frontier Province (NWFP). In Balochistan he gave his blessings to an all-out civil war, the consequences of which continue to the present day (A. Khan 2009).

The link of regionalism to leftist parties until the 1970s, and the increasing levels of repression targeting these parties, makes any gains that the Left *did* make surprising. This is particularly true for the NAP. However, the NAP's generally poor electoral showing forced it to make compromises that were incompatible with its ideology. For example, when the NAP finished a poor second to a PML faction in the 1970 elections, it was forced to form a coalition in the NWFP with Jamiat Ulema-e-Islam (JUI), an Islamic political party whose ideology was antithetical to NAP's secular ideology of Pakhtun nationalism.

The true test of Wali Khan's mettle as a leader occurred when he was unable to muster a significant protest against the forced resignation of the NAP's ministry in the NWFP by the Bhutto government, in the 1973 firing on NAP workers by a paramilitary force in Liaqat Bagh, or even the high-handed treatment meted out to him by Bhutto in 1975 in the Hyderabad conspiracy case in which he was wrongly accused and imprisoned for the murder of PPP member Hayat Ahmed Sherpao. Wali Khan served a prison sentence and the National Democratic Party emerged as the surrogate party for the Left, but it too eventually disintegrated as the Baloch leaders who had helped found it moved on to forming their own parties or going into exile.

The PPP continued to call itself a party that believed in a loosely defined idea of Islamic socialism, but it crushed workers' uprisings and alienated the more radical leftists within it, and its claim to be a leftist party came to be no longer seen as a serious one. This idea of a combination of Islam and socialism had been touted by the state in the 1950s as well, but in all such accounts socialism remained undefined and temporally contingent. For the workers and peasants involved in the movement against Ayub Khan, the cohesion meant something a lot more expansive, including redistribution; there were even rumors of poorer people earmarking houses in wealthier localities that would be theirs after the revolution (Jones 2003, 299). Factory workers thought the movement would take the factories back from employers, and in some notable incidents they locked the employers out (Shaheed 2007). One interviewed labor leader in Lahore stated, "*Socialism aaway hee aaway, jayda waaway oh hee khaway*" (Socialism is coming, he who tills the land will be the one who eats).[4] Clearly those who raised this and other similar slogans in rallies had a specific understanding of the goals of the Left in Pakistan: the movement would change property rights in the country. Bhutto's violent crackdowns on protestors, however, showed them that their belief that the PPP could represent their demands was misplaced (K. A. Ali 2005). By the time Bhutto was ousted by General Zia-ul-Haq, some of the older leftists who had supported Bhutto in the initial phases reportedly celebrated his macabre demise.[5]

Left-Wing Parties in the 1980s and 1990s: The Politics of Disappointment and Repression

In 1977 General Zia-ul-Haq, through a "coup of the ultra-right" (A. Ahmad 1978, 96), ushered in a new era of severe repression characterized by prolonged detentions, public floggings, torture, and the intimidation tactics of a military dictatorship. The only real resistance to the regime came from the Movement for the Restoration of Democracy (MRD). The MRD was geographically limited to Sindh and consisted of eight political parties, not all of whom identified as leftist (Sayeed 1984). Older left-wing parties like the MKP and the Qaumi Mahaz-e-Azadi, joined the MRD. The NAP, however, initially supported Zia's martial law because Wali Khan believed that the ousted PPP government should be held accountable for its past misdeeds. But Wali Khan's stubborn anti-PPP stance proved to be his undoing because even though he reluctantly joined the MRD, his ambivalence alienated his supporters and led to a devastating loss in the 1988 elections at the hands of his own constituency, the former bastion of the Khudai Khidmatgar Movement.

From 1983 to 1989 the military, under direct orders from Zia-ul-Haq, systematically disempowered and suppressed the nonviolent proponents of the MRD, which included leftist parties particularly in rural Sindh (Gazdar 2006). Despite the extreme state repression encountered, the MRD brought the otherwise disparate resistance movements closer. For example, the Sindhiani Tehreek spread and mobilized at this time (Khan and Saigol 2004). At the national level the only parties that were given greater space to function were religiously affiliated. In line with his Islamization program, Zia-ul-Haq patronized parties like the Jamaat-e-Islami, a party that had historically been in conflict with the Left, which, under the PPP, had erupted into armed battles on university campuses and led students to search for alternatives (T. Ali 1970, 99; Nelson 2011). In the 1980s, however, the patronage extended to Jamaat-e-Islami meant that it took over campuses and trade unions, places where previously it had competed with left-wing groups. Effectively this also meant a further erosion of the traditional Left support base.

Two other wider changes were afoot. First, Pakistan imbibed the international environment of neoliberalism and moved toward increasingly greater labor flexibility and privatization of public enterprises. This move further weakened the ability of the Left to draw support from among their old constituencies, particularly the working classes (Candland 2007a). Second, Pakistan's geostrategic position in the 1980s with respect to the Afghan War (and later with the War on Terror) meant that the large amounts of funding pouring into the country came with conditions. This led to a proliferation of nongovernmental organizations around whom progressives rallied, changing their politics from radicalism to development-oriented policymaking. This depoliticization undermined the mandate of leftist movements that could have fed, or developed, into political parties.[6] It is no surprise, then, that "by the end of the 1990s the left had become a political non-entity" (Akhtar 2015, 106).

It was also during Zia-ul-Haq's tenure that the NAP underwent another change in nomenclature. In 1986 four progressive and nationalist parties under the leadership of Wali Khan formed the Awami National Party (ANP), a conglomerate of leftists, nationalists, and autonomists all rolled into one.[7] After Zia-ul-Haq's demise in 1988, Pakistan entered into a democratic interregnum. During the 1990s a series of elections were held in which no government completed its term because each time the Parliament was dissolved by executive fiat. It is no surprise that voter turnout dropped through the 1990s to an all-time low of 20 percent in the 1997 elections (Wilkinson 2000, 223). The disenchantment with politics was another important factor explaining why no leftist party succeeded electorally.

The (Brief) Rise and Fall of the ANP: 2008 and 2013

By the end of the 1990s left-wing political parties in Pakistan were fragmented and extremely wary of the state and elections in general. Given the decades of repression to which they had been subjected, it is no surprise that left-identifying parties made only very limited headway in elections.

The one exception to this was the ANP, which survived through coalition governments, primarily in Khyber Pakhtunkhwa, and, for a brief period after the 2008 elections, in Karachi. There was no parallel survival of the party's factions in Balochistan, in large part because some major army offensives had been launched in that province (A. Khan 2009; HRCP 2013). Further, the politicization of ethnic identity meant that groups like the NAP in Balochistan were no longer remembered as being left-wing or being part of any sort of revolutionary movement. This was compounded by national curricula that sought to elide the role of leftists. Even today no curriculum includes details of movements like the one in 1973 in which the London Group, a small group of left-wing students, came to Balochistan to fight with the Baloch against the Pakistan Army after the dismissal of the NAP government.[8]

The decimation of the ANP in KP has been much more recent. In the 2008 general elections the ANP won the largest number of seats in the KP provincial assembly. In the following election of 2013, however, the ANP won barely any seats and was effectively routed by Imran Khan's Pakistan Tehreek-e-Insaf (PTI). In 2018 the ANP was unable to make an electoral comeback, once again being defeated by the PTI.

The story of the ANP after the 2008 elections is one that illustrates the effects of the most obvious form of repression: physical repression leveled by terrorists against the ANP leadership. The ANP came to power in a province that previously had been under the rule of the right-wing religious leadership of the Muttahida Majlis-e-Amal (MMA). The MMA, an avowedly secular party, adopted a tough stance against militancy—notwithstanding some exceptions, including in Swat, where the ANP signed a peace deal with the Tehreek-Nifaz-i-Shariat-i-Mohammadi (see Abbas 2010 for more details). Subsequently, ANP leaders were targeted by militants in the region, continuing all the way to the 2013 elections in KP. It quickly became apparent that while the ANP leaders received death threats and were wary with every move, leaders of right-wing parties were able to hold their rallies openly and with impunity. Between 2009 and 2013 nearly one thousand ANP members were killed by the Taliban.[9] The victory of the PTI in KP in 2013 was made possible in part because of an emaciated ANP.

The manner in which the repression of the Left created the space for other political actors to emerge is crucial to understanding why the Left has ostensibly done poorly in electoral competitions. The repression leveled by the state onto political actors in the 1950s was not as severe or as visible as it would become in later years, particularly given the protracted war in the northern regions of Pakistan that began in earnest after 2001. However, it was enough to raise the costs of collective action in the short term, and over the longer term it made the political network of leftists much harder to sustain, thereby affecting the organization of leftist parties. In addition to this, Pakistan, taking on labor-flexible regimes and seeing the proliferation of an "NGO culture," stripped these parties of much of the radical potential that could have made them more distinct as leftist parties.

Even when restrictions on left-wing parties have been lifted, as smaller political parties they are wary of participating in politics in the open, and as regional parties they are suspicious of the Punjabi establishment. Indeed, for the older cadre within left-wing political parties, acting in suspicion and secrecy has become part of their cultural ethos. In conversations with labor and leftist activists in the mid-2000s I often heard how they mainly worked "underground," how the revolution would come but the work had to be done in secret, and about how their friends had been picked up and tortured. This atmosphere has affected the tactics that activists thought possible, so they have shied away from engaging in the mainstream political terrain.

Hope for the Future of Left-Wing Political Parties in Pakistan?

Nonetheless, there is reason to believe that left-wing political parties may be able to make some headway in the future. The movement against General Musharraf in 2007 brought together young people in Pakistan and injected a certain amount of faith in the political system. The use of new technologies also meant that the movement was coordinated internationally with Pakistanis in major cities in the US and UK (Bolognani 2010). The experience of being part of this movement led to the reformation of the old left-wing student group the National Students' Federation (NSF) as part of a larger initiative to take back university campuses from the groups that had secured their foothold there under the Zia years.

Soon after, an attempt was made by older leftist parties to merge together to form a new left-wing political party (Akhtar 2012, 28). These efforts proved successful in November 2012, when three parties—the Labor Party

Pakistan, Awami Party Pakistan, and the Workers' Party Pakistan—merged to form the Awami Workers' Party. Drawing on a wide range of ideological factions, these groups together contested the 2008, 2013, and 2018 elections, although they have not yet managed to win seats. In the recent 2018 election the AWP fielded seven candidates for the National Assembly: six in the KP provincial assembly, two in Sindh, and two in Punjab. Their failure to win seats is a reflection of the Left's small base in the contemporary period and the limited overall support for the worker and peasant movements they support. The act of fielding these candidates is, nonetheless, important in a country where democracy is fragile and where a small elite has long controlled politics. Making class-based demands and giving tickets to the working class is therefore an important part of the process. For instance, in the 2018 election the candidate who received the AWP ticket from Nasirabad in Sindh had previously been a worker in a rice factory. Similarly, the election manifesto of the AWP strongly focuses on the inequalities generated by class divisions and the need for more substantial land reform.

In this sense the AWP is not unique; left-wing political parties in Pakistan have historically failed to win votes or even contest elections nationwide. Still, they have played an important role in shaping Pakistan's politics by coordinating smaller resistance movements, by creating a new consciousness among traditionally disenfranchised classes, and by providing young people with a platform for collective action. These networks are important because they are the only way that disenfranchised groups within Pakistan can get access to the resources that are necessary to contest and campaign at election time. For instance, in 2013 Veeru Kohli, an activist and escaped bonded laborer, contested the election from Sindh. Activists from Left parties and organizations in Pakistan were involved in gathering funds to make this candidacy possible.

Perhaps more important than left-wing parties in Pakistan are the movements that they ally with and support—movements that are often invisible to the state and mainstream media. The Haqooq-e-Khalq (Human Rights) Movement in Pakistan, for instance, is a recent network consisting of students, faculty, journalists, and activists that highlights progressive causes and holds study circles.

Historically movements like these as well as individual leftist figures have played an important role in creating small pockets of space for the Left within the wider structure of Pakistani politics. For instance, the written works of individuals like Sibte Hassan and Faiz Ahmed Faiz have inspired an entire generation of youths to demand political change. Other well-known activists have thrown their weight behind issues that in the contemporary context have produced collective action demanding women's rights, the rights of slum dwellers, and the rights of laborers and peasants. Leftists in Pakistan have also resisted the "ideological onslaught" of the establishment and religious parties, and in response have advocated democracy and secularism through literature, poetry, and study circles.[10] On the political front, the mobilization capacity of the Left enabled it to provide a platform to nationalist political movements in Sindh, Balochistan, and KP. It was able to bring together otherwise disparate groupings of intellectuals, professionals, and nationalists to bravely resist military dictatorships under Ayub Khan and Zia-ul-Haq. By inserting class into politics and focusing on mobilizing students and the working class, the Left has been responsible for influencing some of the strategies and tactics that were later used by the JI, the MQM (Muttahida Qaumi Movement), and even the PTI. The Left was also the first to introduce anti-imperialist rhetoric, which later morphed into the anti-West rhetoric of religious political parties such as the Muttahida Majlis-e-Amal. Thus, while left-wing political parties may not be poised for electoral victory, their role as resistance movements in support of the disenfranchised continues to ensure their relevance within the Pakistani polity.

Notes

1. Hassan Nasir was allegedly tortured to death in Lahore's Shahi Qila. The editors of *Pakistan Times,* the Urdu daily *Imroz,* and the weekly *Lail-o-Nahr* were taken into custody because they were owned by a publishing house whose major shareholder was veteran leftist Mian Iftikharuddin. See G. Abbas Jalbani, "Rise and Fall," *Herald*, October 1997, 126.
2. See "Regional Autonomy Will Mean Disintegration," *Pakistan Times*, March 24, 1957, 1.
3. Jalbani, "Rise and Fall."
4. Author interview of Bashir Zafar, November 7, 2010, Lahore.
5. Author interview of Tahira Mazhar Ali Khan, February 2, 2008, Lahore.
6. In the contemporary period this has also been the case with the peasant movement in Okara and the Katchi Abadi (Slum Dwellers) Alliance, both of which were movements by the working poor to get their land back from military officials and urban developers (Akhtar 2015).
7. These were the Mazdoor Kissan Party (Laborer peasant party) led by Afzal Bangash, the Pakistan National Party led by Mir Ghous Buksh Bizenjo, the Sindh Awami Terhrik (Sindh citizen movement) led by Rasul Buksh Palijo, and the National Awami Party led by Wali Khan.
8. Siraj Akbar Malik, "Revisiting the Che Guevara–like Days of Baloch Resistance Movement with Asad Rehman," accessed October 2009, http://gmcmissing.word press.com/2009/10/19/revisiting-the-che-guevara-like-days-of-baloch-resis tance-movement-with-asad-rehman/.
9. Jon Boone, "Pakistan's Campaign Trail Politicians Use Stealth to Outwit Taliban Threats," *Guardian*, April 28, 2013. Also see Manzoor Ali, "Undeterred by Blast, ANP Vows to Contest Polls" *Dawn*, July 12, 2018.
10. Jalbani, "Rise and Fall," 129.

6

Religious Parties
The Politics of Denominational Diversity in an Islamic Republic

Johann Chacko

Nearly two dozen Islamic parties are actively involved in electoral politics in Pakistan (Rana 2004). Despite generally unimpressive electoral results (Ullah 2013), they have collectively played an outsize role in national political life, especially in shaping discursive norms. This distinctive trajectory of Pakistan's religious parties has been determined by South Asia's intrasectarian denominational diversity, which operates in the context of competitive politics within a populist Islamic republic overseen by an authoritarian weak state.

There are three key aspects to explicating this argument. First, the political behavior of each party must be understood in the context of its highly specific denominational affiliation. These denominations in turn must be understood as long-established and highly successful social movements competing to transform society in line with their own reading of Islam. Despite a high level of interdenominational competition, the parties have succeeded in operating collectively as a cartel that deny religious authority and legitimacy at will to those who do not share their collective norms or interests—including the state.

Second, the electoral prospects of individual Islamic parties are limited by three factors: (1) the magnitude of political fragmentation in an observant but highly heterogeneous religious population divided between a large number of faction-ridden denominations, (2) the inherent difficulties of social movements in reconciling their wider goals with electoral optimization, and (3) the preference of most voters for patronage over piety from politicians: religious parties are generally not resource-rich nor powerful enough to compete with business figures and feudal landholders for control or influence.

Third, the depth of the popular consensus behind the world's oldest Islamic republic and the decline in the weak state's ability to autonomously assert Islamic credibility has led many Pakistani government administrations, especially those lacking a strong mandate, to greatly depend on at least passive acceptance from contemporaneous Islamic social movements. The fact that these movements collectively helped turn Pakistan into an Islamic republic and are widely regarded as its ideological guardians has proved to be a lasting advantage over their competitors to power, including the security state. As a result, denominational parties dominate the contentious process of defining and defending the boundaries of Islamic identity, especially as a function of governmentality. This helps account for the apparent paradox of highly influential but electorally uncompetitive religious parties. However, much like the state, denominational parties cannot simply command public opinion; they must woo and shape it through populist messaging.

Pakistan's long but intermittent history of electoral politics dates back to the late colonial era and is a rich source of data for those working on democratization theory and comparative politics outside a Western context (Huntington 1968; Nasr 2005). While scholarship has shifted away from a reliance on an Orientalist explanation of the role played by Islam and Islamicate civilization, the change has often come with a loss of religious context. Overcoming this requires bringing religious studies back into dialogue with political science, particularly given that we are in an era that Jürgen Habermas (2008) describes as "post-secular modernity." One avenue is the development and application of social movement theory (SMT) and its toolkits. As we know from examples such as the women's and LGBTQ movements, successful social movements transform the normative values, political discourse, and distribution of power within a society. Although initially applied largely to secular and progressive Western postwar movements of marginalized groups, the body of work on SMT is increasingly being used in non-Western contexts and as related to religious movements (Kirmani 2008). Studies of Middle Eastern and North African Islamic movements now routinely use SMT's frameworks (Wiktorowicz 2004), but this is still extremely rarely done with their South Asian counterparts.

This chapter, therefore, uses the SMT framework to understand the role and behavior of Islamic parties. First some definitional context is given for how Pakistan's Islamic parties differ from mainstream parties. Second is an examination of the linkages between Islamic parties and their *maslaks* (denominations)—to explain why such parties continue to participate in electoral politics despite performing relatively poorly—and a discussion of the impact Islamic parties have had on the state outside of elections. The chapter concludes with a review of how the behavior of Islamic parties has developed over time and concludes with what they might look like in the future.

Islamic Parties in the Pakistani Context

Islamic parties are often thought of as confessional parties, which Stathis Kalyvas (1996) defines as organizations that explicitly utilize aspects of religious identity to recruit supporters and campaign in electoral contests. In the case of Pakistan the definition applies to nearly all major parties, including the Pakistan Muslim League-Nawaz (PML-N), the Pakistan People's Party (PPP), the Pakistan Tehreek-e-Insaf (PTI), and the Muttahida Qaumi Movement (MQM). These parties have appealed to Islamic identity and values, although usually in combination with class interests or ethnicity (Nasr 2005; Verkaaik 2004; Syed 1992). Vali Nasr (2005) refers to the PML-N more specifically as a "Muslim Democrat" party, which echoes the Christian Democrats of Europe in their center-right appeal to bourgeois Muslim identity and values.

What, then, distinguishes these parties from explicitly religious or Islamic parties, which generically refer to themselves as *deeni* (rooted in the Islamic way of life) or *Islam-pasand* (Islam-loving)? Although deeni parties use broad references to Islam and Muslims in their public-facing messaging, each party is imbued with a clear sense of belonging to a particular *maslak* (denomination) and strives to represent and defend the interests of a particular faith community within the political system.

In addition to the sectarian divide between Sunni and Shi'a, denominational differences in South Asia include major intrasectarian divisions *within* both Sunni and Shi'a Islam. This profusion of maslaks reflects Islam's extraordinary social and intellectual diversity in South Asia. Despite common origins in the Sunni revivalist currents of the eighteenth century, the era of British colonial supremacy following the abolition of the Mughal Empire witnessed the emergence of Barelvi, Deobandi, Ahle Hadith, Ahmadi, and Ahle Qur'an maslaks as distinct movements in the latter half of the nineteenth century (Metcalf 1982; Sanyal 2012). The Jamaat-e-Islami (JI), founded much later (in 1941) by Abul A'la Mawdudi, has been perhaps the most politically oriented of all the maslaks (Nasr 1994). In comparison, the Barelvis are by far the largest maslak in Pakistan and the Deobandis are the next largest and among the most politically active (Behuria 2008).

The maslak itself, argues Brinkley Messick (2005) in drawing on comparative religious scholar Stanley Fish (1976), is an enduring "interpretive community"—that is, a group that holds a shared standard on how to read texts. Strong arguments have been made by Ira Lapidus (1997) that these revivalist movements, which emerged in the Muslim world during the eighteenth and nineteenth centuries, should be understood as (confessional) social movements whose goals remain the wholesale transformation of society. What makes them social movements is the commitment of members to working toward the same broadly defined goal (in this case, the realization of a specific reading of Islam) through deliberate patterns of contentious action (Diani and Della Porta 2006, 23). As a result, these communities provide powerfully distinct sources of identity and loyalty. Their ensuing rivalries have been expressed for over a century both through bitter theological polemics as well as a competition for social space (Zaidi 2010; Robinson 2013).

Denominational (*maslaki*) parties, therefore, go much further than their so-called Muslim Democrat competitors in claiming custodianship over the welfare and integrity of Islam itself. This ownership is a reflection of the self-assured spiritual authority held by the professional religious workers who populate the leadership and cadre of these parties (Zaman 2002). But what they share goes beyond a basic commitment to ensuring that the state demonstrates a reverence for Islamic principles; it extends to securing an exclusive role for the *ulema* (religious scholars) in determining those principles and the independence of the various maslak-controlled educational systems that produce the ulema.

This distinction is useful for examining the quite different aims and leadership styles found among various types of denominational parties. Pakistani maslaki parties' programs, for example, may not be consistently aimed at establishing Islamic law (i.e., not Islamist) but may instead promote denominational, sectarian, cultural, and professional interests (Zaman 1998, 2002). Nor are their programs and claims to authority necessarily based on literalist readings of sacred text (i.e., not fundamentalist). Instead, as Buehler (1998) points out, they might be based on the charismatic authority of ulema, *maulvis* (preachers), and *pirs* (divinely empowered holy men) working toward a place where tradition and evolving public sentiment meet.

The Political Relevance of Denominational Parties

Simply tallying the maslaki parties' share of votes and seats, however, would not reflect their considerable influence. Denominational parties have historically remained competitive in the Khyber Pakhtunkhwa (KP) and Balochistan provinces, where they held majority control in provincial legislatures six times (Ullah 2013). On the other hand, they have played only a marginal role in Punjab and Sindh, which together account for 74 percent of Pakistan's population and the majority of parliamentary seats.[1]

The latest major Islamic party to emerge in Punjab and Sindh is the Tehreek-e-Labbaik Pakistan Party (TLP) led by a working-class preacher named Khadim Rizvi. The TLP came into existence in 2015 to capitalize on the Barelvi mobilization in defense of colonial-era blasphemy laws, which had been made more severe through clauses instituted in the 1980s under Gen. Muhammad Zia-ul-Haq and the impunity subsequently enjoyed by anti-blasphemy vigilantism that had grown in its shadow. Although the TLP's rapid growth and its intimidating public shows of strength suggested state support, results in the 2018 general elections did not live up to the party's expectations, yielding only two seats from Karachi in the Sindh provincial assembly. While the TLP came fifth in elections to the National Assembly and sixth in Punjab provincial elections, that translated into only 4 percent and 6 percent of the vote share, respectively, which had largely been cannibalized from the PML-N's electorate.[2]

With the exception of two short-lived coalition governments produced by heavily rigged elections in 1990 and 2002 and the inclusion in the governing coalition as a very junior partner after the 2018 elections, maslaki parties have never been able to sustain an electoral challenge to Muslim Democrat national parties or regional ethnic parties. Given their inability to eclipse the legitimacy of the military, the judiciary, or the Parliament, these denominational parties have had little option but to embrace pragmatism and conform to systemic norms (Kumar 2001; Fair, Malhotra, and Shapiro 2010; ICG 2011; Ullah 2013; Nelson 2017).

Perhaps this is why maslaki parliamentary parties, with the exception of the JI (Nasr 1994), have been given short shrift in the literature, in favor of a focus on armed groups and state-led Islamization. This is unfortunate because, as Zaman (1998, 2002, 2018) convincingly argues, these parties play a crucial role in aggregating and mediating the often-competing interests of various networks within highly decentralized denominational social movements. By acting as an interface among these networks, the voting public, and the state, the parties collectively play a key role in facilitating the establishment of "Islamic" political norms whenever and wherever consensus emerges across the major denominations.

The maslaki parties and their parent movements played a decisive role in establishing Pakistan as the world's first Islamic republic—that is, a nation-state whose internal legitimacy derives simultaneously from the consent of the people and an aspirational commitment to authentic Islamic governance (Binder 1961). Starting in 1951 the state, in alliance with modernists, made multiple determined attempts to shut out these maslaks from the process of defining the country's political ideology and social norms, but these exclusionary efforts ended after the fall of Field Marshal Mohammad Ayub Khan in 1969. The successful national mass mobilization that brought down Ayub made politics in the country far more populist, but the secession of religious minority and Marxist-heavy East Pakistan (now Bangladesh) in the 1971 civil war subsequently swung the new mass politics considerably further to the right, which greatly benefited the maslaki parties (Talbot 2012).

As a result, whenever maslaki parties have achieved consensus on Islamic matters in the post-1971 era they have commanded popular sentiment in a manner that both the state and mainstream political parties can only ignore at significant political cost. The maslaki success in discursively influencing key elements of the constitution, the legal system, law enforcement, foreign policy, education, and gender policy has been a particular source of concern for Pakistani minorities and progressives as well as international actors (Haqqani 2005; Zaman 2018).

In addition to political ideology and social values, other areas of practical cooperation between denominational parties include what could be considered "guild interests" of religious professionals. These include defending the authority of seminary-trained ulema against university-educated Islamic intellectuals, and fending off state regulation of religious institutions—which even defeated military dictators like Ayub Khan and Pervez Musharraf—while gaining greater state recognition and support of *madrasa* (seminary) education (Zaman 2002, 2018; J. Malik 2007).

The Extended Networks of Maslaki Parties

The denominational parties' constituents are not limited to voters who identify with a given maslak through birth or choice; they also include institutions and organizations associated with the maslak itself. These institutions include service delivery NGOs, militant groups, guild lobbies, madrasas, and Quranic schools. The parties are thus best understood as nodes within the extended networks of denominational social movements. However, parties have to do more than just represent their own particular maslak; they must also compete with other parties and leaders from within the same denomination. Despite sharing cross-cutting ties and mutual sympathies, parties from the same maslak can vary significantly in their political praxes, ethnolinguistic composition, and regional strongholds.

For example, the Deobandi Jamiat Ulema-e-Islam (JUI) founded in 1945 experienced a number of splits over the years, largely over ideological differences between conservatives and populists. The JUI's most notable recent cleavage came ahead of the 1988 elections between the JUI-Fazlur-Rehman (JUI-F) and the JUI-Darkhwasti (JUI-D). The question of whether to ally with the military establishment or the left-leaning PPP reflected deeper differences over whether a return to democracy in partnership with Shi'a-friendly liberals was more important than gaining support from authoritarian pro-Sunni Islamization from above. As a result of these ideological differences, many of the most radical madrasas opted to support the conservative JUI-D over the JUI-F. The JUI-D was supplanted in this role by the Jamiat Ulema-e-Islam-Sami-ul-Haq (JUI-S) following the succession of the aging Abdullah Darkhwasti by his one-time deputy, Maulana Sami-ul-Haq, in the early 1990s; Sami ul-Haq's own prominence was owed to his father, Abdul Haq, who had passed away in September 1988. Sami-ul-Haq was assassinated in November 2018. It is unclear yet who will end up leading conservative Deobandis; the faction's name is likely to change once again after a permanent successor leader emerges, even if the party contains many of the same institutions and prominent scholarly families. This highly personalized style of leadership is reflected not only in party naming conventions but in voting patterns as well. The best-performing constituencies for JUI-F and JUI-S are usually in the districts where their leaders' respective extended family networks are based, although this hasn't always been sufficient for victory (Moj 2015, 103; ICG 2011).

One important example of the maslaki political ecosystem's impact is the Khatm-e-Nabuwwat (Finality of the Prophethood) Movement (KNM). The KNM targets Ahmadis, a maslak that has faced widespread theological controversy since the early twentieth century.[3] Political anti-Ahmadi sentiment dates back to the early 1930s, when vigorous campaigns launched by the Punjab-based Deobandi Majlis-e-Ahrar-e-Islam were soon endorsed by Muhammed Iqbal, the iconic poet and intellectual of the Islamic modernist movement.

In the aftermath of Partition, resentment of perceived Ahmadi insularity and disproportionate representation within high-level Muslim politics (now state politics) was increasingly shared by other maslaki groups, which found themselves frozen out of the halls of power by the modernists.[4] This exclusion was especially galling given the emerging national consensus that Pakistan would be an Islamic state of some kind (Binder 1961; Kamran 2015; Qasmi 2015). Just as crucially, these sentiments also found resonance with the Punjabi masses following Partition. The influx of refugees from East Punjab and the competition to win favor from the bureaucracy in land allocation for resettlement amid corruption, food shortages, and inflation created a situation ripe for the politics of resentment. A relatively better-organized and better-educated minority made a compelling target for populist and majoritarian sentiments within conditions of scarcity and ideological and constitutional crises (S. Saeed 2017; Qasmi 2015; Kamran 2015).

The KNM, by its founders' design, became such a test of both Pakistani-ness and Muslim-ness that it has transcended all individual maslaks and is embedded in the consensus-based 1973 Constitution and the ensuing host of laws regulating access to government services, state resources, and official identification. KNM's transformation into one of the ideological and theological pillars of the Islamic republic has ensured that major political figures (even military dictators) must profess a fierce loyalty to KNM's tenets or fear being accused of being either pro-Ahmadi or even crypto-Ahmadi, with potentially devastating consequences for their political standing and physical safety. The result has been the extreme marginalization of the once highly influential Ahmadi community. Comparisons by scholars and human rights observers have frequently been made to the position that Jews held in Germany of the 1930s following the passage of the Nuremberg Laws (S. Saeed 2017; Qasmi 2015; Talbot 2012).

Another example of the kind of mobilization produced by intra-maslak political ferment is the Ahle Sunnat Wal Jamaat (ASWJ), formerly known as Sipah-e-Sahaba Pakistan, a movement dedicated to politically and legally marginalizing the Shi'a along the same lines as the Ahmadis. The ASWJ first emerged from JUI-D's KNM network as an autonomous local chapter in the town of Jhang in central Punjab, but it quickly established itself as a party in its own right. Ethnically the ASWJ's strength in Punjab also differs from all JUI factions, which rely on Pashtun votes in KP and Balochistan. The ASWJ's ability to grow not only in Punjab but also in the provinces of Gilgit-Baltistan, Balochistan, and Sindh arguably makes it the most dynamic current actor among all maslaki parties. The ASWJ's populism, on the one hand, distinguishes it from the JUI-S, while its openly Sunni-supremacist sectarian message, on the other, sharply contrasts with the JUI-F's generally highly pragmatic approach to politics (ICG 2011).

Why Do Maslaks Participate in Electoral Politics?

Despite its colonial origins and frequent dysfunctionality in the postcolonial era, representative democracy facilitated anticolonial emancipation, social change, and local representation in South Asia. Electoral competition also played a significant part in the communal polarization of politics, culminating in the All-India Muslim League's decisive victories of 1945–46, which in turn played a key part in the establishment of Pakistan itself (Barlas 1995). This may help explain why neither ineffectual civilian governments nor authoritarian military ones have been able to fatally delegitimize democracy among the Pakistani public. Additionally, the state even at its most authoritarian has been unable to exercise effective control without the support of local notables, who tend to favor competitive electoral contests (Malik 2010). The inevitable unpopularity of most dictators and the resilience of democracy makes it unwise for denominational parties to forgo participation.

Nationalist and progressive elements of the Deobandis, led by Mahmud al-Hasan, established the Jamiat Ulema-e-Hind (JUH) in 1919, making the Deobandis the first maslak to embrace modern politics. The JUH acted as a mass-mobilizing force working in concert with the larger nationalist anti-colonial movement (particularly the Indian National Congress) in exchange for influence over Muslim affairs. Although controversial among conservative elements, involvement in politics was declared a necessary means to achieving the Deobandis' larger mission of preserving what they regarded as authentic Muslim life.

The JUI, the JUH's successor and competitor, became its mirror image by partnering with the All-India Muslim League during the Pakistan Movement. The military intervention that ended the Deobandi-led Punjab Disturbances of 1953 and the subsequent Munir-Kayani judicial court of inquiry (see Lahore High Court 1954) instituted to investigate the violence made amply clear that the temporary special relationship between the Deobandi maslak and the state had irretrievably broken down over the question of a special constitutional role for the ulema in governance.[5] The dominance of Euro-American modes of government meant that future influence on the state and its laws required an independent parliamentary presence and the embrace of direct electoral competition (Binder 1961). Other maslaks subsequently followed suit along a broadly similar path, although on different time lines.

While postcolonial dictatorships, like colonial regimes, have been able to ignore pressures to allow meaningful democratic governance for years at a stretch, the legislative and the common law legal system have repeatedly worn down dictatorships and shielded maslaki parties from repression. Considering Pakistan's upheavals since Partition, the major denominational parties have long recognized that they have extremely limited chances of seizing power through either revolution or state collapse. This resilience and persistence creates conditions that favor engagement with the Pakistani nation-state via constitutional democracy (Nelson 2017).

Although denominational parties are unlikely to form a national government through free and fair elections, maximizing their vote share in as many constituencies as possible allows them to increase bargaining power with all other players in the system. The ability of maslaki organizations to act as influencers and mobilize reliable blocs of votes has consistently proved a valuable commodity, particularly in a fragmented political landscape where even the largest parties have difficulty performing competitively in every province and every region. Ullah (2013) notes that 5 to 7 percent of the vote is often enough to swing an election. This provides an additional basis for maslaki parties to become part of what Anas Malik (2010), drawing from selectorate theory, describes as the "winning coalition." Since 1988, all told the maslaki parties have used these margins to bargain for twenty federal ministerial positions and four assembly speaker positions in provincial legislatures (Ullah 2013).

The electoral participation of any individual maslak creates competitive pressure on others to follow suit or risk losing relevance. Additionally, in particular since the formulation of the National Action Plan in December 2014, the authorities have engaged in selective "mainstreaming" of certain state-allied militant groups. Public office offers opportunities for ambitious individuals and organizations to enrich themselves and raise their profiles. The electoral route to prestige and power is particularly attractive if *jihad* has been constrained by policy changes intended to deescalate domestic and international conflicts. However, serious questions remain as to whether this represents a deweaponization of religion or merely a repurposing for use against the military's political foes.[6]

The Puzzle of Maslaki Electoral Mediocrity

Although the "horse-trading" of parliamentary politics—such as the JI's influence on the 1973 Constitution—can explain some maslaki electoral successes, it is insufficient for explaining others.[7] For example, there has been no clear explanation of why the progressively oriented PPP in power suddenly abandoned its Ahmadi backers in 1974 despite overwhelming parliamentary majority, nor why secular opposition parties subsequently joined the PPP and other maslaki parties to unanimously pass a constitutional amendment excommunicating the Ahmadis from Islam (Qasmi 2015).

One approach has been to explain this disjuncture through covert parapolitical interventions by the Pakistani national security state or foreign powers such as Saudi Arabia and the United States (Z. A. Bhutto 1979; J. Malik 1996, 2007). Methodologically this explanation poses serious problems for scholarship. Covert transnational funding is by its nature highly secretive and opaque, as are the finances of denominational organizations in general.

More importantly, while these explanations could account for these groups punching above their weight with the state, they fail to account for maslaki groups' electoral *underperformance* relative to the strength of the public's Islamic sentiments (Fair, Malhotra, and Shapiro 2010, 2012). Given that Pakistan's population has remained over 96 percent Muslim following the creation of Bangladesh in 1971 (I. Malik 2002), and given the pioneering influence of figures such as Muhammad Iqbal and Mawdudi on Islamist movements in the Arab world, why haven't Pakistan's maslaki parties collectively done at least as well as, say, the Muslim Brotherhood in Egypt or Hezbollah in Lebanon?[8] Fragmentation of the vote along maslak lines does not provide sufficient explanation for their poor performance.

The evidence suggests that only a minority of the South Asian electorate are "values voters" who are mobilized primarily on the basis of religious ideals. Pragmatic considerations favor patronage, "feudal" obligations, kinship ties (*biraderi*), and ethnolinguistic or regional identity over ideas or values as the basis for casting votes. Rural areas in particular are dominated by powerful intermediary local figures who have enough influence to deliver votes for candidates on a quid pro quo basis (Mitra, Enskat, and Spiess 2004; Khan Mohmand 2014). Though most voters might agree that love for Islam and its propagation is a virtue, these sentiments are easier to mobilize in favor of policies rather than candidates. The willingness of the JUI (later JUI-F) to operate like a conventional Pakistani political party has played a significant role in its comparative success. This approach has enhanced Fazlur Rehman's political influence while simultaneously reducing his moral authority (Pirzada 2000).

The tension between embodying voters' virtues and appealing to voters' material interests encapsulates the challenges maslaki parties face in deciding what sort of organization they want to be. For most denominational parties the struggle to represent the maslak in the face of competition (from within and without) limits the energy available to focus on voter needs. The ability to mobilize opinion on matters of conscience or faith thus does not necessarily translate into the ability to mobilize voters in elections. This is hardly atypical; successful social movements rarely thrive simultaneously as political parties, even in less patronage-driven political systems. McAdam and Tarrow (2010, 537) point out that there is "an inherent tension between the logic of movement activism and the logic of electoral politics. . . . Electoral politics turns on a centrist, coalitional logic. Movements, on the other hand, tend toward narrow—sometimes extremist—views and an uncompromising commitment to single issues."

Yet it is not impossible to manage this tension. The MQM in Karachi has shown for decades that it is possible to simultaneously sustain a fervent movement and a tightly run political party (see chapter 4 in this volume). The party was aided by the fact that urban Pakistanis are much more likely to make individual decisions on voting; increasingly they are demanding not only better public service but a commitment to ethical governance (Mustafa and Sawas 2013). Given the rapid urbanization of Punjab, these factors may come to favor maslaki parties not perceived to have "sold out" to conventional politics (Iqtidar 2011).

The Impact of Maslaki Parties on the State

Cooperation with the state is driven by two complementary factors. On the one hand, denominational parties find themselves isolated from political decision-making whenever their relationship with the state is antagonistic. On the other hand, Pakistan, like the majority of postcolonial polities, is a weak state, but one that is unusually reliant on its Islamic credentials (credentials that it has been unable to validate or deploy without the support of the ulema and their representatives in maslaki parties) (Malik 2010).

Weakness here does not refer to the willingness or ability to deploy force. Rather, it is the capacity to collect revenue from its citizens and maintain compliance with laws and regulations (Migdal 1988). The British colonial state in South Asia suffered similar problems and relied heavily on favored local intermediaries to manage its relationship with the bulk of the population. While the ulema of the various maslaks mourned the loss of Islam's official status as state religion and the loss of state patronage after the advent of British colonial rule, they also gained much greater autonomy and authority following the retreat of the non-Muslim state from religious oversight. In the aftermath of the Pakistan Movement and the temporary shared use of Islamic symbols, the state (dominated by Muslim modernists) and the ulema both attempted to encroach on each other's areas of authority, setting the stage for a generation-long conflict (Zaman 2018).

Leaders from Mohammed Ali Jinnah to Ayub Khan, although often described as secular (a contested term), consistently instrumentalized Islam in order to establish and secure Pakistan's existence. However, they also simultaneously sought the authority to define Islam in terms that suited their agendas of modernization and nationalism, which inevitably brought them into conflict with the ulema (Jalal 2000; Zaman 2018).

Modernist Islamic intellectuals, with the exception of Mawdudi and the JI (who remained allied with the ulema after 1948) shared the state's interest in unmooring authenticity in Islam from the ulema and traditional Islamic methods of jurisprudence and education and in establishing the (Pakistani) state as a source of religious authority in its own right, which the colonial state had surrendered. The modernists' background in secular educational institutions that were first established under the colonial Raj rendered them ideologically and socially antagonistic to the ulema and their maslaks.

This conflict reached its peak under the government of Ayub Khan in 1958 and ended with his fall in 1969 (Qasmi 2010). Some areas of state policy on which the ulema and maslaki parties clashed—family planning and the use of interest in banking and finance—were to be expected, given their importance for effective technocratic government. More revealing was when relatively marginal issues turned into major flashpoints, such as the use of modern versus traditional methods to sight the moon ahead of the festival of Eid-ul-Fitr and the resultant discrepancy between the dates declared by the state and the ulema in 1967 (Zaman 2018). While the state-modernist alliance succeeded in shutting out the maslaks from political decision-making for a generation, it was unable to replace the authority of the ulema at the mass level. As a result, the alliance found itself being forced into progressively greater compromises as the state's crisis of legitimacy deepened. For their part the Pakistani ulema have largely embraced the modern nation-state, with its political structures and processes and its pursuit of economic and technological modernization. The military's reconciliation with the ulema and with competitive party-based democracy in 1969 ended the Islamic modernists' position of privilege.

In particular, the ulema took over the Council for Islamic Ideology (CII), the key component in the ideological state machinery of the Ayub administration. It is notable that the CII went on to survive the Yahya, Bhutto, Zia, and post-Zia periods while most other consultative bodies saw suspension and summary personnel changes. Given the collapse of the Pakistani state's authority on Islamic issues and the need for trusted intermediaries with the Pakistani population, government reliance on maslaki organizations went far beyond providing deniable jihadi instruments for covert warfare in Afghanistan and India (from the 1970s and 1990s onward, respectively). Military dictatorships and elected governments with weak popular mandates have been particularly dependent on Islamic credentials for popular legitimacy. However, even popular governments have relied on the articulation, distribution, and validation of an Islamic national identity to enhance the central government's authority, especially against local separatist challenges (in Balochistan, for example) and cross-border identities (Punjabi, Pashtun, and Muhajir), both of which were regarded as major vulnerabilities. Maslaki parties have also periodically played an important role since 1969 in building ideological relationships with other Islamic states such as Saudi Arabia needed in order to secure vital military, economic, and diplomatic support for Pakistan. In exchange, the status of traditional Islamic educational systems, although not restored to the level of the Mughal era, has been at its highest since the British abolition of the Mughal Empire in 1857. Other crucial benefits to the maslaks range from gaining greater access to state funding to experiencing greatly reduced levels of state repression (Malik 2010; Cohen 2004; Nasr 2000).

Notwithstanding the state's weakness, it remains unwise to directly confront the state's considerable brute force power beyond the dialogue over a handful of core issues such as madrasa reform. Given that denominational parties have no chance of either seizing power or winning power in elections, partnership with the state remains a logical and appealing option (Haqqani 2005; Zaidi 2005).

The effort to establish an explicitly Islamic political ideology for South Asian Muslims was initiated in the 1930s by sections of the modernist, university-educated Muslim intelligentsia. Mediated through the process of strategic syncretism with Hindutva, the Christian West, Zionism, and atheistic communism, these politically assertive "others" were simultaneously resisted and imitated (Reetz 2006). By the late 1930s the existing "politics of self-expression" had grown into a politics of national self-determination. Following Partition, this program ("Nazariya-e-Pakistan" in Urdu) quickly became official and thus something that the maslaks attempted to participate in, even if only from the outside. The result of this cross-fertilization was that denominational parties, such as the JI and elements of the Deobandis who opposed Partition, were able to appropriate Muslim nationalism, while relatively secular colonial-era institutions (such as the military officer corps and legal bar associations) first embraced Jinnah's Muslim nationalism and more gradually an Islamic identity. However, the modernists retained then and now a strong antipathy for sectarianism, for tests of piety, for madrasa education, and most of all for the ulema, who tended to favor all of these things (Cohen 2004).

The emergent maslaki ideological consensus reshaped the public sphere following the modernists' loss of power in 1969. While individual causes may have started out championed by a particular maslak, their resonance with the Muslim public often led to adoption across denominational lines. Major elements included the marginalization of modernists and severe penalties on "heretical" competitors such as the Ahmadis (originally a Deobandi cause), the punishment of "blasphemous" speech (a Barelvi touchstone), the enforcement of fasting during Ramadan, the suppression of un-Islamic vices (such as alcohol and "obscenity"), and resistance to changes in laws governing marriage age, divorce, standards of sexual consent, and domestic violence (Durrani et al. 2017).

Denominational parties have pushed Pakistan to ever more aggressively police the markers of Islamic identity that enjoy public appeal. These shared practices and beliefs are presented as boundaries that protect Muslims from both internal and external threats. This often manifests as a competition to demonstrate piety and devotion by intensifying the classic Islamic principle of *Amr bil Maroof wa Nahi'anil Munkar* (Enjoining the good and forbidding the bad) (Zaman 2018). Its defense must be maintained and progressively strengthened, either by the state or, failing that, by vigilante citizen action. Yet because this is an expression of what Gilmartin (1991, 128–29) describes as "politics of the heart" as mediated by populism rather than legal processes, the obligations imposed often go far beyond what has been traditionally mandated by Islamic law, such as forcing non-Muslims, children, the sick, and the elderly to fast in public during Ramadan. Moreover, this syncretism explains the fact that no maslak in Pakistan has proved either immune to taking up militantly exclusivist positions or capable of maintaining leadership over broad public opinion through such means (White 2012).

Conclusion

The record since Partition suggests that single-issue mobilizations employing a mix of parliamentary and extra-parliamentary politics have granted denominational parties their most impactful achievements. This includes the passage of the Objectives Resolution in 1949, the ejection of modernist competitors from the CII in 1969, and the inauguration of anti-Ahmadi laws from 1974 on. This should not be surprising given the fact that the country was itself founded through an electorally minded social movement that mobilized religious identity. In this regard it is probably unwise to overlook the denominational parties' continued potential to achieve major changes. The key elements that have structured Islamic politics in Pakistan—denominational diversity, ulema authority on Islamic matters, state weakness, public support for an Islamic republic, competitive elections, and military interference in democracy—are all likely to remain in place for the foreseeable future.

The 1954 report from the Munir-Kayani court of inquiry scathingly suggested that the problem with declaring Pakistan an Islamic republic was that the only way to keep all the denominations on board was by ensuring the term remained an utterly empty signifier, a mere flag of convenience for the state (Lahore High Court 1954). Arguably the maslaks have succeeded in defining many of the republic's most crucial terms of reference—especially the relationship between Muslimness, citizenship, and rights—through a common appeal to majoritarian populism. As Qasmi (2015) suggests, the court's justices underestimated the concept's viability in their rush to discredit it while at the same time tacitly acknowledging its popular appeal.

The question, then, is how notions of an Islamic republic might develop further. The 2012 Pew Muslim World Survey indicates that 61 percent of Pakistani Muslims do not believe in multiple interpretations of sharia—in fact, 34 percent of the sample believe sharia should apply to all citizens of the country, including non-Muslims.[9] Additionally, the 2013 follow-up survey indicates that 76 percent of Pakistani Muslims favor the death penalty as punishment for conversion out of Islam.[10]

On the one hand, this hardening of boundaries increases political players' need for Islamic credentials, which only improves the leverage of maslaki parties. On the other hand, Pakistan's denominational diversity means that the level of denominational and sectarian polarization may well result in increased conflict. In a political system where faith holds such overwhelming importance, any uncertainty over what actually counts as Islamic and the ensuing fears over loss of authenticity provokes political crises and creates opportunity for religio-political entrepreneurs. Given the cross-maslak consensus needed to establish this authenticity, the stakes in a many-sided competition are more akin to a "loser loses all" situation (as exemplified by the Ahmadis) rather than a "winner takes all" scenario. Other risks include a further reduction in tolerance for diversity, setting the stage for further conflict.

An alternative path would require consensus from a critical mass of ulema across the major maslaks that pluralism within the faith is in fact Islamic and that equal rights for all citizens, regardless of denomination or religion, is also Islamic. The progressive decentralization of authority within these movements and the fragmentation of political representation have increased the space for lower-ranking religio-political entrepreneurs to further aggravate polarization within the public sphere.

Hopes that strong state action might avert this are likely misplaced. Pakistan remains a weak state, where three out of four military dictatorships have been brought down by popular mobilization or its threat. General Zia's regime successfully avoided such a fate but did so in part by going the furthest yet to co-opt the forces of Islamic populism alongside new levels of surveillance and repression. The dictatorships of Ayub Khan, Muhammad Yahya Khan, and Musharraf for their part all saw the influence of maslaki parties grow through partnership with government despite occasional conflicts with the state. In short, the more authoritarian the state, the more vulnerable it is to pressures from Islamic populism.

In the current post-Musharraf era all players continue to vie for support from maslaki groups, while the army's leadership and civilian politicians struggle

for control over decision-making power. The result has been a shared willingness to "mainstream" banned extremist and militant groups such as the Ahle
Hadith's Jamaat-ud-Dawa/Laskar-e-Taiba/Muslim Milli Party, the Barelvis'
Tehreek-e-Labaik Party, and the Deobandi ASWJ. While it is possible and
even likely that participation by these groups in mainstream electoral politics
will encourage pragmatism, it is also likely that the ever-present dynamic of
competitive imitation means that such participation will also further radical-
ize the consensus-based definition of the Islamic republic.

The record suggests that popular opinion has a powerful shaping effect
on the opportunities available to religious and political elites alike, selecting winners among ideas and institutions. As a result, monitoring changes
in popular attitudes on issues like sectarian polarization is likely to signal
political change earlier and more clearly than electoral results and levels of
violence. Pakistani society is undergoing enormous structural changes that
will have consequences for the country's political economy and religious sociology and which we cannot fully predict. Addressing the interplay between
all of these elements requires much more study of maslaki parties as part of
larger social movements engaged in contentious politics inside and outside
the formal political system. Such efforts will be essential to delivering insight
into the political conditions to be found in the Pakistan of tomorrow.

Notes

1. Pakistan Bureau of Statistics, "Provisional Summary Results of 6th Population
   and Housing Census–2017" (Islamabad: Ministry of Statistics, 2017), http://
   www.statistics.gov.pk/assets/publications/Population_Results.pdf.
2. Gallup Pakistan, "Near Majority of Tehreek-e-Labbaik Pakistan Voters in Gallup
   Exit Poll Survey Said They Had Voted for PML-N in General Election 2013,"
   accessed June 30, http://gallup.com.pk/wp-content/uploads/2018/07/Gallup
   -Pakistan-Exit-Poll-2018-Who-did-TLP-voters-vote-in-2013-GE-1.pdf.
3. The Ahmadi movement, founded by Mirza Ghulam Ahmad, emerged in Punjab
   in 1888. Perceptions that the Ahmadis were intolerant toward other maslaks,
   that they benefited from their friendly relations with the British Raj, and that
   their theology—which provided a central role to Ahmed with some Ahmadi
   groups believing him to be a divine prophet (S. Saeed 2007, 135)—generated
   significant religious controversy but little political impact (Kamran 2015). In the
   aftermath of Partition resentment of perceived Ahmadi insularity and coloniza-
   tion of high-level Muslim politics (now state politics) was increasingly shared
   by other maslaks, which found themselves marginalized by the modernists. The
   influx of refugees from East Punjab and the competition to win favor from the
   bureaucracy in land allocation for resettlement amid corruption, food shortages,
   and inflation created a situation ripe for the politics of resentment (S. Saeed 2017;
   Qasmi 2015; Kamran 2015).

4. The modernist movement sought to define Muslimness in modern ways, envisioning a public role for Islam that was compatible with the ideals of democracy, civil rights, and rationality. In Pakistan this strain of thought was represented by leaders such as Muhammad Ali Jinnah (see Kennedy 1996).

5. The Punjab Disturbances were a series of anti-Ahmadi riots that broke out in 1953, prompting martial law to be imposed in Lahore. In the aftermath a judicial inquiry was constituted and the resulting report, the Justice Munir-Kayani Report, condemned the violence and hinted that religion and state should be kept separate since it was very easy to whip up mob hysteria on the basis of religious fervor (see Qasmi 2015).

6. Syed Arfeen, "Can Pakistan's Banned Organizations Rejoin the Mainstream?," *Diplomat*, June 20, 2017, https://thediplomat.com/2017/06/can-pakistans-banned-organizations-rejoin-the-mainstream/.

7. The term "horse-trading" is commonly used in Pakistan to refer to party defections that occur when politicians are promised material incentives in exchange for allegiance in legislative voting.

8. Pakistan Bureau of Statistics, "Population by Religion" (Islamabad: Ministry of Statistics, 2017), http://www.pbs.gov.pk/sites/default/files//tables/POPULATION%20BY%20RELIGION.pdf.

9. Pew Research Center, "The World's Muslims: Unity and Diversity," August 9, 2012, http://www.pewforum.org/2012/08/09/the-worlds-muslims-unity-and-diversity-executive-summary/.

10. Pew Research Center, "The World's Muslims: Religion, Politics and Society," April 30, 2013, http://www.pewforum.org/2013/04/30/the-worlds-muslims-religion-politics-society-overview/.

Part II

The Functions Served by Pakistan's Party System

7

Who Do Politicians Talk To?
Political Contact in Urban Punjab

Asad Liaqat, Ali Cheema, and
Shandana Khan Mohmand

Fareed goes back and forth between tales of how close he is to all residents of his ward and how close he is to Sheikh *sahib*, the National Assembly member (MNA) within whose constituency his ward lies. Fareed is one of six general members in his union council (UC); twenty-one union councils constitute Sheikh sahib's National Assembly constituency in the heart of Lahore.[1] Yet Fareed claims to be one of his closest and most cherished aides:"Sheikh sahib gets reports about who is doing what in their areas, and the people of my ward say only good things about me."[2]

Later in the office of Farzand, Sheikh sahib's son and de facto political manager, Fareed is less boastful. He wants to get Farzand's attention for more than a few seconds so that he can explain exactly why the streetlights in his ward are more important than the streetlights about which Farzand no doubt is also being asked. Responding to a question about how he comes to know how popular and hardworking the councilors in his area are, Farzand scoffs dismissively and uses the question as an excuse to lecture the few councilors present in the room, including Fareed. "I don't trust these union councilors and workers to keep in touch with my constituents for me. Anyone who has a problem can come directly to me," he tells us later.[3] On the face of it the latter part of his statement is true. His office is full of visitors, only a couple of whom are elected union councilors. He shows us documents on his computer that list the nearly four thousand visitors to his office over the years. Remarkable as that number is, it is smaller than the number of citizens with whom the more than one hundred local politicians in the NA constituency speak in a week.

One year earlier and a couple of hundred kilometers away, then–federal minister Chaudhary sahib—like Sheikh sahib, a member of the Pakistan

Muslim League-Nawaz (PML-N)—walks into a large room adjacent to his home office within his constituency headquarters on a hot Sunday in July. While he tries to make this trip from Islamabad every week, ministerial duties sometimes prevent it, and on those weeks his son, Muhammad, the mayor of the district council in which Chaudhary sahib's constituency lies, walks into the room instead, usually to encounter a smaller crowd.[4] There are almost fifty men in this room and only a handful of women; they are all here to see Chaudhary sahib. They are all residents of his constituency, which Chaudhary sahib has won repeatedly in the last few elections. His manager, Haji sahib, has already been hard at work for the past hour documenting every visitor's stated problem or complaint. By far the most common problem raised is that of employment, or the lack thereof. The supplicants are mostly educated; they are largely hoping to get hired for the government or professional jobs that are scarcely available. Chaudhary sahib alternates between dispensing career advice, referring to stringent recruitment criteria, promising help, and making phone calls to the right people on the spot. He is attentive and patient and refuses to listen to only one person who, after Chaudhary sahib's questioning, turns out to be from the neighboring constituency. The discovery leads Chaudhary sahib to turn his attention to those who are part of his potential vote bank.

Meanwhile, Muhammad is holding meetings with locally elected union councilors in an adjacent office. As we make our way to an event nearby where Chaudhary sahib is set to give a speech, he remarks that this Sunday gathering allows him to remain in touch with citizen needs.[5] We cannot help but wonder which of the two gatherings he is referring to.

On a later trip about half an hour from Chaudhary sahib's home, during which we speak with three union councilors in his National Assembly constituency, we are told that few residents from their wards even know about these Sunday gatherings at his home.[6] "We know what their problems are, and we spend our days and nights trying to solve them, and still they complain. But these problems are not things for which they would need to go to Chaudhary sahib," one tells us. These men, despite being elected union councilors, are probably less educated than most of the men in Chaudhary sahib's home office that Sunday, and the problems they are talking about are decidedly different from the ones being brought up by the supplicants in the minister's constituency office.

These anecdotes emphasize how the structure and membership of political machines and the manner in which these machines engage with voters have important implications for whose preferences get heard or have a chance of being represented in decision-making. These political party organizations—usually headed by a single boss, family, or small group that is in the business of organizing votes (Gosnell 1933; Scott 1969; Gans-Morse, Mazzuca, and Nichter 2014)—are complex and varied. They contain a mixture of elected local "lower-tier" politicians and unelected party workers who expend considerable time and effort, both during elections and outside of election campaigns, maintaining contact with citizens. These machines are organized by "higher-tier" politicians competing for higher office—typically for national and provincial assembly seats—and their family members. The machines' most important task is to garner votes for higher-tier politicians during general elections. In cases where members of these machines, whether local politicians or unelected party workers, have a personal following of their own, their relationship with higher-tier politicians is more symmetric, with the latter often having a great deal of trouble in keeping together rival local factions within the machine under the party banner. Local politicians and party workers are also valuable to higher-tier politicians for another reason: they act as aggregators of information about voters. Because citizens come to them with a range of municipal and nonmunicipal issues, they arguably know a lot more about citizen preferences than higher-tier politicians.

This chapter provides a description of political machines in urban Punjab and develops a typology of linkages between citizens and local politicians in order to shed light on how local politicians access information about voters and how machine structures facilitate or discourage the transmission of citizen voices. We consider three types of linkages between citizens and political actors: voters being targeted by a political machine for door-to-door election campaigns, voters initiating contact with members of the machine outside of an election campaign, and voters being personally known to local politicians.

To investigate the question of which voters are in contact with local politicians and whether they differ systematically from those with whom the politicians are not in contact, we draw on an original survey in 2017 of 2,150 adult males and females of voting age in forty-three union councils within four provincial assembly constituencies in Lahore. The four selected provincial assembly constituencies reflect a mix of competitive and non-competitive neighboring constituencies in the heart of the city. The two highly competitive provincial constituencies, PP-147 and PP-148, are within National Assembly constituency NA-122; the two other constituencies with less competition at the provincial and National Assembly levels are PP-146 in NA-121 and PP-149 in NA-124. The four constituencies are adjacent to each other in central Lahore.[7] In addition, we conducted semistructured interviews with thirty-three higher-tier local politicians in Lahore and other districts of Punjab province, plus a survey of sixty local politicians in Lahore district. All of this together provides a rich description of the characteristics of political machines and the demographic and political characteristics of voters with whom local politicians come into contact or know well.

In our surveys local politicians in Lahore state a preference for contacting opposition voters and those with unclear affiliations before contacting voters from their own parties during election campaigns. From voter surveys, however, we find that undecided voters are no more likely to be targeted by parties during election campaigns. Instead of targeting undecided voters, parties target illiterate and male voters and those who have a high propensity toward political participation or a higher level of trust in democracy. This finding is consistent with theories that suggest that parties mobilize voters who are more likely to turn out on election day but do not possess the fine-grained information required to target other kinds of voters on the basis of their political inclinations or partisan affiliations (Stokes 2005, 2007; Stokes et al. 2013; Finan and Schechter 2012; Larreguy, Marshall, and Querebin 2016).

While undecided voters are no more likely to be targeted during campaigns, outside of election campaigns they are in fact more likely than decided voters to initiate contact with both government and opposition local politicians themselves. Compared to men, women are less likely to contact local politicians who are members of political machines organized by higher-tier politicians of the ruling and opposition parties, which is possibly due to structural and norm-based constraints to female political participation.

Using voters' beliefs about whether and how well their local elected officials know them, we find that local politicians are much less likely to know both undecided voters and opposition voters. The same is true for poorer, less social, and female voters when controlling for contact during campaigns, demographic factors, and political affiliations. This implies that the voters local politicians know well are different from the voters who contact local politicians themselves and that local politicians are much more likely to know their own supporters and much less likely to know those who are marginalized in society. Whether a politician in a local context knows a voter well or not is mediated by a range of sociopolitical factors, of which a voter's preferences or partisan affiliation is only one. Nonetheless, a key implication of these findings is that politicians' views of their constituencies are segmented and potentially exclude those who may need their attention the most. In fact, we find that within a union council of roughly twenty to twenty-five thousand voters, members of political machines are most likely to know higher-income male voters of their own party; this suggests both an anti-women and an anti-poor bias in the information that is transmitted upward to higher-tier representatives.

This chapter proceeds as follows. The first section presents a brief review of the literature on citizen politician linkages broadly and in Pakistan specifically. Next is a description of the structure of political machines and the strategy political machines use to aggregate citizen voice. The third section introduces the three types of citizen-politician interactions, describes the data used to explore these interactions, and presents results on what kinds of voters are in contact with party machines The chapter concludes with a brief look at whether these findings can extrapolate to the rest of Pakistan.

Literature on Citizen Politician Linkages

A large body of literature on clientelism conceptualizes the relationship between voters and political parties in developing countries to be primarily about the distribution of benefits to voters and higher-tier politicians attempting to hold voters accountable for their vote. Susan Stokes et al. (2013) focus on the distinction between programmatic versus nonprogrammatic distribution and conditional versus unconditional benefits to draw out a "broker mediated theory of clientelism." In doing so they acknowledge the limitations of the earlier unitary party theories that assumed that parties act as single unitary agents when interacting with citizens. In the theory of broker mediation, voters view parties through key members of political machines organized by higher-tier politicians who act as the imperfect agents of parties on the ground, doling out benefits in a conditional and largely clientelistic manner that is based on votes or turnout. Brokers are imperfect agents because their actions are not observed by higher-tier politicians, which gives them space to undertake or shirk actions that maximize their return even if it comes at the expense of their bosses.

Using an original survey of Argentinian brokers, Stokes et al. (2013) argue that brokers have a great deal of knowledge about the voters in their areas. This informational advantage makes them valuable to parties, though not always trustworthy, and makes it possible to sustain clientelistic exchange. Meanwhile, Mark Schneider (2019) finds that brokers do not have the claimed informational advantage in the case of opposition and nonpartisan voters and have only a slight advantage over a random guess in the case of partisan voters. The literature is undecided on the informational advantage of brokers, depending on whom brokers target on behalf of parties.

Most of the work on party-voter linkages focuses on elections and the exchanges that precede them. The question of how party machines and voters engage outside of election campaigns has received far less attention. Adam Auerbach (2016) conducted one of the first attempts at studying the consequences of interactions between local brokers and voters outside an election setting. Using survey data on almost two thousand households in Jaipur and Bhopal, India, he shows that the density of party workers in a slum is positively associated with service delivery outcomes. Interactions between voters and party machines, then, are not simply about exchanges of small favors for votes at election time.

The study of party-voter linkages in Pakistan is at a nascent stage and focuses more on rural settings. Shandana Khan Mohmand (2014) draws on previous research in Pakistan to identify four possible explanations for how politicians and parties connect with voters: that feudal landlords aligned with parties dictate the preferences of voters (e.g., Alavi 1983), that clientelistic exchanges similar to those highlighted here occur between parties and voters (e.g., Keefer, Narayan, and Vishwanath 2003), that voters organize and connect upward along kinship lines (e.g., Wilder 1999), and that party identification has started to matter (e.g., Wilder 1999; Jones 2003). Khan Mohmand concludes through a longitudinal study of a village in Sargodha district that all four explanations lack completeness, primarily because they fail to consider the objectives and incentives of local actors that mediate party-voter linkages. The focus here is on these local actors and how political machines function in urban Punjab.

The comparative literature on party-voter linkages and Khan Mohmand's conclusions point to two aspects of the next frontier of work in Pakistan: detailed microlevel analyses of voter attitudes and behaviors and more emphasis on urban areas (given Pakistan's rapid urbanization that has weakened traditional kinship-based explanations). A broader typology of party-voter interactions beyond the election cycle is needed as well as an understanding of information transmission in the political space, with the voter being the initiator rather than recipient.

In the context of urban Punjab, the local councilor, party broker, and local actor that mediates between voters and parties may all be the same person. Entrepreneurial local intermediaries who are trusted by communities may often be picked up by parties as identifiable brokers that can formally organize the local vote, and party brokers who do well in this context may be rewarded with a party ticket when the local government election comes around.

Political Machines in Urban Punjab

The political system in Punjab relies on local political machines for the upward transmission of preferences and demands and the downward transmission of programmatic policies, clientelistic exchanges, and campaign promises. Political machines tend to operate at the level of the provincial or National Assembly constituency, with each major candidate running for the National Assembly seat piecing together local-level coalitions to mobilize voters and win elections. In cases where a party's candidates for MNA or provincial assembly member (MPA) are strongly aligned, they share this machine. Of the sixty local politicians surveyed, forty-three (72 percent) had campaigned for both an MNA and an MPA candidate, eleven (18 percent) had campaigned for only one, and six (10 percent) had not participated in any higher-tier politician's campaign (where a higher-tier politician is defined as one contesting for or holding an MNA or MPA seat). Candidates for local elections are typically nominated by the party's MNA and MPA candidates for the area that houses the union council. This allows the MNAs and MPAs to exercise significant influence over local politicians. In fact, recent evidence shows that the strength of connections between local and higher-tier politicians is an important determinant of the success of local candidates in union council elections because voters tend to reward more connected candidates (Liaqat et al. 2019).

These local political machines are consequential for a variety of reasons. The most obvious is the large size of political constituencies—the average National Assembly constituency in Lahore as delimited for the 2018 general elections, for example, had a population of more than 750,000. This necessitates the existence of intermediaries that help aggregate and transmit information upward and promises and services downward. Higher-tier politicians place a great deal of value on members of their machines—local politicians or political workers—and recognize that voters value local politicians' connections to higher-tier politicians who are members of the provincial or National Assembly (Liaqat et al. 2019). An examination of the nature of these local political machines is therefore central to understanding the linkages between political parties and voters.

Political Machine Membership and Roles

Layers of political actors between the voter and the elected parliamentarian create the political machine. These actors are referred to as brokers, workers, or influencers in the literature of comparative politics (Auerbach and Thachil 2018; Schneider 2019; Stokes 2005). Because the term "broker" has a negative connotation, some Pakistani politicians instead refer to them as workers or organizers. With the reinstatement of a tier of local elected leaders in 2015, a significant portion of these actors have become local elected politicians in their own right. In this discussion, those who contest in a local election are referred to as "local politicians"; those who do not contest elections but are affiliated with and act on behalf of or in alignment with a party or politician are "political workers." There is considerable overlap between these two categories, with an endogenous process of self-selection and nomination of local politicians from a group of political workers.

Each local and higher-tier politician interviewed confirmed that most of those who fall into the local politician category in Punjab today would have been classified as political workers before the local elections in 2015. In other words, before local elections allowed these individuals to contest for elected office themselves, they had already been acting as political workers for higher-tier politicians. Our survey of sixty local politicians in Lahore district confirms this: these politicians had been involved in politics for an average of fifteen years, and twenty-six out of the sixty had contested an election before 2015.

Local politicians in Lahore and in Chaudhary sahib's constituency informally estimate that somewhere between thirty and one hundred active political workers operate in a union council. Using our voter survey data from forty-three union councils in three NA constituencies in Lahore, we calculate a "party network density" of about 0.85 political workers for every thousand residents, which means that between seventeen and twenty-five political workers operate in each union council. This number is a little lower than the estimate provided by Auerbach (2016) from his work on urban slums in Jaipur and Bhopal. The difference could be explained by India's longer experience with democracy, but more likely it is the difference in the political environment of slums versus formal settlements, as in the case of our Lahore sample. Close to twenty-five individuals in each union council can be considered local politicians at a minimum: thirteen of these sit on the council.[8] A higher number would usually have contested council seats but lost; some would either have chosen not to contest or did not receive tickets. With the introduction of elected local governments in 2015 the importance of local politicians vis-à-vis unelected political workers has increased.

In order to be effective, political workers and local politicians—the key agents of a political machine—must spend a lot of time in their localities, and in cases where their work takes them out of the UC area on a regular basis, they tend to suffer political costs.[9] These actors have a range of occupations, including local business owners, lawyers, or government employees. For some, such as shopkeepers, their occupation involves a fair amount of public dealing, which can be integrated into their role as political workers. Political workers and local politicians allocate a significant portion of their time to politics. The major activities in this broad ambit are (1) fixing citizens' municipal services problems through relevant political and bureaucratic channels; (2) supervising infrastructure and development projects being undertaken in their union council areas; (3) arbitrating household disputes; (4) strategically attending weddings, funerals, and related events; and (5) campaigning for their candidates during election time. While these actors' primary sources of income are their business, agricultural, or professional positions, they may derive rents from politics as well. This rent may come in the form of direct payments from politicians, but more frequently it comes in the form of indirect payments from projects in their areas and also in the form of heightened social standing.

Relationships between Political Workers and Higher-Tier Politicians

There is enormous diversity in political workers' loyalty to parties and politicians. They may have a clear party affiliation, which sometimes flows through generations of workers. In a situation akin to the generational transmission of party identity in the United States, several workers in Chaudhary sahib's constituency and Lahore district stated that they defaulted into being part of the PML-N: their fathers acted as workers for the party and they simply took over from their fathers. There are cases in which the loyalty toward the politician is stronger than their loyalty to the party.

Pir sahib, a contender for a Pakistan Tehreek-e-Insaf (PTI) seat and the son of a well-known PTI MNA, described two categories of political workers that predominantly form his family's political machine. The first is the worker who has been loyal to his father since he joined politics in the late 1980s and who seamlessly switched with him from the PML-N to the PPP in the mid-1990s and from the PPP to the PTI in 2011. The second type of worker—much less common—is the PTI loyalist who became part of the political machine only after his father joined the party. Sardar sahib, the son of a prominent PML-N member of the National Assembly from Lahore, reports similar dynamics.[10] When asked about the strength of their affiliation to the party versus to the higher-tier politician with whom they are associated, forty of the local politicians surveyed report that their affiliation with the party is stronger, ten report that their affiliation with the politician is stronger, and the remaining ten report that their degree of affiliation with the party and the politician is equal.

The power relationship between higher-tier politicians and members of their political machine may be clearly asymmetric in favor of the politician or more symmetric, with the local politicians and political workers having a lot of leverage due to their personal local followings. To the extent that a party's voters at the local level are loyal to local politicians and party workers directly, the members of the machine are able to exercise influence over the higher-tier politicians. Higher-tier politicians tend to be heavily dependent on local politicians and political workers not only during campaign times but also during the implementation and monitoring phases of development projects. One member of the provincial assembly commented that one of his main headaches is to keep together factions of local politicians who are aligned with him but are sometimes inclined to switch allegiance due to internal factionalism.[11] Because parties lack formal systems and criteria for recruiting local workers, and because so much depends on how entrepreneurial a worker appears to the higher-tier politician, local competition between brokers can be intense even when they all work for the same party. This entails recruiting groups of voters and then jealously ensuring their loyalty through delivering benefits or solving other problems. Higher-tier politicians may often be required for such solutions, thus many of the requests that reach them are related to the imperatives of local-level competition between party workers. Workers who do not receive sufficient attention may be courted by candidates from other parties that are looking to strengthen their local presence. It is against this backdrop that we examine how political machines aggregate and transmit citizen voice.

Transmission of Information

Higher-tier politicians typically communicate directives to members of their political machines, whether that be the planning of a gathering or corner meeting in their locality, indicating the area's priorities and needs, or supervising the implementation of a project in the area. The union council chairperson has become pivotal in the electoral machine since the revival of elected local governments in 2015, in particular in the allocation of projects and funds within the council area. The local politician usually tries to convince the higher-tier politician to allocate projects using special MNA funds or, of late, district council funds; higher-tier politicians typically allocate based on a combination of electoral targeting concerns, maintaining loyalties of workers, and convenience. Higher-tier politicians often have little to no information about active local politicians aside from the union council chairperson, except for a small number of favorites.

Citizens' voices reach higher-tier politicians primarily through the machine and in particular through union council chairpersons. The local politicians interviewed were typically confident that they knew their constituents' preferences and needs, political affiliations, and household circumstances. For instance, a union council vice-chairperson from Lahore insisted: "Take me to any street in my union council and I can tell just by looking at a house's gate who lives there and who they vote for."

However, higher-tier politicians on more than one occasion expressed concern that they may be getting a distorted picture. One MNA candidate commented that he was aware that local politicians regularly bad-mouth certain individuals and regularly praise others.[12] Some try to bypass this situation by occasionally visiting localities themselves. One reported that when he visits localities himself, if the local politician becomes aware that the senior politician has some direct information as well, the local politician will change his report.[13] These higher-tier politicians are aware that winning elections requires putting together a broad coalition of voters through patronage and service delivery to ensure a majority. The question is, How well placed are their local political machines to deliver on this expectation?

Contact and Linkages

How does this political machine develop linkages with citizens, and what are the prevalent forms of contact between citizens and political machines? We describe and present correlates for three main forms of contact between citizens and members of political machines: (1) door-to-door canvassing during election campaigns, (2) voter-initiated contact with party workers or local politicians outside of election campaigns, and (3) citizens' personal knowledge of party workers or local politicians.

Door-to-Door Canvassing during Election Campaigns

Conversations with sitting MNAs and MNA candidates of the two main political parties, the PML-N and PTI, reveal how campaigns are typically planned at the level of the national constituency. This constituency is divided into smaller units, and lists of active party workers are drawn up for each of these units. With the reintroduction of a tier of local elected leaders, these smaller units are likely to correspond to union councils. Party workers are tasked with going door-to-door in their localities to deliver the party's message, to inquire how the family intends to vote, to thank those who indicate their intention to vote for the party, and to persuade those who do not intend to vote for the party (by offering promises or, in the case of incumbents, by relying on targeted delivery before and/or after elections).

In one of our sample NA constituencies the political manager claimed an intention to visit every household in the constituency at least once during the election campaign. In another constituency the opposition candidate from PTI played down the importance of door-to-door campaigns, insisting instead that messaging delivered through the media played a larger part in persuading voters.[14]

Despite the political manager's claim that PML-N workers visit every household during an election campaign, only 30 percent of voters surveyed in his constituency reported that their household had received a visit from a representative of a party.[15] Between the central plan to visit all households and the execution of such a plan by party workers, several decisions are made about how to allocate a limited amount of workers' time to household visits. It is important to investigate which individuals receive visits from party workers during campaign time because of these decisions.

We ran a simple regression (table 7.1 column 1) of a binary variable on a range of demographic variables for whether the respondent was contacted during an election campaign by political workers of any party.[16] As one would expect, women are much less likely to report contact during election campaigns by political workers. Even though the survey question asked about whether the *household* received a visit from any political worker, women are 10 percentage points less likely to say they did. This suggests that women are often so far removed from the political process that they might not even know if their own household was contacted by a political worker, let alone have a direct conversation with a visiting party worker. Those who are less educated and have strong social linkages (i.e., those who report having more friends in the community and having attended more weddings in the previous three months) are somewhat more likely to be contacted. This indicates some amount of targeting based on visibility (for the more social) and low social status (where educational attainment is used as a proxy for social status).

Table 7.1. Correlates of politician–voter contact

	(1) Campaign contact (0–1) b/se	(2) Voter-initiated contact with local PML-N politicians (0–1) b/se	(3) Voter-initiated contact with local PTI politicians (0–1) b/se	(4) Knowing UC chairperson well (1–5) b/se
PTI voter	−0.017	−0.040**	0.023	−0.154**
	(0.029)	(0.018)	(0.014)	(0.072)
Small-party voter	0.080	0.001	0.027	0.143
	(0.113)	(0.069)	(0.055)	(0.294)
Undecided voter	0.023	0.054***	0.053***	−0.228***
	(0.022)	(0.013)	(0.011)	(0.057)
Female	−0.096***	−0.081***	−0.062***	−0.736***
	(0.020)	(0.012)	(0.010)	(0.051)
Age	0.001	0.001	0.000	0.001
	(0.001)	(0.001)	(0.000)	(0.002)
Education	−0.010***	−0.002	−0.000	−0.000
	(0.003)	(0.002)	(0.002)	(0.008)
HH expenditure	−0.063	−0.020	−0.002	0.438***
	(0.042)	(0.025)	(0.020)	(0.106)
Migrant	−0.025	0.033**	0.027**	0.020
	(0.024)	(0.015)	(0.012)	(0.062)
Friends	0.004**	−0.002**	−0.003***	0.030***
	(0.002)	(0.001)	(0.001)	(0.004)
Participation index	0.566***	0.641***	0.504***	1.740***
	(0.074)	(0.045)	(0.036)	(0.180)
Trust index	0.099***	0.025***	0.013**	0.133***
	(0.012)	(0.007)	(0.006)	(0.033)
Constant	0.002	−0.069	−0.044	1.079***
	(0.081)	(0.050)	(0.039)	(0.211)
R-squared	0.111	0.192	0.173	0.279
Observations	1951	1938	1949	1765

** $p < 0.05$

***$p < 0.01$

Source: Original survey data.

Note: Each column shows a separate OLS regression. The dependent variable for column (1) is a binary variable for whether the respondent stated that his or her household was visited by a member of any party during the 2013 election campaign. The dependent variables for columns (2) and (3), respectively, are binary variables for whether the respondent stated that he or she had contacted a local PML-N or PTI politician, since the 2015 local election; the dependent variable for column (4) is the respondent's answer to the question, "How well do you think your union council chairman knows you?" on a scale of 1–5, with the scale ranging from 1 = not at all to 5 = very well. Sampling point fixed effects are included and standard errors are reported in parentheses.

Contrary to the existing literature that finds that parties focus on swing voters during election campaigns (Larreguy, Marshall, and Querebin 2016; Stokes et al. 2013), our evidence finds no significant difference in the political affiliations of those visited by parties during election campaigns. Undecided voters are not any more or less likely to be the target of political campaigns compared to partisan PML–N or PTI voters.

The literature also finds that local party workers' responsiveness is positively associated with the density of party workers in a locality (Auerbach 2016). Again, contrary to the literature, we do not find a strong correlation between the extent of campaign contact with political party workers and the density of political worker networks.[17] In other words, it is not the case that the mere presence of more political workers results in more campaign contact (see figure 7.1).[18] This indicates that the main factor constraining these visits is not the number of party workers and that more competition at a local level does not induce greater effort on the part of party workers.

Voter-Initiated Contact outside Election Campaigns

Outside of election campaigns, voters initiate contact with local politicians and party workers primarily for resolving service-delivery issues or disputes. During these meetings it is natural that voters complain about certain local service-delivery issues or, less frequently, national-level policy issues. It is largely through these meetings that local politicians obtain information about what citizens care about and about which way their political affiliations and service-delivery preferences might be leaning. This is also critical information that allows politicians and party workers to engage in targeted delivery. In our sample of sixty local politicians, the median number of citizens who visit politicians in a week is thirty-eight. Roughly twenty-seven of these are men and eleven are women. According to these local politicians, the most common reasons for male citizens to contact them are drainage issues, issues with the police or local courts (*thana katchery*), and disputes outside the neighborhood. Female citizens, on the other hand, are said to most commonly discuss interpersonal domestic issues, water supply, and gas-supply concerns.

Which voters are most likely to contact local politicians?[19] The answer to this question has implications for politicians' beliefs about the policy positions and political attitudes of their constituents. In the case of voter-initiated contact, we do find evidence of undecided voters being significantly more likely to contact party workers from both the PML–N and the PTI (table 7.1 columns 2 and 3). There is also clear partisanship in voter-initiated contact. PML–N voters are much more likely to contact PML–N workers as compared to PTI workers. PTI voters stay away from PML–N workers despite

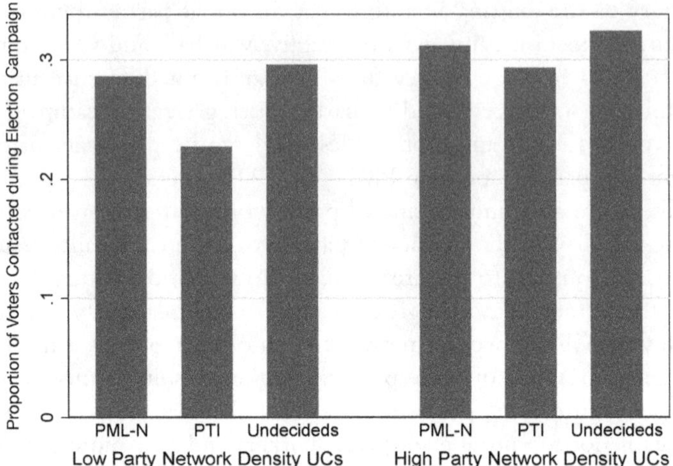

Figure 7.1. Extent of campaign contact between voters and politicians

Source: Original survey data.
Note: The figure shows the proportion of respondents of different party affiliations who reported being contacted by a representative of any political party during the 2013 election campaign. The bars show campaign contact in union councils where Party Network Density is below the median (left side) and above the median (right side).

the PML-N being in power at the time of the survey and controlling access to service delivery at the local, provincial, and national levels.

Columns 2 and 3 of table 7.1 also show that gender is a stark predictor of voter-initiated contact—women are 8 percentage points less likely to contact PML-N workers and 6 percentage points less likely to contact PTI workers. This is consistent with a model in which household bargaining leads to an equilibrium in which the men specialize in the political space and the norm proscribes female political participation. Figure 7.2 also shows that in union councils with higher worker density, more voters contact party workers. This implies that while denser machines may not be better at campaigning, they do allow citizens to reach out to them in higher numbers.

Citizens Knowing Party Workers or Local Politicians Personally

The third and final measure is a measure of closeness—specifically, a response to survey questions about how well the voter believes he or she is known by the union council chairperson and their local councilor(s). The politician in question could know the voter through a political channel or simply by virtue of living in the same locality or being part of the same networks.

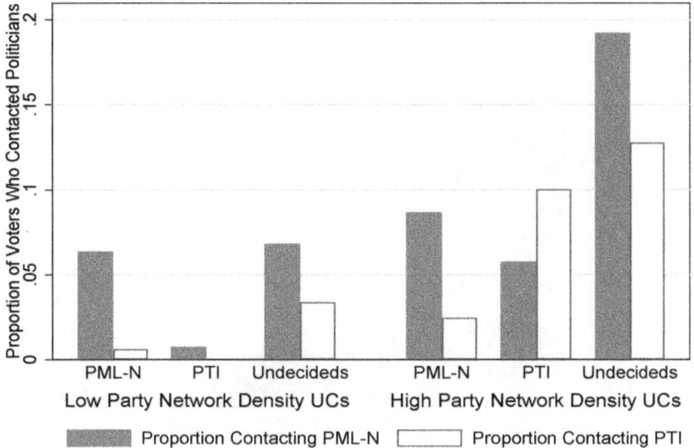

Figure 7.2. Extent of voter–initiated contact with political parties

Source: Original survey data.

Note: The figure shows the proportion of respondents of different party affiliations who reported that they had contacted local politicians since the 2015 general election. The bars show campaign contact in union councils where Party Network Density is below (left side) and above (right side) the median, respectively. The dark bars show the portion of respondents who reported contacting PML-N local politicians; the white bars show the portion of respondents who reported contacting PTI politicians.

Whatever the channel, personally knowing a voter makes it much more likely that the politician is aware of the voter's preferences as opposed to the preferences of other voters.

As shown in figure 7.3, a majority of citizens report that their union council chairperson does not know them at all, while about 11 percent report that their chairperson knows them well or very well. Given that in 2015 each union council had an average of fifteen thousand registered voters, this is perhaps not unexpected, although the rates are much lower than those claimed by local politicians themselves.[20]

Which voters are more likely to report that their union council chairperson knows them well? The answer is shown in table 7.1 column 4. The outcome variable in each case is on the 1–5 scale shown in figure 7.3. In addition to the expected gender difference, the starkest difference between the characteristics of the voters who are known to politicians and those who are not is whether the voter is undecided. Undecided voters are much less likely to say that their local politician knows them, indicating a major difference in the subset of voters who contact politicians versus those who are known well by the politicians. PTI voters are also significantly less likely to say that local politicians know them, which is expected given that most elected union

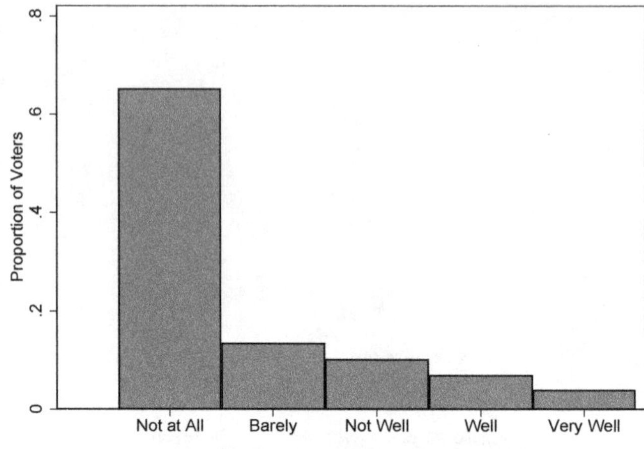

Figure 7.3. Closeness between UC chair and citizens

Source: Original survey data.
Note: The figure shows responses to the question, "How well do you think your union council chairman knows you?" on a scale of 1–5, where 1 = not at all and 5 = very well.

council politicians belong to the PML-N. Another important difference is that politicians are significantly more likely to know richer voters, voters with strong social linkages, and voters who place higher trust in democracy.

This implies that local politicians' personal networks are highly skewed. Outside of the average of five voters who contact them in a day, politicians are mostly surrounded by citizens who support their party, who are far richer than the average voter, and who are predominantly men. If a politician is basing his or her beliefs about what voters care about solely through their interactions with these voters, their beliefs may be largely reflective of only richer male voters who are affiliated with their own party.

Conclusion

Political contact and closeness takes many forms, and while the immediate reasons for the initiation of political contact may be linked to electoral campaigning or the resolution of service-delivery issues, contact and closeness also serve as the primary vehicles for the transmission of citizen preferences to politicians and party workers. Those who are in contact with or close to politicians have markedly different characteristics from the average voter. To the extent that politicians derive their beliefs about citizen preferences from these forms of contact and closeness, and to the extent that they take political decisions based on their own beliefs about citizens' preferences, these findings have important implications for the representation and implementation of citizen preferences. They also demonstrate the critical role that political machines play in transmitting information about citizen preferences up to higher-tier politicians.

Unaddressed here is an assessment of the next link in the chain: When politicians are exposed to voters whose personal characteristics, political affiliations, and policy preferences are different from those of the average voter, do they indeed form beliefs about citizens' preferences that are biased, and do they act on these beliefs in a manner that is detrimental to the representation of citizens' preferences? This question is taken up by Asad Liaqat (2019), who finds that local PML-N politicians in Lahore have highly inaccurate beliefs about citizens' preferences but, encouragingly, respond to accurate information about citizens' preferences by moving their recommendations closer to these preferences.

Some of these findings may extrapolate well to the rest of Pakistan. The size of electoral constituencies is large across the country, and political machines exist in some form or other across all provinces. The informational gap between members of political machines and voters may, however, be lower among highly rural constituencies. At the same time, it is unlikely that selection in political contact does not take place along some dimension of privilege since rural politics often exhibit more rigid hierarchies than urban politics. One important caveat is that Lahore is the political heartland of both the PML-N and the PTI. Party identification is perhaps more salient in Lahore than most other parts of Pakistan, which means that the results on partisanship in voter-initiated contact may not extrapolate well to other parts of Pakistan where party identification is weaker.

Notes

1. *Sahib* is a term of address or honorific for men used commonly in the subcontinent. Union councils are the lowest elected unit of local government in Pakistan's Punjab province. Each union council is divided into six electoral wards that elect one representative each via the first-past-the-post system.
2. Asad Liaqat interview of Fareed, February 2018. Names have been changed to maintain confidentiality.
3. Asad Liaqat interview of Farzand, February 2018.
4. Under the terms of the Local Government Act of 2013, "district council" is the term for the local government of the rural areas of a district.
5. Asad Liaqat interview of Chaudhary sahib and Muhammad, June 2017.
6. Asad Liaqat interviews of three councilors, July 2017.
7. Within each provincial constituency all UCs were included in the sample, with two exceptions: two UCs in PP-147, which had very high income and wealth levels and were composed predominantly of elite government or private housing, and four UCs in which only a minority of polling stations fell inside the sample provincial constituencies while a majority fell outside the sample provincial

constituencies. The excluded union councils constitute only 9.3 percent of the registered voters in the sample constituencies, with vote shares of dominant parties and voter turnout rates within 1 percentage point and 2 percentage points of included UCs, respectively. Within a UC the sampling strategy was as follows: five random GPS points were dropped within each UC's boundary. The surveyors were equipped to accurately reach these points in the field. Once the surveyors reached a point, they surveyed five households around that point using a right-hand rule to ensure randomization. Within each household one female and one male surveyor conducted an interview with a randomly selected female and male registered voter, respectively. The survey was conducted on tablets using SurveyCTO software, and extensive field and remote monitoring was conducted to ensure high-quality accurate survey data.

8. These include the union council chairperson, the union council vice-chairperson, six general members, two women councilors, one youth representative, one working-class representative, and one minority representative. It is perhaps inaccurate to consider all youth, all working class, and all minority representatives as local politicians, because anecdotally these are often token nominations from the party. In the case of women councilors, the situation is a bit more complicated because even if the nominations come from the party and appointment is contingent on the election of UC chairperson and vice-chairperson candidates, they are later tasked with mobilizing female voters. Union councils are set to be replaced by nonpartisan neighborhood councils under the Local Government Act of 2019.

9. Asad Liaqat interview of a UC vice-chairperson from Lahore, July 2017.

10. Asad Liaqat interviews of Pir sahib, July 7, 2017, and of Sardar sahib, February 2017.

11. Asad Liaqat interview of Khawaja sahib, June 2017.

12. Ali Cheema and Asad Liaqat interview of Malik sahib (PTI MNA candidate), June 2017.

13. Asad Liaqat interview of District Council Mayor Muhammad, August 2017.

14. These examples are not necessarily reflective of the campaign strategy of PML-N and PTI candidates in general; there are certainly cases of PTI candidates who run extensive door-to-door campaigns.

15. Political contact during a campaign is measured as the response to a question asking whether the household received a visit from any representative of any party during the 2013 general election.

16. We use a novel estimation strategy to isolate the variation that stems from a very small geographical area with a radius of about 20 to 30 meters. This is achieved through a sample that is obtained by randomly dropping 5 GPS points per sample UC and surveying five households at each of these points, using a random walk rule. In the regression we employ "point" fixed effects to ensure that the variation exploited comes only from within the five households surveyed at each point and not from the range of political, geographical, and service-delivery differences that one would expect to exist across a range of these points.

17. These densities are calculated as the average number of political workers re-

ported in a union council by an average of fifty survey respondents in each union council. Low- and high-density union councils are defined as those in the bottom and top half of the party network density distribution, respectively, with the cutoff being at 0.83 workers for every one thousand residents.

18. While figure 7.1 does show slightly higher rates of contact in high-density union councils, the differences are marginal and not statistically significant. Only PTI voters are significantly more likely to be contacted in high-density union councils compared to low-density councils.

19. We are not making any causal claims here. It could well be that certain characteristics make voters more likely to contact voters. On the other hand, it could be the case that political machines target voters with certain characteristics.

20. It is not the case that citizens are more likely to report that their ward councilor/ general member knows them well. In all, 59 percent report that their councilor does not know them at all, and 13 percent report that their councilor knows them well or very well.

8

Candidate-Party Linkages in Pakistan
Why Do Candidates Stick with Losing Parties?

Hassan Javid and Mariam Mufti

During trips in 2006 and 2013 to NA-67 Sargodha, a constituency in central Punjab, voters spoke favorably about Anwar Ali Cheema, a candidate belonging to the Pakistan Muslim League-Quaid (PML-Q). In contrast to most politicians from the district who were accused of being both corrupt and incompetent, Cheema had managed to build a reputation as an honest and hardworking representative who listened to the demands of his constituents and who had managed to initiate—and complete—a range of developmental projects in the small villages dotting his constituency.[1] Cheema's reported virtues as a leader and politician were reflected in what was then a unique record: since his first foray into electoral politics in 1985 Cheema had not lost an election to the National Assembly, winning seven times in a row. Yet, for all his apparent popularity and electoral achievements, Cheema lost his seat in the 2013 elections to Zulfiqar Bhatti, a relatively unknown candidate from the Pakistan Muslim League-Nawaz (PML-N).

A similar dynamic was at play for Nadeem Afzal Chan, a young politician from the Pakistan People's Party (PPP) who had won in NA-64—another constituency in Sargodha district—in 2008. Despite enjoying a reputation for being an active and accessible legislator, many voters confirmed that they would nonetheless be voting for his most significant opponent, Pir Hasnat Shah of the PML-N.[2]

In both cases voters who were otherwise sympathetic to Cheema and Chan deployed similar arguments to justify their decision not to vote for them. Although Cheema and Chan were good leaders, the voters explained, their lack of affiliation with the PML-N—the incumbent party at the provincial level that was widely tipped to win power at the federal level in the 2013 elections—meant that they would be unable to tap into the networks of influence and patronage that would allow them to effectively discharge their responsibilities as representatives.

The results of these two elections from Sargodha raise interesting questions about the relationship between voters, candidates, and political parties in Pakistan. If voters support particular candidates on the basis of their potential ability to dispense patronage once in government, as opposed to supporting an ideology or policy, then are parties relevant to the electoral process only insofar as they provide future legislators with a collective platform through which to control the levers of state power? This question becomes all the more relevant when confronted with the historical success of traditionally "electable" politicians, defined as those politicians whose independent support bases make them well placed to win elections and who are, therefore, desirable candidates for recruitment and retention by different political parties. Such electables are able to come to power by calling on relatively stable vote banks that are cobbled together by using economic and social resources such as control over land and labor as well as the manipulation of extended kinship networks and alliances. In the presence of these independent sources of social power, the precise role played by parties in the electoral process remains unclear. Indeed, in this context why do otherwise viable electoral competitors like Cheema and Chan choose to stick with losing parties?

In this chapter we examine the nature of candidate-party linkages in Pakistan through the lenses of both candidate-centered and party-centered approaches. We categorize electoral candidates along four types based on their levels of autonomy and commitment to the party: the party heavyweight, the independent electable, the party worker, and the aspirational candidate. The party-centered approach sheds light on which of these candidates is most frequently recruited by political parties to contest elections on the party's behalf. We find that the larger and more electorally successful parties like the PPP, the PML-N, and the Pakistan Tehreek-i-Insaf (PTI) select candidates who have typically displayed high levels of autonomy and low levels of commitment to the party, while smaller parties like the Muttahida Qaumi Movement (MQM), the Awami National Party (ANP), and the Jamaat-e-Islami (JI) select candidates with high levels of commitment to the party. The intersection of the supply of candidates with the demand for autonomous politicians who have independent sources of power results in undisciplined political parties that are unable to elicit credible commitment from their politicians. While some candidates switch party affiliation prior to an election in the quest for the "right" party ticket, several candidates who might otherwise be expected to do so choose instead to remain loyal to their political parties. We argue that parties that are expected to win an election use the promise of access to state resources and prestigious political appointments to elicit loyalty from their candidates. However, parties whose electoral prospects are dim can invoke social factors such as marriage and kinship ties to bind candidates to party leaders. In addition to incentives provided by parties, candidates often exhibit loyalty regardless of electoral outcome because they realize that elections are not a one-off game and that staying with a party provides an opportunity to become closer to party leadership so they are willing to wait for an anti-incumbency advantage in the next election.

The arguments presented in this chapter are based on extensive field-based research conducted between the years 2006 and 2018 across Pakistan by both authors. Our observations are based on semistructured interviews with political elites and observation of the ways in which they execute their political obligations. While we are conscious that this kind of qualitative data is difficult to gather and makes the research design cumbersome to replicate in other political contexts, we contend that our observations reflect the nature of candidate and party interactions in the many developing countries that are also clientelistic and patronage-based. We also argue that knowledge creation through thick description serves as a necessary foundation for more quantitative projects because it can capture the complexity of the more informal aspects of politics. Moreover, a longtime window with repeated visits allowed us to gather qualitative panel data. For example, we followed the career paths of several politicians to reach our conclusions. Similarly, we examined candidate selection prior to two different elections and examined party dynamics with different political parties in power.

This chapter proceeds as follows. Our first step is to present a typology of candidates based on the level of autonomy received from and the level of commitment to the party. Next we shed light on the process of recruitment and selection of candidates by political parties to explain why candidates with high levels of autonomy are usually preferred as party ticketholders instead of those with high levels of commitment. Finally we describe the prevalent phenomenon of party-switching and explain why some candidates are more likely to express loyalty to their political parties despite having high levels of autonomy.

A Typology of Candidates

The relationship between a candidate and a party is typified by two attributes: the candidate's level of autonomy and his or her commitment to the party. Political autonomy refers to the extent to which candidates are able to campaign and operate independently of parties; it is determined by attributes like the candidate's economic status, his or her membership within a strong kinship network, individual connections to the state, and symbolic status (often but not exclusively rooted in religion). Commitment, on the other hand, indicates the degree of loyalty a candidate may display for a party and

		Autonomy	
		High	**Low**
Commitment	**High**	Party heavyweight	Party worker
	Low	Independent electable	Aspirational candidate

Figure 8.1. Typology of candidates

is determined by factors such as ideology, a shared history of political work and struggle, and the social constraints imposed by familial connections and factional rivalries. By evaluating the association between levels of autonomy and commitment we can identify four types of candidates in Pakistan: the party heavyweight, the independent electable, the party worker, and the aspirational candidate (see figure 8.1).

Autonomy

Much of the literature and discourse on Pakistani politics assumes that electoral politics is dominated by so-called electables (see Wilder 1999; Waseem 2006; Khan Mohmand 2014). The attributes that make these political elites such formidable political contenders are diverse and vary from place to place, but it is nonetheless possible to discern a few common qualities that characterize Pakistani politicians.

FINANCIAL RESOURCES. Access to financial resources enables politicians to fund their political ambitions. Financial strength is also a prerequisite for contesting elections, as most political parties, including the PPP, the PML-N, the PTI, and the ANP, require a ticket application fee. However, these parties, unlike the MQM and the JI, do not finance their candidates' electoral campaigns.

Based on the declaration of assets by legislators in the 14th National Assembly, the predominant sources of wealth include landholdings and businesses. Agricultural land is listed as the main source of income for 75 percent of legislators, 29 percent of whom solely rely on agricultural land; the remainder have diversified landholdings and include commercial and residential properties as well. Furthermore, many land-owning politicians have diversified their financial portfolios by investing in CNG filling stations, the food-processing and textile industries, or transport and construction companies.[3]

Historically, control over land was a source of both economic and social power, with the former rooted in the ability of landlords and landowners to appropriate much of the surplus produced on their land and the latter tied to the control over labor that came with ownership of land. The political power of the landed elite was entrenched and institutionalized by a colonial regime that relied on them for local-level support. It was precisely this framework of politics that Pakistan inherited in 1947 (Javid 2011). Indeed, in the immediate aftermath of Partition close to 90 percent of legislators in the provincial and constituent assemblies were part of the traditional landed aristocracy (Maniruzzaman 1966). While this percentage has declined over time with urbanization and the expansion of industry, traditional landed elites continue to play a significant role in Pakistan's politics, particularly in the countryside, where many politicians can trace their own political and economic successes to a history of landownership by their families.

Landownership in Pakistan confers both social status and political advantage. While prestige and influence are measured by the size of the landholding, *izzet* (honor and respect) in the eyes of the people is measured by the landowner's generosity in the form of food and money at life-altering events such as births, marriages, and deaths (S. Ahmad 1977; Lyon 2004). A landowner's generosity is deemed to be a matter of honor and pride for the villager on whom it is bestowed. Landowners also use their social and economic networks to help villagers access the benefits of the state, which offers few institutionalized channels through which it could otherwise be approached. For example, landowners devote a large portion of their time and effort to interacting with state officials and local law enforcement to resolve local disputes (*thana-katcheri*) and secure funding for development projects such as the construction of a tube well, a school, or a basic health unit.

These personalized connections—maintained through a display of wealth, accessibility to the people, and involvement in constituents' daily lives—feeds the perception of the landowner as an ideal caretaker of the villagers' interests. Due to the vertical alignment of interests between a landowner and villagers, the latter forms a personal vote bank for the former. However, landowners cannot simply rely on their economic superiority over villagers in order to manipulate the vote in rural constituencies. In fact, Khan Mohmand (2014) convincingly argues that landed politicians today must additionally demonstrate an ability to deliver political goods and services in exchange for votes because they need the "right" party ticket to increase their odds of winning by adding the votes of party supporters. This explains why, for example, Abida Hussain, an elected representative from Jhang, has been quoted as saying, "Land is our essential link to the people and our voters" (Lieven 2011, 219).

SUPPORT NETWORKS. Politicians with high levels of political autonomy use widespread social networks within their constituencies to enable them to secure more votes than their opponents. In rural constituencies familial, kinship, and factional networks are particularly advantageous, while in urban constituencies access to groups that organize the associational life of citizens, such as trade union and chambers of commerce, are an important support network (Javed 2014). In both instances access to local government is integral in order to serve as an effective conduit between state and citizen.

Even a casual observer of Pakistan's politics is bound to notice both the dynastic or quasi-dynastic nature of party leadership and the overrepresentation of certain families. The British encouraged this tendency by making the political influence given to the indigenous rural elite a hereditary privilege, which led to the development of political legacies of families such as the Daultanas, the Tiwanas, and the Legharis in Punjab; the Khuhros, the Bhuttos, and the Jatois in Sindh; the Bilours, the Hotis, and the Khattaks in Khyber Pakhtunkhwa; and the Mengals, the Bugtis, and the Jamalis in Balochistan. According to Ali Cheema and colleagues (2013), approximately two-thirds of the elected legislators in the National Assembly from Punjab between 1985 and 2008 were dynastic, meaning that multiple family members had contested national and provincial elections in the past.

To maintain their local prestige and influence, political families need access to state resources, such as development funds and projects, to oblige their constituents (Javid 2015). As a result these families have tended to back the ruler of the day, be it the British, the military, or political parties. Political families perpetuate their power by strategically placing members of their families in all the major political parties to ensure that, regardless of which party or alliance forms the government, benefits will accrue to the entire family. These families have also expanded their political networks through marriage into other well-placed political families and diversifying their economic assets to include industrial and commercial enterprises.[4] Furthermore, these families have further embedded themselves by actively taking part in local government as district councilors and *nazims* (mayors). In this way they are able to maintain their contacts with the police and courts (who aid them in solving legal issues faced by their constituents) and the local bureaucracy (who provide the protection of the state and an additional network of patronage in the form of development funds).

Additionally, in Punjab, from where 55 percent of Pakistan's legislators are elected, the kinship-based system of occupational stratification that is found in the countryside (*biraderi*) has placed landowners at the top of the agrarian hierarchy, which reinforces their economic power by providing them with control over traditional informal institutions, such as the *panchayats*, which are tasked with dispute resolution and arbitration (Alavi 1972a; S. Ahmad 1977). Biraderi also form the basis for mobilizing support; extended kinship networks, marital alliances, and direct ties of dependence between landowning and nonlandowning biraderis form the basis for the formation of voting blocs. These vote blocs, built on networks of kinship, have also come to be shaped around the provision and receipt of patronage.

However, political autonomy stems from both access to personal networks like family and biraderi as well as the capacity to mobilize support across different classes and biraderis. Hence, linkages established with faction (*dhara*) leaders enable politicians to bypass party organizations to mobilize voters. These faction leaders allegedly maintain relations with local law enforcement and village *goondas* (thugs) to intimidate rival factions and elicit cooperation from villagers by affording them protection in village-level disputes. Faction leaders, who owe their allegiance to landowning politicians, often advance their own political status by contesting local government elections and becoming involved in local party organizations.

CHARISMA. One final source of autonomous political power is personal charisma, that is, the possession of personal attributes or qualities that inspire devotion from followers. In the context of Pakistan's electoral politics, two sources of charisma appear to be significant: spiritual authority and effective performance in public office. The first category encapsulates individuals such as the traditional caretakers of Sufi shrines (*sajida nashins* and *pirs*) or recognized religious authorities, both of whom possess the legitimacy required to make effective appeals for political support on the basis of religion (Malik and Mirza 2015). The politically illustrious Qureishi family of Multan, keepers of Sheikh Bahauddin Zakaria's shrine, exemplifies a family that traces its descent from a much-venerated saint and has used its status to entrench itself in politics by supporting the ruling establishment and delivering both economic and spiritual patronage (Jafri 2007, 341–52). The second category arguably includes politicians like Anwar Cheema and Nadeem Afzal Chan, who may be part of the overarching system of patronage politics but who are also able to command support because they are perceived as men of integrity and honesty. Their willingness to "be at one" with and be accessible to them earns them this reputation.

Independent electables are candidates who demonstrate high levels of political autonomy and have the ability to operate independently of political parties because they possess the political resources to maintain stable and reliable vote blocs, which are crucial for reelection and maintaining political careers. These politicians have little incentive to remain loyal to particular parties. Instead, their relationship with parties is likely to be transactional, revolving around the extent to which the party provides access to public office and the privileges that accrue from it. Such politicians are prone to defection and opportunistic political decision-making, shifting from one party to another or even aligning with military-led governments, while relying on their vote blocs to continue providing them with electoral support.

While they may choose to join a party on a transactional basis, independent electables do not necessarily need, nor do they always seek, a party ticket to contest elections. In 2013, for example, 2,377 independent candidates contested elections, of which 28 candidates won the election with a total vote share of 13 percent. Not all of the independent candidates who took part in the elections would have been characterized as independent electables; many fall in the category of *aspirational candidate*, but those who were significant electoral contenders participated knowing that their lack of a party label would not necessarily impede their political ambitions.[5] Indeed, of the 28 independent candidates who won, 16 subsequently joined the governing party, the PML-N, after the election, claiming that being a part of the government party gave them crucial access to state resources, which was essential because *"logon kay ziyati kaam karane hotay hain"* (personal delivery of services to the masses is a necessary part of the job).[6]

Party heavyweights enjoy a level of autonomy similar to that of independent electables and therefore are not dependent on their chosen political party for continued electability. Confident of the resources they bring to the table, party heavyweights seek a political party not on the basis of party ideology or policy platform but rather because they seek the "right" party ticket: the political party whose support base in the constituency serves to increase their odds of electoral success. Consequently, their party loyalty is not credible—and they may very well choose to remain loyal only so long as access to the party label helps them win. Of course, they may also switch party alliances prior to an election based on the variety of factors outlined earlier. One key difference between party heavyweights and independent electables is that the heavyweights can be induced to remain part of a chosen party simply because of the existence of social constraints, ideological affinities, and shared history.

Commitment

A second dimension of our typology measures levels of political commitment, that is, the long-standing dedication of a candidate to a political party. This commitment can stem from similar ideological proclivities and shared histories but may also be a result of individual social ties of friendship or marriage.

IDEOLOGY AND SHARED HISTORY. Although Pakistan's political parties are not typically described as having distinct programmatic agendas (Gazdar 2008), their origins are defined by ideological commitments that stem from the politicization of societal cleavages. The MQM and the ANP, for example, trace their origins to the struggle for political autonomy by an ethnic group—the Muhajirs in the case of the MQM and the Pashtuns in the case of the ANP. Although it has not politicized a societal cleavage, the PPP traces its founding to four principles: "Islam is our faith, democracy is our politics, social democracy is our economy, and all power to the people." These ideological principles have provided party candidates with a common rhetoric to use during election campaigns and to publicly demonstrate commitment to the political party.

A shared history of struggle can also form the basis for enduring relationships between a party and its members. Interviews with political elites reveal that political parties are often placed on a continuum ranging from being pro-establishment to anti-establishment, where the word "establishment" is understood to describe the military-bureaucratic axis that has long dominated Pakistan's political system.[7] Parties like the PPP that have historically pitted themselves against the military have also nurtured an image of being a persecuted party and forged ties of solidarity among their members by participating in anti-military movements like the Movement for the Restoration of Democracy (MRD). PPP party workers, known as *jiyalas*, often demonstrate their commitment to the party by making sacrifices such as going to jail or into exile and suffering at the hands of the military during periods of authoritarian rule. These sacrifices help cement their bond with the broader party organization and membership and introduce ideological and personal impediments to party-switching and defection.

DEDICATION TO THE PARTY LEADER. Party leaders in Pakistan, especially those in the PPP and the PML-N, have paid scant attention to membership development and have generally ignored intraparty elections. Although it can be argued that this is a function of weak organizational capacity and limited resources, it also exists because party leaders have typically portrayed themselves as the embodiment of the political party itself, using charismatic authority to create a cult of personality around themselves. Consequently, climbing up the ranks by party members is an exercise in making oneself visible and proving one's worth to the party leadership. In the PPP, ideological commitment to the party has been reduced to a commitment to the Bhutto family, wherein a display of ardent self-sacrificing behavior in the name of the Bhuttos is seen as a measure of good performance in the party (see chapter 2 in this volume for more on the Bhutto family and the PPP). The MQM is also an interesting case in point: a central tenet of party membership under the leadership of Altaf Hussain was to have blind faith in the party leader (Farooq 1989), and, until recently, members of the MQM swore an oath of allegiance to Hussain, who as *Quaid-e-Tehrik* (leader of the movement) maintained undisputed control over the party (see chapter 4 for more on the MQM).

SOCIAL CONSTRAINTS. Loyalty and commitment to political parties have also been the consequence of social obligations that stem from marital and kinship ties. For example, Anwar Ali Cheema, who had defected from PML-N to join the PML-Q, was unable to switch back to his parent party prior to the 2013 elections even though he could clearly see a decline in the PML-Q's electoral fortunes. As a party heavyweight he could have mustered his eighth consecutive electoral victory had his association with the unpopular PML-Q not tainted his campaign. But because Cheema's son is married to the niece of Chaudhry Shujaat Hussain, the leader of the PML-Q, his familial obligations compelled him to stay with the PML-Q. Similar kinds of personal relationships permeate Pakistan's party system, with marriage and kinship being potent mechanisms for securing the allegiance of otherwise powerful politicians. Party heavyweights can both benefit from their connection to the party (by always getting the ticket they want or advancing within the party) and suffer from it (when they would rather switch to another party).

Although candidates with autonomous power tend to dominate national and provincial elections, there are instances where candidates lacking independent bases of support nonetheless engage in electoral contests. As shown in figure 8.1, these candidates can be divided into two main types: *party workers* and *aspirational candidates*.

Party workers, found primarily in parties like the MQM and the JI, have a history of loyalty to the party. Their performance within the party allows them to rise through the ranks and eventually receive the support of their parties in the form of a party ticket to contest elections. Candidates nominated through this route are reliant on the identity and resources of their parties to mobilize support for their electoral campaigns. They are consequently much more dependent on their parties for their political survival than are more autonomous politicians. As candidates they also are unlikely to find much success outside their parties because they lack the vote banks and independent appeal that would make them attractive targets for recruitment by other parties—or would assure their success as independents.

Aspirational candidates lack both autonomous political power and commitment to any given party. However, aspirational candidates do display a high level of commitment to advancing their political careers. A large number of them contest elections as independents or as nominees from smaller, lesser-known parties, knowing full well that their chances of success are remote at best. In 2013 more than 90 percent of the candidates contesting as independents received less than 12.5 percent of the vote. Aspirational candidates are not necessarily motivated by a desire to win as much as they are by the social status conferred by participation in an election. Participation in an election campaign, even as a marginal candidate, can raise a person's social profile and, perhaps more important, help establish his or her credentials as an important member of their community and a potential electoral candidate for larger parties in the future (Gulzar and Khan 2017). However, some aspirational candidates—like Jamshed Dasti, who surprised many by defeating the politically entrenched Khar family in Muzaffargarh—are also able to win substantial majorities.

These four types of candidate—the independent electable, party heavyweight, party worker, and aspirational candidate—are not intended to be viewed as immutable labels. For instance, it is common for party workers to acquire autonomous power over time, rise through the ranks (often through initial experiences in local government or student politics), or acquire political power and its attendant resources (social and economic). Similarly, it is possible to trace a career trajectory for some heavyweights being sidelined by their parties, often as the result of political intraparty maneuvering, but some will also nonetheless find themselves unable to defect to rivals, either out of enduring feelings of loyalty to the party or due to the absence of viable opportunities to do so. On the other hand, party heavyweights, who usually remain loyal to a single party over the span of their careers, have also been known to switch parties when offered better positions or even as a response to changing external political circumstances (with defections to military-backed governments or rising parties like the PTI being a prime example).

Having examined the nature of candidate-party linkages from the perspective of candidates, we now turn to political parties to see how they determine which of the four possible types of candidates should represent them in an election.

Explaining Recruitment and Candidate Selection

Pakistan's political parties have historically been characterized by relatively limited amounts of organizational capacity and ideological coherence. One of the main reasons for this has been repeated episodes of military rule: all four of Pakistan's military governments cracked down on political parties upon assuming power, utilizing a range of repressive measures including outright bans, the confiscation of party funds, and the persecution of political leaders (Kennedy 2006).

This problem has been compounded by the tendency of the military establishment, both when in power and behind the scenes during periods of ostensibly democratic rule, to generate support for itself and its agenda through the co-optation of pliant civilian politicians. In practice this has led to the disruption of political parties through the creation of new parties comprised of politicians peeled away from already existing parties (for example, the Republican Party and the Convention Muslim League under Ayub Khan, or the PML-Q under Musharraf) and the use of forward blocs—coalitions of politicians who defect from their parties—to undermine majorities in Parliament. Furthermore, many of the politicians collaborating with the military establishment have been drawn from among the traditional land-owning political elite and have successfully been able to use their alignment with the military to further entrench their influence and power within the broader political system (Mufti 2011).

Consequently, when contesting elections Pakistan's political parties have always been confronted with a dilemma: whether to engage in the difficult and costly task of constructing an effective party machinery by carving out a distinct ideological identity and crafting effective policy narratives or to rely instead on the services of local politicians who already possess solid vote banks and the means to win elections. The nature of Pakistan's first-past-the-post electoral system disincentivizes the first strategy. The plurality formula of counting votes compels political parties to select the candidate who can win the most votes, but in a context where more opportunistic rival parties deploy locally influential politicians to win quick and easy electoral victories, the less costly electoral strategy is always to select a candidate with high levels of autonomy and local influence. This situation leads to an electoral race to the bottom in which parties continue to vie for the support and loyalty of independent electables and party heavyweights across the country. Over time this has further undermined, if not precluded, attempts to develop robust party apparatuses and perpetuated a political status quo in which independent electables and party heavyweights have been able to further consolidate their power and influence (Waseem 2016). Significantly, catch-all parties like the PPP and the PML-N do not finance the electoral campaigns of their candidates and even demand a ticket application fee to be considered for candidacy. Hence the loyalty of the candidates selected is often self-serving and directed to the local interests that supported their reelection.

The dilemma confronting Pakistan's larger parties is best captured by the experience of the PTI. As a relatively new player in the 2013 elections, the PTI had been able to ride a wave of apparently populist support following a long-running campaign that sought to discredit the party's opponents by accusing them of rampant corruption. However, when faced with the challenge of dislodging the entrenched candidates fielded by its rivals, the PTI continued to campaign against corruption while simultaneously accommodating politicians that defected from the other political parties, including former party heavyweights such as Shah Mehmood Qureshi and Javed Hashmi and independent electables such as Jahangir Tareen (see chapter 3 for more on the PTI's evolution). The irony of this situation was not lost on the party leadership: Imran Khan acknowledged that "one man alone without an electable team can only do so much" and that he could not "find angels to join the PTI."[8]

There are several mechanisms through which parties can attract electables to their side; the most significant is by acting as the conduit for state patronage. While arguably the absence of ideological and programmatic differences between the mainstream parties, as well as their limited organizational capacity, suggests that electable politicians and voters are both indifferent to party labels, one important function that parties continue to play is to serve as the platforms through which individual politicians and, by extension, their clients, constituents, and supporters can gain access to the state. As such, a party that is likely to win an election or at least secure enough seats in Parliament to be able to leverage its position to wrest concessions from its larger rivals can plausibly promise the provision of patronage to electable candidates who agree to contest elections under its banner.

Patronage of this sort can assume different forms. Legislators in both the upper and lower houses of Parliament have since 1985 been entitled to constituency development funds that are disbursed, increased, or even withheld at the direction of the parties heading the relevant provincial or national governments (Tsubura 2013).[9] Being in power or aligned with the party in government provides access to networks of power and influence in the state that can be used to further strengthen a politician's ability to deliver goods to voters and supporters. The value of this alignment was demonstrated during the local government elections held in Punjab in December 2015, when the PML-N won 44 percent of the available seats; an additional 39.4 percent were won by independents. This result was particularly interesting because the vast majority of these independents were subsequently absorbed into the PML-N, as the party had signaled, prior to the election, that it would be willing to work with whichever candidates won.

Other forms of patronage and rewards that can compel electable candidates to support political parties include offers of high office, ranging from cabinet positions to senate nominations. Federal and provincial cabinets in Pakistan have historically been large (and have increased in size over the past decade), with dozens of ministerial posts and the lure of these positions, as well as their attendant perks and privileges, being deployed to retain, discipline, and reward both independent electables and party heavyweights (Mufti 2015a). Immediately after the elections of 2008, for example, a number of legislators who defected from the PML-Q to the PML-N were rewarded with ministerial posts in the Punjab government. Similarly, smaller parties with coalition potential, like the JUI-F, have long been able to use their relatively minor electoral presence to wrest ministries and senate nominations away from successive governments at the provincial and national levels.

In contrast with the PML-N and PPP, smaller parties like the ANP and MQM contest elections in their ethnically defined, geographic strongholds and are not burdened by the need to be nationally representative. Similarly, political parties like the JI and the JUI-F (Jamiat Ulema-e-Islam-Fazlur Rehman) rely on religious appeals to generate support, giving them a clear and distinct identity among sections of the electorate. The MQM, for example, contests elections in predominantly safe seats where a high level of party identification among the voters sharply increases the importance of the party label. Party leaders retain the prerogative of recruiting and selecting candidates who can demonstrate this ideological commitment to the party. In the case of the MQM and the JI in particular, the strength of party-voter linkages is also enhanced by the fact that both parties appeal to an urban voter base not under the influence of traditional landowning elites.

The consequence of this for candidates and intraparty dynamics are clear. As opposed to the larger catch-all parties, the MQM and the JI typically field party worker candidates in elections and provide them with organizational and financial support in their campaigns. Not coincidentally, both parties also have relatively well-developed party apparatuses complete with intraparty democracy and mechanisms through which workers can rise through the ranks of the organization. This does not mean that the JI and the MQM lack electable politicians of their own; many of their leaders enjoy independent support, either due to their societal position or their charisma. However, what differentiates these electables from their counterparts in the larger parties is the relative bargaining power they enjoy: due to their lack of reliance on electables, the two parties can afford to alienate their leaders to a much greater extent than their political rivals. For example, when Nabil Gabol, a long-standing member of the PPP, briefly switched to the MQM and was awarded a ticket to contest his traditional constituency in Karachi, his candidacy was not accompanied by any greater prominence or position within the party nor any significant input into the party's broader decision-making process.

In sum, the larger catch-all political parties in Pakistan like the PPP and the PML-N—which together have made up 71 percent of the vote share and 73 percent of the seat share between 1988 and 2013—cannot seriously threaten candidates by withholding nominations because recalcitrant politicians do not have to *credibly* demonstrate their commitment or loyalty to the party. A candidate's reelection does not depend on having both party support and maintaining personalized linkages with his or her voters. The autonomy of the candidates selected by the PPP and the PML-N is in direct contrast with candidates selected by smaller political parties, which either contest safe seats in their traditional strongholds or seek candidates with strong party credentials. These parties control access to the party label, which is crucial to the electoral success of the candidates, who in turn rely on the party for both financial and organizational support to mount their campaigns. It is therefore unsurprising that party leaders prioritize party workers who demonstrate high levels of commitment to the party as their candidates (see table 8.1).

To Defect or Not to Defect?

As the preceding discussion shows, parties and politicians are engaged in a constant process of negotiation; electable candidates with high levels of autonomy are actively courted by parties that lack effective organizations of their own and require their support for electoral success. This support is cultivated through promises of patronage and offers of high office, and candidates themselves are typically on the lookout for better opportunities in every electoral cycle. Exceptions to this occur either when parties are able to create direct linkages to voters on the basis of identity or ideology or when electable candidates develop high levels of commitment to their parties.

The dynamics of the negotiations underpinning candidate selection and recruitment can be illustrated through an analysis of the relatively widespread

Table 8.1. The distribution of different types of candidates as a percentage of total candidates from a given political party in the 14th National Assembly

	Party heavyweights	Independent electables	Party workers	Aspirational candidates
PPP (n = 36)	92	0	8	—
PML-N (n = 146)	82	12	6	—
PTI (n = 28)	71	0	29	—
MQM (n = 18)	6	0	94	—
Religious political parties (n = 12)	50	0	50	—
Independent parties (n = 9)	0	100	0	—
Other parties (n = 20)	85	0	15	—

Source: Data based on election results from May 11, 2013, and exclude by-election results unless a seat was vacated under Article 223. Elections were terminated in NA 38, 83, and 254 and thus are not considered.

phenomenon of party-switching in Pakistan. According to one estimate, an average of 19 percent of all candidates switched from one party to another in every election held between 1990 and 2008, with 60 percent of these candidates having ranked among the top three candidates in their constituencies during the previous election (Qadri 2014). According to the Free and Fair Election Network (FAFEN), however, defections reached a historic peak in 2018 when 248 politicians at the national and provincial levels switched parties between January and May, with 92 of them choosing to join the PTI, 48 switching to the PPP, and a mere 29 opting for the PML-N.[10] Several factors can explain this. Political rivalries rooted in local-level conflicts and enmities can lead candidates to move to parties that are not aligned with their antagonists. Candidates may also decide to switch parties if it becomes apparent that their current party is unlikely to win—or remain in—power (the wave of defections accompanying the collapse of the PML-Q in 2008 being a case in point).

However, Zhirnov and Mufti (2019) have also shown that defection is strongly correlated with high levels of electoral volatility, meaning that candidates are more likely to switch when levels of party identification are low. In this context the electoral race to the bottom helps explain party-switching. As they compete with each other to recruit electables with high levels of autonomy, the parties end up engaging in a process of outbidding, making offers of patronage and position in exchange for electoral support. The cumulative effect of this across successive electoral cycles is a progressive weakening of party structures, which simply ends up strengthening the very tendencies that prompt party-switching in the first place, namely, an inability to generate voter identification with parties and dependence on the autonomous power of electable candidates.

Taken to its logical conclusion, this view suggests that once parties are unable to satisfy the demands of their electables, defections are likely to ensue. However, there are numerous instances of otherwise autonomous candidates choosing to stick with parties that are unlikely to win power or credibly be in a position to provide patronage or other rewards to their supporters. In this case understanding how candidates develop *commitment* to parties is crucial. Party heavyweights differ from independent electables on the basis of their demonstrated loyalty to particular political parties. In some cases genuine adherence to the ideology of a party, or aversion to the ideologies of its rivals, might lead some candidates to stick with their party; a shared history of struggle or allegiance to a particularly charismatic or inspiring leader might do the same. Social constraints also play a role here, as the case of Cheema vividly demonstrates: marital links between his family and that of the PML-Q leadership prevented him from defecting to another party in 2013.

There is, however, one more set of factors that might prevent a party heavyweight from defecting to a rival party. Despite his defeat in 2013, Chan continues to be a part of the PPP as of March 2018, even as many of the party's more senior leaders in Punjab have defected to the PML-N and the PTI in response to the PPP's increasingly dismal electoral prospects in the province. Chan did, however, resign from his position as the party's general secretary in October 2017, claiming he needed to do so on a point of principle.[11] What this principle might have been remains unclear, although it is perhaps not coincidental that his younger brother, Waseem Afzal, defected from the PPP to join the PTI that very same month. As one of the PPP's few remaining influential and electable candidates in Northern Punjab, Chan arguably stands to gain a lot from his continued presence in the party, especially considering how the PPP's government in Sindh and its significant presence in the senate continue to provide supporters and candidates across the country with access to the corridors of power. Chan's resignation from his post amid defections from other leaders could have simply been a part of his broader strategy for negotiating with the PPP, considering how his brother's move to the PTI might have demonstrated the potential frailty of the links connecting Chan to his party. Or Chan's continued commitment to the party might be more the result of a strategic calculation than any deeper loyalty to it: recognizing that elections are not one-off games, he and others like him might simply be hedging their bets, counting on increased patronage and positions within their current parties as subsequent electoral cycles alter the balance of political power across the country.

Conclusion

This chapter has focused on explaining the understudied linkages between political parties and candidates by answering two questions: What function do political parties serve beyond providing candidates with a collective platform from which to contest elections, and why do candidates remain loyal to political parties despite having control of resources and vote banks and the ability to win an election independently? Four categories of candidates, based on level of autonomy and commitment to a party—party heavyweights, independent electables, party workers, and aspirational candidates—determine the importance of a party label to a candidate's political career. The case of independent electables and party workers is straightforward, wherein independent electables have no need to affiliate with a party to win an election and party workers cannot contest elections without the party's backing. However, the dynamic between party heavyweights and political parties is intriguing. These are highly autonomous candidates from political parties yet they seek party tickets prior to an election to cement their electoral victories. They are not credibly loyal to their political parties because, while some party heavyweights have switched party affiliation with little impunity, others choose to remain loyal to their parties. We conclude that political parties use their proximity to the state to promise the provision of state resources and access to prestigious political appointments in order to elicit loyalty from candidates that may be self-serving or reliant on their local constituencies for electoral success. In patriarchal contexts that accord high importance to family, marital, and kinship structures, these connections can also informally bind together candidates and parties.

Our findings suggest that unless political parties make a concerted effort to strengthen local party organizations, increase levels of party identification, and tighten access to the party label by genuinely making loyalty to the party an integral candidacy requirement, a candidate-centered party system prone to factionalization and party-switching is likely to prevail.

Notes

1. Fieldwork by Hassan Javid in Sargodha, June to August 2006.
2. Fieldwork by Hassan Javid in Sargodha, April 2013.
3. Unpublished data from "Declaration of Assets" (Islamabad: Election Commission of Pakistan, 2013).
4. See Baxter (1974) and *Herald,* Special Election Issue on Political Dynasties, May 2013.
5. In 2018 the same pattern is observed: of the 3,400 candidates who contested an election, 1,597 were independent candidates. Another 13 independent candidates won the election, and 9 of these joined the government-forming PTI.
6. Mariam Mufti interview with a candidate from Sindh in Islamabad, August 21, 2008.
7. Mariam Mufti conducted interviews during a research trip to Pakistan in May–June 2012 and May 2016.

8. Fahd Hussain, "The Great Leap Forward: Imran Khan's Soaring Popularity," *Newsline,* November 30, 2011; A. Rafiq, "The Imran Khan Phenomenon," *Foreign Policy*, January 12, 2012.

9. The 18th Amendment, which devolved power to the provinces, has arguably provided to the parties in power at the provincial level, with even greater control over the disbursement of patronage (Adeney 2012; Waseem 2015).

10. FAFEN, *General Election 2018: Update- V*, July 1, 2018, http://fafen.org/wp-con tent/uploads/2018/07/FAFEN-Pre-Election-Observation-General-Election -2018-Update-V.pdf?x22764.

11. Mubashir Hassan, "Nadeem Chan Resigns as PPP Punjab General Secretary," *Nation*, October 20, 2017.

9

Women in Electoral Politics
An Account of Exclusion

Sarah Khan

During the 2018 general election in Pakistan, Syeda Zahra Basit Bukhari was one of fourteen women candidates fielded by the winning party, the Pakistan Tehreek-e-Insaf (PTI), for a National Assembly seat. She was the only woman contesting the election from the NA-184 constituency, which is located in the Muzaffargarh district in southwest Punjab. Bukhari was a new entrant in politics, and conventional wisdom deemed her a "weak candidate."[1] Her husband, Syed Basit Sultan Bukhari, had already served two terms in the National Assembly and was contesting the 2018 election as an independent candidate in the neighboring constituency; he joined the PTI after he won. The PTI election campaign poster for NA-184 carried Syeda Zahra Basit Bukhari's name but a picture of her husband's face rather than her own. In the lead-up to the election, the Pakistan Muslim League-Nawaz (PML-N) candidate for the NA-184 seat, Syed Haroon Ahmed Sultan, was caught on video at a public meeting with constituents asserting that voting for women candidates was *haram* (prohibited). Sultan was a member of the Punjab provincial cabinet at the time and was contesting elections from one additional national constituency and two provincial constituencies on PML-N tickets. In 2010 he had been the subject of a police complaint for allegedly beating his wife until she fainted and threatening to kill her.[2] He was required to appear in front of the Election Commission for his statement about women candidates, but he ended up contesting the election anyway.

Zahra Bukhari's experience as a faceless candidate—included on the ballot largely by virtue of her husband's involvement in politics and the only woman candidate in her constituency facing an opponent who publicly engaged in misogynistic speech and was alleged to have committed domestic violence in private—may not be a universal experience, but it is not atypical either. The 2018 election in Pakistan saw the highest number of women candidates running for National Assembly seats in a general election to date. There were a number of uplifting stories of women breaking barriers, such as the one of Zartaj Gul, a young woman from Waziristan with no political family connections who started her political career as a member of the PTI's student wing, the Insaf Student Forum, in 2005 and rose up through the party ranks to defeat two strong political stalwart candidates for a National Assembly seat in Dera Ghazi Khan district. At the same time, and despite there being a record number of women candidates competing, fewer women (eight) actually *won* National Assembly seats in 2018, compared to elections in 2008 (sixteen) and 2013 (nine).

Electoral politics in Pakistan today remains a male-dominated affair. Men heavily outnumber women as elected representatives at all levels of government, in party leadership positions, and even on the electoral rolls. This pattern of women's exclusion and underrepresentation is of course neither unique to Pakistan nor to the sphere of formal politics. Indeed, men outnumber women in positions of political decision-making across countries at differing levels of development and across different regime types; women's relative absence from politics in Pakistan also mirrors their absence from other formal workplaces and public spaces more broadly. The female labor force participation rate for women in Pakistan in 2016 was 25 percent, which is lower than countries with similar income levels. Moreover, most of the women in the labor force are employed in rural agricultural work or the informal sector (Field and Vyborny 2016).

In this chapter I highlight some key factors shaping the systematic exclusion of women from electoral politics in Pakistan. I focus on four main channels of women's entry into electoral politics—political parties, electoral institutions, families, and voters—and explore how features of each channel perpetuate the exclusion of women. I also consider the effectiveness of various institutional solutions, such as mandating women's presence through a historical guarantee of reserved seats, and, more recently, party candidate quotas. While these solutions do well in achieving numerical targets, they do little to change party incentives for greater inclusion beyond minimums. I conclude with lessons for more effective institutional design for making progress toward women's inclusion in politics.

Parties and the Institutional Environment

Political parties serve as the primary gatekeepers of individuals' entry into electoral politics. Existing research from various contexts has identified certain characteristics of parties—their ideological leanings and party organizational structures (Caul 1999), the presence of women among party elite (Kunovich and Paxton 2005), and their rules for candidate selection (Pruysers, Cross, and Gauja 2017)—to explain differences in their selection and support of women as electoral candidates. Similarly, we may look to the characteristics of individual political parties in Pakistan to understand the extent to which their structures and strategies are inclusive of women. Among the large mainstream parties, the Pakistan People's Party (PPP), which is historically left-leaning and socially progressive, has had two women, Nusrat Bhutto and Benazir Bhutto, serve as party chair. The substantive character of women's inclusion in the Jamaat-e-Islami (JI)—the oldest Islamist party in Pakistan—is entirely different. While women are essentially absent from the JI's central party leadership, its women's wing operates as a highly active yet separate structure within the party (N. Siddiqui 2010). However, a comparison of Pakistani parties on their promotion of women as electoral candidates shows that parties that are otherwise ideologically and organizationally quite different look remarkably similar. Figure 9.1 shows the percentage of women among the candidates fielded by major parties for general seats in the 2018 general election.

This relative *lack* of variation across parties regarding the nomination of women is at least in part a product of the common institutional environment that all parties face. The design of electoral institutions has implications for women's overall presence (or, more accurately, absence) in electoral politics. Multiple empirical studies on women's presence in parliaments around the world confirm that women's descriptive representation is higher in countries with proportional representation systems compared to majoritarian electoral systems, when accounting for other factors (Wängnerud 2009). Moreover, within proportional representative systems, greater district magnitude (i.e., more seats per electoral district) appears to facilitate greater entry of women (Norris 2006). On the other hand, single-member majoritarian districts—as in Pakistan—imply higher barriers to entry for new parties as well as new candidates within existing parties. When a party can award only a single ticket within a constituency, it is often the women within parties, who are perceived as less competitive or "risky" candidates, who lose out. "When nominating candidates for an election in single-member districts, a party can exclude women and then justify it by arguing that they chose the best person for the job (oftentimes, this candidate is a male)" (Johnson-Myers 2016, 12).

Another feature of the 2018 nomination numbers shown in figure 9.1 is that all parties nominated at least 5 percent women candidates in compliance with Section 206 of the Election Act 2017, which required that when selecting candidates for general seats, parties "shall ensure at least five percent representation of women candidates." The provision marked the first instance of party-based candidate quotas for women and was enforced prior to the 2018 general election by the Election Commission of Pakistan. Noncompliance with Section 206 leads to political parties not being allotted electoral symbols.[3] Nevertheless, parties' compliance with the requirement can only be described as minimal, as the largest percentage of women candidates was

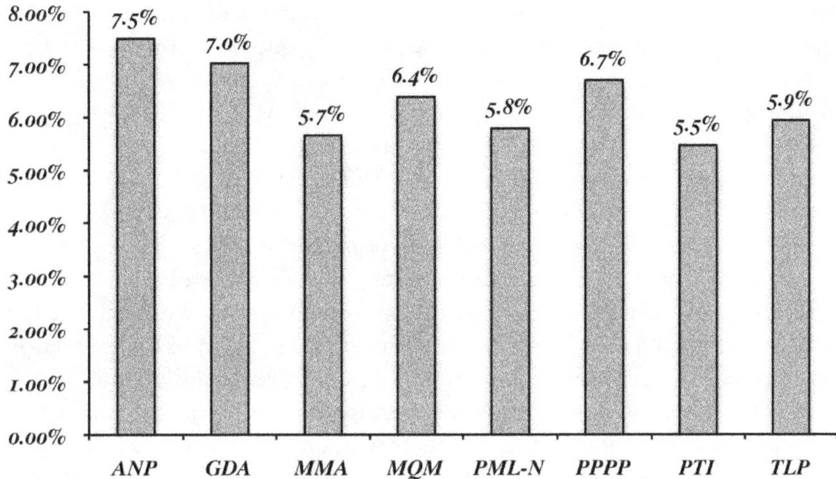

Figure 9.1. Women as a percentage of total candidates fielded on general seats for the national and provincial assemblies in 2018, by party

Source: Election Commission of Pakistan, "Statement Showing the Five Percent Women in General Seats under Section 206 of the Election Act, 2017," July 6, 2018.

still the paltry 7.5 percent put up by the Awami National Party (ANP). Moreover, women candidates across parties complained that they had been fielded in uncompetitive constituencies.[4]

Reserved Seats

Prior to the 5 percent provision of 2017, the main institutional tool for ensuring women's numerical presence in political decision-making was the mandated seat reservations in the legislature. The question of mandated presence of various groups in legislative bodies predates Pakistan's independence. As Jensenius (2015) notes, the subject of quotas first entered the stage during the drafting of the 1909 Indian Councils Act (Morley-Minto Reforms), which legitimized the election of Indians to legislative councils for the first time during the British Raj. The 1909 act guaranteed representation for Muslims as well as certain interest groups (e.g., landowners, tea planters), but mandatory representation for women was not on the table at the time. The 1935 Government of India Act, however, included provisions for reserved seats for women as well as for other communal groups in various assemblies (Htun 2004; Krook and O'Brien 2010).

Following independence, the Indian Constituent Assembly granted electoral quotas (that is, reserved seats) to scheduled castes and tribal groups (SCs and STs) but not to Muslims or women. It was not until the 1970s that the debate around reservations for women was revived in India, where women's representation had become inseparable from the question of representation of other groups. Htun (2005) notes that the Indian Committee on the Status of Women considered the position of women only vis-à-vis other groups and drew an explicit distinction between women as a "category" and caste and religious groups as a "community" or "minority." Htun (2005) and Jensenius (2016) both note that the controversy surrounding reserved seats for women stemmed from anxiety that such reservations would privilege upper caste Hindu women, especially at the state and national levels. This framing of reservations for women as a tradeoff has sometimes posed obstacles to the adoption and expansion of such reservations. While electoral representation of religious minorities has been a source of controversy and violent clashes in Pakistan, the issue has remained separate from the issue of women's representation.[5] Indeed, although the efforts of women's rights activists in Pakistan have frequently been accused of being "elitist" (Saigol 2016), the trade-off argument has not been a salient one in Pakistan. On the one hand, the absence of such obstacles in Pakistan has allowed for relatively easier consensus around the principle of reservations for women. On the other hand, this has meant that the political discourse around women's reservations in Pakistan has been largely bereft of considerations of intersectionality or a real discussion of how the *type* of representational disadvantage faced by women may be similar or different to that faced by other groups. Although women's rights activists and scholars have raised the issue of limitations of reserved seats as a solution to women's underrepresentation, it was not until the 2017 Election Act that a different institutional tool (party candidate quotas) was seriously considered and adopted.

Pakistan upheld reservations for women in its first constitution of 1956: 10 seats in the 310-member unicameral parliament for a period of ten years. While the number of reservations for women varied between the 1956 and 1962 Constitutions and the 1969 Legal Framework Order, the provision remained intact. The 1973 Constitution introduced a bicameral legislature with 10 seats reserved for women in the 210-seat National Assembly for a period of ten years; by presidential order in 1985 the reservation was increased to 20 seats for women and an additional 10 seats for minorities.[6] The provision for reservations reached its ten-year expiry mark before the 1990 elections, and reservations were not revived until 2002. Figure 9.2 shows the proportion of women as contesting candidates and as members of the National Assembly in elections held since 1977. The terms lacking reservations (for assemblies elected in 1990, 1993, and 1997) saw the lowest presence of women in Parliament.

The restoration of quotas in Pakistan under Gen. Pervez Musharraf's military government in 2002 came on the heels of increased international activism around gender quotas leading up to the 1995 Beijing Conference and from the sustained in-country efforts by domestic activists and civil society organizations following it (see A. Khan 2018). One contemporaneous report by a leading domestic nongovernmental organization states,

> With Aurat Foundation taking the lead, several women's rights organizations organized a round table discussion in July 1995 with representatives of three major political parties of the country—PPP, PML-N, and ANP—on the issue of women's reserved seats. The discussion resulted in signing of a joint declaration by the party representatives to restore women's reserved seats and extend the provision to the Senate.... In 1998, a country wide signatures campaign was undertake[n] by advocacy organizations to secure support for the principles of reservation and a 33 percent representation. Wide-spread endorsements were received from more than 1500 Civil Society Organizations; thousands of individuals; opinion leaders; legislators of 19 political parties; [and] some ministers and office bearers of several women wings of political parties. (Aurat Foundation 2012, 32)

Scholarship devoted to explaining the global proliferation of gender quotas emphasizes the role of international and regional norm–diffusion (Krook 2006), international democracy promotion efforts (Bush 2011), collective action by women (Htun 2016), the formation of women's coalitions (Kang and Tripp 2018), and the structure of party competition (Weeks 2018). While each of these factors may have contributed to the adoption of expansive reservations for women at all levels of government in Pakistan in 2002, it is worth noting that Pakistan is one of five countries that already had quotas for women prior to the 1970s, so the 2002 reservations were a restoration and expansion of the quota policy, not a new adoption per se.[7]

Nevertheless, the 2002 reforms guaranteed a significant increase in the proportion of seats reserved for women in national and legislative assemblies (to 17 percent) and expanded this guarantee to the newly established local governments under the Local Government Ordinance 2001 (to 33 percent). Over thirty-six thousand women came into power at the union council, *tehsil,* town, and district levels through the first elections held under the Local Government Ordinance 2001 (Reyes 2002). Civil society organizations and international aid agencies capitalized on this window of opportunity for women's political entry to encourage novices to run for local office and later to train the newly elected women entrants. The 33 percent reservation, combined with the sheer number of positions available and lower resource-based barriers to entry at the local level, created space that was truly accessible to a diverse set of entrants: "While very limited information is available on this subject, existing studies show that most [women councilors] are less than 45 years old (57 percent); more than half are illiterate (53 percent); most are

housewives (73.7 percent); very few own land; and an overwhelming majority has never contested elections (79 percent), neither have their families (64
percent)" (Bari 2001, xiii–xiv).

The introduction of local governments represented a shift in the mechanism by which reserved seats would be filled: at the union council level
women were to be elected to reserved seats through direct rather than indirect elections. However, the elections—held under military rule—were non-
partisan, which meant that despite facilitating the entry of tens of thousands
of women into the formal electoral arena, the reform had limited implications for providing incentives to political parties to include more women in
their ranks.

Do Reservations "Work"?

A large body of literature is dedicated to examining the effects of quotas
for women—in their various forms—on outcomes of interest, for example,
increased presence of women after quotas are removed (Bhavnani 2009), the
substantive representation of women's policy preferences (Chattopadhyay
and Duflo 2004), or changes in voter evaluations of women as leaders (Beaman et al. 2009). Some recent scholarship also points to the limitations of
what quotas can reasonably be expected to achieve. In the case of quotas for
women in Latin America, Htun (2016, 69) notes, "Quotas gave women presence in power, but not the power to make effective use of their presence."

The question of whether reserved seats for women in legislatures "work"
depends in no small part on what metric is used to measure effectiveness.
Certainly, reserved seats mechanically ensure that women are present in legislatures—and as the data presented in figure 9.2 show, in the absence of
reservations (1990–97) women are essentially absent from Parliament. Such
presence may be normatively desirable in and of itself. Nevertheless, existing studies on the effectiveness of quotas have tried to compare men's and
women's relative effectiveness in legislatures by examining metrics such as
attendance, the content and substance of speeches made, the questions asked,
bills proposed, and bills passed. In the case of Pakistan, women legislators in
the National Assembly during 2017–18 were more likely than their male
counterparts to be present at hearings, and they contributed to 39 percent
of all parliamentary business despite making up only 20 percent of the membership.[8] While performance data is collected for all legislators, Bari (2015,
11) notes that performance has been used disproportionately to scrutinize
the performance of women legislators. This double standard is not lost on
women. Bari quotes one legislator's frustration: "Why is everyone interested
to assess our performance? How about men? They don't even bother to
attend parliamentary sessions. What have they done? Why no assessment is

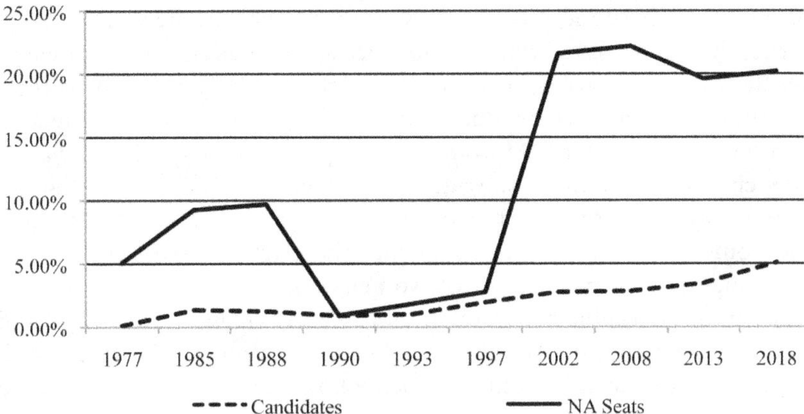

Figure 9.2. Women as a percentage of total candidates contesting election to general seats in the National Assembly and as a percentage of all sitting legislators in the National Assembly, 1977–2018

Sources: Based on calculations from Mehdi 2010; NDI and ANFREL 2013; and Colin Cookman, *Pakistan Elections Data 2018*, accessed October 30, 2018, https://github.com /colincookman/pakistan_elections.
Note: To the greatest extent possible, single candidates standing (and winning) for multiple constituencies are counted only once.

being done on their performance?" Murray (2014, 520–21) attributes this tendency, which spans policy and academic debates on the effectiveness of quotas to the way quotas are framed as a solution to the underrepresentation of women rather than the overrepresentation of men:

> The focus on women's underrepresentation has the unintended consequence of framing men as the norm and women as the "other." With men's presence already accepted as the status quo, the burden of proof for justifying presence lies with the outsiders wishing to enter politics (women), rather than with those already present in excessive numbers (men). Men are required neither to prove their competence nor to justify their inclusion. This is not to say that individual men are immune to all scrutiny, but rather that the competence of men as a category is not questioned. Women, in contrast, are placed under close scrutiny to ascertain whether they "deserve" a greater presence in politics.

Certainly the very design of Pakistan's quotas—reserved seats that are allotted to women through indirect election on a party basis *in addition to* (rather than as a proportion of) the general seats that a party has already won—reflects an unwillingness to formulate the core problem of unequal representation as one of men's overrepresentation (as Murray suggests) rather than simply women's underrepresentation.

One less problematic metric for assessing the effectiveness of quotas is whether they "normalize" women's presence and thus allow more women to enter the electoral arena in the future. This seems to be the case for village-level quotas in India, where Bhavnani (2009) finds that in constituencies that have had reservations for women in the past, women candidates have a higher chance of winning in subsequently held elections even in the absence of a reservation. He suggests this happens both because reservations introduce women who can win elections into the electoral arena and because they change parties' perceptions of women's ability to win elections. In a rich study of the candidate-selection process in Pakistan, Mufti and Jalalzai (2017) assess whether similar gains are observed in Pakistan. They approach the question by studying whether women who enter Parliament on reserved seats subsequently seek seats in general elections and suggest that "pervasive clientelism and patriarchal family structures deter women from entering politics and makes it too costly for political parties to nominate aspiring women to general seats" (4).

An important point of difference between the effects of reservations in India versus Pakistan is that the *design* of reservations in Pakistan precludes the channels for normalization identified by Bhavnani (2009). Since reserved seats for women are filled by indirect rather than direct election, they do not afford women entrants the experience of contesting an election nor do they signal to political parties that women are capable of doing so. Moreover, as Mufti and Jalalzai (2017) note, the lack of an electoral constituency for women on reserved seats excludes these women from the opportunities and incentives to nurture electoral connections that would make them viable candidates in the future. The lack of a constituency is then somewhat self-fulfilling in that women on reserved seats who start out without one are also ostensibly not spending the time to cultivate one for the future. In a single-member district, of course, it is possible that any effort to do so could be seen as an attempt to displace the male legislator(s) or aspirant(s) from their party. The high productivity of women in the legislative arena may well come at the opportunity cost of time spent in constituency service, which is arguably more highly rewarded by voters and would make women electorally viable candidates for general seats.

All in the Family

Despite performing poorly on most indicators of women's inclusion in electoral politics, Pakistan is one of seventy countries to have had a woman prime minister or president to date. This apparent paradox is not specific to Pakistan: cross-country research shows that, if anything, the presence of a woman head of state is correlated with *lower* levels of gender equality on a number of indicators (Jalalzai 2008; Jalalzai and Krook 2010). The puzzle of women breaking the glass ceiling of the highest political office in countries with low levels of gender equality is often understood through the lens of kinship or dynastic politics (Jalalzai 2008). Indeed, in the South Asian cases of Bangladesh, India, Pakistan, and Sri Lanka, the women who have held the highest elected office—Khaleda Zia, Sheikh Hasina, Indira Gandhi, Benazir Bhutto, Sirimavo Bandaranaike, and Chandrika Kumaratunga—have all succeeded fathers or husbands in those positions.

Alongside political parties, families and kinship networks serve as important gatekeepers for entry into the electoral arena in Pakistan. Cheema, Javid, and Naseer (2013, 1) describe the political class of Punjab as "heavily dominated by dynasties, held together by ties of blood and marriage, which impede the participation of non-dynastic aspirants to public office." While dynastic connections are important political currency for both men and women, they seem to be especially important for understanding women's entry into and trajectory within electoral politics. Chandra (2016, 21) discusses this reality in the case of India: "Dynastic Members of Parliament (MPs) are found in significant proportions across gender categories. But women MPs are considerably more likely than men to have dynastic ties. 58 percent of women MPs in 2004, 69 percent of women MPs in 2009 and 43 percent of women MPs in 2014, compared to 17 percent, 25 percent and 19 percent of male MPs in these respective parliaments."

A similar pattern holds up in Pakistan and is, in fact, a far starker situation. Figure 9.3 shows the proportion of winning candidates (male and female) in general elections from 1985 to 2008 who are dynastic. A winning candidate is coded as dynastic if he or she was preceded in electoral office by a family member who was a legislator. The gender gap in dynastic connections for winning candidates is large, and in the 1990, 1993, and 1997 elections *all* women who won general seats were preceded by family members who served as legislators.

How should we understand the gendered role of dynastic connections in electoral politics? While the preponderance of dynastic politicians is often seen as a mechanism for excluding and impeding new entrants, Chandra (2016) and Basu (2016) view family as an "equalizing force" for women's entry into the electoral sphere in a context where systematic barriers in party structures and, as in the case of India, a lack of national- and state-level reservations otherwise prevent entry. An alternative read, of course, is that dynasticism is a barrier rather than a channel, as nondynastic women have a much harder time entering than do nondynastic men. It is important to note that family connections seem less important when barriers to entry are lower—that is, at the local levels of government. In the case of India, Basu (2016) cites a 2000 study of *panchayats* (local councils) in the states of Madhya Pradesh, Uttar Pradesh, and Rajasthan and finds that unlike at the national and state levels, most women representatives at the panchayat level *did not* come from political families. This is similar to the earlier cited finding from a study of local bodies in Pakistan, which finds that 64 percent of women who were elected in the 2002 election did not have a family member who had previously contested an election, which is in stark contrast to the high proportions in national and provincial legislatures visualized in figure 9.3.

To understand the differential role of dynastic connections for men and women, Folke, Rickne, and Smith (2017) draw on work on women's entry into labor markets to develop a theory in which dynastic connections serve as a signal of candidate quality to both parties and voters. Since fewer women are present in the electoral arena and parties and voters have lower levels of experience with women candidates and representatives, they both may rely more heavily on this signal than they would for male candidates, who are present in larger numbers and for whom they have more information on past performance. Folke, Rickne, and Smith's theory has a dynamic component: they predict that as more and more women enter politics over time, parties and voters will gain greater information on women's performance and their reliance on political connections as a sign of performance will decrease, allowing more nondynastic women to enter. While a rigorous empirical test of their theory in the Pakistani case is beyond the scope of this chapter, a decline has occurred in the share of dynastic legislators among women legislators in 2002 and 2008 (see figure 9.3) concurrent to the expansion of reservations that brought more women into office. This drop in the share of winning women candidates with dynastic connections at the provincial and national levels is also consistent with a competing explanation related to an increased *supply* of nondynastic women candidates. If the experience of holding local-level positions is a potential pathway for women to contest general elections and seek higher office, then the large numbers of nondynastic women who had the chance to run for and win local office in 2002 may affect the composition of the pool of women candidates in subsequent elections.

The role of family in women's political entry goes beyond just dynastic connections. Family members may also be important players in the decision about whether individual women run for office or not, either by explicitly exercising control over a woman's decision to participate or by implicitly influencing an individual woman's ability to balance family and household responsibilities with a political career. These same considerations, however, generally affect women's entry into the labor market, not specifically politics. Basu (2016) suggests that while political family connections may offer women some modicum of protection from violence in the political sphere, it is important to remember that the threat of violence for women is often greatest inside the home and coming from other family members. For women who choose to enter politics, or any career, against the wishes of family members, there is a real threat of retributive violence within the

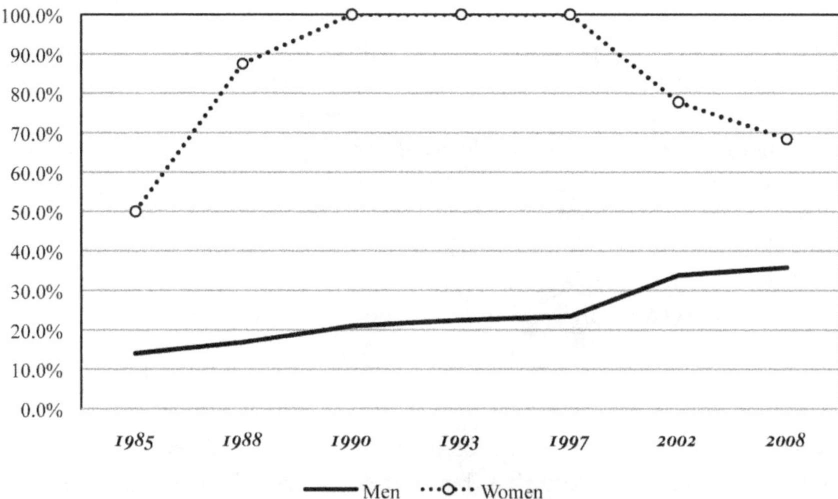

Figure 9.3. Proportion of winning candidates, in general elections to national and provincial assemblies, who are dynastic, 1985–2008

Source: In-progress data collection and research project, "Dynastic Politics in Pakistan" at the Institute for Development and Economic Alternatives (IDEAS), Lahore.

Note: The figure shows winning candidates on general seats; women legislators entering on reserved seats are not included. Thanks to Ali Cheema, Farooq Naseer, and Luke Sonnet for providing the gender disaggregated summary statistics.

family. Instances of such violence are documented in a set of biographies of thirty-six women who were elected as local government representatives compiled by the Aurat Foundation (2008, xiv):

> There were some women who had to face so much family opposition and hostility that they suffered severe mental stress and even physical abuse. . . . Zaib-un-Nissa Bhatti's brothers used to beat her when she went out to help the people of her area. . . . Khadeeja Bibi's husband locked her [in her] room for three days so that she would not be able to file candidacy papers. Shameem Ara's family and in-laws were both violently against her taking part in politics. Her brothers went around the area, forcing people to swear that they would not vote for her.

However, there are just as many or more instances of active family support: "The majority of women councilors had the support of their families to enter politics" (Aurat Foundation 2008, xiii). Nonetheless, the possibility of violence from family members suggests that it is precisely the women with supportive families who disproportionately enter into politics. For those who genuinely fear lack of support or retribution, it would be only a strategic decision to opt out.

Family considerations may also shape the trajectory of women's participation after entering politics. The relatively public nature of a political life means that women may be more restricted by gendered norms of public behavior than they would in some other career. An important area in which this phenomenon manifests is electoral campaigning. While many women candidates ran active campaigns in the 2018 elections, there were also many women nominees who ran limited or no campaigns. In the opening anecdote the absence of Zahra Bokhari's own face from her election poster was explained by her campaign manager as being due to the fact that she belonged to a "Syed family" and "our women do not publicize their pictures."[9]

Voters

While political parties exercise control over candidates' nominations, it is ultimately voters' decisions that determine candidates' fortunes in the electoral arena. Even in the party-controlled selection process strategic elites try to nominate candidates who they think will be preferred by voters and are hence "electable." A number of studies have examined voter preferences for women candidates in various contexts to unpack the "demand-side" explanations for why women may be underrepresented among candidates and representatives: it may simply be that there are fewer women in politics because that is what voters want.

Measuring whether and how voters use gender as a metric for evaluating a candidate is a complicated task. In 2018, 4.5 percent of all women candidates who contested general elections for the National Assembly won seats, while 8.7 percent of male candidates did. At first glance these numbers may suggest that women face an electoral disadvantage and voters penalize women candidates. However, in the 2018 election in particular, women candidates complained about being fielded from uncompetitive constituencies by their parties. If parties disproportionately field women candidates from constituencies where the party itself is uncompetitive, it is unclear whether it is really voters who are penalizing women or if parties are just setting up their women candidates to lose.

Nevertheless, we may look to data on public attitudes toward women in politics for suggestive evidence on Pakistani voters' preferences. Figure 9.4 displays survey responses from the sixth wave of the World Values Survey (conducted in fifty-nine countries) to the question of whether respondents agree with this statement: "On the whole, men make better political leaders than women do." In the case of Pakistan, an overwhelming majority of respondents (72 percent) either strongly agree or agree with the statement, which is high both in absolute terms and relative to the proportion in other countries surveyed that year.

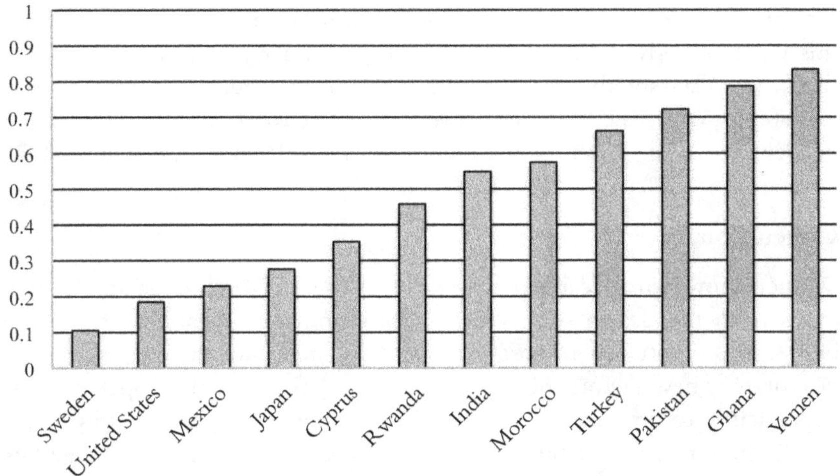

Figure 9.4. Proportion of respondents, by country, who agree or strongly agree with the statement, "On the whole, men make better political leaders than women do."

Source: Dataset from R. Inglehart et al., eds. (2014), "World Values Survey: Round Six, Country-Pooled Datafile Version," http://www.worldvaluessurvey.org/WVSDocumentation WV6.jsp (Madrid: JD Systems Institute).
Note: In each country the survey was conducted among 1,200 respondents weighted to be nationally representative using the most recent census numbers available at the time. Full details on the survey sample and methodology are available in the WVS-6 documentation: http://www.worldvaluessurvey.org/WVSContents.jsp.

Additionally, in a survey conducted before the 2018 elections among 2,500 households in Lahore, Cheema et al. (2019) found that a sizable proportion of respondents (40 percent) think it is inappropriate for women to stand as candidates in elections, and a third (both men and women) believe that merely *discussing* politics is solely a man's job. Similarly, in a 2016 survey of eight hundred men and women in the Faisalabad district, Khan (2017) found that only about half (53 percent) of women respondents say they would feel comfortable disclosing their support for a candidate that others in their household did not favor. In contrast, 80 percent of men said they would feel comfortable doing so. Women are not only excluded from formal positions of power but also appear to be systematically excluded from informal political conversations in their own homes.

These findings on public opinion may lead us to be pessimistic about the prospects of women's entry into electoral politics in Pakistan in the future. However, over time it may be possible to counter voters' apparent bias against women candidates and representatives if parties were to endorse more women and voters were exposed to greater numbers of women. The Indian case provides reason for some cautious optimism for long-term change on this front: a study on the effects of village-level reservations for women finds that villages with a female head of the village council saw "improve[d] perceptions of female leader effectiveness and weaken[ed] stereotypes about gender roles in the public and domestic spheres" (Beaman et al. 2009, 1,497).

Conclusion

Women's low numerical representation in the electoral arena in Pakistan stems from the design of electoral institutions, the incentives of political parties, the constraints imposed by families, and gender biases among the electorate. These factors interact with each other, rather than operating independently, to produce the condition of women's low presence in politics. While there is no silver bullet that can address all of these factors together, ignoring how they interact can lead to poor policy design with unintended consequences. The 5 percent women candidate nomination requirement is an example. While the rule mechanically forced parties to nominate a minimum proportion of women candidates, it did not change party incentives—under a majoritarian electoral system coupled with a perception of women candidates as electorally weaker—to nominate women beyond uncompetitive constituencies. Even though women nominees protested against being given tickets for uncompetitive districts, the presence of reserved seats in addition to party quotas potentially served as a "safety valve" for party elites who could reassure the women fielded from uncompetitive districts that they would be accommodated on a reserved seat were they to lose in general elections. In this way a lack of consideration of how other factors might shape party incentives meant that a well-intentioned policy failed to achieve greater inclusion of women in the electoral arena.

It is entirely possible that effectively changing party incentives to include greater numbers of women in high-stakes provincial and national elections is simply very difficult. On the candidate supply side, the high barriers to entry for this level of election (e.g., needing family connections to be a viable candidate) seem to be even higher for women. Local-level elections, on the other hand, provide a lower-stakes, lower-barriers space where parties may be more easily convinced to take a chance on women candidates and a more diverse set of women candidates may be able to contest. The varied composition of the cohort of women councilors who came to power in the 2002 elections is a testament to this possibility. Moreover, the experience of contesting elections and holding office at a lower level may have "knock-on" effects for the supply of women candidates seeking higher levels of office in the long run.

On the voter side, exposure to women in positions of local leadership may have the additional effect of reducing gender bias among the electorate, as evidence from neighboring India suggests. While similar documented evidence does not exist regarding exposure to women in higher positions of power, it is possible to imagine why it may be difficult to see similar gains. Voters may be able to brush off instances of women in positions of high leadership as rare exceptions rather than as the norm, and they may not shift their perceptions about women as leaders more generally. Moreover, such shifts in perception may require greater access to and sustained contact with a female representative, which is difficult for a provincial or national representative to provide but is in fact the intended goal for local representatives in a decentralized system. Moving beyond indirectly electing women to reserved seats at the national and provincial level to directly electing them on reserved seats in local government may allow for greater inclusion, both instantaneously and in the longer term by durably shifting party and voter perceptions of women as leaders.

Notes

1. Mian Abrar, "PPP, Independents to Make Hay on PTI's Flawed Ticket Distribution in Muzaffargarh," *Pakistan Today,* July 14, 2018.
2. "MPA Beats Pregnant Wife, Threatens Her with Death," *Express Tribune,* September 25, 2018.
3. Election Commission of Pakistan press release, May 11, 2018, https://www.ecp .gov.pk/PrintDocument.aspx?PressId=55126&type=PDF.
4. Jahangir, Munizeh, "The Invisible Candidates Shut Out of Pakistan's Election," *Guardian,* July 24, 2018.
5. In particular the question of separate versus joint electorates for election to seats reserved for religious minorities in national and provincial assemblies was a source of controversy from the 1950s until 2002, when separate electorates were finally abolished.
6. The mechanism of seat reservation for women and minorities was different, however. For women, "the members to fill seats reserved for women which are allocated to a Province under clause (4) shall be elected in accordance with law on the basis of the system of proportional representation by means of a single transferable vote by the electoral college consisting of the persons elected to the Assembly from that Province." For minorities the seats would be filled under a separate electorate system, with the entire country serving as a single constituency. President's Order No. 14 of 1985, *Gazette of Pakistan*, Extraordinary, part 1, March 2, 1985.
7. Bush (2011) excludes Pakistan from her quantitative analysis on the grounds that it is "an outlier that involves different causal processes."
8. Free and Fair Elections Network, "Women MPs Contribute 39 Percent Parliamentary Business during 2017–18," accessed October 2018, http://fafen.org/women -mps-contribute-39-parliamentary-business-2017-18/.
9. Benazir Shah, "A Female Candidate's Faceless Election Campaign," *Geo News,* July 20, 2018.

10

Governance Amid Crisis
Delegation, Personal Gain, and Service Delivery in Pakistan

Sameen A. Mohsin Ali

Although substantial information exists on what parties and politicians in Pakistan must do to gain power (Mufti 2011, 2016a; Khan Mohmand 2014; Martin 2016), little consideration has been given to *what* they do and *how* they do it once they are in government. Yet the role of parties in power is both multifaceted and crucial to governance: they pursue legislative agendas, they formulate and oversee policy implementation, they form and maintain coalitions, they engage with opposition parties, and they dispense patronage to their supporters.

Parties in power adopt a range of tactics to consolidate power and govern, including the development of oversight mechanisms and the manipulation of state resources and services. This chapter focuses on how party leaders establish patron-client relations with and politicize the appointments of favored bureaucrats.[1] This tactic serves as a precursor and enabler for other strategies that parties adopt in pursuit of their particular objectives—personal ones (granting a tender to a particular vendor), electoral ones (garnering voter support through targeted service delivery), and bureaucratic ones (in increased efficiency, such as speeding up the completion of an underpass construction project). Understanding patterns of bureaucratic appointments helps us understand patterns of governance: why certain policies get implemented quickly when others do not, why some projects are swiftly completed while others languish, and why certain communities benefit over others.

In this chapter I explore the objectives and appointment strategies of the three parties that have dominated Pakistan's politics and governance since 2002: the Pakistan Muslim League Quaid (PML-Q), the Pakistan People's Party (PPP), and the Pakistan Muslim League Nawaz (PML-N). These parties exemplify three variants of politician-bureaucrat interaction, namely, delegation, the pursuit of personal gain, and the pursuit of service delivery.

Variations in politician-bureaucrat interaction across these parties depend on two factors: the balance of power between the military and the government during the parties' terms in office and the differing attitudes and experiences of party leaders. These two factors explain the differing nature of each party's ties with the bureaucracy despite all three parties being weakly institutionalized and highly centralized in their decision-making and all three trying to maintain their political space in a precarious political environment.

In particular, the PML-Q's strategy of entrusting decision-making in government to selected bureaucrats was shaped by its rise to power on the coattails of Gen. Pervez Musharraf and the party leaders' lack of interest in policymaking and implementation. With the end of President Musharraf's rule the military took a step back from direct involvement in politics. During this time the PPP appointed bureaucrats to profit from public office and to insulate party members and their cronies from accountability investigations as a result of a crisis in party leadership following Benazir Bhutto's assassination and the rise of Asif Ali Zardari, a man whose rent-seeking and acquisitive politics shaped the behavior of party members. Moreover, the PML-N's strategy of appointing favored bureaucrats to key posts to enhance its bureaucratic performance suited its own service delivery agenda and was the consequence of the party leadership's taste for micromanagement and their intention to prove themselves to voters and their opponents upon returning from exile.

The findings outlined here are based on fieldwork conducted in Punjab between 2014 and 2016, including over 150 interviews of politicians and bureaucrats, semiparticipant observation in government offices, and an analysis of primary sources such as newspaper archives and court judgments. Although access to politicians, bureaucrats, and bureaucratic records was frequently hampered due to suspicion of my motivations, this qualitative work permitted the tracing of appointment pathways and was critical to disentangling the ties between politicians and bureaucrats. In the absence of existing data, newspaper reports proved useful both for informing the interview questions and for verifying claims made by interviewees. Newspaper stories often provide the only publicly available accounts of bureaucratic appointments and politician-bureaucrat interactions in Pakistan. As the bureaucracy's role has expanded (in Punjab in particular) and with increasing court scrutiny of bureaucrats' behavior, the English-language press has produced detailed coverage on bureaucratic appointments, particularly of elite cadres. Some of this coverage draws on and develops reports made in the Urdu press and on television news channels, making them even more substantial accounts of politician-bureaucrat behavior.

This chapter proceeds in four parts. The first elaborates the history of military intervention—direct and indirect—in Pakistan's politics and the weakness and centralization of Pakistan's political parties, then links these two factors to the politicization of bureaucratic appointments. Each of the subsequent three sections provides a review of the PML-Q, the PPP, and the PML-N, in turn, and explains the variations in the parties' relationships with the bureaucracy.

Military Interventions and Weak Parties

Grzymala-Busse (2003, 2007) and O'Dwyer (2004, 2006) argue that in the Eastern European context, party competition is inversely related to the politicization of bureaucratic appointments, provided that some certainty and stability exists in the political system. Parties in Pakistan, once in government, face precarious circumstances due to the military's repeated intervention in politics and party indiscipline due to factionalism, party-switching, and lack of ideological commitment by party members (Mufti 2016a). However, political competition between parties remains robust since winning state power is of substantial value. Elections (except in 2002) are meaningful contests, and parties outside government provide opposition to parties in power. But party competition has not limited the politicization of the bureaucracy. Rather, bureaucrats have sought political patronage to guarantee their own careers throughout democratic periods in Pakistan's history and will continue to do so in the absence of meaningful civil service reform.

Pakistan also does not meet Grzymala-Busse's or O'Dwyer's condition for certainty and stability in the system. Pakistan has a history of military intervention, with coups occurring in 1958, 1969, 1977, and 1999 (Jalal 1995; Rizvi 2000). Like Field Marshal Mohammad Ayub Khan had done before him, Gen. Muhammad Zia-ul-Haq (1977–88) set up a nonparty local government system and held party-free elections that created and empowered a new political class (Waseem 1989; Jaffrelot 2015). Nawaz Sharif, for example, was a direct beneficiary of the military-led regime. After Zia's death the military backed the Islami Jamhoori Ittehad (IJI) to balance the power of the PPP under Benazir Bhutto. At the same time, constitutional engineering during periods of direct military rule have empowered the office of the president at the expense of prime ministers and their cabinets (Waseem 1989). Therefore, between 1988 and 1999 the military continued to destabilize elected governments in collusion with the presidency, vetoing their policy decisions and dismissing them under the infamous Article 58 Section 2b and with the aid of the judiciary (Newberg 1995).[2] This pattern of military intervention in politics continued until 1999, when the military decided to once again intervene directly in politics as Musharraf took over in a military coup and exiled the leadership of both the PPP and the PML-N (see chapter 12 in this volume).

The precarious nature of Pakistan's politics has meant that parties in Pakistan are well aware that even with a comfortable majority in the legislature, they may not complete their term. In contradiction to Kopecky's (2011, 728) argument that dominant parties are less likely to politicize the state due to the "luxury of long-term horizons," Pakistan's political parties face short-term horizons. Therefore, parties in power have no incentive to refrain from politicizing the state.

The politicization of the state involves ensuring that key bureaucratic offices (provincial chief secretaries, secretaries of government departments, directors of autonomous bodies and authorities, and heads of key administrative districts) are staffed by party loyalists such that governmental decision-making favors the party's agenda. Elite bureaucrats, such as members of the Pakistan Administrative Service (PAS), are recruited through an extensive testing process (the Central Superior Services examination). Their subsequent promotion and transfer are determined by the federal Establishment Division and at the senior levels by the prime minister's office. Although there are detailed rules regulating the appointment of bureaucrats, these rules are often manipulated by politicians and bureaucrats to make politicized appointments. Politicization is hardly a surprising phenomenon—like politicians, bureaucrats are also in search of patrons to cement their own positions and ensure career stability in an unstable political environment. They seek out patrons to help them achieve it, and in return the bureaucrats assist their patrons in achieving specific objectives.[3]

In the past bureaucrats in Pakistan sought patrons among the military. Alavi (1972b) describes how a military-bureaucratic oligarchy dominated Pakistan's politics in its early years, but by the time Zia-ul-Haq took charge the bureaucracy was no longer an equal partner with the military. This was due to two events: first, Bhutto's reforms of the civil service weakened constitutional protections for bureaucrats (Kennedy 1987), and second, Zia's lateral induction of a significant number of personnel from the armed forces into the civil service disrupted the senior bureaucracy's relatively stable service structure (Jalal 1995). Musharraf later also inducted military officers into the civil service on a contract basis; an example of such an inductee was Lt. Gen. Tanvir Naqvi, who headed the National Reconstruction Bureau, the organization in charge of institutional reform brought about by the Local Government Ordinance 2001.

During the 1990s, as the government changed hands between the PML-N and the PPP, the bureaucracy was less a means of enhancing government performance than a means for the ruling party to cling to the few vestiges of power left behind by nongovernmental forces. Each of the parties wanted to work with their loyalists, so a change in government meant a reshuffle to replace one set of favorites with another. In other words, politicians and bureaucrats were brought together by the instability of the system itself.

The instability of Pakistan's political parties is enhanced by the parties themselves—none of the major parties campaign on programmatic platforms, and internally they are undemocratic, weakly institutionalized, and overly centralized (Waseem and Mufti 2012; Mufti 2016a). Their membership orbits around the party founder and the founder's family; party members are loyal less to a party or its ideology and more to its leaders.

On matters of governance and policy, directions flow from party leaders to party members. As Waseem and Mufti (2012, 93) note, the drafting of the party manifesto and policymaking are all "leader-centric" exercises that are "not open to review and consultation." For instance, in the PML-N, Nawaz Sharif is known to make important party and policy decisions in consultation with his kitchen cabinet, known as the *panj pyaray* (five favorites) (37). Meetings are held simply to inform senior party members of decisions that have already been made, leaving no room for debate on party priorities (38).

Since most legislators are excluded from party decision-making, they have little interest in legislating or providing oversight, and their lack of expertise in policymaking allows them to be easily sidelined by the bureaucracy and their own party leadership. Keefer (2007, 820) argues that the low credibility of politicians and parties leads to a situation where the only viable means of gaining electoral support is through "high targeted spending, high rent seeking, and low levels of non-targeted good[s] provision." Both Wilder (1999) and Khan Mohmand (2014) reach similar conclusions while studying linkages between parties and voters in Pakistan. Indeed, what matters most to Pakistani politicians—and therefore to political parties—is doling out patronage in the form of targeted goods (such as jobs), which are enjoyed only by citizens who have promised to support the politician in elections. The provision of nontargeted or public goods (health and education provision by the state, for example) is less useful to the politician: if everyone benefits from the services the state is providing, the politician cannot claim credit for it nor use it to appeal for support.

In other words, the PML-Q, the PPP, and the PML-N are centralized and personalized political parties that seek to dispense patronage to voters through the distribution of targeted goods. What does this mean for politician-bureaucrat interactions? When a party is in power its ties with the senior bureaucracy are mediated through the party's leadership. Consequently, in terms of responsibilities and objectives, parties in power expect the bureaucracy to be a function of the party leaders' leadership style and priorities.

The literature on bureaucratic appointments tends to focus either on initial appointments upon recruitment into the bureaucracy or during postings in the wake of elections (Grindle 2012; Iyer and Mani 2012; Akhtari, Moreira, and Trucco 2017). But politicized appointments can take place at any point during a bureaucrat's career (S. Ali 2018). This is a crucial notion because, regardless of the objective a party in power has in mind (personal, electoral, or bureaucratic), the specific timing of an appointment often comes down to finding the right bureaucrat for the job. Ideally this would be an official with whom the politician or bureaucrat has worked before or one recommended by a key bureaucratic ally—that is, not a new recruit (S. Ali 2018). Politicians and bureaucrats establish relationships of trust and mentorship with bureaucrats, and these relationships become the bedrock of future ties between these actors. In addition, bureaucrats maintain extensive networks of ties among themselves, especially the elite cadres of the PAS. Furthermore, bureaucrats with ties to prominent politicians often mentor junior officials and bring them to the attention of party leaders.

The PML-Q and Delegation: Bureaucratic Carte Blanche

In 1999 the PML-N's leadership was exiled when Musharraf took over as martial law administrator. A faction within the PML-N at the time, led by Chaudhry Shujaat Hussain and Chaudhry Pervaiz Elahi, broke away and formed the PML-Q. The newly formed party did not have sufficient traction among the political elite to contest and win an election on its own. Therefore they became Musharraf's "king's party" (Waseem and Mufti 2012, 39), with Musharraf convincing locally influential politicians in various districts to defect to the PML-Q. Because of this political engineering and the disqualification of many candidates on the basis of a new law that required candidates to have a bachelor's degree, the PML-Q won the 2002 election and formed the national government and the provincial government in Punjab.

Meanwhile, the exile of Nawaz Sharif and his brother Shahbaz Sharif led to the exile of bureaucrats who had worked closely with them from 1997 to 1999. The leaders of the PML-Q—Shujaat (prime minister) and Elahi (chief minister Punjab)—placed their own favorites in the vacated senior posts at the federal level and the local level in Punjab. Some of the most prominent officials during the PML-Q's tenure had close personal links with the party leadership and their families. Consequently, they were implicated in corruption cases with the political leaders under whom they served. For example, the chief secretary of Punjab, Kamran Rasool (2003–5), was an employee at one of Chief Minister Pervaiz Elahi's businesses before rejoining the civil service to (legally) take up the post of chief secretary.[4] He was later implicated in the Bank of Punjab corruption case over a public-sector bank's extension of credit to buy a sugar mill owned by the chief minister's family.[5]

However, PML-Q bureaucrats who served as departmental secretaries or district coordination officers (DCOs) in Punjab demonstrate a critical difference in the way the party leadership conducted itself while in power as compared to the PML-N.[6] Elahi and Shujaat claimed that they wanted to improve governance but knew their own limitations and were therefore willing to leave development policy to the bureaucrats—those whose training had prepared them for making those kinds of decisions. Even when it came to appointing bureaucrats to various posts, Elahi relied on the recommendations of senior bureaucrats.[7] And, once appointed, that bureaucrat usually had carte blanche to make decisions related to his department with little interference from the offices of either the chief minister or the prime minister. For example, the PML-Q government did not interfere in the World Bank–funded Punjab Irrigation and Drainage Authority, which, contrary to the Punjab government's tendency to centralize and politicize control of the irrigation system, sought to devolve water management to the farmer organizations at the local level. In fact, the government-appointed secretary, Arif Nadeem, actively encouraged the devolution.[8] It was not until 2009, when the PML-N had returned to government, that these reforms began to stall due to a lack of interest by the department secretaries.

However, the reasons behind the PML-Q's delegation strategy within the bureaucracy were not simply a matter of the party leadership realizing its limitations as policymakers. As the "king's party" the PML-Q was under the direction and scrutiny of Musharraf, Naqvi of the National Reconstruction Bureau, and military appointees to the civil service, many of whom were retired military officers.[9] Within the political space that the PML-Q had left, delegating decision-making to the bureaucracy arguably gave the party leadership plausible deniability on policy decisions. Furthermore, it ensured that the military's ambition to contain political forces was achieved: the PML-Q stayed in its lane with politicians focused on constituency-level patronage politics and leaving governance to the military and, as a significantly junior partner, the bureaucracy.

But the seemingly easy interaction between the PML-Q and the bureaucracy was soon disrupted by Musharraf's local government reforms, which introduced changes that threatened the hold of the powerful District Management Group (DMG), now known as the Pakistan Administrative Service, at the district level. The prestigious (and colonial-legacy) post of deputy commissioner was dissolved and the new DCO post was created but stripped of magisterial powers. Moreover, and far worse in the DMG's view, the district *nazim* (mayor) became the supervisor of the DCO (previously the most senior bureaucrat in the district and typically a PAS officer) and responsible for signing off on the DCO's performance evaluations and holding ultimate say over which bureaucrat was appointed to which district (see Cheema, Khwaja, and Qadir 2006; S. Ali 2018). Although DMG officials deeply resented the new *nazims* and the party leadership that had facilitated their election, the ones most closely associated with the PML-Q leadership remained loyal due to their personal ties of exchange (Shafqat 2013; Jaffrelot 2015).

By the time of the 2008 election, and with the return from exile of Benazir Bhutto and the Sharif brothers, few bureaucrats serving in Punjab felt any compulsion to help the PML-Q garner support among voters. Instead, bureaucrats willingly sought political patronage from other avenues, namely the newly resurgent PML-N, which was equally opposed to the local government reforms. As a result the PML-Q was defeated handily in Punjab, bringing the PML-N to power in the province. The federal government, however, went to the PPP as the head of a coalition government.

The PPP and the Pursuit of Personal Gain: The Case of the Supreme Court

The PPP has always had a reputation among elite and midtier bureaucrats (as well as among voters and even its own party members) of indulging in widespread petty corruption both in seeking their own cut in government bids and contracts and even in minor transactions involving citizens—for instance, demanding a bribe from a voter for putting in a good word with a bureaucrat about a job.[10] Much of this activity takes place in Sindh, the PPP's heartland, and is arguably one of the reasons Sindh continues to lag behind on development indicators.[11] There is no single explanation for why the PPP fails to deliver nontargeted goods to its heartland whereas the PML-N delivers in Punjab. One possible explanation is that outside of Karachi the PPP has never had a serious competitor for votes in Sindh and has therefore never been pushed to perform or reform. This has not been the case in Punjab: despite the PML-N's dominance in the province over the last decade, it has not been without electoral competitors. Another possible explanation is that Karachi and Hyderabad absorb much of the Sindh government's attention and budget, which leads the rest of the province to lag behind.[12] Whatever the reason, many PAS bureaucrats resist postings in Sindh or even Karachi, preferring the administrative "culture" in Punjab and Islamabad to the "self-seeking" culture in Sindh.[13] They speak of the PPP with disdain, contrasting it unfavorably with the PML-N, a party that is acknowledged to be corrupt but also perceived to be in pursuit of a development agenda. In terms of governance, then, the main problem for the PPP has always been an internal one since the party's leadership appears to consistently prioritize personal gain over the benefit of their voters.

During the PPP's term in federal government from 2008 to 2013, the government was plagued by a series of challenges stemming from the uneasy alliance among the governing coalition of political parties, the mushrooming of private media houses, and the judicial activism of the chief justice of the Supreme Court, Iftikhar Chaudhry. In particular the PPP leadership's dealings with the bureaucracy came under extensive scrutiny by the Court and the media, and judgments often led to embarrassment for the prime minister and his cabinet.

Perhaps the PPP under Benazir Bhutto's leadership would have weathered these storms better: if nothing else, party members likely would have remained loyal to her. Although Bhutto's death in December 2007 may have been a factor in the PPP's electoral win in 2008, it did nothing to endear her husband to her own party. The ascent of Asif Ali Zardari—also known as "Mr. Ten Percent" (Kochanek 2010, 373), a nickname that refers to his alleged propensity to demand bribes while his wife was prime minister—to the post of party co-chairperson (alongside his son, Bilawal Bhutto) tainted the party. Party members, opposition parties, bureaucrats, and voters all spoke of him with suspicion and questioned his ability to set aside his personal interests to run the party.[14] Hence an already enervated, overly centralized party found itself floundering because it was seen as being led by an individual who prioritized personal gain over the party. As Zardari's ethos of financial gain, protection from prosecution, and distribution of jobs to family spread throughout much of the party's upper echelons, the PPP became a party that was simultaneously left-leaning and constitutionally principled but whose members were frequently caught politicizing the state in ways that would benefit them and their cronies.

The most famous clash between the PPP and the bureaucracy was the Anita Turab case.[15] Turab had filed the case following the removal of the establishment secretary from his post by Prime Minister Yousaf Raza Gilani for obeying the Supreme Court's orders to reinstate the accountability officer investigating the Hajj scam involving the prime minister and his family. For Turab the incident was the culmination of numerous incidents of politicized appointments by the PPP government that had demoralized and insulted the bureaucracy as an institution. She appealed to the Court to order the government to follow the established regulations for bureaucratic appointments rather than using its discretion to reward and punish bureaucrats.[16] Although the case against discretion in making bureaucratic appointments was filed by just this one official, the media coverage (particularly of Turab's seemingly punitive suspension) and the subsequent court ruling laid bare both the PPP government's dubious interactions with the bureaucracy and the party's priorities during its time in power.[17] From that point on every round of bureaucratic appointments and promotions approved by the prime minister came under scrutiny by the courts.[18] In some cases bureaucrats took the risk of airing the bureaucracy's dirty linen in public—something most tight-lipped bureaucrats frown on. Behind closed doors, however, these bureaucrats were supported in their drive to limit the PPP's politicization of bureaucratic appointments for personal gain.

Suo moto actions by the Supreme Court frequently implicated the PPP's leadership in corrupt practices, such as in the 2011 Hajj scam case.[19] In other cases PPP leaders attempted to protect their allies, which resulted in direct clashes with opposition parties. In 2011, after transferring senior bureaucrats from Rawalpindi to Balochistan, Gilani attempted to (extra-legally) transfer an officer to protect Malik Riaz (a property magnate and "kingmaker") from an accountability investigation.[20] The leader of the opposition, Chaudhry Nisar of the PML-N, was furious at the removal of his favored bureaucrats from his electoral district in Rawalpindi and threatened to remove all of Gilani's favorite officers from the latter's home district of Multan (in Punjab). Gilani was forced to back down.[21]

By the time the 2013 election campaign began, the general feeling among voters was that the PPP had achieved little during its term. However, there were two exceptions. The first was the Benazir Income Support Program (BISP). The program started out with a distinctly electoral gain focus—families were recommended for the program by parliamentarians—which led to allegations of vote-buying. In the last few years, with the PML-N government at the center, the program has continued to grow in its ability to alleviate poverty (even if only marginally).[22] The BISP is a rare example of policy programs that continue even though the party in power has changed. The second exception is the PPP's legislative achievements, the foremost of which was the passing of the 18th Amendment to the 1973 Constitution. However, the PPP's policymaking and legislation failed to win the PPP votes, at least in part due to its inability to ameliorate the suffering caused by the energy crisis during its term.

During its time in power the PPP's attempts to forward its policy agenda were constantly thwarted by the actions of the party leadership itself. Their pursuit of personal benefits (in the guise of enrichment and protection of themselves and their allies) led to constant scrutiny and criticism, frequent clashes with the courts and opposition parties, and reversals of their decisions. Furthermore, the practice of petty corruption by the PPP's leadership has never endeared them to the bureaucracy, a situation made worse by constant media coverage and the Court's scrutiny of bureaucratic appointments. For members of the PPP, the party's ideological roots and even its viability as a national political party were lost with the death of Bhutto and the rise of Zardari and his brand of rent-seeking politics. The party leadership's priorities—personal gain and protection of their moneyed donors—created a situation where the party had become so *badnaam* (vilified) among both voters and party members and workers that its support plummeted.[23] In the 2013 election the party won only in Sindh and won just 2 percent of National Assembly seats in Punjab.

The PML-N and the Duty to Deliver: The Vision of the *Khadim-e-Aala* (Servant in Chief)

PML-N party members often refer to the "vision" of their party's leadership, suggesting that they see their own role as limited to fulfilling that vision in their own constituency rather than contributing to its development.[24] The vision of party leader Nawaz Sharif and his brother Shahbaz Sharif was shaped by the PML-N's factionalization in 1999 and its leaders' period of exile in two ways. First, the experience of being ousted by Musharraf and being forced out of the country changed the PML-N's perspective on the military. Previously the PML-N had been patronized by the military and regarded as a pro-establishment party. It is now firmly critical of military involvement in politics and allied more deliberately with the bureaucracy. During their exile both Sharif brothers were helpless to prevent the defections of party members to form the PML-Q; this exile had caused them to value loyalty as an important quality of their associates. Upon their return they found that many bureaucrats with whom they had worked closely between 1997 and 1999 had indeed remained loyal, keeping a low profile during the Musharraf and PML-Q years by taking extended leave or opting for transfers abroad. Second, the Sharifs' time away from politics seemed to impart them with a missionary zeal to "deliver" to the people upon their return. In 2008 the brothers' priority was to establish the PML-N as the party that "gets things done," a marked contrast to the PML-Q's term in office and a particularly effective contrast to the hamstrung central government of the PPP.

The PML-N placed a priority on service delivery, which bucked the trend of parties in nascent democracies that focus on dispensing patronage to voters through the distribution of targeted goods (Keefer 2007). The PML-N did, of course, dispense patronage to its voters, but it also ensured the provision (imperfect as it may be) of at least some nontargeted goods (i.e., public goods, which an entire community may enjoy), even in an environment where their provision was dis-incentivized. It did this by ensuring that "patronage was adapted to competence" (Grindle 2012, 55); that is, politicized appointments to the bureaucracy were made such that bureaucratic performance and nontargeted service delivery were enhanced (S. Ali 2018). Though the PML-N's service delivery was focused mainly on urban areas in northern and central Punjab, the party's heartland, it is undeniable that its performance was in sharp contrast to the performance of the PPP in Sindh, as the PPP's own members acknowledged.[25]

To achieve speedy and effective service delivery that would reestablish the PML-N in the eyes of voters, the party required a bureaucracy that was not just efficient but also attuned to the needs and outlook of the party leadership. Between election day in 2008 and the day the PML-N officially took over the Punjab government, much upheaval occurred in the provincial bureaucracy as the PML-Q's people moved out and were replaced by the PML-N's favorites (S. Ali 2018). The first of these appointments, and the one with the furthest reach, was that of Punjab's chief secretary. Javed Mahmood's extra-legal discretionary appointment as chief secretary caused considerable friction within the elite PAS since he was too junior for the post, leapfrogging over others higher on the seniority list.[26] Mahmood and Chief Minister Shahbaz Sharif had previously worked together from 1997 to 1999 and saw eye to eye on their role as administrators, prioritizing service provision to citizens through improving accessibility (S. Ali 2018).[27] The two men viewed themselves as the *khadim* (servants) of the people, and together they ensured that appointments to key posts throughout the province's administrative structure went to handpicked bureaucrats who shared their vision and work ethic. Many of these bureaucrats had either worked in previous PML-N governments or proved themselves by delivering desired results in difficult circumstances (see S. Ali 2018). Consequently, the mantra of service delivery soon became the predominant driver of governance in Punjab. This was quite dissimilar to the methods of the PPP, whose demands of bureaucrats were often related to the party leadership's personal gain or protection. And, unlike the PML-Q, which handpicked a team of bureaucrats, set targets for them, and then left them to get the job done, Shahbaz Sharif remained closely involved both in setting targets and ensuring compliance. In other words, Sharif was a micromanager who often made impossible demands of his chosen officials; his behavior was replicated by his chosen bureaucrats, leading to similar micromanagement and close monitoring of midtier levels of the bureaucracy.[28] Nevertheless, although there was no doubt corruption and malfeasance along the way (for instance, contracts were granted to favored firms without due process and budget tampering occurred), bureaucrats were not appointed solely for personal gain.

The Government of Punjab "Delivers" Education

One of the most significant aspects of the Punjab Education Sector Reform Program was the merit-based recruitment of teaching staff. The recruitment of teachers—junior civil servants—has traditionally been a heavily politicized process, and for two reasons: first, teaching jobs are a convenient means of doling out patronage. The thousands of available posts are spread out across districts, which allows access to government resources (such as budgets and buildings). As these are civil servant jobs, the posts provide pensions and protection from dismissal. For politicians the ability to distribute jobs among voters and party workers is the easiest way of guaranteeing not just the individual's vote but often the vote of the teacher's family as well. Second, teachers are the civil service officers deployed to conduct the census, verify and compile voter lists, and staff polling stations during elections.[29] In rural areas in particular the control over these officials can be critical in manipulating not just the results but who gets to vote. For instance, barring women from voting requires the collusion of politicians and at least some polling staff.[30]

Any attempt to regulate the appointment and transfer of teaching staff is a fraught exercise and can effectively damage the electoral prospects of a party's local politicians. Nonetheless, the Punjab government has made significant strides in streamlining the teacher appointment and transfer process. Most important has been the display of merit lists for public viewing. When a teacher applies for a position, the application is processed and the applicant is placed on a merit list; available posts are filled in accordance with the publicly displayed list. This relatively small innovation has made it more difficult for bureaucratic staff (clerks and data entry officers, among others) to tamper with the merit list or "misplace" an application. At the same time, teacher transfers have been regulated by imposing a ban on all transfers during the school year (except for family reasons). Although the arbitrary patronage-based transfers that plagued the education department have been reduced, the appointments process continues to be subject to manipulation and there remains a significant difference between the ability of both senior and junior politicians and bureaucrats to dispense patronage (S. Ali 2018, 2019).[31] While the chief minister and senior members of the PML-N and the bureaucracy have praised these reforms, many politicians have found it difficult to cope with patronage avenues being closed to them. As a result, the implementation of these reforms has required a firm hand in dealing with demands made by politicians to make patronage appointments in violation of the new policies.

The bureaucrat handpicked for the post of secretary of the School Education Department at the critical moment of implementation of the reform program, Abdul Jabbar Shaheen, was an officer familiar to the chief secretary at the time. Shaheen had the reputation of being intractable when it came to demands made by local politicians, even those from the ruling party. He could afford such an attitude because he had the backing of the chief secretary, and through the secretary the chief minister, which meant that he had little need for local political goodwill (S. Ali 2018). Subsequently, when politicians made demands for patronage, Shaheen would direct them to the chief secretary.[32]

Shaheen's (legal) appointment was ideal: not only was he able to handle politicians' demands, he was also willing to work closely with the chief minister's secretariat. Many junior politicians and ordinary citizens would get short shrifted because demands for patronage dispensation made by the secretariat and the chief minister's allies would be fulfilled quickly and quietly regardless of new regulations on teachers' appointment and transfer (S. Ali 2018, 2019).[33] In the offices of the additional and deputy secretaries of the department, the right kind of *sifarish* (intercession) would be quickly redirected to the secretary, while sifarish from the less well-connected would be written on a slip of paper, which often ended up on the floor.[34] It was no wonder that the ruling party's junior members of the provincial assembly lamented their inability to have constituents appointed or transferred as teachers.[35]

The PML-N in Federal Government

Punjab is Pakistan's political heartland, and in recent years Lahore became not just the center of power but the testing ground for Sharif's pet projects. Projects initiated in the city, such as the metro bus, were replicated elsewhere.

The governance of Punjab fed into governance at the center. Most bureaucrats serving in Islamabad had at some point served in Punjab under Sharif and been, so to speak, "trained' by him. While the Sharif brothers occupied both the prime minister and Punjab chief minister posts, bureaucrats were often recommended by the latter for posts in the prime minister's office or in federal departments and, once posted, brought with them the same "delivery" ethos that characterizes the chief minister and senior bureaucracy in Punjab. Fawad Hasan Fawad, for instance, who went on to become secretary to the prime minister, had worked closely with the chief minister Punjab in a variety of posts from 2008 to 2015. Once in the prime minister's office, Fawad was soon making decisions that were beyond his remit (per the 1973 Civil Servants Rules [on appointments, promotions, and transfers]), most significantly the transfer and promotion of PAS bureaucrats.[36]

Conclusion

Discussions about what Pakistani political parties do once they are in power must acknowledge the constraints within which governance in Pakistan takes place. Repeated military interventions in politics—direct and indirect—have created a situation in which parties see little incentive to invest in anything that might produce long-term returns. At the same time, political parties in Pakistan are personalized, centralized, and oriented first and foremost toward patronage politics. In the PML-Q, the PPP, and the PML-N, decisions with regard to governance priorities and policy are made by party leaders and their kitchen cabinets with no input from the parties' larger membership. This centralization and exclusion in Pakistan's political parties means that ideology has little value when it comes to party affiliation or loyalty by party members and voters alike. Instead, politicians and parties focus on dispensing patronage through the delivery of targeted goods to win over and retain voters.

Party leaders contend with instability by forming relationships of patronage with senior bureaucrats and making politicized bureaucratic appointments to key posts in order to achieve their own objectives. The form of these relationships and the demands made of bureaucrats depend on the party leadership's attitudes and experiences. Where party leaders are hamstrung by direct military intervention in politics and have little interest in policymaking, as in the case of the PML-Q, they delegate decision-making powers to appointed bureaucrats. Where party leaders prioritize financial benefit and protection from accountability over governance, as the PPP does, they make bureaucratic appointments to advance personal gain, which only attracts scrutiny and alienates party members. Where party leaders make it a mission to improve governance, as the PML-N did, appointments are made to enhance bureaucratic performance and deliver nontargeted goods to citizens.

How the Pakistan Tehreek-e-Insaf, which won the general elections in 2018, will interact with the bureaucracy while in government remains an open question. It is too early to make any concrete surmises about the PTI's governance strategy vis-à-vis the bureaucracy, but it would be fair to say that thus far it has acted similarly to the PML-N, with a focus on reform and service delivery. However, the PTI government has been hampered by the discrepancy between its anticorruption, reform-oriented rhetoric and the demands for access to patronage from party members.[37] In September 2018 the PTI government faced considerable embarrassment as politicians sought to influence the appointment of street-level bureaucrats in their constituencies, leading to bureaucrats filing official complaints against them with their respective district commissioners and the Election Commission.[38]

At the same time, heightened scrutiny by the courts and investigative agencies (such as the National Accountability Bureau) has meant that the bureaucracy has been hesitant to take any action for fear of being hauled into court. Particular attention has fallen on the numerous companies set up by the PML-N to deliver services (e.g., the Punjab Saaf Pani [clean water] Company and the Punjab Safe Cities Authority), and on both the bureaucrats who were hired at enhanced salaries to head them and the bureaucrats who were responsible for awarding contracts for various projects.[39]

Furthermore, elite power dynamics in Punjab's coalition government—between the relatively inexperienced Usman Buzdar (chief minister), the disqualified Jahangir Tareen (adviser), and political heavyweights Chaudhry Pervaiz Elahi and Chaudhry Sarwar (speaker of the Punjab assembly and governor of Punjab, respectively)—have led to infighting, confusion, and near paralysis within the bureaucracy. In the absence of an experienced chief minister, the PTI has struggled to govern.[40] There is no doubt the PTI has a long way to go, and it is unfair to judge it on the performance of just a few months. However, its brief time in power is an example of an idealistic opposition party morphing into a politically pragmatic party finally in power (see chapter 3 in this volume for more on the PTI).

Three variants of politician-bureaucrat interaction appear within the PML-Q, the PPP, and the PML-N, and each party has had a unique approach to bureaucratic appointments. It is clear that Pakistan's history of military intervention, the weakness of its parties, and the politicization of its bureaucracy have come together to impact governance.

Notes

1. These appointments include the elite cadres of the civil bureaucracy in Pakistan but exclude appointments made to the judiciary or police service of Pakistan.
2. The Eighth Amendment Act of 1985 introduced Article 58 Section 2b to the

1973 Constitution of Pakistan. It gave the president the power to dissolve the national assembly and dismiss the prime minister and his or her cabinet if, in his or her opinion, "a situation has arisen in which the Government of the Federation cannot be carried on in accordance with the provisions of the constitution and an appeal to the electorate is necessary."

3. See Kennedy (1987) for a history of the Pakistan bureaucracy and Ali (2018) on bureaucrat preferences.

4. "New Chief Secretary Assumes Charge," *Dawn*, December 27, 2003.

5. "Hamesh Seeks Pardon to Reveal All Secrets," *The News*, June 18, 2010.

6. Interviews of former civil servants, both of whom served in Punjab under the PML-Q government, April 14 and 16, 2015.

7. Interview of a former bureaucrat who served in Punjab under the PML-Q, April 16, 2015.

8. Interviews of Punjab Irrigation Drainage Authority (PIDA) employees, April 6, 2015.

9. Aminullah Chaudhry, "Military in Civil Service," *Dawn,* September 3, 2011.

10. Interviews of PAS bureaucrats, September 18 and 29, October 28, 2014, and with members of the PPP, February 12 and 19 and April 28, 2015.

11. Hasan Mansoor, "Sindh in Poor Shape Despite PPP Allocation of Rs. 700 bn for Uplift Projects in Eight Years," *Dawn*, October 30, 2014.

12. Umair Javed, "'Liberating' Sindh," *Dawn*, November 24, 2014.

13. Interviews of PAS bureaucrats, September 29, 2014, and May 6 and April 16, 2015.

14. Interviews of PAS bureaucrats, September 18 and 29 and October 28, 2014, and with members of the PPP, February 12 and 19 and April 28, 2015.

15. Constitutional Petition 23 (2012), http://www.supremecourt.gov.pk/web/user _files/File/const.p.23of2012.pdf, accessed January 30, 2018.

16. Interview of Anita Turab, October 28, 2014.

17. "Woman Officer Suspended for Calling a Spade a Spade," *The News*, January 10, 2013. See also "Bureaucracy Icon Anita Turab Slapped with Dismissal Notice," *The News*, June 8, 2013.

18. See Constitutional Petition 22 (2013), http://www.supremecourt.gov.pk/web /user_files/File/Const.P.22of2013.pdf; and the Tariq Aziz ud Din case (2010 SCMR 1301), accessed January 30, 2018, http://www.supremecourt.gov.pk /web/user_files/file/hr8340of2010.pdf.

19. "SC Orders Reinstatement of Hajj Probe Chief," *Express Tribune*, July 26, 2011.

20. "War over Officers Intensifies between PM, Chaudhry Nisar," *The News*, November 5, 2011.

21. "Gilani, Nisar Fight 'War of Cops,'" *The News*, October 22, 2011.

22. BISP, *BISP Policy Brief*, accessed January 17, 2018, http://bisp.gov.pk/wp-con tent/uploads/2017/02/BISP-Policy-Brief.pdf.

23. Interviews of members of the PPP, February 12 and 19 and April 28, 2015.

24. Interviews of PML-N members of the Punjab Provincial Assembly, March 17 and 20, May 25, and June 11, 2015.

25. Interviews of members of the PPP, February 12 and 19 and April 28, 2015. See also Hasnain (2008) and "Sindh Assembly Debate: Treasury, Opposition Not Happy with PPP's Style of Governance," *Business Recorder*, April 27, 2016.

26. Sumra Anwer, "Senior Officers Acquiesce to Junior Head of City Govt.," *Express Tribune*, October 28, 2010.

27. See also Sameen M. Ali, "Good Sifarish, Bad Sifarish: A Look at PML-N's Selective Anti-Corruption Drive," *Dawn,* April 19, 2018.

28. Interviews of PAS bureaucrats, September 19 and October 2, 15, 16, and 29, 2014, and April 13 and 14, 2015.

29. Interviews of School Education Department staff, September 13 and 24, 2014. See also Aasim Sajjad Akhtar, "A Rigged System," *Dawn*, December 4, 2015.

30. Free and Fair Elections Network, "PK-95 By-Election: Candidates Collude to Bar Women from Voting," May 8, 2015, http://fafen.org/pk-95-by-election-candidates-collude-to-bar-women-from-voting/.

31. See also Ali, "Good Sifarish, Bad Sifarish."

32. "Power Players Playing on Project Funds," *Dawn*, December 18, 2008.

33. See also Ali, "Good Sifarish, Bad Sifarish."

34. Semi-participant observation in the Punjab School Education Department, January 29 and February 17, 2015. See also Hull (2012).

35. Interviews of PML-N members of the Punjab Provincial Assembly, March 17 and 20, May 25, and June 11, 2015.

36. "Captain Safdar Assails PM Office, Bureaucrats," *Dawn*, November 19, 2016; and Nokhaiz Sahi, "Fawad's Wings Clipped," *The Nation*, August 20, 2017.

37. Waseem Abbasi, "Punjab Bureaucracy Appears in Revolt," *The News*, September 5, 2018.

38. Mansoor Malik, "Two Complaining Punjab DCs Get Notices under Removal from Service Law," *Dawn*, September 15, 2018; and Mansoor Malik and Tariq Saeed Birmani, "Another DC in Punjab Reports MPs' Meddling in Official Matters," *Dawn*, September 5, 2018.

39. Syed Irfan Raza, "PM Vows to Depoliticize Bureaucracy," *Dawn*, February 9, 2019.

40. Waseem Abbasi, "Is PTI in the Driving Seat in Punjab?," Geo TV, November 14, 2018.

11

Opposition Parties and Regime Uncertainty in Pakistan

Sahar Shafqat

The role of opposition parties is crucial in any democracy. Robert Dahl (1966, xiii) argues that "the right of an organized opposition to appeal for votes against the government in elections and in parliament" is one of the "three great milestones in the development of democratic institutions." Opposition parties can be pivotal in their ability to legitimize democratic regimes and competitive electoral systems. Indeed, if we conceptualize democracy as "institutionalized uncertainty" (Przeworski 1991) then it is critical that the losers of an election—more so than the winners—accept the results. As Dahl (1966, xviii) states, "Today one is inclined to regard the existence of an opposition party as very nearly the most distinctive characteristic of democracy itself." In most developed democracies the traditional notion of a "loyal opposition" that criticizes the governing party on substantive grounds but does no damage to the system itself is deeply ingrained (even if this notion is, in some cases, more imagined than real).[1]

However, that does not mean that an institutionalized opposition is an easy milestone to reach. Dahl notes that institutionalized opposition parties emerge when governments refrain from using their coercive powers over opposition elements; this happens when the following conditions are met: "elites and the general population of a country develop a sense of nationhood that includes the opposition; [there is] a distaste for violence; a commitment to a liberal ideology; [with] economic and social goals that require internal stability" (xvi). But even among Western countries the behavior of opposition parties has varied greatly, with opposition parties sometimes challenging fundamental principles of the political system (see Von Beyme 1987). Kolinsky (1987a) notes that the emergence of new social movements in Western Europe in the 1960s and 1970s changed the landscape for opposition parties and created new "sites" of opposition that were outside Parliament (see also Amyot 1987; Capitanchik 1987; Kolinsky 1987b). Broadening the analysis further, Su (2015) examined antigovernment protests in 107 democratic countries from 1990 to 2004 and found that opposition parties were a significant source of antigovernment protests, clearly demonstrating that extra-parliamentary mobilization is not necessarily an aberration within democratic politics and must be considered as one of the tactics that opposition parties use to achieve their political goals.

It is therefore not surprising that in developing democracies such as Pakistan we observe opposition parties behaving differently than the idealized version; sometimes they turn to mobilization outside Parliament in order to achieve their political goals. The incentives for doing so are exacerbated by the uncertainty that exists around elections, around Parliament, and around other democratic institutions, which is largely the result of the influence of the military. Even when the military does not intervene directly in the form of military coups, it continues to exert great influence to pressure civilian governments behind the scenes (Waseem 2016, 67). This renders a challenging environment for political parties. They cannot reliably assume open electoral competition and they cannot assume that even if competitive elections exist, they will continue to exist for the long term. This failure to assume repeated competitive electoral interactions with other parties is a central feature of the party systems of developing democracies, and this uncertainty about future interactions helps to explain why opposition parties behave in seemingly unexpected ways.

The conventional wisdom on Pakistani parties in opposition is that they have "hindered democracy in Pakistan by engaging in adversarial politics, instead of offering a credible alternative and holding the ruling party accountable."[2] Certainly the Pakistani opposition has generally not acquitted itself well overall. Yet little attention has been paid to the specific functioning of opposition parties in the country, particularly the structural conditions that provide incentives for their behavior. I argue that the presence of certain structural conditions, particularly the existence of regime uncertainty, provides incentives for opposition parties to use extra-parliamentary tactics, including protests, agitation, and a kind of permanent campaigning that serves to discount parliamentary procedures and democratic norms. However, moments do exist when opposition parties acting in response to regime uncertainty can bolster and not just hinder democracy.

This phenomenon is explored using two case studies from recent Pakistani political history that were selected because they reveal how opposition parties might behave under two different systemic conditions. The first is the case of the Pakistan Muslim League-Nawaz (PML-N) and its involvement in the Lawyers' Movement of 2007–9. This period marked a transition from military dictatorship to competitive electoral democracy. The second is that of the Pakistan Tehreek-e-Insaf (PTI) and the strategies that it employed after the 2013 election. This period was one of electoral democracy and one in which democratic consolidation might have been expected. The cases chosen allow for a comparison between the behavior of opposition parties and the ways in which they may both reinforce or undermine democratic institutions. I use a mixed-methods approach based on my fieldwork from 2014 to 2015, during which time I interviewed civil society activists and lawyers to better understand the role of parties in the opposition, specifically the relationship of various parties to civil society and events such as the Lawyers' Movement. In addition, I analyze the rhetoric used by party leaders using evidence from newspaper accounts, interviews, and their own speeches to examine how opposition parties make appeals to the electorate in Pakistan.

A System Marked by Uncertainty

Developing democracies are characterized by uncertainty, defined as "imprecision with which actors are able to predict future interactions" (Lupu and Riedl 2013, 1344). Lupu and Riedl identify three main kinds of uncertainty: regime uncertainty, economic uncertainty, and institutional uncertainty. The current focus here is how regime uncertainty affects the behavior of opposition parties in Pakistan. Lupu and Riedl define regime uncertainty as the likelihood that competitive party politics may not last for the long term: "In developing democracies, the very newness of democratic institutions means that actors ascribe a nontrivial probability to the possibility of authoritarian reversal. . . . Regime uncertainty thus makes the longevity of many institutions of political interaction difficult to predict" (1345).

Regime uncertainty affects the behavior of political parties in multiple ways. First it may influence the formation of ideological cleavages in the party system between parties that are pro- and anti-regime (1348). Regime uncertainty may also impact party mobilization, particularly "the strategic choices of political parties, both in terms of their interactions with voters and in terms of their interactions with competing political parties" (1350). The typical distinction scholars have made is between programmatic and clientelistic strategies, but "regime and institutional uncertainty means that democratic political institutions are in flux and may not be reliable avenues for expressing voter preferences" and thus may determine the strategies that parties select (1351). Parties may not always focus on maximizing votes. Instead they may seek to maximize office and current access to resources since they are not certain of continued electoral competition. Regime uncertainty also leads to parties having greater interest in engaging in extra-parliamentary action, especially in coordination with citizen groups and other civil society actors.

Opposition parties have strong incentives to coordinate with civil society actors and social movements. Su (2015) notes that opposition parties "often use both institutional and non-institutional means to influence the policy process" and are especially incentivized to coordinate with social movement actors when they are "building social coalitions for electoral purposes" (151). The compounding factor in the case of Pakistan, of course, is that since elections may always be just around the corner, opposition parties can reasonably believe that it is opportune to build electoral constituencies at any time.

Regime uncertainty has differing effects on political parties depending on whether the party is in power or not. While it is dangerous for ruling parties that may be swept out of power as a result of a reversion to authoritarianism, such a change is also appealing for opposition parties because the lack of competition can create an opening for one's own party. However, uncertainty means that even military rulers may not always be able to rely on a continued hold on power, leading to a change of regime from authoritarianism to democracy.

In Pakistan regime uncertainty rests primarily on the disproportionate power of the military establishment, also known as the "deep state."[3] Pakistan has been dominated by its military establishment since its creation in 1947 and under direct military rule for nearly half of that time.[4] The problem of finding mechanisms to restrain the military exists in all postcolonial societies, but Pakistan's experience suggests an especially overdeveloped military with concomitantly weak civilian institutions. Even during periods of civilian rule the military has exercised a great deal of control over policy decision-making (especially toward India) and resource allocation. As opposed to other traditional militaries, Pakistan's military has also defined domestic security as part of its mandate over national security, especially in the aftermath of the 1971 civil war that led to the secession of erstwhile East Pakistan to form the independent nation of Bangladesh (see Jalal 1990). Siddiqa (2007) argues that the military's frequent interventions into politics are explained by its need to protect its vast business empire, which is estimated to be in the billions of dollars. The result has been military penetration into virtually every sphere of public life, including the government bureaucracy and the media, with almost no role for civilian institutions, including the judiciary. This overdeveloped military dominates Pakistani society, working through allies in such a way as to control decision-making very broadly, both directly and indirectly.

The behavior of two opposition parties in Pakistan—one an opposition party acting against a military dictatorship and then subsequently under a democratically elected government (the PML-N) and one an opposition party acting against a democratically elected government (the PTI)—demonstrates this point. Regime uncertainty has led opposition parties to behave in ways that further destabilize the system. However, parties' anti-system behavior has also reinforced democracy (perhaps accidentally) when the given party was in opposition under a military government and disrupted democratic consolidation and when the party was in opposition under a democratically elected government. In both cases under examination the opposition parties engaged in tactics that relied on extra-parliamentary mobilization in coordination with civic actors and appealed to segments of the populace in an attempt to mobilize populist sentiment in their favor. Both parties were able to do so in part because they were able to draw on *dharna* (sit-in) politics, a mode of protest that has deep roots in Pakistani and in South Asian history (see Mulla 2017). In one case the opposition party's actions helped to usher in a democratic transition; in the other the opposition party's actions worked to undermine democratic institutions. However, the implications of their actions for democratic consolidation were mere side effects of their actions; they were not the parties' intended goals. The parties were merely pursuing political power in an environment of regime uncertainty.

The PML-N as Opposition Party: 2002–8

The PML-N has its roots in the party of independence, the Pakistan Muslim League, and represents the faction that is affiliated with Nawaz Sharif. The PML-N emerged as one of the two major political parties in Pakistan in the 1990s (the other being the Pakistan People's Party, PPP); it is generally considered right-of-center on economic and social issues as well as foreign policy. The party has historically been closely linked to the military establishment, and Sharif received patronage early in his career from Gen. Muhammad Zia-ul-Haq (see Waseem and Mufti 2012 and chapter 1 of this volume). After the end of the Zia dictatorship, the PML-N succeeded in winning elections three times, and the landslide victory of 1997 allowed it to form a majority government on its own. However, the party used this majority to enact some far-reaching legislative changes and challenge the supremacy of the military establishment, which led to the October 1999 military coup led by Gen. Pervez Musharraf.

Musharraf's coup ended Pakistan's decade-long experiment with democracy in the 1990s, during which the PPP and the PML-N had alternated their control of government but failed to complete their terms of office due to being dismissed (usually on charges of corruption). Another military dictatorship was not new for Pakistan, but the style of Musharraf's governance differed in some important ways from the past. Musharraf was noticeably Westernized and sought to project an image of "enlightened moderation" in which he called for a liberal version of Islam.[5] This approach disarmed many liberals, and the immediate response to Musharraf's coup was relatively muted, with some even celebrating what might otherwise have been received as a terrible reversal for Pakistani democracy (see Zaidi 2008).

In the face of what appeared to be public support for the coup and with little international attention being paid to Pakistani domestic politics, the

PML-N was severely constrained in its strategic response. The most direct target of the coup was Sharif himself. The PML-N had tried to use constitutional means to assert control of the elected government over the military by naming a successor to Musharraf (who was chairman of the Joint Chiefs of Staff). Sharif timed the announcement to be released while Musharraf was in Sri Lanka for an official visit. But Sharif proved to be no match for the Pakistani deep state, and within hours he was under house arrest, Musharraf had declared a state of emergency with himself as chief executive, and all legislative assemblies were suspended. The state of emergency and the coup were legitimized by the Supreme Court under the "doctrine of state necessity" (see Kalhan 2013).

Sharif was arrested, tried, and found guilty of hijacking by a military tribunal, then sentenced to life imprisonment. But he was eventually allowed to go into exile in Saudi Arabia through a deal brokered by Saudi Arabia. With the party out of power and its top leadership living in exile, the PML-N had reached its nadir, especially as other parties began to exploit the opportunities presented to them in the aftermath of 9/11 and the reality of the new Pakistan-US alliance, which greatly empowered Musharraf and the military establishment.

During Musharraf's rule several policies of liberalization were instituted that created new opportunities for opposition actors. While the deep state continued to consolidate its control over society, Musharraf engaged in a series of actions that helped to liberalize the political system. These policies were designed to take Pakistan in a more liberal direction, especially in response to the War on Terror and Western pressure. Most notably these policies included a strengthening of the judiciary and liberalizing economic policies, especially as manifested in an aggressive program of privatization of state-owned enterprises (see Khan and Bari 2004) and led to the rise of a larger urban middle class. Musharraf also deregulated the media, which resulted in the proliferation of dozens of private television and radio broadcasters (Mulla 2017) and the mushrooming of electronic media.

However, these policies also had the unintended effect of creating cracks in the establishment. Even while Musharraf was implementing these liberal reforms his regime was also engaged in harsh repression. This created internal conflicts within the regime, and the resulting contradictions were received with alarm, especially in liberal intellectual circles (for example, see HRCP 2006). The logic of his dictatorial rule started to wear thin. All dictators rely to some degree on performance legitimacy (see Huntington 1991), the appeal to suspend democratic norms in order to tackle some sort of crisis. But as dictatorial rule wears on and the "crisis" appears to be unresolved, people often grow restive about having traded their civil rights and liberties for a controlling power that seems unable to tackle the very problem for which it had given itself a mandate. Musharraf's main rhetorical appeal had been the necessity of tackling the problem of terrorism and of economic crisis, but as time went on these problems not only failed to ease and even grew in scale and scope.

The logic of regime uncertainty suggests that even in a military dictatorship actors may not reliably assume that the regime will persist, and this was very much true of the Musharraf dictatorship, especially since Pakistan's history has plenty of examples of past dictatorships that ultimately gave way to democratic governance. Coupled with the pressure from the United States to implement some democratic reforms, the major political parties began to envision the possibility of a return to competitive party politics. The leadership of both the PPP and the PML-N were in exile during Musharraf's rule and began to engage in discussions about the future of Pakistani politics and their potential return. Although these opposition parties were very weak, regime uncertainty meant that they could direct some party resources into future strategies. The PML-N expected that it would be one of the two major parties in the country after the resumption of competitive politics, and in 2006 it negotiated the Charter of Democracy with the PPP, which established the rules that both parties would adhere to in the event of their return to Pakistan.[6] The agreement included a robust set of principles, including constitutional measures and acknowledgment of the supremacy of Parliament, which were intended to reinforce democratic institutions.

The PML-N and the Lawyers' Movement

While the PML-N leadership was negotiating a return to Pakistan, developments within Pakistan—where the Supreme Court had become an unexpectedly robust institutional check on the military executive—seized control of party negotiations in London. A constitutional crisis was brewing. The Supreme Court had historically legitimized military coups before, including in 1999 with the Musharraf coup as well. But the political reality had shifted and the judiciary was paradoxically empowered, partially as a result of Musharraf's liberal reforms. In 2007 the judiciary and Musharraf clashed over the latter's desire to remain in power past his constitutional term. When the Supreme Court ruled against him he cracked down on the judiciary and on civil society actors, sacking all judges of the higher judiciary and installing compliant judges of his own. These actions prompted a lawyers' movement led by the judiciary but joined by other civil society actors as well, all of whom had turned against Musharraf because he had failed to deliver on his liberal reforms (see Ghias 2010; Kalhan 2013; Shafqat 2017).

The PML-N saw an opening in this moment and positioned itself ideologically as a champion of the judiciary. Supporting the movement was risky because there was no guarantee that it would gain any traction and the PML-N probably would have had a safer path back to competitive party politics by continuing to cooperate with the Musharraf regime. However, the potential payoff was dislodging Musharraf from power. The PML-N began to make public statements in support of the judiciary and its restoration; indeed, the Lawyers' Movement did eventually succeed in forcing Musharraf from power and initiating a transition to democracy, but the movement remained largely led by nonparty actors. The PML-N offered vocal support but no direct involvement in the movement (see Kalhan 2013). After competitive elections in 2008 the PPP came into power. The PML-N accepted the election results and offered the ruling party its parliamentary coalition support. This appears to have been a calculated decision on the part of the PML-N, perhaps because of its erstwhile commitment to the Charter of Democracy.

The PML-N was strongly associated with the cause of the judiciary. Indeed, it performed better than expected in the 2008 election partly due to championing this cause: "The P.M.L.-N, in particular, far exceeded expectations—because, it was widely believed, the party had made the restoration of the judges its top priority."[7] Although the PPP government was nominally committed to restoring the sacked judges to the higher courts, it resisted doing so (in part because it believed the replacement judges were more favorable to its interests and in part because it did not want to upset the delicate balance it was attempting to achieve with the military). As it was the opposition party that had campaigned on the issue of the restoration of the judiciary, the PML-N raised the issue in Parliament but showed remarkable restraint even when it did so. Perhaps the party reasoned that regime uncertainty meant that the military establishment could upend democracy once again, so it took pains not to undermine the PPP's status as ruling party.

Meanwhile, the Lawyers' Movement itself was growing frustrated with the promises that had been made, and by mid–2008 it launched another street mobilization, called the Long March, which aimed to march to Islamabad to pressure the government to restore the judges. The Long March was intended to culminate in a dharna until the protesters' demands were met. But the movement leadership abruptly called off the dharna, apparently in exchange for another commitment from the PPP government.[8] Later, when the PPP had not delivered on its promise to restore the sacked judges, the PML-N did not use the issue to attack the PPP even though it could have gained considerable leverage by doing so.

It was not until early 2009, when the PPP federal government dismissed the PML-N provincial government in Punjab, that the PML-N actively began to mobilize against the PPP. The Lawyers' Movement planned another march on Islamabad, culminating in a dharna in March 2009, and this time the PML-N publicly affiliated itself with the Long March and mobilized its members to participate in the protests. One of the activists of the Lawyers' Movement told me,

> After the failure of the first Long March . . . I think not even the leaders of
> the Lawyers' Movement believed that the chief justice would be restored.
> I think they were all so ready to accept some kind of compromise . . . I
> think it's just that the PPP eventually played their hand badly. When the
> second Long March was announced, they were stupid in dissolving Shah-
> baz Sharif's government. Because there was a very strong lobby within
> the [PML-N] against a Long March, it was against destabilizing the gov-
> ernment, and there was always that threat that if we keep fighting, then
> maybe the army will come back in . . . they said, "We have a government
> in Punjab, why should we jeopardize it for a lawyers' long march and
> for Iftikhar Chaudhry. Most of the judges are back anyway." But if the
> PPP hadn't dissolved the Punjab government, I don't think the [PML-N]
> would have participated in the Long March the way that they did. But
> once that happened and they had no stakes left in government, then they
> went all out, and fortune favors the brave.[9]

Nawaz Sharif himself vowed to take part in the protests, but he was detained
in his Lahore home by the Punjab provincial authorities (on the pretext of
security). The PPP government also used the pretext of security to justify
blocking highways out of major cities and into Islamabad, hoping to stop the
Long March from ever taking place. This gave the PML-N an opportunity to
not only champion the Lawyers' Movement but also take rhetorical aim at
the PPP. In a speech at his home at the start of the Long March, Sharif said,

> The actions of the government are unconstitutional. . . . In Pakistan, the
> government has instituted new usurpations everywhere, in little and big
> ways. They have closed streets. These actions are all illegal. They are fabri-
> cating excuses to stop us. These actions are meant to stop good Pakistanis
> from marching. I should be allowed to leave my residence. I demand that
> all of these restrictions on movement should be lifted. They cannot arrest
> the Pakistani spirit. They cannot stop the desire of the people to deliver
> Pakistan to its destiny. We should all salute the passions of the Pakistani
> people, instead of trying to suppress them. . . . They have arrested Nawaz
> Sharif, but I am warning them that this detention is illegal, and they can-
> not forcibly keep me detained. I will never accept these illegal acts. . . . To
> the young men of Pakistan, today is the day for you to leave your homes
> and go into the streets. To the daughters of Pakistan, today is the day for
> you to leave your homes and go into the streets.[10]

This rhetoric clearly criticized the PPP, but interestingly it did so in constitutional and legal terms, which served to reinforce democratic norms. The
Long March eventually went ahead and a dharna was held in Islamabad, after
which the PPP government finally relented and restored all of the judges
who had been sacked (including, most controversially, the chief justice). The

PML-N could have pressed forward and potentially demanded the resignation of the PPP government or attempted to extract other political concessions, but it retreated to Parliament after the Long March was over. The party had joined a street mobilization to press for its demands, but it still saw Parliament as the appropriate venue to resolve differences with the ruling party.

Consequently, observers such as Kalhan (2013) have argued that the PML-N played an important role both during and especially after the movement in fashioning a new civil-military balance in Pakistan. The PML-N helped establish a new balance of power between civilian institutions and the deep state, notably in the form of the 18th Amendment, which devolved many powers to the provinces. Partly as a result, the elected PPP government was able to serve a full term in office, which was an unprecedented event in Pakistani political history, and to some extent the PML-N (and the Lawyers' Movement) can take credit for this result. Omar Waraich and Andrew Buncombe note,

> The opposition, too, is deserving of recognition. In the past, politicians never let an opportunity slip to see their opponents fall, no matter whom the ultimate beneficiary may be. This included enlisting the support of the powerful army. But former prime minister Nawaz Sharif, the main opposition leader, has been seen to show admirable restraint. When his Pakistan Muslim League-N provincial government in Punjab was toppled, Mr. Sharif led marches in protest and in support of the deposed judiciary. When his demands were met, he called an end to the 2009 so-called long march, against the advice of hawks within his party.[11]

The PML-N came to power in the 2013 election but was once again cast into the opposition after its defeat in 2018. The lead-up to the 2018 elections saw the PML-N facing multiple political scandals, including the fallout from the release of the Panama Papers, which led to the ouster of Nawaz Sharif from the office of prime minister and his eventual trial and conviction on corruption charges just before the election.[12] This prompted a major internal debate within the party on how best to present itself in the election campaign: as a party victimized by the military establishment (favored by the Nawaz Sharif faction) or on the strength of its platform, which emphasized bread-and-butter issues (favored by the Shahbaz Sharif faction).[13] Combined with what appears to be a concerted effort by the military establishment to constrain the PML-N's electoral appeal, the party's failure to project a unified message led to a sharp loss in parliamentary seats.[14]

With its popular leader behind bars, the party has struggled to follow a coherent opposition strategy. Nonetheless, it is striking that, at least in its first year in opposition, the party has steered clear of extra-parliamentary action. Indeed, the party strenuously pursued the chairmanship of the powerful Public Accounts Committee in the National Assembly, an important plank of the Charter of Democracy signed by the PPP and the PML-N that allows for a stable framework of parliamentary engagement between the ruling party and the opposition (especially since the bulk of parliamentary work is done in committees).[15] There are three possible reasons for what appears to be the party's continuing commitment to parliamentary engagement. The first is what appears to be an ongoing debate within the party about the proper opposition strategy to take. Playing up the victimization angle requires pointing a finger at the military establishment, which Nawaz Sharif has already done, and also offers opportunities for extra-parliamentary engagement in the future.[16] But there are other party leaders who want to pursue a more cautious approach.[17] Second, the party has lost its most popular leadership with Nawaz Sharif in prison, and there are signs of a tussle for power among various contenders. Finally, there is currently no obvious route to take, unlike the Lawyers' Movement, which provided a ready mass-mobilization vehicle in the party's earlier opposition period.

On the other hand, one must also consider the possibility that the completion of two full parliamentary terms, however compromised they may have been, may be reducing institutional uncertainty. In other words, regardless of the establishment's manipulation of electoral processes, if it seems more likely that Parliament will continue to remain a substantive venue for hashing out policy and politics, it would be rational for the PML-N, even in such a weakened state, to continue to engage with it instead of seeking alternative routes to power.

The PTI as Opposition Party: 2013–18

The second case to consider is that of the PTI, which emerged as one of the major opposition parties to the PML-N after the 2013 election. (It also won a plurality of seats in the 2018 election, enabling it to lead a coalition government.) The PTI had been limited to only one seat in Parliament until 2013, and although it had attracted a lot of attention largely because of its charismatic leader, cricketer-turned-politician Imran Khan, the party had not historically enjoyed electoral success. The party had eschewed traditional politics that require cobbling together coalitions of leaders with their own power bases; instead, it opted for an ideological appeal that highlighted Khan's ability to speak truth to power and to challenge the way the political game had always been played.[18]

In an attempt to make electoral gains the party made a decision to change this approach in the run-up to the 2013 election and began to recruit traditional politicians, including some who had been affiliated with both the Musharraf-supporting Pakistan Muslim League-Quaid (PML-Q) and the PPP. These recruits were helpful in both swelling the popular ranks of the PTI and in making the party appear to be a more credible contender for political office, but the downside was a tarnishing of the party's image of honesty and a reduction in its anti–status quo appeal.[19] Nevertheless, the party campaigned energetically in the run-up to the 2013 election, running on the slogan of "Naya Pakistan" (New Pakistan) and holding rallies in a number of cities, including in Karachi at the Quaid-e-Azam mausoleum.[20] Newly formed alliances and relationships with traditional power brokers gave the party a heft that previously it had lacked in its attempts to gain electoral office.

These alliances paid off electorally, with the PTI winning a total of 28 seats in the general election; with the addition of 6 women's seats and 1 minority seat, the party's total stood at 35 seats. It was the third-largest party in Parliament, losing narrowly to the PPP, which had secured 42 seats. Although it did not win enough seats to form the government, the PTI had succeeded in becoming a leading opposition voice and had two main options before it as a party in opposition.

Traditional theories of opposition parties in established democracies suggest that in preparation for the next election opposition parties typically focus on establishing themselves as a credible alternative to the party in power through programmatic appeals that are designed to highlight both the party's strengths as well as the governing party's weaknesses (see Schattschneider 1942). However, as Lupu and Riedl (2013) have noted, because parties in developing democracies face tremendous uncertainty, they behave differently than they would in established democracies. Indeed, the PTI could have reasonably believed that there was a chance that the current elected government would be dismissed. After all, such an outcome was hardly unprecedented in Pakistan's history. Indeed, the 2013 election marked only the first time that an elected government had been able to complete its full five-year term.[21]

The PTI took a different tack than the PML-N had done immediately after the 2008 election: it claimed the PML-N had been denied an electoral majority and the right to form the government. The PTI had decided to attack the electoral framework as the cause for its loss and claimed that massive election irregularities had caused it to lose, especially in important constituencies. The PTI then proceeded to engage in a series of extra-parliamentary tactics that rejected the legitimacy of the PML-N government. This strategy undermined the democratic framework because, as many theorists have pointed out, the legitimacy of electoral competition depends especially on losers accepting the results of the election (for example, see Anderson et al. 2005). The PTI's response can be seen as a rational decision in the context of regime uncertainty, especially since it was well known that the deep state was especially troubled by the PML-N (see Kalhan 2013).

In the aftermath of the 2013 elections the PTI called for investigations into election rigging and eventually produced a white paper that documented a number of irregularities across Pakistan.[22] Over the following few months the PTI and the ruling PML-N negotiated the issue, with the PTI demanding an independent investigation. But a year into the new government's tenure the PTI appeared to have had enough of the on-again, off-again talks and started to consider calling for street protests.[23]

The PTI-Led Dharna of 2014

After months of calling for investigations into election rigging, the PTI decided to call for a protest march and a dharna in June 2014. Imran Khan announced that the party would march from Lahore to Islamabad starting on August 14 (Independence Day) and stage a dharna in Islamabad until its demands were met. The symbolism of starting the protest march on August 14 was powerful, and indeed the march was renamed the Azadi (Freedom) March after having initially been dubbed the Tsunami March.[24] In a speech at the launch of the march in Lahore, Khan alluded to this symbolism when he said, "Pakistan was liberated from the British by our elders; God willing, today we will liberate Pakistan from the pharaohs who are ruling it now."[25]

In Islamabad the PTI was joined by a citizen's group called the Pakistan Awami Tehreek (PAT) led by the cleric Tahir-ul-Qadri, who had spent many years in exile in Canada but had returned to lead a movement against the PML-N government. Qadri's group had been engaged in antigovernment demonstrations for some years, and he too had announced his intention to march on Islamabad on Independence Day. (His march was to be called the Inquilabi March or the "revolutionary march"). Although the two forces were not formally allied, they both wanted to dislodge the PML-N government and agreed to cooperate and to merge their rallies once they reached Islamabad.[26] Once in Islamabad the party established a more-or-less permanent presence on Constitution Avenue for four months, with the leaders regularly giving speeches to the assembled crowd in what became dubbed "container politics" or "container dharna" (Mulla 2017). The familiar slogan "Go Musharraf Go!" from the Lawyers' Movement was now replaced with cries of "Go Nawaz Go!" as protesters upped the ante and called for Nawaz Sharif's resignation.

The PTI dharna crystallized many of the qualities on which it had been basing its appeal. Speeches painted the PML-N government as corrupt and incompetent and, by contrast, the PTI as a force for honesty and efficiency. In a speech on August 19, early in the dharna, Khan said the following:

Those who have sucked our blood and have reduced the country to a corpse, they have kept their fortunes outside the country. Remember this: I am the only Pakistani politician who made a living outside Pakistan for 18 years, and I sold it all, and all my assets and wealth are in Pakistan. I will live and die in Pakistan. How can someone be a leader of Pakistan, when he has kept all of his wealth and assets outside Pakistan? Who are these leaders who keep going overseas for treatment of every common cold? What kinds of leaders are these? It is these corrupt leaders that I have come to liberate you from! [Crowd chants: Go Nawaz Go!][27]

The party projected itself as having a more tolerant and moderate ideology coupled with a modern middle-class sensibility. Notably, the dharna included a significant presence of middle-class women, and on multiple occasions the crowd danced to music. The presence of these women drew the ire of many religious conservatives.[28] But this was not a new phenomenon for the PTI: it had sought to project this modern image even before the 2013 election. Arsalan Jawaid (2013) describes the attendees at a PTI rally in 2011 in this way: "Khan drew crowds from a cross-section of Pakistani society, from the slums of Karachi to the most elite areas. Girls in T-shirts and jeans mingle with women in burkhas. Young, western-educated businessmen stand with street cleaners, vendors and boys with tattoos."

Mulla (2017) has explored the public image of the PTI further, arguing that the 2014 dharna especially helped to mark the PTI as a modern and urban middle-class party. The party sought to highlight the presence of "well-dressed middle age women sporting sunglasses and handbags, and attractive young women adorned in PTI flag colors"; this image was visually contrasted with the large female presence of burqa-clad, religiously conservative, and lower-middle-class PAT supporters who were also participating in the dharna (Mulla 2017, 4193). At one level this contrast heightened the PTI's contradictory image since it was cooperating with the more conservative PAT, but the dharna itself provided a useful political stage on which to project the PTI's messages and its image, which it would not have been able to do otherwise.

The dharna finally ended on December 17, 2014, and it took an extraordinary and tragic development to end it. The day before, a group of Islamist militants attacked the Army Public School in Peshawar, killing 141 people, including 132 children.[29] The tragedy shifted the political calculus for the PTI, and it became impossible to ignore the impact that the tragedy had on the dharna. Most important, Prime Minister Nawaz Sharif called an all-parties conference in response to the attack. The all-parties conference is a familiar format intended to bring all parliamentary parties together to discuss matters of national importance, and the PTI agreed to join these talks. But the PTI decided to boycott Parliament again in the wake of the Panama Papers revelations in October 2016, even though it returned to Parliament two months later. It nonetheless continued to apply extra-parliamentary pressure on the PML-N government through court petitions for Sharif's dismissal as prime minister on the basis of alleged corruption that had particularly implicated his family in the Panama Papers.[30] This attitude toward Parliament may appear contradictory, but it is part of the PTI's strategy of continuing to use extra-parliamentary maneuvers to gain political advantage as a party in opposition. Indeed, this appears to have been a winning strategy, given that it was victorious in the 2018 election.

An open question is whether the PTI will change strategies and become more inclined to work within democratic institutions after coming into power. Since assuming office the PTI has generally continued to eschew parliamentary engagement with other parties. For example, the party initially refused to allow the PML-N to assume chairmanship of the important Public Accounts Committee—although it eventually relented—in what one observer termed a "perfectly avoidable stand-off between the treasury and the opposition."[31]

It is too early to tell, but it is possible that the PTI may be shifting its behavior now that it is in office, and perhaps the constraints of governing have provided greater incentives for the party to work with opposition parties within a parliamentary framework. It seems unlikely that the PTI will sign on to the Charter of Democracy knowing that it is being exhorted to do so by the opposition PPP.[32] But the PTI may yet find that extra-parliamentary tactics no longer provide the political payoffs it gained as an opposition party. It may also mean that the PTI will be more circumspect with extra-parliamentary engagement once it is back in the opposition, as someday it will inevitably be.

Conclusion

This chapter has examined the strategic actions of opposition parties in Pakistan by focusing on the cases of the PML-N and the PTI during their respective times in opposition. The PML-N behaved more like a "true opposition," with the effect of strengthening democratic institutions; the PTI challenged the ruling PML-N party by attacking some of the very institutions that had served to bring the PML-N to power. In one case the actions of the party reinforced democratic institutions, but in the other they undermined them. It would be tempting to conclude, therefore, that some Pakistani political parties are simply more democracy-accepting and some are simply democracy-averse. But that would be a simplistic reading of the situation.

The point is not that any of the Pakistani parties are either inherently for or against democracy. Rather, they are responding to environmental uncertainty in a way that incentivizes them to act outside of the parliamentary framework, which is consistent with the behavior of opposition parties elsewhere, including in Western democracies. One should expect that when regime uncertainty is reduced, parties will more regularly engage with parliamentary politics. This truth, however, depends on the military establishment's retreat into the barracks, and whether the military will do so remains to be seen.

Notes

1. For example, Potter (1966) says that the British constitution formalizes a role for "Her Majesty's Opposition" (including a salary) but also notes that opposition leaders have often resisted the constraints that this title places on them. See also Von Beyme (1987).

2. "Pakistan Tehreek-i-Insaf: New Phenomenon or Continuation of the Political Status Quo?," *NORIA*, October 22, 2016, https://www.noria-research.com/south-asia-5-pakistan-tehrik-e-insaaf/.

3. Ejaz Haider, "The Democratic Uncertainty of Pakistan," *Himal*, December 2006.

4. Indeed the joke goes that while most countries have an army, the Pakistan Army has a country. See, for example, "Why Pakistan's Army Wields So Much Power," *Economist*, September 20, 2014.

5. Pervez Musharraf, "A Plea for Enlightened Moderation," *Washington Post*, June 1, 2004.

6. "Democracy Charter for Pakistan," BBC News, May 15, 2006.

7. James Traub, "The Lawyers' Crusade," *New York Times Magazine*, June 1, 2008.

8. Traub, "Lawyers' Crusade." See also Shafqat (2018).

9. Interview of Salahuddin Ahmed, March 4, 2015, Karachi.

10. Adil Baig, "Nawaz Sharif Historical Address before Long March on 15th March," video filmed March 2009, 9:50, accessed December 27, 2017, https://www.youtube.com/watch?v=m9ffNAiI38M.

11. Omar Waraich and Andrew Buncombe, "Pakistan Celebrates First Ever Full Term for Democratically Elected Government," *Independent*, March 17, 2013.

12. Memphis Barker, "Former Pakistani PM Nawaz Sharif Sentenced to 10 Years in Jail," *Guardian*, July 6, 2018.

13. Mahboob Mohsin, "An Insider View on How PML-N Went to Pieces during Elections," *Dawn*, July 31, 2018.

14. "'The Angels' at Play in Pakistan's Election," BBC News, July 25, 2018.

15. Shahbaz Sharif was quoted as saying, "Parliament is the 'only hope for the people of this country' and only through the parliament the people's demands could be met. Lawmakers have not come to the legislature to get salaries and stage sit-ins." Amir Wasim, "PML-N to Head 9 NA Standing Committees, Shehbaz to Lead Public Accounts Committee," *Dawn*, September 25, 2018.

16. Douglas Schorzman, "In Pre-Election Pakistan, a Military Crackdown Is the Real Issue," *New York Times*, June 6, 2018.

17. Mohsin, "Insider View."

18. Madiha Tahir, "'I'll Be Your Mirror': What Pakistan Sees in Imran Khan," *Caravan*, January 1, 2012.

19. Tahir, "I'll Be Your Mirror."

20. The mausoleum of Muhammad Ali Jinnah, also known as Quaid-e-Azam, has great symbolic importance as the resting place of Pakistan's founder. It is imbued with patriotic and nationalist meaning.

21. Waraich and Buncombe, "Pakistan Celebrates."

22. Adnan Khan, "Bringing Down the House," *Maclean's* 127, no. 35 (2014): 26.

23. Mariam Mufti, "Divided They Rule," *Herald*, August 12, 2014.

24. Khan, "Bringing Down the House."

25. "PTI Azadi March Begins 14 August 2014," video filmed August 2014 in Islamabad, Pakistan, 2:06, accessed December 26, 2017, https://www.youtube.com/watch?v=d60pWMor8yg.

26. Khan, "Bringing Down the House."

27. Noora Jutt Talk Shows and Latest News, "Imran Khan Speech to PTI Dharna Islamabad 19th August 2014, FUL HD [video file]," (2014), accessed on December 27, 2017, https://www.youtube.com/watch?v=UcopjxYX5g0on.

28. "Dance in PTI Jalsa Face Criticism on Social Media," *Awami Politics Blog*, 2014, http://www.awamipolitics.com/dance-in-pti-jalsa-faces-criticism-on-social-media-17515.

29. Rachel Roberts, "Pakistan: Three Years after 140 Died in the Peshawar School Massacre, What Has Changed?," *Independent*, December 15, 2017.

30. Salman Masood, "Nawaz Sharif, Pakistan's Prime Minister, Is Toppled by Corruption Case," *New York Times*, July 28, 2017.

31. Ahmed Bilal Mehboob, "The First Six Months," *Dawn*, February 17, 2019.

32. "PPP Doubts PTI Support for New Charter of Democracy," *Dawn*, March 17, 2019.

Part III

The Survival of Pakistan's Party System

12

The Kingmaker
Pakistan's Military and Political Parties

Ayesha Siddiqa

The 2018 national elections in Pakistan did not change the country's political scene substantially other than by introducing a new stakeholder: cricketer-turned-politician Imran Khan and his party, the Pakistan Tehreek-e-Insaf (PTI). While the transfer of power from one civilian government to another without prior military intervention did improve the conditions for electoral democracy in Pakistan, the entire political process—of which elections are just one part—continues to demonstrate a pattern of military dominance. The politically strong army appears to have opted for indirect intervention in the country's day-to-day governance rather than directly taking over the reins of government. This governance pattern can be viewed as the maintenance of a hybrid democracy (see Adeney 2017) or, indeed, of a hybrid martial law (see Siddiqa 2019). Greater control of governance without direct intervention may have been deemed necessary to reestablish central control of the bureaucratic state that had begun to dilute after the 18th Amendment to the 1973 Constitution was passed in 2010.[1] Such indirect control over governance rather than direct control of the state provides to the army echelons the opportunity to keep the officer cadre glued to their professional work while ensuring that the echelons' organizational and personal interests are safeguarded. Unlike some other dictatorships around the world that have successfully formed their own political parties, however, the Pakistan Army has consistently engaged in a policy of developing partnerships throughout the political classes, resulting in the military penetrating every political party. Consequently, the political system is influenced in a manner such that no party can imagine gaining power without the support of the Army General Headquarters (GHQ) and its several intelligence agencies. Even if political parties aim to establish control for themselves, their entry into the corridors of power is not possible without the army's support.

This chapter examines the Pakistan military's political philosophy and its linkages with various political parties, in particular why and how the army opted to become an arbiter rather than a direct ruler of politics in Pakistan. I show how the military patronized various political parties as its clients, including the changing relationship between the army and the Pakistan People's Party (PPP), starting from Zulfikar Ali Bhutto's attempts to bring the military under civilian control and culminating in the present-day pariah status of the party vis-à-vis the army. I then turn to explaining how the military helped create the Muttahida Qaumi Movement (MQM) in Karachi before launching an operation against it in the early 1990s; how its long-standing relationship with the Pakistan Muslim League—the party most assumed to be friendly with the army—has recently faltered; its most recent co-optation of the PTI; and the way in which it has used religious parties to aid its strategic objectives.

The Pakistan Army's Role as Arbiter, Not Ruler

A popular joke doing the rounds in Pakistan prior to the 2018 elections was that no matter who you voted for, ultimately the PTI would win. This joke was a reflection not so much about Imran Khan's popularity but more about the support rendered to him by the Pakistani armed forces. Though the PTI did not sweep the elections, it managed to form the government at the center as well as in three provinces. The election results and subsequent government formation suggest that Khan received support in bringing his party into power. The PTI received less than a simple majority in the center (116 seats of 272), it trailed behind the PML-N in Punjab in the initial count, it could not form the Punjab provincial government without independent candidates and groups that helped bring the party to a position of majority (146 of 297 seats), and it received only 6 out of 51 seats in Balochistan (less than three other parties). Still it managed to form coalition governments in all three. This was in addition to Khyber Pakhtunkhwa, where it earned a majority. Khan's political opponents have claimed that pressure was put on voters, political managers, and candidates to ensure the formation of this government.[2]

The 2018 elections are not a simple story about election management. Rather, they reflect the army's overall intervention in the political process. More important, they point to a pattern pursued by Pakistan's army to ensure that the organization remains at the helm of power. In particular, the military controls political outcomes through three methods: first, it plays a role in nurturing and then selecting political leaders; second, it influences the political environment through supporting its most favored candidates; and third, it infiltrates political parties with its favored men at the local level and in Parliament. This strategy has turned the military into a kingmaker. It is central to who comes to power. The longevity of a parliament or a cabinet depends on how these institutions are perceived by the GHQ. In this way the Pakistan military has carved out a role for itself beyond what the Turkish military was able to do as an arbiter until the 1990s, when it ceased to be one as the Justice and Development Party (AKP) gained power. Nor is the Pakistan military a "ruler type," which can be used to describe the militaries in Egypt and Libya: they remain in power through individual leaders. Instead, Pakistan's military has evolved from being a ruler-type to a permanent arbiter-guardian of both the state and the government.

However, this was not always the plan. The country's first non-British army chief, Gen. Muhammad Ayub Khan, who took power in 1958, did not give any indication of wanting to give up power after he altered the political system in 1962. He created a structure for local government, known as basic democracies, which allowed for the selection of a number of new political stakeholders that not only elected him as president in an indirectly held election but also became the military's political clients (Sayeed 1967). Many of these handpicked clients, including Zulfikar Ali Bhutto, Chaudhry Zahoor Elahi, and Khursheed Ahmed Kasuri, became prominent political players during the 1960s and the 1970s. Generals Muhammad Zia-ul-Haq and Pervez Musharraf repeated Ayub Khan's method of creating new stakeholders by headhunting at the local political level. Other generals who did not declare martial law but remained powerful also utilized this strategy. Like Ayub's system of basic democracies, Zia's democracy ordinance and Musharraf's devolution of democracy were aimed at creating new political players who would provide support against established but estranged politicians.

Ayub can also be remembered for setting the precedent of taking over a political party (in his case the Pakistan Muslim League, or PML) and converting it into a "king's party" (the Pakistan Muslim League-Functional, or PML-F). Later Musharraf also tried to experiment with this formula by becoming an informal patron of the Pakistan Muslim League-Quaid (PML-Q) during the 2000s. In both cases the plan of ruling through parties did not work. Rather, both examples demonstrated that an army chief who turns permanently toward politics is powerful only insofar as he remains head of the organization or is not seen as damaging to institutional interests. Ayub Khan lost power the moment he transferred power to army chief Gen. Muhammad Yahya Khan and became field marshal and president of the country. From the army's standpoint and despite his military connections, Ayub could not be supported forever as a military-president, especially when he became unpopular after the 1965 war with India and with the political situation deteriorating in both wings of the country, particularly in East Pakistan. The same situation was true for Musharraf, who was pushed out despite being the army chief when the military found his actions costly to its overall standing in society and detrimental to its military-strategic institutional goals, especially vis-à-vis India. The limited political movement of the lawyers' and media's public protests against Musharraf was essentially the last nail in the coffin (see chapter 11 for more on the Lawyers' Movement). This lack of popularity in the case of both Ayub and Musharraf was a death knell for the political parties they had created and supported. Even senior commanders who had made parties after retiring from service did not succeed. Those names include Musharraf (All Pakistan Muslim League), former army chief Mirza Aslam Beg (Awami Qiyadat Party), and Air Chief Marshal (Ret.) Mohammad Asghar Khan (Tehreek-e-Istaqlal).

The Pakistan Army's preferred role of political guardian, rather than ruler, has evolved over time as the leadership has learned to balance the need to keep the organization professional with its involvement in politics. This professionalism has helped maintain a hierarchical command-and-control structure; the army chief's power is centralized and sufficiently consolidated to prevent a colonels' coup and gives the impression that the officer cadre is a highly professional life pattern designed to not engage in politics (Staniland, Naseemullah, and Butt 2018). However, politics are conducted by the army chief, who is the only one allowed to take extraordinary measures on behalf of the echelons to declare a coup or remove the head of state, and the politics of the officer cadre and the entire organization are centrally expressed. This hierarchical structure ensures that the army chief's power has limits placed on it. The chief is the "first among equals," specifically the corps commanders and other three-star generals from among whom the army chief is selected.

Therefore, despite its political role, the Pakistan Army considers itself as first and foremost a professional army. The popular view within the service is that its main work is external security from which it gets diverted due to the need to bail out the country internally. According to former army chief Ashfaq Parvez Kiyani, political intervention is tantamount to "temporary by passes that are created when a bridge collapses on democracy's highway. After the bridge is repaired, then there's no longer any need for the detour" (Shah 2014b, 1017). From an institutional perspective, acknowledging its engagement in politics or providing help to retired officers in their political careers would politicize the organization much more visibly and could start internal competition against which the army wants to protect itself. For example, when Ayub and Musharraf became unpopular, the army intervened to protect its reputation. Instead, the army has chosen to influence the political environment by infiltrating political parties and nurturing specific individuals.

The Military and Its Political Clients

The inability of political parties to grow, independent of the military, can also be attributed to the role of patronage. Pakistan's political structure is largely patronage-based, with local elites playing a dominant role (Wilder

1999; Lieven 2011; Khan Mohmand 2014). In West Pakistan, where Punjab is the largest province in terms of population and one of the hubs of state bureaucracy, the landowning elite dominated politics. Indeed, it was the Unionist party, dominated by landowning elites, that converted into the PML to ensure that the latter won the referendum for the independence of Pakistan in 1947 (see Talbot 1998). Ayub Khan managed to hijack this same Muslim League and turn it into the PML-F. Ayub's political strategy was based on poaching the Muslim League and building a new clientele through a basic democracy scheme. The general's recruitment drive helped discover new faces, one of the most prominent being Zulfikar Ali Bhutto, who later became Khan's foreign minister. This experience was the beginning of the army's deep entrenchment in politics.

Birth of Politics: The Pakistan People's Party

The Pakistan People's Party (PPP), formed in 1969 by Zulfikar Bhutto, was the first experiment in the military's political patronage (see chapter 2 of this volume for more on the PPP). In addition to his close relations with Ayub Khan, Bhutto's geopolitical philosophy and governing style suited the military. Representing a relatively liberal element within Ayub's cabinet, Bhutto gradually distanced himself from his political mentor. He mustered support among the public but also within segments of the armed forces that had grown disenchanted with Ayub Khan's signing of the Tashkent Declaration to bring an end to the 1965 India-Pakistan War. As foreign minister, Bhutto had supported Operation Gibraltar that led to the war and advised the president against signing a no-war pact with New Delhi. Ayub finally sacked Bhutto on the US's insistence, after which Bhutto carved out his own political future (NA 1967).

According to Aijaz Ahmad (1978), Bhutto built the self-image of a revolutionary leader while turning his party into the apparatus of a reactionary state. The PPP leader's socialist ideology came on the heels of Ayub's era of development, offering a revolutionary but necessary departure from what had been presented in the past (481). More important, Bhutto's image bore fruit at a critical time when the economy had nosedived and the military's morale was at its lowest following the loss of the country's eastern wing in 1971. The government of Yahya Khan, in fact, dispatched Bhutto to represent Pakistan at the United Nations, where he famously tore up his speech and lambasted the international community for not condemning India's aggressive moves. On the whole Bhutto had the image of a nationalist leader who vehemently supported the Kashmir issue and raised the slogan of fighting "a war for a thousand years."[3]

Indeed, it was the defeat at India's hands in 1971 that ultimately forced the military to transfer power to a political leader. Senior army commander Lt.

Gen. Gul Hasan Khan and Air Comm. Sajjid Rahim played an instrumental role in shifting power from Yahya to Bhutto (484). Although Bhutto offered a socialist ideology, in no time leftist elements in his party were sidelined (see chapter 5 in this volume). By the time Bhutto contested the country's second general elections in 1977, the party's politically progressive forces were completely marginalized, leaving greater room for the conservative elite. Instead of empowering his voters, Bhutto strengthened the state bureaucracy, partly through the process of nationalizing businesses and industry.

While the 1970s saw the start of a process of higher defense reorganization with the intention of bringing the armed forces under civilian control, this change went hand-in-hand with appeasement of the military. For example, Bhutto, who took over as chief martial law administrator and president because no alternative constitutional mandate existed, was able to pass an ordinance that made any negative comments about the army over the East Pakistan debacle punishable with a long prison sentence. Bhutto also played a central role in having ninety thousand prisoners of war repatriated from India. The appeasement did not end there. While the country recovered from the financial burden of a lost war, the leader of the PPP spent money on the acquisition of weapons from France, China, and the UK. He also invested in and gave direction to the nuclear program in order to compete with India, which had carried out its first peaceful nuclear explosion in 1974. Notwithstanding the reduction in the organization's overall perks and privileges, the prime minister engaged with the military primarily with the intent of using it to enhance his personal power. For example, Bhutto appointed Gen. Tikka Khan, a man with an atrocious human rights record and known as "the butcher of Bengal," as governor of Punjab. But all this changed with time.[4]

Regarding Bhutto and the military, two narratives emerge. First, until the mid-1970s the prime minister was liked by the men in uniform for restoring their confidence and amplifying their national security narrative. In the process of building ties with China, the Soviet Union, and the Middle East, Bhutto appeased the nation and soothed the army's hurt ego but also provided direction for the army's role in the world. Moreover, the superficial turning away from the United States looked like a firm response to experiences during the 1965 and 1971 wars, during which Islamabad was slapped with an arms embargo. According to Bhutto's law minister, Abdul Hafeez Pirzada, the generals used the PPP leader to their own advantage to rebuild their image and power only to later abandon him.[5]

The second narrative, which contradicts Bhutto's first avatar as a nationalist and committed leader, appeared after 1974. The Bhutto that the army remembers after 1977 is a reckless political leader out to destroy the country. This narrative shift likely happened due to a growing fear among the army echelons that Bhutto was trying to establish himself as a political counterweight. While enhancing the military's significance, he took measures to minimize its structural importance. The PPP government was the only one that introduced organizational reforms meant to bring the military under greater civilian control. This seems to have concerned the generals that had enjoyed autonomy since 1954. The creation of a strong Ministry of Defense and the position of the chairman of the Joint Chiefs of Staff Committee, changing commanders in chief of all three services to simply chiefs of staff, constitutionally designating the prime minister as the supreme commander, and formally determining that a coup d'état was an act of treason punishable by death all signaled a change in the military's overall power.

It is likely that the generals also understood the humiliation that many of the civil bureaucrats had experienced at the hands of the prime minister. According to one retired senior bureaucrat, Bhutto publicly insulted civil servants to create a powerful image of himself among his constituents.[6] His decision to establish the Federal Security Force (FSF) might have been aimed at reducing the military's domestic security role, but it was also driven by Bhutto's feudal instinct to grab power and coerce any opposition. Ultimately Bhutto's personal traits as a feudal lord got the better of him when he selected Zia-ul-Haq as army chief, mistaking the general's effected humility for assured subservience. Bhutto did not hear the footsteps of the coming 1977 coup; he was too absorbed in fighting the opposition-led movement's accusations of rigging elections that year.

Bhutto started to appear increasingly as an embattled politician who would go to any lengths to protect his victory and not to be seen as a "rigger of elections."[7] The generals noticed his desperation, on which they started to build a narrative pitching the military as ethically superior to the PPP's top leadership. In addition to the overall logjam between the PPP and the opposition Pakistan National Alliance (PNA), this superiority was presented as the reason that only the army could avert an impending internal crisis by declaring martial law in July 1977 (M. Ali 1977). One of the pegs on which the military could hang its decision to sack the government was a letter written by Air Chief Marshal Khan to the army chief, imploring him to use his own moral judgment to obey or disobey orders of the political government. Asghar Khan also laid the blame for unrest in East Pakistan on Bhutto's shoulders (Yaseen, Ahmad, and Butt 2016). From this point on the army not only abandoned Bhutto but also invested in building a negative image of him. The allegations against him for ordering the murder of an opposition leader resulted in a questionable Supreme Court decision implemented on April 4, 1979: the former prime minister was hanged.

After 1979, therefore, relations between the military and the PPP deteriorated. Concerned with the party's popularity among the masses, the military adopted three measures. First, it used repression against PPP workers. Bhutto's wife, Begum Nusrat Bhutto, who was now chairperson of the PPP, and his daughter Benazir were often put under house arrest or jailed. On one occasion the Lahore police attacked Nusrat Bhutto with batons.[8] There was also a clampdown on the media meant to curb any sympathy generated for the party, and the party's support base was hit by a ban on student and labor unions.[9] Second, an effort was made to neutralize the party's power by creating counterweights such as the MQM in urban Sindh (the home province of the Bhuttos). Giving birth to and nourishing an ethnic party was mainly intended to counter the resistance in the 1983 Movement for Restoration of Democracy (MRD) in which Sindhi politicians played a role.[10] Third, the army created newer political options to minimize the PPP's influence. For example, nonparty-based elections were held in which the prime minister, Muhammad Khan Junejo, was selected from Bhutto's home province.

The 1980s were a period of political confrontation between the GHQ and the PPP; the latter boycotted both the presidential referendum in 1984 and the 1985 elections. While the army released Nusrat Bhutto from jail in 1981 due to illness, Benazir Bhutto, who was effectively the main anchor of the party, was held in prison until 1984, when she was released due to international pressure. Zia allowed Bhutto to contest elections, but tried to ensure that she could not win by announcing the date of the elections in November when it was suspected that Bhutto would deliver her first child (Khuhro and Soomro 2013).

Zia-ul-Haq's death in a mysterious air crash in 1988 marked the beginning of a new phase of mistrust in the military's relationship with the PPP. The army remained suspicious of Benazir Bhutto for the same reasons it had become suspicious of Zulfiqar Bhutto: her popular support among the masses, which was demonstrated upon her return to Pakistan in 1986 and later in 2007. There was much showboating between the GHQ and the prime minister as Bhutto flexed her muscles to discipline the army and the ISI. In 1989 she made three critical decisions: (1) she removed the director general (DG) of the ISI, Lt. Gen. Hamid Gul, and replaced him with her handpicked official, Lt. Gen. Shamsur Rehman Kallu; (2) she formed an intelligence committee to find ways to curb the ISI's power; and (3) she planned to retire the chairman of the Joint Chiefs of Staff Committee, Adm. Iftikhar Sirohi, to be replaced with the army's chief general, Mirza Aslam Beg (Sekine 2014, 69–75). Bhutto's decisions were considered a violation of the military's sacrosanct domain, and the army struck back with a plan to overthrow her government through a no-confidence vote. Although in 1989 Bhutto's director general ISI discovered the plan—code-named Operation Midnight Jackal—in time the president removed Bhutto using the 8th Amendment to the 1973 Constitution.[11]

The military struggled throughout the 1990s to weaken the PPP's overall position by creating a political counterweight in Punjab province. In particular, Bhutto's power in Punjab was contested by Mian Nawaz Sharif, a leader discovered by the Zia regime (see chapter 1 for more on the PML-N and

Sharif). In 1990 an elaborate plan was launched by the ISI in which money was paid to different politicians to contest against the PPP (M. Khan 2005).[12] The Islami Jamhoori Itihad (IJI) that was formed by the ISI won the 1990 elections.[13] However, the PPP was brought back into power in 1995; two years later its government was dismissed over corruption charges.

The PPP's edge during Benazir Bhutto's lifetime appears to have been her ability to interact with the international community and convince the world of her political strength. This perceived strength helped push the United States to convince Musharraf to continue negotiations with her, resulting in the signing of the National Reconciliation Ordinance (NRO) in 2007.[14] Musharraf agreed to withdraw corruption cases against the PPP leader and her husband that were pending in Swiss courts in return for their support of the general. The idea was also for Bhutto to return to Pakistan. This latter part of the understanding has aroused controversy, as Musharraf alleges that she returned to Pakistan despite instructions not to do so.[15] Musharraf reacted by not providing her security, thus leaving her vulnerable to terrorist attacks. She died in a second assassination attempt on December 27, 2007. The prevailing narrative around the assassination is that it was the handiwork of a Taliban group, although many believe the military had a hand to play (Munoz 2010).[16]

The PPP suffered tremendously after Bhutto's death. The reins of the party were immediately taken over by her widower, Asif Ali Zardari, who managed to win the 2008 elections and formed the government with himself as president. However, Zardari did not demonstrate the sagacity needed to keep party workers motivated. His key strategy remained: test the waters through a variety of challenges to military dominance but withdraw under pressure. He provoked the ire of the GHQ by trying to tinker with the command and control of the ISI. Later he was accused by the armed forces of trying to conspire against them through Hussain Haqqani, his handpicked ambassador to the United States. In a scandal that became known as Memogate, news reports surfaced that Haqqani had written a memo to US Admiral Mike Mullen asking for the American government's assistance in confronting the Pakistan Army, which was accused of planning a coup against the civilian government.[17] The existence of the memo remains unproved, but it hung on the PPP's head; the highest judiciary frequently flagged the case until it was finally dismissed in February 2019.[18] The party lost the 2013 elections mainly due to its poor performance delivering services while in government, and in 2018 it was mainly limited to Sindh. Despite the PPP's inability to recreate its past powerful aura, the military remains suspicious of the party, in part due to the PPP's role in passing the 18th Amendment to the 1973 Constitution. The amendment invoked the wrath of Army Chief Qamar Bajwa, who described it "as big a problem as Sheikh Mujeeb's six points," referring to the disagreement between the eastern and western wings of the country that resulted in the former breaking away in 1971.[19] While Bilawal Bhutto-Zardari, the young current chairman of the PPP, seems to have attracted positive attention due to the friendly tone he adopted toward the army during an interview in Davos, the PPP still remains a pariah in the eyes of the institution.[20] It will perhaps have to recreate itself completely, as well as become relevant politically, particularly in Punjab, to earn a more favorable position with the army.

The MQM: Hitchhiking to Power

The MQM's leadership was discovered by the military during the latter's conflict with the PPP in the 1980s. Hence, the military has always seen the ethnic urban Sindh-based party through a tactical lens. It was only during the Musharraf period that a plan was made for a more strategic engagement with the party, a chance that passed when Musharraf resigned from the position of army chief and president of the country.

The MQM's relations with the army cannot be separated from two structural issues. The first relates to the party's birth in 1984, when it was formed by a group of Muhajir leaders dissatisfied with the government over the distribution of resources and opportunities provided to the city's various ethnic groups. "Muhajirs" is a term loosely used to refer to those people who migrated from Muslim minority provinces of India from 1947 to 1951 and who mainly settled in urban Sindh (see chapter 4 for more on the Muhajir ethnic group and the MQM). According to the 1981 census, of the total Sindh population of 19.3 million, Muhajirs represented 4.6 million. The bulk of this Muhajir population (3.3 million in 1981) live in the largest cosmopolitan city, Karachi (Kennedy 1991, 939). Because at the time 70 percent of Muhajirs—compared to 10 percent of the indigenous population—were literate, and because they had played a disproportionate role in the movement for independence, they became overrepresented in elite groups in the country, including in the army, where in 1968 they held 23 percent of senior positions (brigadier and above) (942–43). This balance began to change initially with Ayub Khan giving preference in the armed forces to fellow Pashtuns, and later, with Bhutto doing the same for other ethnic groups, particularly Sindhis. Furthermore, when Bhutto introduced a quota for government jobs to placate the concerns of other ethnic groups, the Muhajirs' hold over government employment was challenged. Bhutto's nationalization policy also predominantly affected Karachi-based Muhajir entrepreneurs (945–46).

General Zia empowered Muhajir leadership by providing it a political platform and giving it weapons to challenge PPP activists. This violence became ingrained in the party's culture (see Verkaaik 2004) and was tolerated as long as it served the military's tactical plan to ostracize the PPP. However, when the MQM started to target military personnel and began to have an impact on the country's economy, the military became uncomfortable. Moreover, there was little sympathy in the armed forces for the MQM, given the marginalization of Muhajirs in the military. By 1988 the only senior Muhajir officer was Army Chief Gen. Aslam Beg, who had ascended to the position following Zia's air crash. By the late 1980s, 95 percent of the military was either Punjabi or Pashtun, many of whom had little sympathy for the MQM's shenanigans (Kennedy 1991, 946).

Zia's death in 1988 marked the beginning of a new era of MQM-military relations. Although General Beg tried to give a helping hand in settling Biharis—Urdu-speaking Muslim migrants who remained in Bangladesh after its independence from Pakistan in 1971 and were stranded in refugee camps in Pakistan—the move was opposed in Sindh, whose inhabitants feared that the additional population would further disturb the ethnic balance. After Beg's retirement came Gen. Asif Nawaz Janjua, who was not only a strong Punjabi general but also demonstrated little patience for MQM's use of violence. By the early 1990s the army seemed to have returned to its normal functioning pre-Zia, exhibiting less patience with instability in urban Sindh, the country's financial lifeline. Interestingly, rekindling the military's professional ethos reduced the organization's tolerance for becoming involved in non-Punjabi ethnic politics. In 1992 the Sindh police launched an operation to target crime and violence in Karachi. The operation was initiated under Sharif's PML-N government (1990–92) but wasn't fully executed until the PPP government took oath in 1993. Hundreds of Muhajirs were killed and tortured during the operation. Even the MQM leader, Altaf Hussain, had to flee the country and seek exile in the UK, where he continues to live. While the operation was not successfully completed, the effort to weaken the MQM by encouraging a split through the creation of the Muttahida Qaumi Movement-Haqiqi (MQM-Haqiqi) resulted in a period of internecine war in the party and greater violence in Karachi and Hyderabad. In the process of pitching one group against another, the army ended up strengthening all extremist elements (Haq 1995). Urban Sindh became a hotbed of violence that could not be controlled, even with long-term military deployment in the province.

This precarious situation underwent a change after the 1999 Musharraf coup. Musharraf was a Muhajir, and the party considered him one of its own; they received his held-out hand for discussion. A negotiated truce between the army and the MQM was implemented in 2002, which resulted in the streamlining of MQM in Sindh's power politics. The truce included the appointment of an MQM leader as governor of Sindh (Gayer 2007, 535–36) and recognition of the group's hegemony over urban Sindh, an understanding that was underlined by the state taking action against the MQM-Haqiqi. In the later part of 2002, the leader of the MQM-Haqiqi was jailed and its headquarters were bulldozed, which together announced the co-optation of

Altaf by the army (538, 543). During this period the MQM developed an image of being one of the many political right hands of the military. Musharraf later used the party during his own showdown with the deposed Supreme Court chief justice, Chaudhry Iftikhar Hussain.[21] The party disrupted a rally in Karachi on May 12, 2007, that Chaudhry was to address, resulting in the deaths of forty of his supporters and injuring hundreds of others (Davies 2007, 10–11).

The army's misgiving about the MQM and its control of the country's biggest city surfaced after Musharraf's departure from power; apprehension was compounded by internal rifts within the party that resulted in the murder of one of its leaders, Imran Farooq, in London. Fingers were pointed at Altaf Hussain.[22] The situation became even more tense after 2013 when the army appeared to want to rid the country of obdurate leadership in order to pave the way for successful completion of the China-Pakistan Economic Corridor (CPEC) (Wolf 2016). Around the same time the Punjabi-dominated army leadership emerged as an alternative to the country's civilian leadership. And given the rise in tensions, Hussain warned workers of tough times ahead and verbally targeted the military, actions for which other MQM party leaders later were forced to apologize.[23] Much heat was generated when the army launched an operation in 2013 to clean up Karachi once again. Despite resistance, the operation continued even after a story surfaced regarding the alleged confession by MQM leader Tariq Mir to the British police about the party taking money from the Indian intelligence Research and Analysis Wing.[24] The statement pertained to a money-laundering inquiry started in London by the British police after heaps of cash were recovered from Hussain's house in Edgware. The military promptly accused the party of training terrorists in India and using them to carry out attacks in Pakistan.[25] Although no independent inquiry was launched, the army took the opportunity to launch the operation in Karachi against the MQM. A new party, carved out of the old MQM, was launched in March 2016: the Pak Sarzameen Party (PSP) led by the former mayor of Karachi. Reports suggest that people were pressured to join the PSP.[26] The GHQ seems inclined to simultaneously clip the wings of Muhajir politics while maintaining a sanitized version of an MQM that is not under the control of its founder, Altaf Hussain.

Party for Hire: The Military and the Pakistan Muslim League

The Muslim League is one party that the generals have regularly adopted, either as a platform from which to propagate a narrative or as a safeguard for retaining its key hub in Punjab. This is perhaps in part because the party symbolizes the movement to create the country and in part because it has a conservative and nationalist clientele. Whatever the reason, the party has attracted all army generals, from Ayub Khan to Zia-ul-Haq and later

Musharraf. Despite the PTI replacing the PML-N in the 2018 elections in Punjab, the PML-N may not be entirely out of the political game. Some believe that it could still bounce back into power if Imran Khan loses the support of the army top brass.

After Ayub Khan lifted the ban on political parties in 1962 and searched for political clients of his own, he revived the old All-India Muslim League of Muhammad Ali Jinnah and turned it into the Convention Muslim League. This is the platform on which the general-president contested the 1962 elections against Jinnah's sister, Fatima Jinnah, whose platform was the Muslim League (Council) and later the Combined Opposition Alliance. Clearly symbolism was attached with the title. However, Ayub's Muslim League did not survive after he lost his initial luster and was sidelined by Yahya Khan's martial law. The abandoned party then broke into various factions, and in 1973 the Council and Convention wings were brought under the leadership of a feudal landowner from Sindh, Pir Pagaro, with the new title of Muslim League-Functional (PML-F). The PML-F was one of several parties used in the Pakistan National Alliance (PNA) movement against Bhutto in 1977. A segment of the PML-F turned into a smaller party headed by Malik Qasim, which later joined the PPP in its struggle against General Zia-ul-Haq. Nevertheless, the main PML-F cadre stayed the course and was turned into the unified Pakistan Muslim League (PML) to form the government in 1985. These elections were held on a nonparty basis, but one member of the PML-F, Muhammad Khan Junejo, was handpicked by Zia as the prime minister (Ziring 1998). Despite the eventual dismissal of the Junejo government in 1988, Pagaro maintained close links with the military and during the mid-1980s was allegedly involved in negotiating major weapons deals with the navy.[27]

The 1980s marked the formation of the present-day PML-N and also its initial bonding with the army. The leader of the PML-N, Mian Muhammad Nawaz Sharif, the scion of an industrialist migrant family from East Punjab, was reportedly the find of Lt. Gen. Ghulam Jillani Khan, the governor of Punjab and deputy martial law administrator.[28] Initially appointed as finance minister and later as chief minister, Sharif began to symbolize the PML. According to journalist Raza Rumi, though he was initially rather shy, Sharif was groomed to become "the blue-eyed boy of the military establishment and he delivered in terms of consolidating all anti-PPP forces and vote banks through the 1980s. Such was his intimacy with the dictator General Zia that the latter called Sharif his 'son' in public."[29] Sharif's PML was part of the IJI coalition party that had been cobbled together in the late 1980s to oppose Benazir Bhutto. He was also one of the politicians bribed by the military with campaign funds against the rival PPP in the 1990s.[30]

Sharif was sworn in as prime minister on November 6, 1990. Although not as charismatic as Zulfikar Ali Bhutto, Sharif was the first strong Punjabi leader who could claim capital due to both the military's faith and established networks among the Punjabi urban middle class. Nonetheless, his government was dismissed in April 1993, ostensibly on corruption charges but more likely due to differences over the handling of foreign policy (see Mufti 2015b). The Sharif cabinet was also the first to impose taxes on the military's commercial business ventures (Siddiqa 2007). Toward the end of Sharif's tenure, relations with the army were strained. Rumors were even spread about him having a hand in the sudden death of then-army chief Asif Nawaz Janjua (Nawaz 2008).

Sharif returned to power in 1997 with a two-thirds majority in Parliament. This time around he was more confident about his power base and more confrontational. His first act of consolidating power was to amend the 1973 Constitution, removing the president's power to sack a government. This was followed by severe questioning of then-army chief Jahangir Karamat, who was forced to resign after making a controversial statement against government policy on October 6, 1998. Meanwhile, Sharif handpicked Pervez Musharraf as the next army chief, thinking that a Muhajir army chief would feel constrained among his Punjabi colleagues and follow the prime minister's wishes. By the end of 1998 Sharif was on a high: he had taken the decision to carry out nuclear tests on May 28, 1998, in response to India's tests and conducted whirlwind tours of the Islamic world in the hope of collecting money to pay off the country's debts.

But Sharif had too much on his plate. On the one hand, he tried to muzzle the press and mistreat his main opponent, Benazir Bhutto, by initiating corruption cases against her husband and placing him in jail. Bhutto herself left the country to escape persecution.[31] On the other hand, Sharif delved in risky foreign and security policy options, including negotiating a peace initiative with India before consulting with the army. The army's resentment was apparent: all three services chiefs were absent from Wagah when Sharif went to receive Indian prime minister Atal Bihari Vajpayee in February 1999.[32] Within a few months of signing the Lahore Declaration information surfaced that while Sharif was reaching out to his Indian counterpart, his own army was involved in an operation in Kargil to occupy hilltops in the glacial terrain of the Himalayas.[33] The army was certainly unhappy with his peace overtures, knowing it would initiate a process that would eventually undermine the military's raison d'être. According to then-naval chief Adm. Fasih Bokhari, a game of cat-and-mouse was being played by the army chief, who by that time was also given the additional portfolio of the chairman of the Joint Chiefs of Staff Committee, and the prime minister. Each was trying to find an opportunity to sack the other. Sharif made the first move by dismissing Musharraf and replacing him with a new army chief while the latter was away on an official tour of Sri Lanka. Efforts were made to divert

Musharraf's plane and prevent it from landing in Pakistan. The army was too organized to let Sharif play his hand: Musharraf overthrew the government on October 12, 1999.

After initially being jailed following Musharraf's takeover, Sharif was allowed to spend ten years in exile in Saudi Arabia as the result of a secret deal with Musharraf. Sharif claimed that he was sent under duress.[34] The military government aborted his one effort to return to Pakistan without first seeking permission. His party was taken over indirectly when many of its members were diverted to a new faction called the Pakistan Muslim League-Quaid (PML-Q). The PML-Q was intended to function as a "King's" party. Its leaders, who belonged to a family from Central Punjab with political roots in the first military government of Ayub Khan, were given charge of the critical Punjab province. Musharraf had his eyes on the PML-Q winning the 2007 elections, which were later postponed to 2008. However, with his eye on strengthening his government, the general signed the NRO deal with Bhutto to return, which also would allow Sharif to return from exile. Nonetheless, the situation was completely overtaken by the death of Benazir Bhutto, which led to the PML-Q being almost entirely routed in the 2008 elections.

The Charter of Democracy, signed by Sharif and Bhutto in 2006 in London, stipulated a set of principles that underlined not repeating the bitterness and constant opposition of the past. However, this bitterness between the PML-N and the PPP resurfaced after the latter formed a government in 2008. Sharif struggled between adhering to the charter's principles and his eagerness to placate the army and ensure it of his loyalty. The PML-N leader initiated the petition against the PPP in the Memogate case, in effect doing what the army and the ISI chiefs wanted. Much later he expressed regret for his previous actions.[35]

Other actions indicated a major shift in Sharif's strategic approach toward the armed forces. Soon after winning the 2013 elections he announced his desire to make peace with India as being on the top of his agenda. He pursued this goal by inviting Prime Minister Narendra Modi to a private meeting at his residence in Lahore. The army wasn't happy; apprehensive of the hard-line Indian leader, it wanted Sharif to not keep any peace overtures hidden from it. The burden of poor relations between the GHQ and the prime minister' house increased with Sharif initiating a treason case against Musharraf. Eventually Sharif was cut down to size when all extra-parliamentary forces came together to expose Sharif's corruption. On July 6, 2018, the former prime minister was sentenced to ten years in prison. The army continues to be unwilling to accommodate Nawaz Sharif. The relationship is certainly at an impasse for the time being. However, relations may be rekindled, particularly if the army top brass becomes disappointed in Imran Khan's ability to deliver economically.

Fatal Attraction: Discovering the Pakistan Tehreek-e-Insaf

The 2018 elections in Pakistan turned out to be tense, with all fingers pointed at Imran Khan and his party, the PTI, as the military's choice. More than just Khan's competitors from the PPP and the PML-N were concerned; analysts and journalists talked about pressure being placed by state institutions on electable candidates to join his party.[36] Even a senior judge of the Islamabad High Court spoke of the ISI's meddling and forcing judges to write decisions against the PML-N, the PTI's main rival.[37] However, Khan did not gain a safe majority in the National Assembly or even in Punjab, a critical province for the army and the country more broadly. The outcome indicates that the task of bringing a favored candidate into power was shared by the military and the party: the former managed pre-poll manipulation, while the latter mustered support from constituents. In 2018, however, the ordinary voter in Punjab was not weary of Nawaz Sharif, as demonstrated by the fact that five out of six divisions in north and central Punjab—the hub of the civil and military establishment—voted for Sharif. Rather, the transformation was largely restricted to the middle class, whose narrative demanded clearing the country of traditional corrupt politicians and bringing in a third option. Nonetheless, when the military felt constrained by the two main parties, Khan provided some essential breathing space.

Although Khan is known to have been close to the former DG ISI, Lt. Gen. Hameed Gul, he did not catch the military's attention immediately. This is despite the fact that Khan's views about the United States, his sympathy for the Taliban, and his belligerence about Pakistan's recognition in global politics match the GHQ's. In some respects the military's close relationship with Khan started to develop after 2013, especially as the GHQ's unhappiness with the PML-N increased. Reportedly DG ISI Lt. Gen. Zaheer-ul-Islam was instrumental in helping Khan plan and execute a 2014 sit-in in Islamabad to protest alleged election rigging by the PML-N in the 2013 elections.[38] It has also been argued that Khan emerged as a preferred option for the military only after the Panama Papers leaks in April 2016 revealed information about Sharif's undeclared offshore companies. Pakistan senior journalist Muhammad Ziauddin, however, is of the view that a conspiracy to oust Sharif hatched by the army, Khan, and the higher judiciary started after October 2016. Ziauddin claims that while the Supreme Court turned down the PTI leader's petition in August 2016 to disqualify the prime minister, action was taken against Sharif when he confronted the military high command regarding its support for militants, as revealed in the infamous *Dawn* leaks.[39] The civil-military divide on the issue became clear; the petition was accepted and a larger inquiry into Sharif's wealth was initiated by the court. Given the long-standing popular narrative that has painted both the PPP and the PML-N as unreliable and corrupt—a reputation for which the parties are also partly responsible—the military viewed the PTI as a reasonable alternative. It is indeed a new relationship, the success of which will largely be determined by Imran Khan's ability to stabilize the economy and the country in general.

Military and Religious Parties

Although reputed as a nonreligious military, Pakistan's armed forces are known for their warm yet tactical relations with various religious political parties. The Jamaat-e-Islami (JI) was a key partner during the army's operations in former East Pakistan. The JI's militant wings, al-Badr and al-Shams, have been accused of aiding the army in torturing and killing Bengali intellectuals during the 1971 military operation.[40] Similarly, the JI's help was sought in fighting the Afghan War of the 1980s. However, while religious political parties like the JI and the Jamiat Ulema-e-Islam-Fazlur Rehman (JUI-F) were close to the military in the past, it is not clear that the parties electorally benefited from the cooperation.

This changed in 2002, when the Musharraf government cobbled together an alliance of religious parties and formed the Muttahida Majlis-e-Amal (MMA), which won elections and formed the provincial government in Khyber Pakhtunkhwa province (Haqqani 2005, 259–60). The alliance won sixty seats in the National Assembly. From the military's point of view this was a precious partnership to counter the terrorism arising in the areas bordering Afghanistan, as most of the political parties in the MMA were linked with one militant group or the other. The MMA benefited in establishing a foothold in the province and mainstreaming its radical perspective. From 2002 to 2007 restrictions were placed on exhibiting photos on billboards in the provincial capital, Peshawar. Although the MMA lost to the Pashtun nationalist Awami National Party in the 2008 elections, one of its partners, the JI, became a coalition partner of the PTI government after 2013.

The MMA was revived again for the 2018 elections, with the alliance fielding a large number of candidates in the country (460). But it was not the only religious party contesting. The Barelvi Tehreek-e-Labbaik Pakistan Party (TLP) and the Allah-o-Akbar Tehreek Party (AAT), the latter linked with the militant group Lashkar-e Tayyaba (LeT), also contested. The military's linkages with the TLP, which appears to have been created primarily to lure away the PML-N's voters belonging to the dominant Barelvi sect, appear complex and multifaceted. In November 2017 the TLP protested changes in electoral laws by the Sharif government, which they alleged were blasphemous. But in an encounter between the police and members of the TLP, the latter were badly beaten and the police claim that those who used violence were not TLP supporters but military personnel.[41] The matter was eventually settled with the army-dominated Rangers allegedly distributing money to the party.[42] Mobilized primarily for political gains, it is difficult to see how the TLP can be kept completely harnessed moving forward.

Conclusion

Pakistan's political system is as much military as it is civilian. Because the state is inherently a bureaucratic polity, it has acquired a design that is open to intervention by the army. The military views itself as an arbiter that must intervene at critical times. When it chooses to not take over the reins of government, the choice is mainly to protect its own legitimacy. The army's role in politics has been developed through building a narrative of the institution as the only viable alternative protecting the nation against external and, more important, internal threats posed by incompetent and corrupt leadership.

While overtly wishing for a strong party, the military has weighed down the system to the point that only parties that are susceptible to patronage are able to flourish. This in turn has weakened the party system and created a vicious cycle from which it has proved difficult to emerge: political weakness tends to make parties vulnerable to meddling, but at the same time it is this intervention that makes them weak. Over decades the bureaucratic polity has tied the political elite and the military in a tight relationship in which the latter has a major stake in creating and supporting parties. While the people's support is organic, it is the leadership that eventually gets co-opted. Hence, from Zulfikar Ali Bhutto to Imran Khan the country has witnessed three distinct eras of political leaders and their parties coming into power through the assistance of the army or support of some of its segments. While the movements around the parties may be organic, Pakistan has yet to produce a nationwide party whose leadership is able to rise to power and consolidate it without extra help from the military or has been able to survive without becoming the military's client.

Notes

1. This constitutional change financially empowers the provinces and takes away the federal government's total control over resources, which directly impacts the military.
2. Interviews in Lahore, Islamabad, Bahawalpur, and Karachi, September 7–30, 2018. See also Mehreen Zahra-Malik, "Arrests and Intimidation Fuel Fears of 'Dirty Elections' in Pakistan," *Guardian*, July 21, 2018.
3. Zulfikar Ali Bhutto, "Speech in UN Security Council," September 22, 1965, https://www.dailymotion.com/video/x24uvrv.
4. Yaqoob Khan Bangash, "No Lessons Learnt in Forty Years," *Express Tribune*, December 15, 2011.
5. Interview of Hafeez Pirzada, Islamabad, January 5, 2004.
6. Interview of Javed Syed, Oxford, UK, March 3, 2016.

7. Asad Rahim Khan, "Meltdown," *Express Tribune*, August 12, 2014.

8. Nudrat Kamal, "Begum Nusrat Bhutto: March 23, 1929–October 23, 2011," *Newsline*, November, 2011.

9. S. Akbar Zaidi, "Despotic Islamization," *Dawn,* November 1, 2017.

10. Umair Jamal, "Why the Pakistani State Can't Seem to Figure Out the MQM in Karachi," *Diplomat*, August 30, 2016.

11. Shaikh Aziz, "A Leaf from History: When the 'Midnight Jackal' Didn't Howl," *Dawn*, November 27.

12. See also Mariam Mufti, "Who Rigs Polls in Pakistan and How?," *Herald*, July 2018.

13. The IJI comprised nine political parties and groups: the Pakistan Muslim League, the Jamiat-e-Masaikh, the Jamaat-e-Islami, the Jamiat-ulema-i-Islam, the Jamiat-ulema-i-Islam (Darkhwasti Group), the Jamiat-Ahle Hadith, an independent group led by Fakhr Imam, the Nizam-e-Mustafa, and the Hizb-e-Jihad.

14. "Shaukat Aziz Recalls How Sharif's Exile and Benazir's NRO Deals Were Struck," *Dawn,* July 6, 2016.

15. Owen Bennett-Jones, "Benazir Bhutto Assassination: How Pakistan Covered Up Killing," BBC News, December 27, 2017.

16. Ziad Zafar, "Who Killed Benazir Bhutto?," *Dawn*, December 27, 2017.

17. "Memogate Proceedings: Pasha Denies Any Coup Planned after May 2 Raid," *Express Tribune*, April 6, 2012.

18. Hasnat Malik, "SC Wraps Up Memogate Case, Says State Free to Pursue Haqqani," *Express Tribune*, February 14, 2019.

19. Khurram Husain, "Reversing the 18th Amendment?," *Dawn*, March 22, 2018.

20. "Bilawal Displays Diplomatic Chops in Interview to Indian Publication," *Dawn*, January 27, 2018.

21. "A General State of Disarray in Pakistan," *Economist,* May 17, 2007.

22. "Three Indicted in Imran Farooq Murder Case," *Dawn*, May 3, 2018.

23. "MQM-Establishment Love and Hate Relationship," *The News*, September 29, 2014.

24. "Altaf Received Funds from RAW, MQM Man Confesses to London Police," *Pakistan Today*, March 19, 2016.

25. Owen Bennett Jones, "Pakistan's MQM 'Received Indian Funding,'" BBC News, June 24, 2015.

26. Zubair Ashraf, "Sattar Asks CJ, COAS to Take Notice of 'Forced' Switches to PSP," *The News*, April 16, 2018.

27. Author interview of Pakistan Navy officers, 1994.

28. Raza Rumi, "The Fall of Nawaz Sharif," OPEN Magazine, August 4, 2017, http://www.openthemagazine.com/article/world/the-fall-of-nawaz-sharif.

29. Rumi, "Fall of Nawaz Sharif."

30. Rumi, "Fall of Nawaz Sharif."

31. Rumi, "Fall of Nawaz Sharif."

32. Interview of Admiral (Ret.) Fasih Bokhari, Islamabad, December 3.

33. The Lahore Declaration was a bilateral agreement signed by India and Pakistan about the development of nuclear arsenal and the unauthorized use of nuclear weapons.

34. "The Truth about Nawaz Sharif's Exile Deal," *The News*, April 24, 2013.

35. "Nawaz Regrets Being a Part of Memogate," *Pakistan Today*, March 27, 2018.

36. Zahra-Malik, "Arrests and Intimidation."

37. Tahir Naseer, "IHC Judge Makes Startling Allegations against Security Agencies 'Meddling' in Judicial Affairs," *Dawn*, July 21, 2018.

38. "Two Ex-ISI Chiefs Pushed Anti-Govt London Plan of Sit-in: Defense Minister," *The News*, July 13, 2015.

39. Muhammed Ziauddin, "The Devil Is in the Details," *Daily Times*, May 5, 2018.

40. Mofidul Hoque, "Pakistani Viewpoint: Killing of Bengali Intellectuals," *Daily Star*, December 14, 2017.

41. Interviews of on-duty policemen, Islamabad, 2017.

42. Ilyas M. Khan, "Why Was Pakistan General Giving Money to Protestors?" BBC News, November 29, 2017.

13

Judicial Politics in a Hybrid Democracy
Pakistan's Judiciary and Political Parties

Yasser Kureshi

In Pakistan's unceasing political turmoil, with power repeatedly alternating between political parties and unelected civil and military bureaucracies, the superior courts have always been a central feature, defining and redefining the legal framework underlying the distribution of power. Throughout much of its history Pakistan's superior judiciary was seen by democrats as "the junior partner" of the Pakistani military: legitimizing coups, providing the military's political actions legal cover, and undermining democratically elected governments (Oldenberg 2016, 89). However, in recent years the judiciary has charted a more independent course, particularly after the courts clashed with Gen. Pervez Musharraf's regime in 2007, a moment of judicial resolve that catalyzed the end of the military leader's government (Ghias 2010). The question this chapter considers is how variation in the relationship between the military and the judiciary has affected political parties and the prospects of a consolidated elected democracy in Pakistan.

As institutional interlinkages between the military and the judiciary have diminished, the judiciary has shifted from collaborating with the military in sustaining military rule and depoliticizing the state to creating space for political parties to operate and facilitating the state's return to constitutional democracy. However, at the same time the judiciary continues to share the military's disdain for political parties and Parliament and has thus sought to regulate political parties, in turn undermining elected governments.

I integrate methods from both social science and legal studies to explain the evolution of the relationship between the military, the judiciary, and political parties.[1] A longitudinal analysis of the institutional evolution of the judiciary tracks how institutional interlinkages between the judiciary and military evolved over time and then traces the process by which these changes affected the jurisprudence of the courts during alternating periods of military and democratic rule. I select major court decisions from three periods of military rule (1958–69, 1977–88, and 1999–2008) related to questions on the legality of military coups, on legislative actions by the military, on limitations of party activity, and on the detention of major party figures. Comparing these three periods allows me to draw out the divergence between the judiciary and the military over questions of political party operations and democratic rule over time. I also select judgments on two questions the judiciary dealt with within each period of democratic rule: the dissolution of assemblies in the 1990s and the disqualification of prime ministers after 2008. These lines of jurisprudence demonstrate how the judiciary used its powers during democratic periods to manage political parties according to its own institutional interests, as opposed to safeguarding elected parliamentary supremacy.

I collected information on reported court judgments from published annual court reports compiling these judgments.[2] I also collected information on the professional backgrounds of Supreme Court judges from several sources, including the website of the Supreme Court, judges' retirement speeches in published annual court reports, and published biographies of judges. To understand the changing political environment surrounding changes in the Court's jurisprudence, I collected relevant newspaper articles from newspaper archives. Finally, given the limited public information on judicial appointments and judicial deliberation, I interviewed influential lawyers and retired judges to gain more information.[3] Thus, while there are few consolidated sources of information on the Pakistani judiciary, triangulating information from judicial decisions, judges' speeches, newspaper articles, and interviews helps create a more complete picture of the processes underlying judicial decision-making and the relationship between the military, the judiciary, and political parties.

This chapter proceeds as follows. First, it builds on current literature on judicial politics to propose an institutional explanation for how the military and political parties seek to gain the support and acquiescence of the judiciary, either by weakening the courts or, more consequentially, by developing institutional interlinkages with the courts. A comparison of the judiciary's composition and jurisprudence during three periods of military rule shows how diminishing institutional links between the military and the judiciary have led to gradual divergence between the two institutions on questions of military rule and electoral democracy. An examination of the judiciary's composition and jurisprudence during two periods of democratic rule demonstrates how the judiciary's increasing autonomy from the military was not enough to ensure its support for democratic consolidation and the supremacy of elected parties. The final section contains an examination of the tactics used by the Pakistan People's Party (PPP) to gain the support and ac-quiescence of the judiciary and analyzes why these efforts largely failed. This study reveals the strategies that elected and unelected power centers have used to gain judicial support. It demonstrates that an institutionally and atti-tudinally independent judiciary can facilitate democratic transitions but may also undermine democratic consolidation in its pursuit of judicial supremacy.

Institutional Dissonance and Institutional Interlinkages

Pakistan belongs to a group of "hybrid" states in which power remains con-tested and negotiated between political and bureaucratic power centers.[4] During periods of parliamentary democracy, unelected civilian and military bureaucracies remain politically formidable; during periods of dictatorship the military is unable to completely depoliticize the state and rule on its own and must share power with pliable political parties. In such states, power cen-ters develop contrasting visions of the polity that they use to rationalize the preeminent role they seek to play (Shambayati 2008). Brumberg (2001, 33) describes this phenomenon as "dissonant institutionalization" where "com-peting images of political community and the symbolic systems legitimating them are reproduced in the formal and informal institutions of state and society."

The judiciary is placed in a unique position as arbiter of this dissonance as it interprets the constitutional framework underlying the political order of the state. Thus, one characteristic of these states is the judicialization of "megapolitics," where matters of great political significance, including elec-toral outcomes and corroboration of regime change, are decided by the courts (Hirschl 2008, 93). Where the judiciary occupies a position of such relevance, both sides seek it as an ally in legitimizing and sustaining their power.

As the relevance and authority of the judiciary has grown across differ-ent regime types, a growing body of literature has demonstrated the ways in which political parties and state institutions seek to ensure that the judiciary upholds their interests in contests with other actors and institutions. Re-gimes seeking to ensure the judiciary's acquiescence could either weaken or threaten to weaken the courts' authority to keep them in line (Helmke and Rios-Figueroa 2011). Ginsburg and Moustafa (2008) write that the judiciary can be weakened by fragmenting the judicial system into parallel courts and restructuring the power of judicial review and the right to access the courts. Meierhenrich (2008) describes how the South African apartheid govern-ment responded to adverse rulings of the courts by limiting its jurisdiction. Weakening tactics that restrict the authority of the courts and the credible threat of such tactics help ensure that a strategic court remains in line with the threatening institution.

However, a *loyal* court is a more durable ally than a *weak* court, as the loyal court will uphold the institutional interests of its allies even when formal political power shifts hands. Judicial loyalty can be assured when the institutional norms and preferences of the judiciary align with the preferences of the regime (Hilbink 2007). Scholars of judicial politics in new democracies have shown how outgoing regimes design the institutional powers and compose the judiciary to ensure judges act as downstream guarantors of outgoing regimes' interests, even after the regime is removed from power (Ginsburg 2003; Meierhenrich 2008; Bali 2012). Institutionalist scholars have moved beyond questions of institutional design to examine how the culture of judiciaries ensure the construction of norms of loyalty and deference to political parties and military regimes (Hilbink 2007; Couso and Hilbink 2011; Couso, Huneeus, and Sieder 2011). Kapiszewski (2010) explains how the *internal culture* of the judiciary—the interaction of ideas and practices that shape the way high courts engage in politics and policymaking—is influenced by external institutions, namely the formal rules and informal norms guiding the composition and independence of the courts.

Most of the literature on the construction of judicial constraints and culture by civilian and military regimes explains this reality as a product of institutional design and interinstitutional relationships. This current study emphasizes the importance of both the judiciary's institutional relationships *and* its sociology in the development of its institutional culture. There are two means by which external actors can intervene to shape the internal culture of the judiciary: (1) by ensuring that the authorities charged with judicial appointments, promotions, case assignments, and discipline are affiliated with or supportive of the installed regime so that only those judges who support the regime or its affiliated elites move forward, and (2) by ensuring that judges are appointed from social and professional networks tied to the regime.[5] Judges from particular social and professional backgrounds identify with those who share their backgrounds and similar preferences, thus affecting their decision-making.

Both judicial appointment gatekeepers and judicial recruitment networks combine to shape the internal culture of the judiciary. It is through these linkages that external actors, including the military and political parties, can develop interlinkages with the judiciary and shape institutional ideas and practices in their favor.[6] A study of this interactive process of judicial norm formation and change can help us understand both the choices judges make in managing the dissonance of hybrid states and why their choices change over time. Studying interactions and institutional interlinkages between Pakistan's military, political parties, and judiciary sheds light on the processes of judicial norm formation and its consequences for multiparty democracy in hybrid states.

The Judiciary, the Military, and Political Parties

Dissonant institutionalism has been evident in Pakistan since its inception in 1947, when a tradition of bureaucratic authoritarianism was already deeply rooted (Jalal 1990). A powerful set of paternalistic executive institutions had been established by the British Empire, while political institutions were weakly developed (Talbot 1998). After independence, military officers and civil servants imbibed the colonial officials' view that nationalist politicians and political parties were untrustworthy agitators and politics were divisive and parochial; together these necessitated the oversight and guidance of organized professional institutions (Shah 2014b). On the other end, Pakistan's political parties sought to mobilize popular national and subnational identities and patronage networks in order to win parliamentary elections and gain control over the distribution of political resources (Talbot 1998).

Where did the judiciary fit into this civil-military dissonance? Three strands of literature that assess the political role of the judiciary in Pakistan exist. The dominant strand restricts its focus to the period immediately before and after 2007 and identifies factors unique to the judicial assertiveness of that period (M. Malik 2008; Ghias 2010; Cheema and Gilani 2015; Siddique 2015; Shafqat 2017). A second strand focuses on specific prominent decisions in the judiciary's history, such as major military coup decisions, but not on the evolution of judicial institutions (Hasan 2001; H. Khan 2005). A third historicized approach tracks the Supreme Court's jurisprudence over time but seeks to explain the trajectory of the Court primarily through the text of its decisions (Newberg 1995; M. Khan 2015). I use this historicized legal approach combined with an assessment of social science methods to explain the evolution of the relationship between the military, the judiciary, and political parties.

Judiciary in Transition

Following independence, the Pakistani judiciary arrived in two streams: from the civil service cadres trained in the British-run civil service and from lawyers trained to be barristers in the United Kingdom (Braibanti 1999). Hence, the officers of the judiciary, the bureaucracy, and the military all came from the same elite class of British-trained officers who had been trained and socialized in the practices and principles of colonial administration. During this period the final word on judicial appointments lay with the executive branch. The military ruler consulted senior judges but had the final word in judicial selection, ensuring that appointed judges upheld the interests of the regime. Thus, through both the judicial appointment system and the recruitment pool the military had close institutional interlinkages with the judiciary.

However, between 1969 and 1999 the institutional interlinkages between the military and the judiciary steadily diminished. The 1973 Constitution mandated the separation of the judiciary from the executive, ending the civil service as a professional pipeline for the judiciary. After 1973 a majority of high court judges were selected laterally from the bar of professional lawyers; a minority were promoted from within the judicial services of the lower courts. Consequently, over time fewer judges recruited from the elite network of British-trained civil service officers remained, as shown in figure 13.1.[7] In *Al Jehad Trust v Federation of Pakistan* (1996) the Supreme Court amended the judicial appointment process to give the chief justice the primary role in the appointment of high court judges.[8] A former judge explained that prior to this decision, uniformed and bureaucratic contacts "were useful through the mid-90s (for becoming a judge), but the *Al-Jehad* decision changed this."[9] Institutional interlinkages between the military and the judiciary diminished during this period.

Second, from the 1980s onward the bar of professional lawyers, from which judges were being increasingly recruited, grew more politicized, adopting an activist political agenda and mobilizing in pursuit of that agenda. During the 1970s and 1980s political debates of the time permeated the bar as its leaders became more politically active and the proportion of "political lawyers increased, whose real vocation was politics."[10] Soon the bar associations became a venue for criticizing military rule and agitating for a return to constitutional democracy.[11]

Thus the separation of the judiciary from the military and the politicization of most judges ensured that the military's institutional interlinkages with the judiciary diminished and the internal culture of the judiciary changed. The military and the judiciary's visions of the political order grew increasingly dissonant: the judiciary increasingly came to support a more democratic political structure, an expansion of its role, and more space in which political parties could operate and participate.

The Judiciary under Military Regimes

It is useful to understand the impact of the divergence between the military and the judiciary on regarding judiciary's approach toward political parties across three military regimes: that of Field Marshal Mohammed Ayub Khan (1958–1969), of Gen. Muhammad Zia-ul-Haq (1977–1988), and of Gen. Pervez Musharraf (1999–2008).

COLLABORATION IN DEPOLITICIZATION: 1958–69. The deep institutional interlinkages between the judiciary, the military, and the civil service during Mohammad Ayub Khan's regime meant that the judiciary was loyal to the military's vision of the state and used its power to uphold it. The judiciary favored a strong unelected executive that could hold back the tide of mass

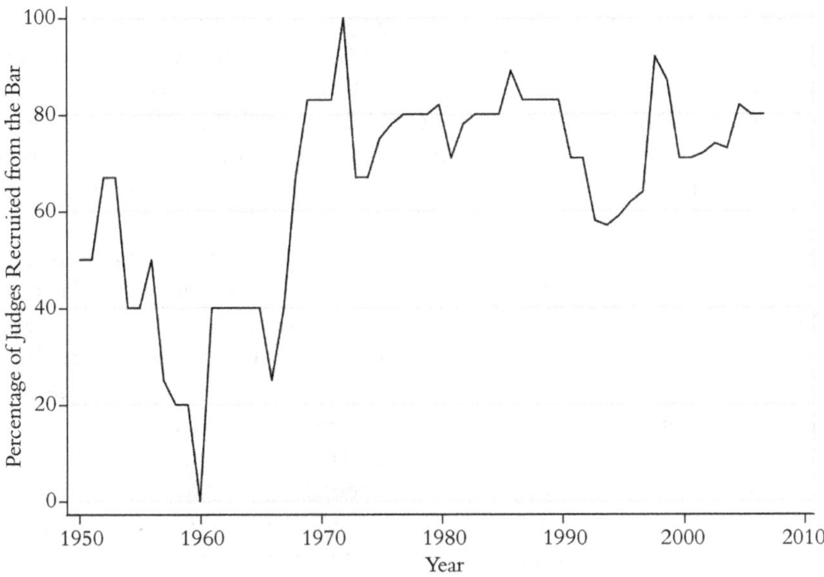

Figure 13.1. Percentage of Supreme Court judges recruited from the bar of professional lawyers

Source: Data compiled by author.
Note: Data includes the professional backgrounds of 102 of the 108 judges appointed from 1950 to 2007.

politics. "Like the colonial judge, the judge of the superior courts thought that the executive and state were synonymous. . . . The principle of the separation of power was not present in the minds of the judges."[12]

In the 1955 cases *Maulvi Tamizuddin* and *Governor General's Reference*, the Supreme Court supported the military-backed governor-generals' dissolution of the elected constituent assemblies, determining that this action was necessary to "prevent the State from dissolution and the constitutional and administrative machinery from breaking down." This formulated legal doctrine became the legal foundation for a series of subsequent military takeovers.[13] In *State v Dosso* (1958) Chief Justice Muhammad Munir "seized on this opportunity to declare Ayub Khan's coup constitutionally valid," upholding martial law and the abrogation of the constitution.[14]

In 1962 Ayub Khan's regime passed the Political Parties Act, which permitted the formation of political parties but restricted political party activities. Judges disagreed over the place of fundamental rights within this new political order, but they did not question the organization of the garrison state. The judiciary overturned the unilateral dissolution of the Jamaat-e-Islami political party, upholding the rights of the party and its members.[15] But its defense of the Jamaat-e-Islami was not extended to rights petitions by left-wing socialist, communist, or nationalist political parties that were viewed as a greater threat to the state.[16] Similarly, the courts upheld the detention of most political figures who rallied against Ayub's regime.[17] The institutional interlinkages between the military and the judiciary ensured that the courts were closely engaged in the antipolitics state-building agenda. They actively collaborated in the military's depoliticization project.

FROM COLLABORATION TO MILITARY SUBORDINATION: 1977–88. The judiciary further collaborated with the military in bringing an end to Zulfikar Ali Bhutto's civilian government in 1977. High court judges willingly swore an oath to the military regime (Sidhwa 1989), and the Supreme Court both upheld Muhammad Zia-ul-Haq's military takeover and removal of the PPP government on the grounds of necessity and approved the execution of Bhutto (H. Khan 2016).[18] After General Zia came to power he banned all political activity and suspended all fundamental rights. The regime targeted political parties and their members, especially the PPP, for arrest and detention and gave martial law administrators and military courts broad powers to detain and try individuals involved in political activity.

The civilian courts became flooded with petitions challenging military court decisions, detentions by martial law administrators, and martial law legislation. Most high court judges at the time were appointed from the more politically engaged lawyers' community, which was reflected in the divergence between the judgments of the Supreme Court and those of other high courts. While the senior-most judges of the Supreme Court upheld the discretionary powers of the military regime, junior members of the changing judiciary sought to limit the regime's discretion. Between 1977 and 1981 the Supreme Court had thirteen reported judgments concerning actions by martial law administrators and military courts; it upheld the military's actions in twelve of the thirteen cases, but as table 13.1 shows, the high courts were more willing to place restrictions on the military regime.

In cases concerning political leaders and political activists, the Sindh and Balochistan high courts limited the regime's detention powers and questioned constitutional orders made by Zia and execution orders made by the military courts (Rizvi 2000).[19] The challenge to Zia's regime from the high courts was limited but significant, indicating a developing divergence.

In 1981 Zia recognized this divergence and chose to weaken the courts and remove all judges who were not willing to acquiesce to the will of the regime. The regime instituted a new provisional constitutional order (PCO) that weakened the judiciary by drastically reducing its powers and jurisdiction and compelling judges to swear a new oath to the regime.[20] Most judges accepted the oath in order to preserve their careers.[21]

In 1985 Zia restored the 1973 Constitution with important amendments that contained dissonant visions of the state: Parliament was restored, but

Table 13.1. Summary of reported judgments by high courts on rulings by military courts and martial law administrators, 1978–79

	Reported judgments by high courts	
	For the regime	*Against the regime*
1978	36	20
1979	16	24

Source: Data compiled by author using publicly reported judgments.
Note: Data includes only 1978 and 1979 because courts were curtailed from hearing such cases in 1980 and ousted in 1981.

the unelected branches were given important controls over the system.[22] Initially Zia permitted only parliamentary elections on a nonparty basis, as political parties were still prohibited from organizing. In the historic 1988 judgment *Benazir Bhutto v Federation of Pakistan,* the Supreme Court overturned Zia's restriction on political parties contesting elections, clearing the path for party-based elections.[23] In supporting political parties the judiciary attempted to create a "symbolic break with the past" of complicity with the military (M. Khan 2015, 306). After years of silence the Court reasserted its fundamental jurisdiction, expanded its original jurisdiction to loosen the requirement of an aggrieved party in a case of public interest, and moved beyond the focus on procedural rights.[24] Zia's period exemplified the early but significant divergence between the judiciary and the military.

FROM SUBORDINATION TO ASSERTION: 1999–2008. In 1999 Pervez Musharraf ousted Nawaz Sharif's elected government. Musharraf's military coup was soon challenged on legal grounds. However, before the Court could hear the petition Musharraf instituted a new PCO similar to the one Zia had installed in 1981 to purge and control the judiciary. This time seven Supreme Court judges refused to take the oath of loyalty, twice as many who had refused in 1981.[25] The newly purged Court once more upheld a military coup.[26] But even as it did it articulated a more expansive role for the judiciary than previous validating courts had, emphasizing the judiciary's independence while claiming that the Court would overturn constitutional amendments that "undermine the independence of the judiciary."[27]

During the initial years of Musharraf's regime, and given the restrictions placed by the PCO, the judiciary remained cautious and muted: it validated Musharraf's run for the presidency while still serving as chief of army staff (COAS) and confirmed his constitutional amendments and referendum.[28]

By the time Musharraf came to power the judiciary had been largely separated from the executive and wielded considerably greater independence and control over judicial appointments. One senior lawyer interviewed stated, "By quality of appointments made, it would not be inaccurate to say quality of judicial appointments improved. Between 1997 and 1999, appointments were of those who . . . had all been successful lawyers."[29] A majority of these judges had been lawyers during the 1980s, when bar associations mobilized politically against the military regime. Also, given the changes that had taken place in the internal culture of the bar and the bench, bar associations targeted and delegitimized judges who collaborated with the military regime.[30] This cadre of judges enjoyed more distance from the military than in any previous era, which was reflected in judicial decisions, particularly after 2005.

Under Chief Justice Iftikhar Chaudhry, who was elevated in 2005, the judiciary intervened in a range of new political, social, and economic activities. At the Supreme Court level the vehicle for this expansion was public interest litigation, which increased dramatically during this period.[31] As the courts expanded their jurisdiction they engaged in high-risk activism by crossing "red lines" with the military government. The judiciary heard cases challenging the military regime's political foundations, accepting petitions challenging Musharraf's prerogative to stand for election, to exile political opponents, and to maintain both the offices of president and COAS (H. Khan 2016). This assertiveness led to increased support by political parties, which came to see the courts as a venue for challenging the regime (Shafqat 2017).

The judiciary's activism was risky, however, and the courts ultimately paid the price. In November 2007 Musharraf tried to bring the judiciary under control by instituting a new PCO, but this time a majority of high court judges, supported by the bar associations, did not take the oath.[32] Political parties aligned with the Court, and an alliance of parties, civil society, and the legal community, helped bring down Musharraf's regime.

By 2007 the judiciary neither collaborated with the military nor was subordinate to it. Instead, it saw itself as equally if not more capable of reshaping and reforming Pakistan's political order. As Justice Ramday opined in *Justice Iftikhar Muhammad Chaudhry v the President of Pakistan*, "The time has come to put the nation on a right path . . . and remove all excessive and colorable exercise of power in each and every sphere of government."[33] The Court was articulating a new vision of judicial supremacy.

Over the course of three military regimes the divergence between the military and the judiciary opened up space for political parties to operate and resist military dominance. Indeed, the judiciary played a significant role in transitioning the state out of military rule.

The Judiciary during Democratic Rule

One question remains: During democratic periods did the divergence between the judiciary and the military help facilitate democratic consolidation? Certainly opposition to military rule does not necessarily imply support for the supremacy of civilian political parties. Leaders of the bar, from which judges were recruited, had little faith in political parties. They viewed the bar as a true reflection of public aspirations and the judiciary as the vehicle for safeguarding fundamental rights and pursuing policies in the public interest. A 1999 speech by the Sindh High Court Bar Association president articulated this perspective: "Our representatives are intellectual destitutes in whom the faculty for thought has become atrophied. The edifice of our democratic system is built upon the foundations of illiteracy and ignorance . . . promises of just governance have become fairy tales. . . . We need to structure a judiciary to even strike down laws which in its considered opinion are harsh, unjust . . . or counterproductive."[34]

During two democratic periods, 1988–99 and 2008–2017, this same attitude of the bar is reflected in the judiciary's decision-making. The judiciary's growing independence from the military did not bring it closer to supporting Pakistan's political parties and parliamentary supremacy.

Between 1988 and 1999 the courts had to rule on the presidential dissolution of the National Assembly on four occasions. The superior judiciary was still mostly composed of judges appointed during Pakistan's earlier military regimes, and the military was still strong enough to wield pressure on it. In *Haji Saifullah* (1988) the Court found President Zia's dissolution order illegal, observing that the power of dissolution can be used by the president only in a narrowly circumscribed set of objectively extraordinary situations.[35] However, the Supreme Court surprisingly did not grant relief for the restoration of the assemblies, commenting that "interrupting the election process was politically infeasible" (Newberg 1995, 209). Some years later the former chief of army staff, Aslam Beg, publicly claimed that he had pressured the Court not to reinstate the assemblies (H. Khan 2016).

In both dissolution decisions pertaining to Muslim League governments (1988 and 1993), the Court rejected the presidential dissolution of power, upholding a restrictive reading of the power of the president to dissolve the assemblies, and in 1993 it restored the dissolved assemblies.[36] On the other hand, in the two dissolution decisions pertaining to the PPP governments (1990 and 1997) the judiciary set a far more lenient and subjective standard for presidential dissolution, expanding the president's discretion to dissolve the assemblies.[37] Siddique (2006, 665) writes that under the lenient standard, dissolution was not only legitimate as a "curative action, but also a preventive one." The contradictory positions taken by the judges in these cases were even more surprising given that it was often the same judges providing dramatically different interpretations of the president's powers.[38]

The jurisprudence of dissolutions provides an important insight into the combination of strategies and attitudes shaping the Court during this period. Why did the judiciary choose to restore Sharif's Muslim League government? First, Sharif had started his political career as part of Zia's regime, and his rise to power had been partially engineered by the military. The judiciary was therefore less concerned about military opposition and retaliation when restoring him. Second, as one lawyer pointed out, "Nawaz Sharif, just like many of these judges, was a product of Zia's establishment. A lot of the judges who approved the restoration of the assemblies in the Nawaz Sharif judgment were judges who formerly belonged to the Lahore High Court (when Sharif was Chief Minister of Punjab) and had close ties to him."[39]

Thus Sharif's Muslim League already enjoyed institutional interlinkages with the judiciary: they belonged to the same politically conservative social networks from which Zia had recruited political and judicial appointees. Chief Justice Nasim Shah, who presided over the bench restoring Sharif's government, was known to be close to Sharif.[40] Chief Justice Saeeduzzaman, Siddiqui's wife, was employed in Sharif's second government, and later Siddiqui himself was appointed governor during Sharif's third tenure.[41] When a group of Supreme Court judges successfully mutinied against Chief Justice Sajjad Ali Shah in 1997, they had Sharif's support (H. Khan 2016). And when Sharif's party workers stormed the Court in a show of aggression in 1997, the same judges who had relied on his support to overthrow Justice Sajjad Ali Shah exonerated Sharif's close aides from any wrongdoing.[42] It is clear the Muslim League benefited from prior linkages with the judiciary, and Sharif continued to rely on these linkages throughout the 1990s.

In contrast, the PPP did not fare as well with the judiciary for two reasons. First, the judiciary was strategically navigating the configuration of power at the time: the military and the presidency actively opposed the PPP, making decisions to restore the PPP governments riskier, especially as the military's ability to pressure the judiciary persisted. Second, nearly all judges appointed by Z. A. Bhutto had been removed from the judiciary by Zia, and most judges appointed during Zia's regime were politically conservative and expected to uphold his Islamization policies and reject the more left-wing politics of the PPP.[43] The PPP did not enjoy any institutional linkages with the courts and remained ideologically at odds with the conservatism on the bench.

Even as the judiciary gained more independence in this era, its commitment to the supremacy of elected government was tempered by pressure it felt from the military, by its close ties with the Muslim League during the 1990s, and by conservatives' distrust of the PPP. Taken together these made democratic consolidation elusive.

After 2008 the judiciary helped bring an end to military rule, but its resistance to Musharraf was triggered by his specific efforts to undermine the judiciary's independence when ousting the chief justice, not by the judiciary's support for elected parliamentary supremacy. Following the events of 2007 this newly independent and assertive judiciary, which enjoyed few interlinkages with the military, with the Muslim League, or with the PPP, leaned toward the notion of judicial supremacy and a judicially regulated democracy. As a lawyer in the 1990s, Justice Asif Saeed Khan Khosa, a prominent judge post–2008, had written that "legislators passed their time passing motions about breach of privileges, and the judiciary had to arrest this repugnancy" (Azeem 2017, 224). The consensus view of the judiciary was that political parties were corrupt and did not act in the public interest and that the judiciary was best suited to tackle this corruption (Aziz 2015). Between 2008 and 2017 the judiciary intervened in all areas of political life, reversing decisions that fell within the regulatory frameworks of other state institutions (Siddique 2015).

Most significant, as part of its drive against political corruption the judiciary ousted two elected prime ministers. The president's power to dissolve elected assemblies had been removed by 2009, but the Supreme Court's power to oust parliamentarians for not fulfilling vague standards of morality and sagacity, as stated under Articles 62 and 63, remained; these powers became the vehicle for the unelected judiciary to manipulate the arrangement of elected authority.[44] In 2012 the Supreme Court ousted Prime Minister Syed Yousaf Raza Gilani (of the PPP) after convicting him of contempt of court because he had refused to write a letter to Swiss authorities to reopen corruption cases against his party leader, Pres. Asif Ali Zardari. Justice Iftikhar Muhammad Chaudhry had ordered Gilani to write this letter simply because the courts were interested in pursuing corruption cases against the PPP leadership.[45]

In 2017 the Court ousted Prime Minister Nawaz Sharif from power under Article 62, based on misdeclaration of assets and allegations of corruption.[46] The judiciary's actions in this case were even more assertive: Gilani's removal was based on an actual conviction, but Sharif had not yet been convicted of a crime. A misdeclaration of assets was considered enough to have him removed from power without the possibility of appeal. Justice Khosa opined that Article 62 "provides a recipe for cleansing the fountainhead of authority of the State so that the trickled down authority may also become unpolluted. If this is achieved then the legislative and executive limbs of the State are purified at the top."[47] Between 2017 and 2018 the Court used Articles 62 and 63 to purge electoral politics of the politicians it deemed unworthy of political office, interpreting violations of the articles as grounds for a lifetime ban from politics. Unlike the 1990s, the ruling Muslim League bore the brunt of the Court's usage of Article 62 and lost its leadership and significant public support as a result of several court decisions. This boosted the electoral fortunes of the Pakistan Tehreek-e-Insaf (PTI), which ultimately won a plurality of seats in the 2018 election and replaced the Muslim League government.[48]

In a period after military rule, democratic consolidation continues to elude the state as the dissonance grows. An independent judiciary may help facilitate democratic transitions but may also undermine democratic consolidation and the supremacy of elected government.

Judicial Strategies of Political Parties

Why were political parties unable to gain the support of the judiciary for elected parliamentary supremacy? The PPP, like the military, tried to both weaken the judiciary and reshape its internal culture to ensure its support. Both strategies backfired because the party had neither the institutional interlinkages with the judiciary nor the centralized coercive power enjoyed by military regimes. The PPP, unlike the Muslim League during the 1990s, consistently faced an adversarial judiciary and was unable to build linkages with the judiciary, which highlights the importance of these linkages in explaining judicial behavior toward political parties.

THE FAILURE OF INSTITUTIONAL WEAKENING. The era of constitutional democratic rule in the 1970s allowed the judiciary to arbitrate the contradiction between the promise of constitutional democratic rule and the quasi-authoritarian limitations on constitutional rights perpetuated by Z. A. Bhutto's PPP government. As his government grew more authoritarian, Bhutto used statutes and constitutional amendments to institutionally weaken the judiciary, imposing restrictions on procedural rights and reducing judicial oversight of executive actions.[49] Bhutto also alienated the legal community, much of which belonged to the more conservative urban middle class that was opposed to his populist alliance of rural landholders and the working class. Particularly in Lahore, leading bar associations openly allied themselves with the Pakistan National Alliance, a coalition of political parties challenging Bhutto's regime.[50]

Bhutto's strategy of institutionally weakening the judiciary and increasing authoritarian suppression of the bar associations placed him at odds with much of the legal community. In 1977 the Lahore high court overturned the declaration of Bhutto's martial law and the establishment of military courts, upholding its own jurisdiction under the 1973 Constitution.[51] However, in the same decision the court held that martial law *can* be imposed if the constitution is abrogated under the doctrine of necessity, signaling its willingness to validate an extra-constitutional intervention against Bhutto. When General Zia-ul-Haq assumed power following a military coup in 1977 that ousted Bhutto's PPP government, the alienated judiciary initially collaborated in the new political order.

FAILING TO BUILD INSTITUTIONAL INTERLINKAGES. Given that the judiciary upheld Zia's coup, sanctioned Bhutto's execution, and dissolved Benazir Bhutto's government in 1990, many members of the PPP believed that a strong institutional bias against the PPP was locked into the judiciary. A lawyer affiliated with the PPP explained his belief this way: "Between 1988 and 1999 there was a compact between the judiciary and the army against the PPP. The Court was anti-Benazir and the PPP. Judges who had convicted and hanged Bhutto [her father] were serving judges on the [Supreme Court] bench."[52]

Benazir Bhutto's government sought to reshape the bench by building institutional interlinkages and appointing judges from networks of lawyers and legal practitioners who belonged to the PPP. In 1994 "Benazir sought to appoint 18 judges to the Lahore High Court all chosen by her, without any input from the judges," which judges feared would "change the entire face of the court."[53] Questions were raised by prominent lawyers and civil society leaders about the credentials and capability of these judicial appointees, which included "people who had not even seen the High Courts, ever."[54]

Bhutto's attempts to alter the recruitment pool of judges deeply aggrieved senior judges. Her actions triggered the famous *Al-Jihad* decision in which the judiciary, with opposition and presidential support, wrested control over the appointment procedure from the executive. Bhutto's attempts to pack the courts with loyalists miscarried, leading to the elected government losing its role in the appointment process.[55] Since the PPP did not enjoy a monopoly over political or coercive power, its strategies of institutional weakening and developing institutional interlinkages were largely unsuccessful, and the judiciary remained an adversary, intervening to challenge the administration's leadership and undercut its governance policies.

Conclusion

The Pakistani judiciary has played a critical role in managing the institutional dissonance between Pakistan's military and its civilian political parties. Both the military and the parties have sought to gain support and acquiescence by pursuing policies of institutional weakening and building institutional interlinkages with the judiciary. As these interlinkages have diminished over time, the judiciary has grown more autonomous from the military and ultimately has played an important role in helping political parties survive and transition the state to civilian democratic rule. However, the examples here show that an independent judiciary may help facilitate a return to democratic rule but may also undermine democratic consolidation because the pursuit of judicial supremacy can lead to a judiciary that regulates political parties, filters their leadership, and picks favorites. The 2018 elections demonstrate the judiciary's impact on democratic consolidation: the courts engineered the political landscape, weakened the incumbent Muslims League party, and set the stage for the PTI to come into power for the first time. Today Pakistan's judiciary has not reconciled the institutional dissonance between the military and political parties. Instead, three institutional visions of the state survive: a military-centered praetorian democracy, a party-centered parliamentary democracy, and a court-centered judicial democracy. These three visions coexist in a state of constant tension, leaving political parties susceptible to interventions by the military and the judiciary and a democracy that is unstable and unconsolidated.

Notes

1. Azeem (2017) and Siddique (2006) also integrate social science into their judicial studies.
2. Only court judgments that carry significance as precedents for future jurisprudence are reported, but this covers all the judgments impactful enough to affect these issues.
3. To protect anonymity, interviewed judges and lawyers are assigned the letters J and L, respectively, and a random number between 1 and 100 generated and assigned to each interview, e.g., J-40. All interviews are referenced only by a code and the interview date.
4. Similar states include Turkey, Nigeria, and Brazil during the 1990s (Adeney 2017).
5. The idea that the social and professional sources of judicial recruitment shape the values and ideals of judges is well-established among law and society scholars (Ladinski 1963; Edelman 1992).
6. By institutional interlinkages I mean that the military and military-affiliated elites are linked to the inner workings of the judicial institutions through their role in setting judicial career paths and judicial recruitment networks.
7. "Certainly Not a Bureaucrat-Dominated Judiciary," *Leader*, September 30, 1995.
8. *Al-Jehad Trust v Federation of Pakistan*. PLD 1996 Supreme Court 324.
9. Interview J-19, April 23, 2017.
10. Interview L-42, April 1, 2017.
11. Interview L-42, April 1, 2017.
12. Interview L-42, April 1, 2017.
13. *Federation of Pakistan v Maulvi Tamizuddin Khan*, PLD 1955 FC 240; *Reference by His Excellency Governor-General*, 1955 PLD FC 435.
14. *State v Dosso*, 1958 PLD SC 533; interview L-42.
15. *Saiyyid Abul A la Maudoodi et al. v The Government of West Pakistan and the Government of Pakistan*, PLD 1964 SC 673.
16. *Mian Iftikhar-ud-din and Arif Iftikhar v Muhammad Sarfaraz*, PLD 1961 Lahore 842.
17. *Malik Ghulam Jilani v The Government of West Pakistan*, PLD 1967 SC 373.
18. *Begum Nusrat Bhutto v the Chief of Army Staff and Federation of Pakistan*, PLD 1977 Supreme Court 657.
19. *Mumtaz Ali Bhutto and Another v The Deputy Martial Law Administrator, Sector 1, Karachi and 2 Others*, PLD 1979 Karachi 307; *Yaqoob Ali v. Presiding Officer, Summary Military Court, Karachi*, PLD 1985 Karachi 243.
20. The PCO was announced at the same time that the Supreme Court accepted a petition appeal challenging the validation of Zia's constitutional amendments.
21. Only four Supreme Court judges did not take the oath, of which at least one, Maulvi Mushtaq, was denied the oath. Eleven high court judges did not take the oath (Rizvi 2000).

22. 8th Amendment, 1973 Constitution of Pakistan (1985).

23. *Benazir Bhutto v Federation of Pakistan*, PLD 1988 Supreme Court 416.

24. "SC Judgment—I—Law, a Vehicle of Social, Economic Justice," *Daily News*, June 30, 1988.

25. The resignation of almost half of the Supreme Court justices raised questions about the legitimacy of Musharraf's government. See "Why the Judges Quit," *Dawn*, January 22, 2000.

26. *Syed Zafar Ali Shah and Others v General Pervez Musharraf, Chief Executive of Pakistan, and Others*, PLD 2000 SC 869.

27. *Syed Zafar Ali Shah and Others v General Pervez Musharraf, Chief Executive of Pakistan, and Others*, PLD 2000 SC 869.

28. *Watan Party v Chief Executive, President of Pakistan*, PLD 2003 SC 74; *Pakistan Lawyers' Forum v Federation of Pakistan*, PLD 2005 SC 719.

29. Interview L-50, May 18, 2017.

30. Naveed Ahmed, "SC Dismisses SCBA Statement as Contemptuous." *The News*, October 31, 2002.

31. In 2004 the number of *suo motu* cases (public interest cases taken up by the Supreme Court at its own initiative) was four; in 2005 this rose to fifteen; and in 2007 to twenty-seven (Siddiqi 2015).

32. Thirteen of seventeen Supreme Court judges and around fifty high court judges did not take the oath in 2007. See "PCO and Its Victim Judges," *Dawn*, January 7, 2008.

33. *Iftikhar Chaudhry v President of Pakistan*, PLD 2007 SC 578.

34. "System of Good Governance Has Collapsed," *Business Recorder*, May 13, 1999.

35. General Zia was already dead by the time the Court announced its decision. *Government of Pakistan v Muhammad Saifullah Khan*, PLD 1988 SC 43.

36. *Muhammad Nawaz Sharif v Federation of Pakistan*, PLD 1993 SC 473.

37. *Khwaja Ahmad Tariq Rahim v The Federation of Pakistan through Secretary, Ministry of Law and Parliamentary Affairs, and Another*, PLD 1992 SC 646; *Mohtarma Benazir Bhutto and Others v President of Pakistan and Others*, PLD 1998 SC 388.

38. Justice Shafiur Rahman authored one decision supporting dissolution and another opposing dissolution.

39. Interview L-3, May 22, 2017.

40. Intikhab Hanif, "Former CJ Nasim Shah Passes Away." *Dawn*, February 4, 2015.

41. Amina Jilani, "In His Own Cause," *Nation*, June 13, 1999.

42. Jalilur Rehman, "SC Played Key Role in Political Scene in '99," *News*, January 8, 2000.

43. Interview L-3, May 22, 2017.

44. "Qualifications for Membership of Majlis-e-Shoora," Article 62, 1973 Constitution of Pakistan; "Disqualification of Membership of Majlis-e-Shoora," Article 63, 1973 Constitution of Pakistan.

45. Criminal Original Petition No. 6 of 2012 in Suo Motu Case No. 4 of 2010, www.supremecourt.gov.pk.

46. Haseeb Bhatti, "Nawaz Sharif Steps Down as PM after SC's Disqualification Verdict," *Dawn*, July 28, 2017.

47. *Imran Ahmed Khan Niazi v Mian Muhammad Nawaz Sharif, Prime Minister of Pakistan*, Constitution Petition No. 29 of 2016, www.supremecourt.gov.pk.

48. Salman Masood and Maria Abi-Habib, "Pakistan Court Releases Nawaz Sharif, Ex-Prime Minister, from Prison," *New York Times*, September 19, 2018.

49. The 4th, 5th, 6th, and 7th Amendments of the 1973 Constitution reduced the judiciary's check on executive authority.

50. "Lawyers Take Out Procession in Lahore," *Dawn*, March 25, 1977.

51. *Darvesh M. Arbey, Advocate v Federation of Pakistan through the Law Secretary and 2 Others*, PLD 1980 Lahore 206.

52. Interview L-1, May 15, 2017.

53. Interview L-88, June 5, 2017.

54. Interview L-88, June 5, 2017.

55. The PPP sought to gain some control over the appointment process again with the passage of the 18th Amendment in 2010, but the Supreme Court overturned these efforts. See Asad Jamal, "Judicial Appointments, Again," *Express Tribune*, October 22, 2010.

14

Parties and Foreign Policy in Pakistan

Christopher Clary

Pakistan was born a frontier state, and it remains one today. Its relations with the United States, China, Afghanistan, and India directly affect the livelihood and security of ordinary Pakistanis. The United States and China have sent tens of billions of dollars in aid and investment into Pakistan in the last decade, while violence from the US global war on terrorism focused on Afghanistan has spilled over into Pakistan, contributing to the deaths of more than sixty thousand Pakistanis from terrorist violence since the attacks of September 11, 2001.[1] Pakistan's own decision to logistically, financially, and militarily support terrorist and insurgent groups operating in India has also led to domestic blowback, with members of those groups sometimes concluding that the harsh obligations of *jihad* also include attacks against Pakistanis. Evidence for why foreign policy does and should matter to everyday Pakistanis is, therefore, overabundant. Yet it is difficult to find sustained, meaningful differences on these important issues at the forefront—or even in the background—of Pakistan's cacophonous political debate. Nawaz Sharif's finances and Imran Khan's romances are the subject of countless political attacks launched with passion and zeal by political opponents. Foreign policy disputes, in contrast, have a scripted, rote quality to them. While political participants can improvise at the margins, the core themes in foreign policy discourse have near-universal adoption.

This situation, as with so many others in Pakistani society, is a result of the structural constraints imposed by civil-military relations on Pakistan's political parties. Pakistan is a praetorian state, that is, a state "in which the military tends to intervene and *potentially* could dominate the political system" (Perlmutter 1969, 383, emphasis in the original). The fact that the military sometimes recuses itself from political power and abstains from the daily machinations of politics does not eliminate the coercive effect created by its potential to intervene.

This chapter focuses on the relationship between foreign policies and political parties. Next to defense policy itself, foreign policy most impinges on the concerns and the prerogatives of the military. Furthermore, the nature of Pakistani democracy devalues programmatic policy generally and appeals on foreign policy especially. Pakistani voters are more concerned with the promise of patronage or ethnic appeals than they are with the intricacies of diplomacy overseas. Such an emphasis is no doubt rational for individual Pakistani voters and is made even more so because focusing ballot attention on foreign policy is particularly ill-advised if politicians are largely unable to alter the foreign policies preferred by military leaders. This combination of a praetorian state and patronage politics means that the potential costs for parties that stake out distinct foreign policy positions are high and the benefits of doing so are low.

Consistent with that logic, this chapter demonstrates that the strong constraints imposed by civil-military relations largely limit foreign policy debates between political parties. This homogenizes party positions and results in less varied elite cues to party supporters, which in turn generates greater consensus on many foreign policy issues in Pakistan than is present in more contentious partisan contexts elsewhere. This is especially the case for the three mainstream parties that have experience leading governing coalitions: the Pakistan Muslim League-Nawaz (PML-N), the Pakistan People's Party (PPP), and the Pakistan Tehreek-e-Insaf (PTI). Nonetheless, important instances exist in which individual civilian leaders have been able to make critical foreign policy decisions at some risk to their political survival. Additionally, while there are limits to the range of messages that political parties can promulgate, there is still variation on those messages within those constraints. Examining that variation is meaningful since it demonstrates the incremental changes parties attempt to make despite the restrictions placed on them.

Existing literature on Pakistan has largely taken for granted the notion that parties have little influence on foreign policy and hence generally avoided discussion of party positions on foreign affairs. Some major accounts of Pakistani political opinion omit foreign policy issues entirely (see Wilder 1999), and analyses that do link Pakistani public opinion with foreign policy tend to provide a cursory examination of party affiliation (Ahmed and Cortright 1998; Pew Research Center 2014). When foreign policy is discussed, most accounts are either focused only on the military's preferences (Waseem 2002) or on civilian disagreements with the military's preferred policies (Blom 2002) rather than on disagreements among civilian parties themselves. When distinct foreign policy approaches are associated with specific parties, such discussions overwhelmingly focus on either Zulfikar Ali Bhutto's unique foreign policy vision (e.g., Cohen 2004: 141–44; Haider 2010, 19–20; Jones this volume) or the ideologically coherent foreign policy of the Islamist Jamaat-e Islami (JI) (Nasr 1994; Bashir 2009). While existing work has understandably focused on the more salient civil-military divide (Shafqat 1997; Talbot 2002), it is important to go beyond existing accounts by identifying and describing areas of party agreement and disagreement on foreign policy. This provides a fuller understanding of beliefs held by party leaders and the appeals they believe are appropriate for their voters as well as some faint indication of what foreign policy might look like if the civil-military divide were to diminish in significance in the future.

The arguments presented in this chapter are supported through a combination of primary sources, including party manifestos and public opinion polling data. Examining primary party documents reveals what parties themselves consider an essential component of party policy and how they reconcile competing voices within the party umbrella. In turn, statistically analyzing public opinion data collected by the Pew Research Center allows us to examine voter preferences and assess whether party policy is constrained or influenced by party leaders' desire to seek votes and retain support.[2]

This chapter proceeds in four parts. First, it describes the nature and extent of constraints placed on politician and party behavior due to the military's dominance of Pakistani politics. It highlights select instances in which individual politicians have pursued distinct foreign policies despite these structural conditions. Second, and cognizant of those constraints, is a review of how parties describe their foreign policy positions in authoritative public statements before, third, turning to an examination of whether party supporters have similar or markedly distinct worldviews as they consider some of Pakistan's most important foreign policy relationships. Finally, alternative explanations for Pakistani domestic opinion and party messaging on foreign policy are given, before concluding that the overwhelming effect of civil-military relations retains explanatory primacy.

The Influence of Political Parties on Foreign Policy

Since independence Pakistan's military has undertaken direct interventions to seize power or remove civilian leaders (in 1958, 1969, 1977, and 1999) and alleged covert interventions to do so (in 1990, 1993, 1996, and 2017). This tendency of the Pakistan Army to intervene in politics when it believes civilian politicians have gone astray—what Aqil Shah (2014a) calls a tutelary norm—is arguably the fundamental feature of Pakistani politics. Gen. Mohammad Ayub Khan told a US diplomat in 1952, "The Pakistan Army will not allow the political leaders to get out of hand," and the Pakistan Army has since behaved as if that task were one of its primary functions.[3]

As a consequence, as Fair (2014, 30) observes, "Given the army's ability to bring down a civilian government through direct or indirect intervention, few politicians are willing to take on the army. Most prefer to defer to the military in exchange for the opportunity to remain in power." This public deference masks private disagreement among politicians and the parties they lead. Sensitive topics are frequently characterized by manufactured consensus (Clary 2016). Politicians have greater freedom to advocate in more hawkish, more nationalistic directions than they do in arguing for more pacifistic policy because the army is comfortable with public hawks, who make the status quo appear moderate by comparison. The army is less willing to accept politicians who advocate policies that have the logical conclusion of greater civilian control of the military and fewer resources for national defense. Behind the scenes, away from television cameras and reporters' microphones, there is greater room for policy heterodoxy, but even here substantive political actions increase the danger of military intervention.

Precisely these discreet settings are the best examples of circumstances where individual leaders have deviated from the military's preferred policy. Though civilian politicians have been unable to transform Pakistan's most important foreign policies toward India, Afghanistan, and the United States, they have been able to alter those policies in meaningful ways, at least temporarily. Benazir Bhutto, during her first term as prime minister (1988 to 1990), reportedly rejected a proposal to increase Pakistan's intelligence support for Sikh separatists in India and instead ordered the sharing of intelligence her country had collected on the separatist movement, information that she subsequently claimed led to "the end of the Sikh insurgency."[4] In her second term in office Bhutto supported the movement that subsequently became known as the Taliban in Afghanistan, helping to shift Pakistani state support away from its previously favored proxy of Gulbuddin Hekmetyar. In this case Bhutto appears to have been motivated by a desire to strengthen her political ally, Maulana Fazal-ur-Rehman of the Jamiat Ulema-e-Islam (JUI-F), and weaken her (and the JUI-F's) political opponent, the Jamaat-e-Islami (JI), which historically had close relations with Hekmetyar. Bhutto may also have hoped to increase Pakistan's trade with central Asia since, given the army's veto-playing role, enhancing India-Pakistan trade was off-limits (Coll 2004, 90–91).

More recently there is circumstantial evidence of civil-military disagreement over intervention in the civil war in Yemen. Perhaps wary of aggravating Sunni-Shia tensions internally, Pakistan's parliament unanimously voted to remain neutral in the conflict rather than side with the Saudi-led coalition confronting the Iran-backed Houthis, who follow a variant of Shia Islam.[5] The Pakistan Army's preferences were and remain opaque, but the army chief at the time of the parliamentary vote, Gen. Raheel Sharif, accepted a prominent appointment to lead a Saudi-organized military coalition of majority Sunni states following his retirement, suggesting that he may have preferred more visible support to Pakistan's traditional ally, Saudi Arabia.[6]

Many of these moves, though consequential, were hidden from the public until years after the fact. Over a year after the initial parliamentary vote on Yemen, the exact contours of the civil-military fight are difficult to discern and even harder to prove. More recent press reporting (in February 2018) that Pakistan will deploy an additional brigade to "train and advise" the Saudi military within Saudi Arabia illuminates the fact that even a unanimous parliamentary motion can be eroded by subsequent policy moves.[7]

Other episodes remain shrouded in secrecy. Nawaz Sharif's second term in office (1997 to 1999) notably included the launch and spectacular collapse of an ambitious peace process with India as a result of the fourth India-Pakistan war that followed Pakistani military intrusions near the Indian town of Kargil in the disputed territory of Kashmir. While there is no doubt that the peace process was Sharif's initiative, there remains considerable confusion as to whether Sharif also was aware of the military's aggressive moves near Kargil, which ultimately proved totally incompatible with a peace initiative. Lt. Gen. (Ret.) Shahid Aziz, who was in charge of analysis for Pakistan's Inter-Services Intelligence during the Kargil event, is probably correct in assessing that Sharif was "not fully in the picture" but also "not completely in the dark."[8] However, other credible recent accounts suggest the prime minister did not know anything of the Kargil operation prior to the onset of major India–Pakistan fighting months after the operation began (Zehra 2018).

This opacity regarding foreign policymaking, while severe in the Pakistani context, is not unique to Pakistan. In recent theoretical work Narang and Staniland (2018) argue that regimes vary on the clarity of responsibility for foreign policy outcomes, that is, the ability of voters to attribute outcomes and punish or reward politicians as a result (see also Tavits 2007, 220). While Narang and Staniland mostly consider complex coalition governments in parliamentary systems, Pakistan's structure follows a similar logic: there is widespread awareness that the military plays an important policymaking role, which makes it difficult for voters to know if a decision is being made by politicians or not and even more difficult to sanction politicians for bad outcomes. Voters have essentially no ability to sanction the military except during periods when military dictators govern overtly. In such an ambiguous environment, Narang and Staniland predict one of two outcomes: for high-salience issues that matter to the public they expect "demagoguery and opportunism" to be the norm, such that whenever "contingent political tides make it worthwhile to intervene in security policy, politicians may do so, but this attention will be variable and unpredictable"; for low-salience issues like the meat-and-potatoes foreign policy actions taken toward less important countries, "little attention [will be paid] to security policy by the vast majority of politicians, and no strong link between the public and foreign policy" (412). Pakistan represents a special case for their argument since even demagoguery and opportunism by civilian politicians are limited by the ever-present risk of military intervention. Only when the military has clearly blundered, such as after the loss of East Pakistan in 1971, have politicians been granted the space for sustained and meaningful critique. Otherwise, rhetoric supporting established policy and repeating old shibboleths is far safer than venturing down new paths.

What Do the Parties Say?

In this context what do Pakistan's political parties say on foreign policy? Consistent with the homogenizing pressures detailed earlier, they offer a fair amount of pablum. When they do venture into more interesting territory, parties feel safer veering in hawkish, well-worn paths, notably anti-Americanism. Islamist parties, which have little chance of governing, have felt more latitude to say provocative things, while even the brashest mainstream party (i.e., the PTI) has tended toward moderation in official statements, especially as its chances for governing grew in 2013 and 2018. The prospect of winning brings sobriety and "embarrassing responsibility" (Waltz 1967, 83). For parties such as the JI, which are perpetually in the opposition, the route to influence may be espousing resonant messages that bring pressure on the ruling dispensation even if they do not persuade voters to back them (Bashir 2009, 26).

Given the advent of cable news and social media in Pakistan, political parties engage in a nonstop stream of messaging. Cataloging the entirety of those communications would be nearly impossible. Prior to each election, however, every party does focus its energies on creating a document that identifies both what the party assesses to be the most important electoral issues of the day and the party's stance on those issues. All of the large parties take the creation of a manifesto at least somewhat seriously, with the 2013 election documents running from 12 pages (for JUI-F) to 110 pages (PML-N), with most between 30 and 50 pages in length.[9]

Manifestos are party-produced documents that represent collective deliberations and may be absent even in the coding of statements by partly leaders (and which could reflect idiosyncratic individual beliefs made off the cuff). There is some evidence from other contexts (notably, India) that more voters read party manifestos or, at a minimum, are familiar with party promises than might be expected (Chhibber and Verma 2018, 154–55). Studying manifestos is not without its drawbacks, however, since parties may pay variable attention to manifesto writing depending on their respective constituencies: some parties are more invested in the programmatic appeals best captured by a manifesto, while other parties focus almost exclusively on patronage. Additionally, the salience of any individual issue (and whether it merits inclusion or exclusion in a manifesto) varies substantially from election cycle to election cycle, meaning silence on a specific issue can imply differing things from year to year (see Volkens, Bara, and Budge 2009). Nevertheless, by looking at manifestos emanating from a wide range of parties over the last two election cycles (2013 and 2018), the problem of variable salience over time is substantially reduced. Taking election manifestos as a point of departure, what do parties say on foreign policy in their most authoritative documents?

The United States

All of the mainstream parties have struggled to create manifestos that acknowledge the importance of Washington regarding Pakistan's fate while simultaneously contending with the occasionally deep unpopularity of US foreign policy. This tension was much more apparent in the 2013 election than in 2018, most likely because of the sharp diminution in US drone strikes and the increasing distance from the Abbottabad raid and the Raymond Davis affair (see Clary and Siddiqui 2017a). In 2013 the PPP, with the special challenge of authoring a manifesto while governing, was least critical of the United States. The PPP argued that Pakistan's alliance with Washington "remained critical" to Pakistan's "struggle for peace and stability" even as it chided the United States for its "counterproductive" continuation of drone strikes (67–68).[10] The PML-N largely avoided clear statements about the United States in 2013, though it partially attributed the worsening of militancy in Pakistan to "intense outrage with U.S. policies in Afghanistan" (85), a sentiment shared in the PTI 2013 manifesto, which blamed the US war on terrorism for creating "polarized and often violent cleavages within Pakistan's polity" (3). Instead, the PTI promised to "implement its 'no to drones' policy" and to "extricate Pakistan from the U.S.-led War on Terror" (9) while attempting to preserve a "constructive" relationship with Washington (7–8). Unsurprisingly, Islamist parties felt less compunction to express full-throated criticism in 2013. The JUI-F repeated its long-standing criticism that Washington's "emotional response" to the events of 9/11 led to policies that had increased rather than decreased terrorist violence, while declaring that "foreign dictation would not be accepted" if the JUI-F were in power. The similarity with PTI's message is apparent and perhaps unsurprising given the importance of constituencies in Khyber Pakthunkhwa for both parties. The JI was most severe: "Our country has fallen into the clutches of American interests in the region. Its espionage apparatus is spread all over the country and we have been obliged to yield to its commands like a slave. Our rulers have turned the army on its own people by asserting ownership of a foreign war" (6). The MQM manifesto did not mention the United States at all.

The 2018 manifestos were generally blander and safer than the 2013 documents. The PPP, freed of governing, made a belated emphasis on sovereignty by reminding potential voters that it shut down a US facility at Shamsi Air Base in Balochistan in 2011. It also promised that a PPP government would "not sign on to agreements that erode Pakistan's authority over its soil, airspace and littoral limits" while also stressing the importance of a "more enduring, balanced, and clearly defined partnership" with Washington (57). The PTI, at the precipice of governing, settled for a vague promise that "reciprocity and mutuality of interest will be the determinants of our relationship" with the United States (55), a theme virtually indistinguishable from the PML-N's pledge to "build relations with the United States on the basis of equality and mutuality of interest" (32). The brief, limited sharpness of the manifestos' criticisms in 2013 had faded into passing and vague appeals to the importance of sovereignty by 2018.

India

All parties genuflect toward the "core issue of Kashmir" in their 2013 and 2018 manifestos, but many are surprisingly moderate in their published stances on India. The PPP argued in 2013 for "honest and sincere dialogue" with India (70) and stressed that a "lack of progress" (73) on one agenda item (i.e., Kashmir) should not impede progress on other priorities. The 2018 PPP manifesto—alone among those of the mainstream parties for the last two elections—avoided direct inclusion of the mantra over the "core issue of Kashmir" though it did not deviate too far from established dogma and repeatedly emphasized the importance of outstanding United Nations resolutions on Kashmir. While the 2013 PPP document on India was moderate, the 2018 document was even more fulsome in its advocacy of normalizing relations with India "without prejudice to the UN Security Council Resolutions" (61). The PML-N largely sidestepped the subject of India in its 2013 manifesto, instead stressing it would pursue "a policy of normalization with countries with which we have differences, . . . especially those that are neighbors" (81). In 2018 India merited passing reference in the PML-N manifesto for "dialogue" to "stabilize relations," even as the government promised to "resource fully" Pakistan's military needs to respond to what it termed "India's colossal military buildup" (31). The PTI 2013 manifesto, too, reflected the moderation of mainstream parties on India, identifying "progressive détente with India" (7) as a long-term goal and specifically calling for dialogue with India on water rights disputes and nuclear weapons issues. In 2018 the PTI settled for short, vague calls for "conflict resolution" with India (55). The MQM claimed in 2013 that it "wants to solve the Kashmir issue through meaningful, sincere and honorable dialogue according to the wishes of Kashmiri people" (21), but little else. Even the generally more provocative JUI-F manifesto did not veer into demagoguery, saying "both India and Pakistan with [utmost] seriousness should work to resolve [the] Kashmir issue, as Kashmiris are becoming disillusioned" (10)—the only time either India or Kashmir are directly mentioned in its 2013 manifesto.

China

Mention of China was largely absent from the 2013 manifestos, and language in those documents typically traveled the well-worn grooves of emphasizing support for Pakistan's "time-tested and abiding friendship" with China, as the 2013 PPP manifesto did (70), or promising to "expand [Pakistan's] traditional strategic partnership with China at multiple levels, especially in the strategic economic field," as the 2013 PTI document did (8). In 2018 China—and the China-Pakistan Economic Corridor (CPEC) specifically—took on a much larger role in mainstream party manifestos. All three mainstream parties argued that they were uniquely capable of harnessing CPEC's potential. The PPP took credit for having "spearheaded a quantum leap forward" (60) during the Zardari government through its efforts to associate Pakistan with the Chinese Belt and Road Initiative. The PML-N government advertised its embrace of CPEC by selling it as a "game changer" (10), while the PTI manifesto promised to "ensure CPEC translates into a game changer" (32). The 2018 document was consistent with prior PTI messaging, which had criticized unfair distribution and corruption in the PML-N central government's handling of CPEC projects and taking great pains to avoid criticizing China—"wax[ing] lyrical about China's ongoing support of Pakistan" in meetings between PTI leader Imran Khan and Chinese diplomats, for instance.[11]

Iran

Even Iran, with which Pakistan has had difficult relations over the years, is portrayed positively in official party messaging. In their 2013 manifestos the PPP, the PML-N, the MQM, and the JI all reference Iran as a source of energy supply, an important electoral issue given the regular brownouts and natural gas shortages across Pakistan. The PPP highlighted its progress in securing Iranian energy supply to the Pakistani grid. The PML-N also emphasized the potential of gains from transmitting energy and pipeline routes from Iran to China and India. The JUI-F omitted mention of neighboring Iran in its manifesto, although the JUI-F's ties to the Taliban (which in 1998 killed Iranian diplomats in Mazar-i-Sharif) have led to signs of JUI-F troubles with Tehran, and vice versa.[12] In the 2018 manifestos Iran was relegated to a catch-all discussion of the PML-N's desire to strengthen relations with Pakistan's neighbors, while the PPP again promised to strengthen trade and resume work on the Pakistan-Iran pipeline. The PTI omitted direct reference to Iran, although it did stress a desire to "play the role of a bridge builder and honest broker amongst the states of the Gulf by adopting a non-partisan role in intra-Gulf conflicts" (55) (an indirect reference to the Shia-Sunni split that has come to dominate contemporary Middle Eastern politics). The PPP manifesto was more direct in calling for a "rational balance in our relations with Riyadh and Tehran to shore up our influence and enhance prospects for engagement with each" (59). Unknowledgeable readers would have little reason to suspect a record of recent Pakistani-Iranian difficulties were manifestos their only reference points.

Afghanistan

Pakistan's other neighbor, Afghanistan, has had as troubled relations with Pakistan as India has over the past decade, but those troubles are largely elided in party manifestos. The PPP 2013 manifesto highlighted the then-incumbent government's support for a stable Afghanistan and pursuit of transit trade ties with it. The manifesto also stressed, in an implicit critique of the Pakistan military but also of the PPP's own actions in the 1990s, "Pakistan's proximity to Afghanistan must not become a motive for meddling in Afghanistan's internal dynamics" (72). The PPP reemphasized "its commitment to non-interference in Afghanistan" in 2018, although it also expressed concern about "terrorist sanctuaries in eastern Afghanistan" that "present a potent threat to Pakistan's safety and security" (60). The 2013 PML-N manifesto emphasized the possibilities of Afghanistan as a bridge to central Asia and Pakistan's potential to "develop a flourishing transit economy" (80) that connects west, central, and east Asia. In 2018 the PML-N highlighted progress on energy pipelines through Afghanistan, restated its commitment to regional connectivity, and underscored its belief that Pakistan and Afghanistan's stability were "inextricably intertwined." It also, however, drew attention to the PML-N government's deportation of "4.3 million illegal refugees back to Afghanistan" (31–32). The only direct reference to Afghanistan in the 2013 PTI manifesto was a commitment to initiate negotiations on water rights over the Kabul River, an important issue in a Pakistani economy that is 25 percent agricultural and whose labor force is over 40 percent employed in agriculture; the 2018 manifesto avoided reference to Afghanistan entirely. The JUI-F encouraged negotiations in Afghanistan and declared itself "vindicated" (10) by growing international acceptance that the Taliban needed to be part of those negotiations. The JI's manifesto, despite the party's long history of involvement in Afghanistan, omitted direct reference to it though elsewhere the JI has called for the withdrawal of "extra regional forces."[13] The MQM's only reference to Afghanistan in its 2013 manifesto was a call to reduce smuggling and money laundering associated with transit trade into Afghanistan, even though MQM leader Altaf Hussain has blamed Afghan instability for the existence of terrorist safe havens in Pakistan.[14]

Rather than using their manifestos to highlight party differences on foreign policies, parties largely gravitate toward safe, bland discussions of foreign policy. To the extent the documents take a stand at all, the subject of conflict resolution is vastly more prominent than conflict escalation. Does this homogeneity in official party documents mask heterogeneity in supporters' beliefs?

Do Party Supporters Disagree?

Kenneth Waltz (1967, 85) wrote, "If the preferences of voters cluster in the center with numbers dwindling as one moves toward either extreme, then the politics of a country will be stable and its policies moderate. If there are two parties in contention, they will be highly similar." Waltz's analysis would have been more accurate had he said that politics would be stable given a clustering of voters around the median viewpoint. But there is no inherent reason to believe that the median viewpoint needs to be moderate in any objective sense.

In Pakistan exactly this sort of attitudinal clustering exists among respondents and is associated with "highly similar" parties, to use Waltz's expression. As figure 14.1 demonstrates, there is overwhelming consensus on most issues. Median respondents across all major parties have very unfavorable views toward the Afghan Taliban and very favorable opinions of China. Similarly, India and the United States are viewed unfavorably by the vast majority of respondents sampled by the Pew Research Center in 2015, representing over 60 percent of supporters from all major parties. Only supporters of the MQM and the PPP are notable for modestly more favorable views—with the median MQM respondent holding only a "somewhat unfavorable" view of New Delhi and Washington and the median PPP respondent holding the same view toward Washington but not New Delhi.

The presence of this consensus does not necessarily indicate that party supporters hold these views strongly. The consensus may represent party supporters' beliefs about where their party stands on a particular topic or more broadly their sense of societal consensus. Respondents may be offering the reply of a good party loyalist or what they view as socially desirable but would not be willing to sanction a political leader who held contrary views.

In separate survey experimental work undertaken in Pakistan in 2015, Niloufer Siddiqui and I find evidence that suggests strong limits on the extent to which voters are willing to sanction politicians who hold discordant views. Randomly varying candidate views on India—whether they favor a hard-line or friendly policy toward New Delhi—only very modestly changes the probability that a respondent would support a candidate with similar views as compared to another candidate that held the opposite view. Of the several candidate attributes tested, candidate views on India were

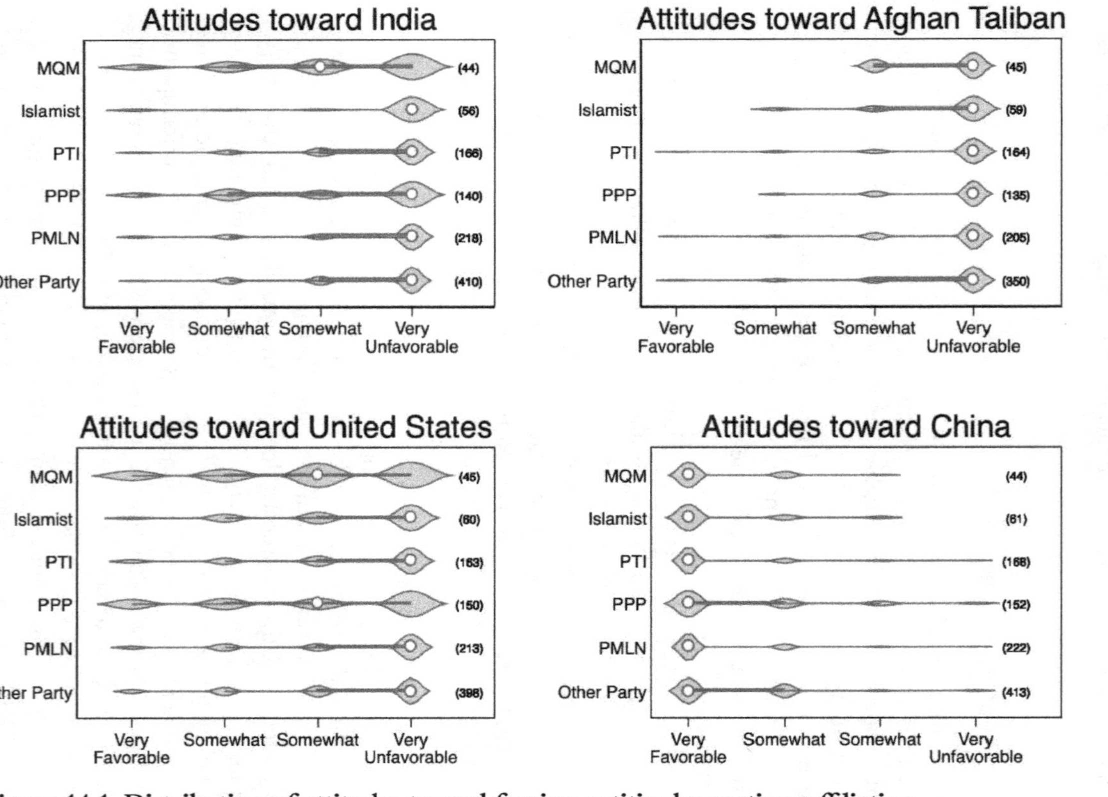

Figure 14.1. Distribution of attitudes toward foreign entities by partisan affiliation

Source: Pew Research Center (2015).

Note: White circle indicates median; thick line indicates interquartile range; shaded area indicates density plot; number of respondents is in parentheses.

one of the least meaningful in terms of respondent choice. Alone, these experimental results do not permit us to discern if Pakistan's policy toward India has low salience for most Pakistanis or merely if the poor clarity of responsibility for foreign policy in Pakistan means that respondents do not exert much effort in ensuring foreign policy conformity for a parliamentary candidate who likely will be unable to affect foreign policy anyway (Clary and Siddiqui 2017b). But the evidence from the content of manifestos and polling data offers yet another reason for parties to deemphasize foreign policy in their public appeals.

What Other Sources Exist for Consensus or Disagreement?

While Pakistan's pattern of civil-military relations has persisted for seven decades, the high levels of consensus might not entirely be the product of military intervention. Nor, it should be noted, is the military the only institution in Pakistani society that pushes for continuity in foreign policy rather than a rupture with the past. In fact, there are reasons to believe that the military has been effective in achieving its preferences in part because it has allied with and convinced civilian bureaucrats and diplomats of the validity of its vision for Pakistani society (see Jalal 1995). Beyond the governing elites—whether politicians, bureaucrats, or soldiers—there are other structural forces that have been identified by political scientists as being associated with divergent (or convergent) foreign policy views, and those forces largely suggest greater accord in Pakistani public opinion than in other societies.

Stepping back, it is puzzling that parties would ever disagree on foreign policy, especially for state-centric accounts of foreign policy behavior. If the international system creates incentives that determine state policy, why then would political parties prefer different paths? Such divergent views could lead to erratic, swerving policy, diminishing state credibility, and, in the process, endangering the state (Waltz 1967, 63–64). Political scientists attempting to explain partisan divergence in the United States and elsewhere tend to point to five different explanations: (1) asymmetric regional consequences; (2) economic class implications; (3) co-ethnic affinity; (4) distinct ideational traditions; and (5) institutional confrontation. Each is worth considering and in turn applying to the Pakistani context. If they are operative, they help outline when, why, and how parties might offer alternative foreign policy platforms.

The idea of asymmetric regional consequences suggests that foreign policy choices do not affect a nation equally but rather impose differential benefits and costs on subnational regions (Trubowitz and Mellow 2005; Trubowitz 1998). Representatives of those regions respond by backing advantageous policies for their regions while opposing costly strategies that might endanger their regional homes. In the Pakistani case the archetypical example might be of Pakistan's former east wing, which Bengali politicians argued was left virtually undefended in the 1965 Indo-Pakistani War initiated from West Pakistan by an army that overrepresented West Pakistanis. As a consequence the Awami League sought greater defense spending in East Pakistan, greater influence in national security decision-making by East Pakistanis, and a more pro-Indian foreign policy. The fact that none of these demands—or any others—generated serious concessions by West Pakistan's military government helped ensure the Awami League's success in the 1970 elections, which set the stage for the 1971 civil war that led to the creation of Bangladesh. More recently this theory has had less explanatory power in the Pakistani case. While each of the largest mainstream parties has a regional stronghold—the PML-N in Punjab, the PPP in Sindh, and the PTI in Khyber Pakthunkhwa—leaders of the PPP and the PTI also know that they can secure national power only with the support of Punjabi constituents. Such national aspirations, in the context of Pakistan's specific post-1971 electoral arithmetic, have mitigated the importance of regionalism on Pakistan's foreign policy.

Foreign policy can have distributional implications for regions and across socioeconomic classes. Parties organized on class lines might find themselves favoring divergent foreign policies as a result. This explanation has been less important in the Pakistani context, given the weakness of working-class political actors and the usurpation of working-class grievances to fuel interethnic political fights (Candland 2007b, 35–37). All of the mainstream political parties rely on cross-class coalitions, with each being reliant to some extent on powerful wealthy elites and their associated lower-class vote banks. On average PTI supporters do tend to be wealthier than PPP supporters, with PML-N supporters in between.[15] But despite class differences in the composition of rank-and-file supporters, the senior leadership of many of the parties draws predominantly on landed families and industrialists.

In ethnically heterogeneous societies such as Pakistan, coethnic affinity (or cross-ethnic antipathy) may generate sorting into political parties that coincides with specific foreign policy preferences. Thus, in India analysts routinely posit that Tamils and Bengalis sympathize with the plight of coethnics across the border in Bangladesh and Sri Lanka and as a consequence favor interventionist foreign policies toward those states (Kapur 2015, 307–8). There is some evidence for this in Pakistan as well. Pashto speakers have somewhat more favorable opinions of the Afghan Taliban and somewhat less favorable opinions of the United States than respondents who speak other languages.[16] Similarly, self-identified Pakistani Shias have more favorable views of Iran than do Sunnis. Given the causal antecedence of ethnic and religious identity, it seems reasonable to suggest that the reason the JUI-F and PTI, the most successful parties in Pashtun areas in Pakistan, are more sympathetic to the Afghan Taliban and more critical of the United States is that they have taken public stances consistent with their supporters. Similarly, some evidence suggests that the PPP, the party most supported by Pakistani Shias, has sought more positive relations with Iran—at least in recent years—during periods when it governed Pakistan.[17]

Even when it appears operative, coethnic affinity can provide only so much analytic leverage. The Awami National Party also cultivates its support from Pashtuns but is ideologically opposed to the Taliban—both the Afghan Taliban and the Tehreek-e-Taliban Pakistan (the so-called Pakistan Taliban). ANP opposition to the Taliban after 9/11 gave room to religious parties like the JUI-F to strengthen their support in Pashtun areas, which they did (Rahman 2010, 236). While the literature on the domestic sources of foreign policy includes the possibility of multiple, distinct strategic cultures vying for dominance, it has had less to say on the sources of party ideology. The ANP case is instructive, however, as it shows that ideology need not flow decisively from some causally prior variable like coethnic affinity. Whether the ANP is an outlier, however, and whether there are distinct strategic cultures within Pakistan are open questions, let alone whether those strategic cultures vary at the level of party (rather than merely at the individual level) (see Fair 2014; Lavoy 2006; F. Khan 2005). Nellis and Siddiqui (2018) argue that Pakistani parties sort into secular and nonsecular categories: the PPP, the ANP, and the MQM are in the former category and all other major parties are in the latter. While the authors convincingly demonstrate that such parties have incentives to prevent religious violence in their constituencies during periods in office, overall the secular-nonsecular distinction does not appear to be closely correlated with the attitudes of party supporters regarding issues of religious violence. Secular party supporters appear to be slightly less worried about Al Qaeda and as worried about the Taliban compared to nonsecular party supporters but somewhat more likely to assess that suicide bombing might be justified in certain circumstances.[18] Again, the nature of Pakistani politics may mean that elites in secular parties hold secular beliefs but feel no need to broadcast those beliefs to their constituencies, resulting in the absence of elite cueing to generate revised beliefs among supporters. For example, private secular beliefs by political elites can result in actions—such as encouraging the close monitoring of religious radicals by law enforcement—that are largely unseen by the public but lead to changed outcomes (a reduction in religious violence) even if public attitudes have not changed. Thus it is quite possible for Nellis and Siddiqui to be correct that secular party elites work to prevent religious violence even if overall their secular party supporters have indistinguishable views on religious violence from their nonsecular party counterparts.

Finally, there is a temporal component to partisan policy preferences. In British politics one old aphorism with a nineteenth-century lineage declares that the duty of a parliamentary opposition is to "oppose everything" proposed by the governing coalition. The structure of competition incentivizes opposition parties to oppose unpopular but necessary policy choices, such as acquiescence to austerity measures demanded by international lenders or making compromises in negotiations with India, or criticize governing mistakes, such as failures to stop terrorist attacks. There is a certain hypocritical amnesia that comes with opposition status. While Kenneth Waltz (1967, 87) is correct that a party "cannot change policies as an actor changes costumes, without gaining thereby a damaging reputation for inconstancy," that reputation may not meaningfully sway partisans or swing voters and may give the party considerable latitude to change stances opportunistically. So, despite a history of rapprochement with India under PPP rule and the necessity of such rapprochement in order to alter the civil-military balance in Pakistan, PPP leaders were eager in 2016 to criticize Nawaz Sharif for his "friendship" with Indian prime minister Narendra Modi, which the PPP alleged was "causing irreparable damage to the Kashmir cause."[19]

Combined with the secrecy, personalism, and incrementalism that can accompany major foreign policy moves in Pakistan, which together result in ambiguous cueing for partisans when policy changes are afoot, this oppositional opportunism further confuses things. The result should be the appearance of consensus among partisans even when leaders may hold differing private views regarding the wisdom of policy courses that they advocate publicly. The hostile attitudes of PPP supporters toward India changed little from when the PPP governed Pakistan to when they lost power to the current PML-N government, but PPP leaders could offer anti-India messaging after 2013 whereas structural pressures forced them to stay quiet before then. Similarly, despite strong indications that Nawaz Sharif's PML-N government has sought improved relations with India, PML-N supporters held no more favorable opinions toward India in 2015 than they did in 2012.

Conclusion: Do Parties Matter?

Devesh Kapur argues, "Among the many factors that drive a country's foreign policy, the least understood is the role of public opinion" (Kapur 2015, 298). This confusion has manifold bases. The public is frequently ill-informed and its views can shift, often quite rapidly, based on cues sent by elites. When elite views—or at least public statements—and public views conform, it is difficult to discern the direction of causality. Have past elite statements generated the elite-public consensus of today, or are elites parroting their supporters? Even if public beliefs are ambiguous, the masses do appear to adhere to certain core values and principles. Elites may stray from those core public beliefs, but doing so is dangerous and at a minimum requires a certain degree of rhetorical creativity to reshape new positions out of existent resonant views widespread among supporters (Samuels 2005, 7–8). Recognizing a transitory idea versus a deeply held belief is difficult prior to an occasion when leaders attempt to sway their partisans to a different position, and even these rare circumstances are rarely exogenous. Leaders may stray from the party line only when they sense a certain pliability of their followers or a latent willingness to move in a new direction.

As a consequence, knowing cause and effect—the great challenge of contemporary political science—is incredibly difficult. Informed observers such as William Milam and Matthew J. Nelson (2013) can conclude, "The effect of public opinion on [Pakistan's] politics, including its foreign policy, may be critical." But the degree to which Pakistani foreign policy behavior is "shaped from below," as Milam and Nelson argue, versus being manipulated by elites from above, is an open question. The ability to test these rival hypotheses is further limited by the reality of civil-military relations in Pakistan: civilian leaders are wary of testing the military's preferred worldview lest they provoke military intervention that complicates their lives or endangers their political survival. More extensive survey and survey experimental work is necessary to tease out how voters assess heterodox foreign policy opinions and interviews with elites to discern elite perceptions of public views and the latitude they perceive in contradicting them.

Notes

1. "Fatalities in Terrorist Violence in Pakistan 2003–2018," South Asia Terrorism portal, accessed March 21, 2018, http://www.satp.org/satporgtp/countries/paki stan/database/casualties.htm.

2. Unless otherwise stated, data are from the Pew-funded nationally representative face-to-face survey of adults in Pakistan carried out by Princeton Survey Research Associates International, April 6–30, 2015. Pew's repeated surveys in Pakistan provide one of the few recurrently collected sources of data on Pakistani public opinion, and because Pew has fielded similar surveys in many countries over many years the data permits cross-national and temporal comparison.

3. Memo of conversation between Gen. Mohammad Ayub Khan, Commander-in-Chief, Pakistan Army, and Raleigh A. Gibson, American Consul General Lahore, to the Department of State, Foreign Service Despatch no. 105, December 23, 1952, http://www.icdc.com/~paulwolf/pakistan/ayubkhan23dec1952.jpg.

4. Shaikh Aziz, "A Leaf from History: The Rise and Fall of the Khalistan Movement," *Dawn*, July 12, 2015. See also Neena Gopal, "I Kept My Word, Rajiv Didn't," *Outlook India*, December 31, 2007.

5. Tim Craig, "Defying Saudis, Pakistani Lawmakers Vote to Stay Out of Yemen," *Washington Post*, April 10, 2015.

6. Salman Masood and Ben Hubbard, "Pakistan Approves Military Hero to Head Tricky Saudi-Led Alliance," *New York Times*, April 2, 2017.

7. "Pakistan to Send Troops to Saudi Arabia to Train and Advise," Reuters, February 16, 2018. See also Nadir Guramani, "Senator Babar Fears Pakistani Troops Could Get Sucked into Yemen 'Quagmire,'" *Dawn*, February 20, 2018.

8. Quoted in Khaleeq Kiani, "Kargil Adventure Was Four-Man Show: General," *Dawn*, January 28, 2013.

9. Discussion includes 2013 manifestos belonging to parties that received at least 5 percent of the votes cast for National Assembly in the 2013 elections as well as the two largest religious parties that year. For 2018 the manifestos belonging to the three mainstream parties, the PML-N, the PPP, and the PTI, are included. PTI, "Inshallah Naya Pakistan: PTI Manifesto Election 2013," accessed February 10, 2018, http://www.insaf.pk/about-us/know-pti/manifesto; PTI, "The Road to Naya Pakistan: PTI Manifesto 2018," accessed April 15, 2019, http://www.pmo.gov.pk/documents/manifesto-pti.pdf; PML-N, "National Agenda for Real Change: Manifesto 2013," accessed February 10, 2018, http://pmo.gov.pk/documents/manifesto.pdf; PML-N, "Vote Ko Izzat Do—Khidmat Ko Vote Do; Manifesto 2018," accessed April 15, 2019, https://www.thenews.com.pk/assets/docs/PML-N-Manifesto-Booklet-min.pdf; PPP Parliamentarians, "Manifesto 2013," accessed February 10, 2018, http://www.citizenswire.com/wp-content/uploads/2013/03/PPPP_Manifesto_14_3_13.pdf; PPP, "Election Manifesto 2018: BB Kaw Aada Nibhana Hai Pakistan Bachana Hai," accessed April 15, 2019, https://www.thenews.com.pk/assets/front/pdf/PPP_Manifesto_2018.pdf; MQM, "Empowering People: 2013 Manifesto," accessed February 10, 2018, http://www.mqm.org/Assets/MQM-Manifesto-2013-Eng.pdf; JI Pakistan, "Manifesto." accessed February 10, 2018, http://kurzman.unc.edu/files/2011/06/JI_2013_English.pdf; and JUI Pakistan, "Manifesto for Election 2013," accessed February 10, 2018, http://kurzman.unc.edu/files/2011/06/JUI-F_2013_English.pdf.

10. All parenthetical references following quotes from manifestos refer to the page of the manifesto where the quote was found or the page of the PDF version of the manifesto.

11. Khawar Ghumman, "Protests Not against CPEC, PTI Chief Assures Chinese Envoy," *Dawn*, October 19, 2016.

12. "JUI-F Delegation Fails to Get Iran Visa," *Dawn*, May 14, 2015.

13. JI Pakistan, "Situation in Afghanistan and Its Implications on the Central Asian Regions," accessed February 13, 2018, http://jamaat.org/en/articledetail.php?id=11.

14. MQM, "MQM Founder Leader Mr. Altaf Hussain Deplores Loss of Lives in Kabul Suicide Attack," accessed May 31, 2017, http://www.mqm.org/englishnews/39572/mqm-founder-leader-mr-altaf-hussain-deplores-loss-of-lives-in-kabul-suicide-attack.

15. For instance, in the 2015 Pew data, PPP supporters had a median monthly income of Rs.7,000–10,000 (approximately US$60–$90), PML-N supporters had

a median monthly income of Rs.10,001–15,000 (US$90–$135), and PTI supporters had a median monthly income of Rs.15,001–20,000 (US$135–$180).

16. Pew Research Center (2015) data. Pew did not ask respondents either their ethnicity or their mother tongue, so the language in which the interview was conducted is used as a proxy.

17. Muhammad Akbar Notezai, "Iran-Pakistan at the Crossroads?," *Diplomat*, July 9, 2017.

18. Results of two-sided t-tests on Pew 2015 data. The ANP, the MQM, the Balochistan National Party, and the Pukhtunkhwa Milli Awam Party (PKMAP), and the PPP and its offshoots were coded as secular parties, while all others were coded as nonsecular. Respondents who did not support a party were excluded from the analysis.

19. Zulqernain Tahir, "'Sharif-Modi Friendship' Damaging for Kashmir Cause, Says Bilawal," *Dawn*, July 11, 2016.

Conclusion
Political Parties in an "Establishmentarian Democracy"

Mohammad Waseem

In a way this book wrote itself by fulfilling the need for focusing on the most visible, consistent, and resilient actors on Pakistan's political stage. The editors set out for themselves an ambitious task of pulling together the current academic research on political parties and integrating its main findings. Lest we forget, the first major lesson of the book is that there is no democracy without political parties. This applies firmly to Pakistan as a functioning democracy in which parties operate as contenders for power. The scheme of the book neatly falls into three categories: institutional design (form), relevance of parties for the hybrid political system (function), and resilience in the face of challenges from extra-parliamentary forces (survival). This innovative heuristic model defines the research problematic through a schematic approach to the body politic and goes beyond analyzing political parties merely as election entities within a quantitative matrix that often ends up in "abstracted empiricism" (Mills 1959). The essays give due weightage to mainstream, ethnic, and Islamic parties in the institutional design and pose the question, Is the shell full or empty? The answers point to the organizational and ideological orientation of parties in the first case and patronage politics at the constituency level in the second.

The book explores "form" in all three types of parties. It finds the mainstream parties—the Pakistan Muslim League-Nawaz (PML-N), the Pakistan People's Party (PPP), and the Pakistan Tehreek-e-Insaf (PTI)—to be organizationally weak. Although in both the PPP and the PTI strong ideological orientations operated in the initial stages of party development—as reflected in the populism of the left and the populism of the right, respectively—periodic and selective co-optation by the military has long shaped party politics, not least because of the wavering loyalty of loose-ended "electable" politicians. As a result, patronage clusters have often emerged as factions opting out of existing political parties, sometimes en masse, as was the case with the Pakistan Muslim League-Quaid (PML-Q) in 2002. As for ethnic parties, apart from the Muhajir Qaumi Movement (MQM) in Sindh and the Awami National Party (ANP) in Khyber Pakhtunkhwa, a plethora of ethnic parties from Balochistan—the Jamhoori Wattan Party (JWP), the National Party (NP), the Balochistan National Party-Mengal (BNP-M), and the Pukhtunkhwa Milli Awam Party (PKMAP)—represent "tribal family politics" and have passed through numerous internal splits and horizontal mergers. Ethnic politics is sometimes accompanied by violence, such as the MQM's war of attrition in Karachi or the Marri-led guerrilla warfare in Balochistan. Islamic parties have generally operated as street agitators, as a religious lobby, and lately as militants whose votes can tip the balance in favor of one candidate over another.

Moving from inside to outside the party, the book focuses on party-voter links: How and why does a person become a party voter? In addition to the conventional wisdom about the nature of partisan ties through kinship, the caucuses of influential persons, and the communal ties of caste, sect, and tribe, the authors raise questions about the application of a rational voter model—with a focus on the transactional aspects of voter behavior—to the Pakistani context. They distinguish between "constituency politicians," who are rather freewheeling in terms of their party loyalties, and "party loyalists," who represent the public profile of parties in terms of policy and ideology (see also Mufti 2011). Even independents who win elections look for endorsements from political parties. This testifies to the role of political parties as "agents." The authors, therefore, seek to understand what "functions" of political parties make the parties relevant to the political system in the face of supra-parliamentarian forces that carry immense destabilizing potential. This in turn raises the question of the very "survival" of political parties within a potentially unfavorable political environment.

The chapters in this volume make clear that the "establishment"—shorthand for the military-bureaucracy nexus—is a permanent feature of the way political parties define their goals and means. Thus Pakistan is an "establishmentarian" democracy. The rise and fall of political parties must be analyzed with reference to the establishment, which has been responsible for dominating the political system, manipulating political parties, engineering elections, shaping the media, and controlling all other manifestations of a free democratic order. While the illiberal hybrid regime model has become the conventional wisdom about countries such as Pakistan (Adeney 2017; Samad 2017) and is supported by many of the authors in this volume, its analytical utility is questionable on two counts. First, such a categorization groups together all countries that are not "liberal" (in contrast to mature democracies) and which are therefore hybrid (that is, mixed with some undefined nondemocratic elements). This makes the approach teleological in the same way that modernization theory was once criticized. Defining one cluster of countries in terms of another remains problematic unless fully conceptualized. Second, the determinants of hybrid democracy are insufficiently analyzed in terms of bringing out the potential—or the lack of it—to transform to a mature democracy. For example, the hybrid democracy model is applicable only to the "differentiated social formations," whereby a modern state rules a traditional society, rather than to "undifferentiated social formations," where the state has a traditional tribal base (Lapidus 1996, 25–26).

The establishment's hegemony over party politics in Pakistan can be traced to Mohammad Ayub Khan's martial law regime, which subordinated all other institutions—bureaucracy, judiciary, Parliament—to the security apparatus and turned the political class into its client. Civilian supremacy over the armed forces was briefly restored during the PPP's rule (1971–77). However, any gains made by the political elite during this period were lost during Muhammad Zia-ul-Haq's martial law. The Afghan war mobilized a divine source of legitimacy that produced the garrison-*mullah* alliance (Haqqani 2005). Moreover, the dismissal of four prime ministers by the president on behalf of the army under Article 58 Section 2b (in 1988, 1990, 1993, and 1996) essentially discounted the mass mandate of political parties as the constitutional source of legitimacy.

By 2007, however, the Lawyers' Movement had largely diminished the possibility of direct military rule in Pakistan. Political mobilization of large sections of the population, the fallout of the third wave of democratization, and the fact that all South Asian countries are currently under democratic rule have collectively created an impression in the region that democracy is the only game in town. In the 2018 election the establishment in Pakistan learned to play the game accordingly. It undermined some political parties and promoted others, particularly the PTI. The leaders of the incumbent parties, the PML-N and the PPP, faced numerous cases of corruption under the National Accountability Bureau. Coupled with the establishment's muzzling of press freedom to ensure that election coverage was reflective of its broader agenda, almost all of the opposition parties lost their nerve and opted against protesting the blatant pre-poll and polling day rigging.

Whether Pakistan will remain an "establishmentarian democracy" for the foreseeable future remains an open question. The collection of chapters in this volume provide us some insight. The individual party profiles describe the role of the establishment in making and breaking Pakistan's political parties. Elections are held within the framework of an establishmentarian democracy. This model fulfils the main legal, formal, and procedural requirements of electoral democracy, but the Pakistani system functions under the rules of the game set by the unelected institutional apparatuses of the state, which ultimately define the legality and legitimacy of the political stakeholders. The black letter law has been consistently interpreted by the logic of the unwritten law that draws on this institutional imbalance. While political parties shy away from crossing "the red line," their struggle to compete for the mass mandate is dependent on the political imagination and support of society at large—a task that requires the ability to dole out patronage and underlies its legitimacy.

Saeed Shafqat's chapter on the rise and fall of the PML-N under Nawaz Sharif's leadership provides insight into this complex and transactional nature of the relationship between the military and the political class. He chronologically traces how the Muslim League underwent a number of splits and mergers to finally emerge as the PML-N. However, the electoral fortunes of the party have waxed and waned with the changing dynamics of civil-military relations. Sharif was nurtured by his military benefactors in the 1980s to become the prime minister in 1990. But as he asserted himself in foreign policy and enacted legislation to exercise executive privilege, the same establishment clipped his wings through Pervez Musharraf's military coup. Differences on policy toward India, Afghanistan, the United States, and the Taliban led to civil-military tension under Sharif's third tenure (2013–17) and ultimately to the PML-N's defeat in the 2018 elections. Although the PML-N began its third stint in power with a parliamentary majority, it was quickly hampered by the PTI's 2014 sit-in—which the establishment did not hesitate to support—and an underperforming economy. Charges of corruption ultimately led to Sharif's disqualification as prime minister. The inclusion of intelligence agencies' personnel on the Joint Investigation Team (JIT) for the Panama case further contributed to the death knell of Sharif's rule.

The PPP traversed a similar path for survival in politics. Philip Jones analyzes the party's march to victory in 1970 with reference to Z. A. Bhutto's embrace of a leftist ideology at the crest of a rising socialist movement. Bhutto heralded the common man's entry into the political field by striking against the oppressive hold of Ayub Khan's system. However, as a charismatic populist leader Bhutto discounted the need to organize the party and soon dispensed with the ideological cadres. Under Zia's martial law an unbridled process of Islamization fostered the rise of Islamic parties and the enhanced security agenda dispensed with PPP-style politics for good. Under the rule of troika (1988–99), comprising the chief of army staff, the president, and the prime minister (in that order), Benazir Bhutto twice failed to snatch the political initiative from the establishment. When her husband, Asif Zardari, became president, he generally operated through elite bargaining but nonetheless alienated the establishment on policies relating to the United States, which led to a media blitzkrieg against him. As expected, the erosion of party support during the 2013 and 2018 elections has confined the PPP's presence primarily to Sindh.

While research on the PML-N and the PPP focuses on the wider contextual framework of power, the study of the PTI by Tabinda Khan brings out its internal dynamics. Most typically, the PTI sought to become a catch-all party through a reduction of its ideological baggage and the virtual de-acknowledgement of ordinary party workers. While the PTI started as a mode of defiance against political dynasties, it eventually opened its ranks to turncoats from other parties as potential election winners. The party projected a profile as a political situation beset by corrupt politicians, poor health and education, and a nonperforming economy. As a celebrity Imran Khan nurtured a cult of personality and attracted maximum on-screen time to give voice to the frustrations and expectations of the disillusioned middle classes, especially after the latter were mobilized during the 2007 Lawyers' Movement. Activists and cadres from other parties such as the PPP, PML-N, Jamaat-e-Islami (JI), Jamiat Ulema-e-Islam (JUI), MQM, and PML-Q flocked to the party as the perception of Imran Khan as the establishment's blue-eyed boy spread. The new entrants—powerful electables—were able to marginalize the "old guard" ideological cadre, some of whom eventually left the party. Accommodation of pro-establishment elements has made the PTI a status-quo party par excellence, which accounts for its victory in the 2018 elections.

While mainstream parties have "negotiated" with the system in this way, ethnic parties have drawn on linguistic, sociological, and regional identities—local or migrant—to challenge the prevalent scheme of things. In his study of the MQM, Tahir Naqvi examines its central strategy for mobilization as the adoption of a discourse of sacrifice and deconstructs it as psychological essentialism. Sacrifice served the ethnic imaginary of Muhajirs by characterizing Muslim nationalism as a "universalizing ideal" heralding the movement for Pakistan, on the one hand, and the multiethnic reality of living in Sindh on the other. Sacrifice provided a transcendental frame for the MQM's movement. While two-thirds of all migrants from India were assimilated into Punjab, one-third of them remained unassimilated in Sindh (Waseem 1999). Over the course of two generations the latter moved from a classic Muslim nationalism assemblage to an ethnically marked restive community. Although the MQM renamed itself as *Muttahida* (united) in recognition of the ethnically plural character of Sindh and Pakistan, its members' sense of sacrifice and their resolve to assert the party through affect and action has become the defining feature of MQM factions as the party atrophied before and during the 2018 elections.

Parallel to the MQM, leftist parties have their own story of rise and fall, although theirs has followed a different trajectory. The left's initial activism was followed by a gradual decline in the face of state oppression, a reassertion as part of the larger populist movement of the PPP, and then a prolonged process of degeneration as a viable political actor. In Anushay Malik's view, since those who espoused the causes of the left and provincial autonomy often operated from a common organizational platform—such as that of the National Awami Party (NAP)—the state's crackdown on autonomists as potential secessionists further weakened the left (Nasr 2001). Like elsewhere, the left in Pakistan operated against the status quo, with class as the pivot of its rhetoric, neoliberalism as its ultimate liquidator, organized labor as its mainstay, and anti-imperialism as its ideological position (L. Khan 2009). In Pakistan the state's suspicion of the left's links with India and its need to establish its anticommunist credentials for entering into military alliances with the West led to its suppression. In the twenty-first century the left in Pakistan faces the challenge of the all-pervasive influence of neoliberalism, on the one hand, and nongovernmental organizations pursuing progressive causes within that framework, on the other.

Johann Chacko describes a politics of denominational diversity among religious parties that are low on votes but high on discourse. They are strongly divided on how to bring about the rule of sharia but are typically united on the agenda of denying legitimacy to the state's power to exercise religious authority. The failure of denominational parties to win elections is rooted in the parties' lack of capacity to provide patronage to their clients as compared to the larger mainstream political parties. The fact that voters tend to favor candidates who carry the potential to deliver in terms of material benefits explains the gap between the Islamists' single-issue movements and voting patterns at large. Nonetheless, elections have provided these parties with bargaining power, as they carry small vote margins that can tip the balance in favor of their preferred candidates. Given the inability of denominational parties to occupy the seat of government, their ultimate response is to work in partnership with the establishment. Meanwhile, the hardening of denominational boundaries (Shia, Sunni, Barelvi, Wahabi, Ahmadi) has increased sectarian conflict. Examples of the denominational ecosystem's impact include the emergence of groups united around protecting the finality of prophethood by targeting Ahmadis and, to a lesser extent, Shias.

The chapters go beyond examining the broader context of political competition between the military and political parties to focus on how parties fulfill their functions as conduits for the interests of the citizens to the state, and vice-versa. The study of political contact in urban Punjab by Asad Liaqat, Ali Cheema, and Shandana Khan Mohmand, for example, takes the reader beyond the ideational framework of party politics. It focuses on the layered pattern of communication among party leadership, cadres, and workers at one end, and sections of society commensurate with their respective social, economic, and political status at the other. The study deals with the different electoral contexts at the federal, provincial, and local government levels and relates them to the way in which higher-tier and lower-tier politicians operate within the party organizations. The importance of local politicians is highlighted as brokers of the citizen-party linkage, which is based on the provision of patronage. Lower-tier politicians bring information about citizen demands and preferences, develop strategies to give priority to committed or undecided voters during election campaigns, and are able to focus on active voters more than passive sympathizers. Party machines in Punjab thus transmit public demands upward and policies and patronage downward. Local politicians link up with higher-level politicians representing their respective factions. The gap between voters and party machines increases when moving from rural to urban constituencies. Thus, voter-initiated partisanship in the cosmopolitan world of Lahore may not reflect the ground reality in other parts of the country.

Parallel to party-voter linkages, candidate-party linkages are equally important for understanding the electoral context. Hassan Javid and Mariam Mufti provide a typology of electoral candidates underscored by two attributes: autonomy, which draws on the social and economic status of candidates and their strong kinship ties, and commitment, which means loyalty to the party or leadership determined by ideological or familial ties. This typology identifies four kinds of candidates. The first is party heavyweights, who enjoy financial power relating to landed property and increasingly to business concerns but are committed to a single political party. Second is independent electables, who have their respective stable vote blocs and can therefore bargain with political parties from a position of strength. Third is party workers, most typically from the MQM, who lack an independent vote bank of their own. Finally, aspirational candidates, usually social climbers, stake their claim to a public role and often make it in the end. Party leaderships opt for candidates who have their local strongholds so that the party does not incur the cost of investment in building the party. However, strong candidates in turn opt to join a "winning" party in order to gain access to state patronage. The implication of this typology is the authors' key takeaway: low levels of party identification and reliance on party heavyweights and independent electables has made political parties prone to shifting party loyalties. Indeed, time and again this vulnerability of political parties has been manipulated successfully by the establishment to shape electoral outcomes in its favor.

By and large politics is a male-dominated arena in which women are systematically underrepresented, a fact that speaks volumes about the health of Pakistan's democracy. Sarah Khan's chapter describes the myriad ways in which women are excluded from politics. Within political parties, patterns of recruitment and selection explain why women are sparingly awarded party nominations; even when parties award tickets to women candidates, they tend to field these candidates in uncompetitive districts. Although reserved seats for women have helped to increase women's representation, the fact that they are indirectly elected seats means that women candidates are unable to gain experience in electoral campaigning. Within the private sphere, families primarily structure women's participation in electoral politics through dynastic connections, which means that nondynastic candidates are discouraged from participating. Still, there was a slight decrease in dynastic candidates with a concurrent increase of women's reserved seats in the 2002 and 2008 elections. It is clear that gender bias exists among voters, with high percentages of Pakistani voters expressing skepticism that women political leaders can be effective.

While political parties grapple with establishing contacts with voters and prospective election candidates, what happens when they are obliged to deliver on governance once they occupy office? From the pursuit of legislation, maintaining coalitions, and formulating policy to initiating and completing development projects, they depend on civil bureaucracy. Sameen Ali argues that different parties develop different models of relations with the higher bureaucracy and politicize the appointment of bureaucrats based on the party's relation with the military and the attitudes and experiences of party leaders. In the context of an establishmentarian democracy, political parties have a short-term perspective that increases their dependence on the bureaucracy to operate as channels for providing targeted goods (as patronage) rather than nontargeted goods (as policy). It is instructive to compare the politician-bureaucrat relationship under three successive governments. The PML-Q (2003–8) effectively delegated power to bureaucrats and focused on patronage politics at the constituency level, not least because of the empowerment of district politics under the military-imposed Devolution Plan in 2001. The PPP government under Zardari (2008–13) politicized the appointment of bureaucrats to pursue the party's traditional practice of delivering targeted goods under a grand patronage strategy. Meanwhile, the PML-N government (2013–18) allied itself with the bureaucracy, partially because it drifted away from the army after the Sharif brothers came back from exile. The party focused on service delivery and gaining nontargeted goods through crony bureaucrats.

The third set of chapters grapples with the question of party survival in the face of external forces. Political parties are continually being challenged and often undermined by both electoral and nonelectoral forces, and this is especially true of Pakistan's establishmentarian democracy.

The role of opposition parties is explored by Sahar Shafqat through the conceptual framework of institutionalized uncertainty that has resulted from the tutelary influence of the establishment and has spread its tentacles to strategic areas of public policy, administrative hierarchy, and the media. While mature democracies have an in-built role for opposition without coercion, the classic parliamentary role of the opposition has recently undergone a change by opting for public demonstrations and street politics in pursuit of new social movements, among other tactics. Pakistan's regime uncertainty, which casts a shadow on the legitimacy of electoral politics and legislative activity, promotes an extra-parliamentary role for the opposition. Shafqat focuses on two examples: the 2007 Lawyers' Movement against Musharraf that was later joined by the PML-N against the PPP's government in 2008–9 and the PTI movement against the Nawaz Sharif government in 2014. These examples drive home the point that, even if not in government, political parties can have long-lasting implications for democracy through their mobilization activities.

Ayesha Siddiqa argues that rather than ruling directly, the military operates more as an arbiter by supporting political leaders through the electoral process. The army's preference for client parties is ultimately responsible for keeping the party system weak and vulnerable. Its role vis-à-vis the creation of the MQM, the PML, the PTI, and various religious parties is a testimony to its deep involvement with political parties. However, by putting all eggs in the army's basket, a party runs the risk of underestimating other relevant factors. For example, to claim that the rise of Bhutto was meant to strengthen a reactionary state grossly bypasses the revolutionary potential of his populist movement (K. A. Ali 2015). Indeed, the Bhutto era was the only period of qualified civilian supremacy. Later PPP governments were dismissed by the army and suffered acute distrust. The later creation of the MQM is also generally attributed to Zia's move to counter the PPP's popular base in Sindh (A. R. Siddiqui 2008). Later, as the MQM's militant politics in urban Sindh spiraled out of hand, the army created a new MQM faction—*Haqiqi*—and then, in 2016, the army put an end to Altaf Hussain's leadership role after his "treasonous" speech against Pakistan. Nawaz Sharif's three terms in office (1990–93, 1997–99, and 2013–17) similarly succumbed to civil-military tensions.

In the context of the never-ending civil-military crisis, the judiciary has played a pivotal role in tilting the balance in favor of the military. Yasser Kureshi focuses on the concept of dissonant institutionalization whereby the competing profiles of the community and their legitimation strategies keep the state from depoliticization, contrary to the wishes and efforts of military dictators. This dissonance provides a role for the judiciary as an arbiter of "megapolitics." This process brings about a pattern of interaction between the internal culture of the judiciary, as defined by its daily brush with the black letter law and court cases on one end, and the outermost formal structure and institutional ethos of the judiciary on the other end. The Pakistani judiciary has transitioned from supporting the military against elected party leaders (citing "state necessity"), to challenging Zia's martial law regulations in civil courts, to becoming assertive about the judiciary's institutional privileges in the midst of litigation surrounding Iftikhar Chaudhry's suspension. Chaudhry's removal was followed by the suspension of a series of judges under emergency in November 2007; the post-2009 judiciary has taken pride in ushering in an era of democracy, but it has chosen to do this by raising suspicions about politicians and bad governance. In contemporary Pakistan, institutional dissonance among the army, the judiciary, and the political parties continues to destabilize democracy.

Foreign policy is a relatively underutilized policy area for political parties, a topic that Christopher Clary explores in some detail. Pakistan's citizens are more concerned about issues nearer to home—tribe, caste, ethnicity—than issues abroad. In Pakistan it is risky for parties to deliberate on foreign policy issues because of the army's tutelary control over diplomacy. The military welcomes only hawks in pursuit of the declared national policy. The stated policies of party manifestos in 2013 are a good indicator of their respective positions about international relations. The key question, however, is whether these positions have any salient impact on policymaking. Although Clary acknowledges the primacy of military interests in Pakistan's foreign policy, his examination of party manifestos shows political parties subtly differ in their stances than the military does in its messaging to voters. Of course, foreign policy can have asymmetrical levels of acceptance across the country. Cross-border ethnic affinity, for example, has been noticed among Pashtuns for the Taliban and among Shias for Iran.

The underlying role of the establishment pervades the author's argument in every chapter of this volume. A recurrent theme is that the establishment has assumed the role of the real "agent" by other means beyond the doctrine of separation of powers, while political parties operate as "proto agent." If democracy is the only game in town, the establishment has demonstrated that it is ready to play ball—a situation unlikely to change in the near term. In the context of an establishmentarian democracy, then, the authors demonstrate that political parties may be catalysts of democratic competition as much as they are blockers of the military's hegemonic institutional dominance.

Appendix: Pakistan Electoral Results, 1988–2018

Table A.1. Pakistan electoral results, 1988–2018

1988			1990			1993			1997		
Party	Vote share	Number of seats	Party	Vote share	Number of seats	Party	Vote share	Number of seats	Party	Vote share	Number of seats
PPP	38.52%	93	IJI	37.37%	105	PML–N	39.85%	73	PML–N	45.83%	135
IJI	30.21%	54	PDA	36.83%	44	PPP	37.84%	86	PPP	21.74%	18
IND	19.52%	40	IND	10.30%	22	IND	7.40%	15	IND	14.24%	21
PAI	4.39%	3	HPG	5.54%	15	PML-J	3.90%	6	HPG	4.00%	12
ANP	2.09%	2	JUI-F	2.94%	6	PIF	3.24%	3	PPP-SB	1.98%	1
JUI-F	1.84%	7	ANP	1.68%	6	IJM	2.40%	4	ANP	1.87%	9
NPP-K	0.50%	1	JUP-N	1.47%	3	ANP	1.67%	3	JUI-F	1.71%	2
PDP	0.41%	1	PNP	0.60%	2	MDM	1.09%	2	BNP	0.65%	3
PNA	0.36%	2	JWP	0.61%	2	PKMAP	0.49%	3	NPP	0.45%	1
JUP-D	0.23%	1	PKMAP	0.35%	1	NDA	0.32%	1	JWP	0.35%	2
Other (18)	1.93%	0	Other (18)	2.31%	0	JWP	0.27%	2	Other (38)	8.39%	0
Total	100.00%	204	Total	100.00%	206	PKQP	0.27%	1	Total	100.00%	204
						NPP	0.24%	1			
						BNM–H	0.24%	1			
						BNM–M	0.23%	1			
						Other (27)	0.55%	0			
						Total	100.00%	202			

2002			2008			2013			2018		
Party	Vote share	Number of seats	Party	Vote share	Number of seats	Party	Vote share	Number of seats	Party	Vote share	Number of seats
PPP	26.05%	63	PPP	30.87%	89	PML-N	32.53%	127	PTI	31.89%	116
PML-Q	25.66%	79	PML-Q	23.18%	42	PTI	16.92%	28	PML-N	24.41%	64
PML-N	11.66%	15	PML-N	19.64%	68	PPP	15.42%	34	PPP	13.07%	43
MMA	11.41%	44	IND	10.95%	29	IND	13.08%	28	IND	11.41%	13
IND	9.31%	28	MQM	7.45%	19	MQM	5.39%	18	MMA	4.85%	12
NA	4.77%	13	MMA	2.22%	6	JUI-F	3.25%	11	GDA	2.38%	2
MQM	3.19%	13	PML-F	2.04%	4	PML-Q	3.08%	2	ANP	1.54%	1
ANP	1.03%	0	ANP	2.04%	10	PML-F	2.34%	5	MQM	1.38%	6
PML-F	1.00%	4	NPP	0.43%	1	JI	2.11%	3	PML-Q	0.98%	4
PML-J	0.97%	3	PPP-S	0.41%	1	ANP	1.03%	1	BAP	0.51%	4
PTI	0.83%	1	BNP-A	0.21%	1	PKMAP	0.47%	3	BNP	0.41%	3
PAT	0.69%	1	Other (32)	0.57%	0	NPP	0.43%	2	AMLP	0.23%	1
PPP-S	0.34%	2	Total	100.00%	270	PML-Z	0.28%	1	JWP	0.04%	1
PKMAP	0.33%	1				AMLP	0.20%	1	Other (73)	6.90%	0
JWP	0.33%	1				AJIP	0.16%	1	Total	100.00%	270
PML-Z	0.27%	1				BNP	0.16%	1			
BNP	0.27%	1				NP	0.13%	1			
MQMP	0.18%	1				All PML	0.12%	1			
PSPP	0.15%	1				QWP	0.10%	1			
Other (41)	1.56%	0				Other (91)	0.60%	0			
Total	100.00%	272				Total	100.00%	269			

Sources: Election results from 1988 to 2008 are taken from Mehdi (2010). Election results from 2013 are based on Election Commission of Pakistan, "Report on the General Election Pakistan," vols. 1 and 2 (Islamabad: ECP, 2013). Election results from 2018 are provisional and based on Form 47, available at www.ecp.gov.pk, accessed May 2, 2019.

Note: The results presented here are of electoral contests in single-member districts and do not include reserved seats. Results of the 1970, 1977, and 1985 elections are not included for a number of reasons: the 1970 election was held in East Pakistan and West Pakistan, but this book focuses on politics in the latter only; an accurate record of election results from 1977 do not exist (and it has been reported that the military had the results destroyed); and in 1985 the election was held on a nonparty basis. Results of elections to the National Assembly districts 16, 21, and 62 in 1988; 91 in 1990; 26, 34, 60, 72, and 123 in 1993; 1, 121, and 143 in 1997; 41 and 42 in 2008; 38, 83, and 254 in 2013; and 60 and 103 in 2018 are not included because election results were either delayed or the proceedings were terminated. All results presented here reflect vote counts on polling day and are not updated to include the results of by-elections.

References

Abbas, Hassan. 2010. *Militancy in Pakistan's Borderlands: Implications for the Nation and for Afghan Policy.* Washington, DC: Century Foundation.

Adams, James, Andrea B. Haupt, and Heather Stoll. 2009. "What Moves Parties? The Role of Public Opinion and Global Economic Conditions in Western Europe." *Comparative Political Studies* 42 (5): 611–39.

Adeney, Katharine. 2012. "A Step towards Inclusive Federalism in Pakistan? The Politics of the 18th Amendment." *Publius* 42 (4): 539–65.

———. 2017. "How to Understand Pakistan's Hybrid Regime: The Importance of a Multidimensional Continuum." *Democratization* 24 (1): 119–37.

Adorno, Theodor. 2000. *Problems of Moral Philosophy.* Stanford, CA: Stanford University Press.

Afzal, M. Rafique. 1986. *Political Parties in Pakistan: 1947–1958.* Islamabad: National Institute of Historical and Cultural Research.

———. 1987. *Political Parties in Pakistan: 1958–1969.* Islamabad: National Institute of Historical and Cultural Research.

———. 1998. *Political Parties in Pakistan: 1969–1971.* Islamabad: National Institute of Historical and Cultural Research.

Ahmad, Aijaz. 1978. "Democracy and Dictatorship in Pakistan." *Journal of Contemporary Asia* 8 (4): 477–512.

Ahmad, Mujeeb. 1993. *Jamiat Ulema-i-Pakistan, 1948–1979.* Islamabad: National Institute of Historical and Cultural Research.

Ahmad, Saghir. 1977. *Class and Power in a Punjabi Village.* New York: Monthly Review.

Ahmed, Feroz. 1972. "Interview Ishaque Mohammad." *Pakistan Forum* 3 (1): 5–9.

Ahmed, Saifuddin, and Marko M. Skoric. 2014. "My Name Is Khan: The Use of Twitter in the Campaign for 2013 Pakistan General Election." In *Proceedings of the 47th Annual Hawaii Institute Conference on System Sciences,* 2242–51. Piscataway, NJ: IEEE Computer Society. https://doi.org/10.1109/HICSS.2014.282.

Ahmed, Samina, and David Cortright. 1998. "Pakistani Public Opinion and Nuclear Weapons Policy." In *Pakistan and the Bomb: Public Opinion and Nuclear Options,* edited by Samina Ahmed and David Cortright, 3–27. Notre Dame, IN: University of Notre Dame Press.

Ahmed, Wajihuddin. 2014. *Election Tribunal Order*. Lahore: privately printed.

Akhtar, Aasim Sajjad. 2006. "The State as Landlord in Pakistani Punjab: Peasant Struggles on the Okara Military Farms." *Journal of Peasant Studies* 33 (3): 479–501.

———. 2012. "Twenty-First-Century Socialism in Pakistan?" *Economic and Political Weekly* 47 (45): 27–29.

———. 2015. "The Socialist Imperative: Left Politics in Contemporary Pakistan." *Capitalism Nature Socialism* 26 (3): 102–14.

———. 2018. *The Politics of Common Sense: State, Society and Culture in Pakistan*. Cambridge: Cambridge University Press.

Akhtar, Hameed. 2009. *Kali Kothri* [Black Cell]. Lahore: Book Home.

Akhtari, Mitra, Diana Moreira, and Laura Trucco. 2017. "Political Turnover, Bureaucratic Turnover, and the Quality of Public Services." OpenScholar Working Paper 468671. Cambridge, MA: Harvard University.

Alavi, Hamza. 1971. "The Politics of Dependence: A West Punjab Village." *South Asian Review* 4 (2): 111–28.

———. 1972a. "Kinship in West Punjab Villages." *Contributions to Indian Sociology: New Series* 6: 1–27.

———. 1972b. "The State in Post-Colonial Societies: Pakistan and Bangladesh." *New Left Review* 1 (74): 57–81.

———. 1983. "Class and State." In *Pakistan, the Roots of Dictatorship: The Political Economy of a Praetorian State*, edited by Hassan N. Gardezi and Jamil Rashid, 40–93. London: Zed.

Ali, Kamran Asdar. 2005. "The Strength of the Street Meets the Strength of the State: The 1972 Labor Struggle in Karachi." *International Journal of Middle East Studies* 37: 83–107.

———. 2015. *Communism in Pakistan: Politics and Class Activism, 1947–1972*. London: I. B. Tauris.

Ali, Mehrunissa. 1977. "Pakistan: Aftermath of the March 1977 Elections." *Pakistan Horizon* 30 (3–4): 77–102.

Ali, Sameen A. M. 2018. *Staffing the State: The Politicization of the Bureaucracy in Pakistan*. PhD diss., School of Oriental and African Studies, University of London.

———. 2019. "Party Patronage and Merit-Based Bureaucratic Reform in Pakistan." Working paper presented at the 77th Annual Midwest Political Science Association Conference, Chicago, April 4–7.

Ali, Tariq. 1970. *Pakistan: Military Rule or People's Power*. London: Jonathan Cape.

Amyot, Grant. 1987. "Non-parliamentary Opposition in Italy: The New Social Movements." In *Opposition in Western Europe*, edited by Eva Kolinsky, 353–74. New York: St. Martin's.

Anderson, Benedict. 1991. *Imagined Communities: Reflections on the Origin and Spread of Nationalism*. New York: Verso.

Anderson, Christopher J., Andre Blais, Shaun Bowler, Todd Donovan, and Ola Listhaug. 2005. *Losers' Consent: Elections and Democratic Legitimacy*. Oxford: Oxford University Press.

Anwar, Raja. 1997. *The Terrorist Prince: The Life and Death of Murtaza Bhutto*. New York: Verso.

Appadurai, Arjun. 1998. "Full Attachment." *Public Culture* 10 (2): 443–49.

———. 2006. *Fear of Small Numbers: An Essay on the Geography of Anger*. Durham, NC: Duke University Press.

Auerbach, Adam M. 2016. "Clients and Communities: The Political Economy of Party Network Organization and Development in India's Urban Slums." *World Politics* 68 (1): 111–48.

Auerbach, Adam M., and Tariq Thachil. 2018. "How Clients Select Brokers: Competition and Choice in India's Slums." *American Political Science Review* 112 (4): 775–91.

Aurat Foundation. 2008. *From Home to House: Experiences of Women Councillors in Local Government, Vol 3*. Lahore: Aurat Publication and Information Service Foundation.

———. 2012. *Legislative Quotas for Women: A Global and South Asian Overview of Types and Numbers*. Lahore: Aurat Publication and Information Service Foundation.

Ayres, Alyssa. 2009. *Speaking like a State: Language and Nationalism in Pakistan*. New York: Cambridge University Press.

Azeem, Muhammad. 2017. *Law, State and Inequality in Pakistan: Explaining the Rise of the Judiciary*. Singapore: Springer International.

Aziz, K. K. 1976. *Party Politics in Pakistan: 1947–58*. Lahore: Sang-e-Meel.

Aziz, Sadaf. 2015. "The Politics of Anti-Corruption." In *The Politics and Jurisprudence of the Chaudhry Court*, edited by Moeen Cheema and Ijaz Shafi Gilani, 253–80. Karachi: Oxford University Press.

Aziz, Sartaj. 2009. *Between Dreams and Reality: Some Milestones in Pakistan's History*. Karachi: Oxford University Press.

Bali, Asli. 2012. "The Perils of Judicial Independence: Constitutional Transition and the Turkish Example." *Virginia Journal of International Law* 52: 235–320.

Bari, Farzana. 2001. *Local Government Elections, December 2000 (Phase I)*. Islamabad: Pattan Development Corporation.

———. 2015. "Bridging the Fault Lines? Rethinking the Gender Quota Approach in Pakistan." In *Reviewing Gender Quotas in Afghanistan and Pakistan*, edited by Jennifer Bennett, 7–27. Islamabad: Heinrich Boll Stiftung.

Barlas, Asma. 1995. *Democracy, Nationalism, and Communalism: The Colonial Legacy in South Asia*. Boulder, CO: Westview.

Bashir, Omar S. 2009. "Explaining Islamist Pressures on State Behavior: The Jamaat-i Islami and Pakistani Foreign Policy." MPhil thesis, University of Oxford.

Basu, Amrita. 2016. *Women's Movements in the Global Era: The Power of Local Feminisms*. New York: Avalon.

Baxter, Craig. 1974. "The People's Party vs. the Punjab 'Feudalists.'" In *Contemporary Problems of Pakistan*, edited by J. Henry Korson, 6–29. Leiden: E. J. Brill.

Beaman, Lori, Raghabendra Chattopadhyay, Esther Duflo, Rohini Pande, and Petia Topalova. 2009. "Powerful Women: Does Exposure Reduce Bias?" *Quarterly Journal of Economics* 124 (4): 1497–1540.

Behuria, Ashok K. 2008. "Sects within Sect: The Case of Deobandi–Barelvi Encounter in Pakistan." *Strategic Analysis* 32 (1): 57–80.

Bhavnani, Rikhil R. 2009. "Do Electoral Quotas Work after They Are Withdrawn?

Evidence from a Natural Experiment in India." *American Political Science Review* 103 (1): 23–35.

Bhutto, B. 2008. *Reconciliation: Islam, Democracy and the West.* New York: HarperCollins.

Bhutto, Z. A. 1969. *The Myth of Independence.* New York: Oxford University Press.

———. 1979. *If I Am Assassinated.* New Delhi: Vikas.

Binder, Leonard. 1961. *Religion and Politics in Pakistan.* Berkeley: University of California Press.

Blom, Amélie. 2002. "The 'Multi-vocal State': The Policy of Pakistan on Kashmir." In *Pakistan: Nationalism without a Nation?*, edited by Christophe Jaffrelot, 283–310. New York: Zed.

Bolognani, Marta. 2010. "Virtual Protest with Tangible Effects? Some Observations on the Media Strategies of the 2007 Pakistani Anti-emergency Movement." *Contemporary South Asia* 18: 401–12.

Brader, Ted, and Joshua Tucker. 2012. "Following the Party's Lead: Party Cues, Policy Opinion, and the Power of Partisanship in Three Multiparty Systems." *Comparative Politics* 44 (4): 403–20.

Braibanti, Ralph. 1966. *Research on the Bureaucracy of Pakistan.* Durham, NC: Duke University Press.

———. 1999. *Chief Justice Cornelius of Pakistan: An Analysis with Letters and Speeches.* New York: Oxford University Press.

Brumberg, Daniel. 2001. *Reinventing Khomeini: The Struggle for Reform in Iran.* Chicago: University of Chicago Press.

Buehler, Arthur. 1998. *Sufi Heirs of the Prophet.* Columbia: University of South Carolina Press.

Burki, Shahid Javed. 1988. *Pakistan under Bhutto, 1971–1977.* 2nd ed. United Kingdom: Palgrave Macmillan.

———. 1992. "Pakistan's Economy under Zia." In *Pakistan under the Military—Eleven Years of Zia-ul-Haq,* edited by Craig Baxter and Shahid Javed Burki, 112–16. Boulder, CO: Westview.

Bush, Sarah Sunn. 2011. "International Politics and the Spread of Quotas for Women in Legislatures." *International Organization* 65 (1): 103–37.

Butler, Judith. 1997. *Excitable Speech: A Politics of the Performative.* New York: Routledge.

———. 2005. *Giving an Account of Oneself.* New York: Fordham University Press.

Butler, Judith, Ernesto Laclau, and Slavoj Žižek. 2000. *Contingency, Hegemony, Universality: Contemporary Dialogues on the Left.* London: Verso.

Butt, Ahsan. 2016. "Street Power: Friday Prayers, Islamist Protests, and Islamization in Pakistan." *Politics and Religion* 9 (1): 1–28.

Candland, Christopher. 2007a. *Labor, Democratization and Development in India and Pakistan.* Oxon, UK: Routledge.

———. 2007b. "Workers' Organizations in Pakistan: Why No Role in Formal Politics?" *Critical Asian Studies* 39 (1): 35–57.

Capitanchik, David. 1987. "Non-parliamentary Opposition in Great Britain: The Case of the Trade Unions." In *Opposition in Western Europe,* edited by Eva Kolinsky, 265–88. New York: St. Martin's.

Carothers, Thomas. 2002. "End of the Transition Paradigm." *Journal of Democracy* 13 (1): 5–21.

Caul, Miki. 1999. "Women's Representation in Parliament: The Role of Political Parties." *Party Politics* 5 (1): 79–98.

Chandra, Kanchan. 2004. *Why Ethnic Parties Succeed.* Cambridge, UK: Cambridge University Press.

———. 2016. "Democratic Dynasties: State, Party, and Family in Contemporary Indian Politics." In *Democratic Dynasties: State, Party, and Family in Contemporary Indian Politics,* edited by Kanchan Chandra, 12–56. New York: Cambridge University Press.

Chatterjee, Partha. 1993. *The Nation and Its Fragments: Colonial and Postcolonial Histories.* Princeton, NJ: Princeton University Press.

Chattopadhyay, Raghabendra, and Esther Duflo. 2004. "Women as Policy Makers: Evidence from a Randomized Policy Experiment in India." *Econometrica* 72 (5): 1409–43.

Cheema, Ali, Hassan Javid, and Farooq Naseer. 2013. "Dynastic Politics in Punjab: Facts, Myths, and Their Implications." Working Paper No. 01–12. Lahore: Institute of Development and Economic Alternatives.

Cheema, Ali, Sarah Khan, Asad Liaqat, Shandana Khan Mohmand, and Anam Kuraishi. 2019. "Women's Political Participation in Pakistan's Big Cities: Evidence for Reform." IDS Policy Briefing 166. Brighton: IDS.

Cheema, Ali, Shandana Khan Mohmand, and Asad Liaqat. 2017. "Competing to Deliver? Political Workers and Service Delivery in Pakistan." Making All Voices Count Research Briefing. Brighton: IDS.

Cheema, Ali, Asim Ijaz Khwaja, and Adnan Qadir. 2006. "Local Government Reforms in Pakistan: Context, Content, and Causes." In *Decentralization and Local Governance in Developing Countries: A Comparative Perspective,* edited by Pranab K. Bardhan and Dilip Mookherjee, 381–483. Cambridge, MA: MIT Press.

Cheema, Moeen, and Ijaz S. Gilani. 2015. *The Politics and Jurisprudence of the Chaudhry Court.* Karachi: Oxford University Press.

Chhibber, Pradeep K., and Rahul Verma. 2018. *Ideology and Identity: The Changing Party Systems of India.* New York: Oxford University Press.

Clary, Christopher. 2016. "Pakistan: The Nuclear Consensus." In *The Nuclear Debate in Asia: Risks and Rewards,* edited by Deepa Ollapally and Mike Mochizuki, 221–44. Lanham, MD: Rowman & Littlefield.

Clary, Christopher, and Niloufer Siddiqui. 2017a. "Obama and the U.S.-Pakistan Marriage of Convenience." In *The World Views of the Obama Era: From Hope to Disillusionment,* edited by Matthias Maass, 283–307. New York: Palgrave Macmillan.

———. 2017b. "Voters and Foreign Policy: Evidence from a Conjoint Experiment in Pakistan." Paper presented at the International Studies Association Annual Conference, Baltimore. February 23.

Cohen, Stephen. 2004. *The Idea of Pakistan.* Washington, DC: Brookings Institution Press.

Coll, Steve. 2004. *Ghost Wars: The Secret History of the CIA, Afghanistan, and Bin Laden, from the Soviet Invasion to September 10, 2001.* New York: Penguin.

Conroy-Krutz, Jeffrey, Devra Moehler, and Rosario Aguilar. 2015. "Partisan Cues and Vote Choice in New Multiparty Systems." *Comparative Political Studies* 49 (1): 1–33.

Couso, Javier, and Lisa Hilbink. 2011. "From Quietism to Incipient Activism: The Institutional and Ideological Roots of Rights Adjudication in Chile." In *Courts in Latin America*, edited by Gretchen Helmke and Julio Rios-Figueroa, 99–127. New York: Cambridge University Press.

Couso, Javier, Alexander Huneeus, and Rachel Sieder. 2011. *Cultures of Legality: Judicialization and Political Activity in Latin America.* New York: Cambridge University Press.

Dahl, Robert. 1966. "Preface." In *Political Oppositions in Western Democracies,* edited by Robert Dahl, xiii–xxi. New Haven, CT: Yale University Press.

Davies, Liz. 2007. "Pakistan Dictator Takes on His Judiciary." *Socialist Lawyer* 47:10–11.

Diani, Mario, and Donatella Della Porta. 2006. *Social Movements: An Introduction.* New York: John Wiley & Sons.

Dryland, Estelle. 1992. "Perspectives on Socialist Realism in Asian Literature." *Journal of South Asian Literature* 27 (2): 175–85.

Durrani, Naureen, Máiréad Dunne, Kathleen Fincham, and Barbara Crossouard. 2017. "Pakistan: Converging Imaginaries in an Islamic State." In *Troubling Muslim Youth Identities,* edited by Naureen Durrani, Máiréad Dunne, Kathleen Fincham, and Barbara Crossouard, 77–125. London: Palgrave Macmillan.

Easwaran, Eknath. 1984. *Nonviolent Soldier of Islam: Badshah Khan, a Man to Match His Mountains.* Tomales, CA: Nilgiri.

Edelman, Martin. 1992. "The Judicial Elite of Israel." *International Political Science Review* 13 (3): 235–48.

Elischer, Sebastien. 2013. *Political Parties in Africa: Ethnicity and Party Formation.* New York: Cambridge University Press.

Fair, C. Christine. 2014. *Fighting to the End: The Pakistan Army's Way of War.* New York: Oxford University Press.

Fair, C. Christine, Neil Malhotra, and Jacob N. Shapiro. 2010. "Islam, Militancy, and Politics in Pakistan: Insights from a National Sample." *Terrorism and Political Violence* 22 (4): 495–521.

———. 2012. "Faith or Doctrine? Religion and Support for Political Violence in Pakistan." *Public Opinion Quarterly* 76 (4): 688–720.

Farooq, Imran. 1989. *Nazm-o-Zabt Ki Takazay* [The Needs of Discipline]. MQM pamphlet.

Field, Erica, and Kate Vyborny. 2016. *Policy Brief on Female Labor Force Participation in Asia: Pakistan Country Study.* Asian Development Bank Briefs No. 70.

Finan, Fredrico, and Laura Schechter. 2012. "Vote-Buying and Reciprocity." *Econometrica* 80: 863–81.

Fish, Stanley E. 1976. "Interpreting the Variorum." *Critical Inquiry* 2 (3): 465–85.

Folke, Olle, Johanna Karin Rickne, and Daniel M. Smith. 2017. "Gender and Dynastic Political Recruitment." IFN Working Paper No. 1233. Stockholm, Sweden: Research Institute of Industrial Economics.

Gans-Morse, Jordan, Sebastian Mazzuca, and Simeon Nichter. 2014. "Varieties of Clientelism: Machine Politics during Elections." *American Journal of Political Science* 58 (2): 415–32.

Gayer, Laurent. 2007. "Guns, Slums and 'Yellow Devils': A Genealogy of Urban Conflicts in Karachi, Pakistan." *Modern Asian Studies* 41 (3): 515–44.

———. 2014. *Karachi: Ordered Disorder and the Struggle for the City.* New York: Oxford University Press.

Gazdar, H. 2006. "Counter-Insurgencies in Pakistan." *Economic and Political Weekly* 41 (20): 1952–53.

———. 2008. "Pakistan's Precious Parties." *Economic and Political Weekly* 43 (6): 8–9.

Gerth, H. H., and C. Wright Mills. 1947. *From Max Weber: Essays in Sociology.* London: Kegan Paul.

Ghias, Shoaib. 2010. "Miscarriage of Chief Justice: Judicial Power and the Legal Complex in Pakistan under Musharraf." *Law and Social Inquiry* 35 (4): 985–1022.

Gilmartin, David. 1988. *Empire and Islam: Punjab and the Making of Pakistan.* Berkeley: University of California Press.

———. 1991. "Democracy, Nationalism and the Public: A Speculation on Colonial Muslim Politics." *South Asia* 14 (1): 123–40.

———. 1998. "Partition, Pakistan, and South Asian History: In Search of a Narrative." *Journal of Asian Studies* 57 (4): 1068–95.

Ginsburg, Tom. 2003. *Judicial Review in New Democracies.* Cambridge, UK: Cambridge University Press.

Ginsburg, Tom, and Tamir Moustafa. 2008. "Introduction: The Function of Courts in Authoritarian Politics." In *Rule by Law: The Politics of Courts in Authoritarian Regimes,* edited by Tom Ginsburg and Tamir Moustafa, 1–22. Cambridge: Cambridge University Press.

Goodnow, Henry Frank. 1964. *The Civil Service of Pakistan.* New Haven, CT: Yale University Press.

Gosnell, Harold F. 1933. "The Political Party versus the Political Machine." *Annals of the American Academy of Political and Social Science* 169 (1): 21–28.

Government of Pakistan. 1978. "White Paper on the Conduct of the General Elections in March 1977." Rawalpindi: Government of Pakistan.

———. 1979. "White Paper on the Performance of the Bhutto Regime." 4 vols. Islamabad: Government of Pakistan.

Grindle, Merilee S. 2012. *Jobs for the Boys: Patronage and State in Comparative Perspective.* Cambridge, MA: Harvard University Press.

Grzymala-Busse, Anna. 2003. "Political Competition and the Politicization of the State in East Central Europe." *Comparative Political Studies* 36 (10): 1123–47.

———. 2007. *Rebuilding Leviathan: Party Competition and State Exploitation in Post-Communist Democracies.* New York: Cambridge University Press.

Gulzar, Saad, and Yasser Khan. 2017. "Politicians: Experimental Evidence on Candidacy and Performance." Center on Global Poverty and Development Working Paper, Stanford University.

Gunther, Richard, and Larry Diamond. 2003. "Species of Political Parties: A New Typology." *Party Politics* 9 (2): 167–99.

Habermas, Jürgen. 2008. "Notes on Post-Secular Society." *New Perspectives Quarterly* 25 (4): 17–29.

Habib, Hassan. 1973. *Babus, Brahmins and Bureaucrats*. Lahore: People's Publishing House.

Haider, Ziad. 2010. *The Ideological Struggle for Pakistan*. Stanford, CA: Hoover Institution.

Haq, Farhat. 1995. "Rise of the MQM in Pakistan: Politics of Ethnic Mobilization." *Asian Survey* 35 (11): 990–1004.

Haqqani, Hussain. 2005. *Pakistan: Between Mosque and Military*. Washington, DC: Carnegie Endowment for International Peace.

Hasan, Abrar. 2001. *Constitutional and Extra-Constitutional Decisions by Superior Courts of Pakistan*. Karachi: Asia Law House.

Hasan, Arif, Muhammad Younus, and S. Akbar Zaidi. 2002. *Understanding Karachi: Planning and Reform for the Future*. Karachi: City Press.

Hasnain, Zahid. 2008. "The Politics of Service Delivery in Pakistan: Political Parties and the Incentives for Patronage, 1988–1999." *Pakistan Development Review* 47 (2): 129–51.

Helmke, Gretchen, and Julio Rios-Figueroa, eds. 2011. *Courts in Latin America*. New York: Cambridge University Press.

Hicken, Allen, and Erik Kuhonta. 2011. "Shadows of the Past: Party System Institutionalization in Asia." *Comparative Political Studies* 44 (5): 572–97.

Hilbink, Lisa. 2007. *Judges beyond Politics in Democracy and Dictatorship*. New York: Cambridge University Press.

Hirschl, Ran. 2008. "The Judicialization of Megapolitics and the Rise of Political Courts." *Annual Review of Political Science* 11: 93–118.

Horowitz, Donald J. 1985. *Ethnic Groups in Conflict*. Berkeley: University of California Press.

HRCP (Human Rights Commission of Pakistan). 2006. *State of Human Rights in 2005*. Lahore: Human Rights Commission of Pakistan.

Htun, Mala. 2004. "Is Gender like Ethnicity? The Political Representation of Identity Groups." *Perspectives on Politics* 2 (3): 439–58.

———. 2005. "What It Means to Study Gender and the State." Politics and Gender 1 (1): 157–66.

———. 2016. *Inclusion without Representation in Latin America: Gender Quotas and Ethnic Reservations*. New York: Cambridge University Press.

Hull, Matthew S. 2012. *Government of Paper: The Materiality of Bureaucracy in Pakistan*. Los Angeles: University of California Press.

Huntington, Samuel, P. 1968. *Political Order in Changing Societies*. New Haven, CT: Yale University Press.

———. 1991. *The Third Wave: Democratization in the Late Twentieth Century*. Norman: University of Oklahoma Press.

Hussain, Akmal. 1990. "The Karachi Riots of December 1986: Crisis of State and Civil Society in Pakistan." In *Mirrors of Violence: Communities, Riots and Survivors in South Asia,* edited by Veena Das, 185–94. Delhi: Oxford University Press.

Hussain, Altaf. 2011. *My Life's Journey: The Early Years (1966–1988)*. Karachi: Oxford University Press.

Hussain, Zahid. 2007. *Frontline Pakistan: The Struggle with Militant Islam*. London: I. B. Tauris.

ICG (International Crisis Group). 2011. *Islamic Parties in Pakistan*. Asia Report No. 216. Brussels: International Crisis Group, December 12.

Inayatullah, Sohail. 1963. *Perspectives on the Rural Power Structure in West Pakistan*. Washington, DC: USAID Development and Research Evaluation Group.

Inglehart, R., C. Haerpfer, A. Moreno, C. Welzel, K. Kizilova, J. Diez-Medrano, M. Lagos, P. Norris, E. Ponarin, and B. Puranen, eds. 2014. *World Values Survey: Round Six-Country-Pooled Datafile*. Madrid: JD Systems Institute.

Iqbal, Muhammad. 1992. *Stray Reflections: The Private Notebook of Muhammad Iqbal*. Lahore: Iqbal Academy.

Iqtidar, Humeira. 2010. "Jamaat-e-Islami Pakistan: Learning from the Left." In *Beyond Crisis: Re-evaluating Pakistan,* edited by Naveeda Khan, 245–69. New Delhi: Routledge.

———. 2011. *Secularizing Islamists?* Chicago: University of Chicago Press.

Iyer, Lakhshami, and Anandi Mani. 2012. "Traveling Agents: Political Change and Bureaucratic Turnover in India." *Review of Economics and Statistics* 94 (3): 723–39.

Jaffrelot, Christophe. 2004. *A History of Pakistan and Its Origins*. New York: Anthem.

———. 2015. *The Pakistan Paradox: Instability and Resilience*. Gurgaon: Random House India.

Jafri, Aqeel Abbas. 1995. *Democracy and Authoritarianism in South Asia: A Comparative and Historical Perspective*. New York: Cambridge University Press.

———. 2000. *Self and Sovereignty: Individual and Community in South Asian Islam since 1850*. New York: Routledge.

———. 2007. *Pakistan kay Siyasi Waderay* [Pakistan's Landowning Elite]. Pakistan: Jahangir.

Jalal, Ayesha. 1990. *The State of Martial Rule: The Origins of Pakistan's Political Economy of Defence*. New York: Cambridge University Press.

———. 1995. *Democracy and Authoritarianism in South Asia*. New York: Cambridge University Press.

———. 2000. *Self and Sovereignty: Individual and Community in South Asian Islam Since 1850*. New York: Routledge.

Jalalzai, Farida. 2008. "Women Rule: Shattering the Executive Glass Ceiling." *Politics and Gender* 4 (2): 205–31.

Jalalzai, Farida, and Mona Lena Krook. 2010. "Beyond Hillary and Benazir: Women's Political Leadership Worldwide." *International Political Science Review* 31 (1): 5–21.

Javed, Umair 2014. "Associational Politics in Punjab." *Economic and Political Weekly* 49 (26–27): 53–54.

Javid, Hassan. 2011. "Class, Power, and Patronage: Landowners and Politics in Punjab." *History and Anthropology* 22 (3): 337–69.

———. 2015. "Path Dependence and the Persistence of Landed Power in the Punjab." In *State and Nation-Building in Pakistan: Beyond Islam and Security*, edited by

Roger D. Long, Gurharpal Singh, Yunus Samad, and Ian Talbot, 35–59. Oxon, UK: Routledge.

Jawaid, Arsalan. 2013. "Game Changer." *World Policy Journal* 29 (4): 106–15.

Jensenius, Francesca R. 2015. "Mired in Reservations: The Path-Dependent History of Electoral Quotas in India." *Journal of Asian Studies* 74 (1): 85–105.

———. 2016. "Competing Inequalities? On the Intersection of Gender and Ethnicity in Candidate Nominations in Indian Elections." *Government and Opposition* 51 (3): 440–63.

Johnson-Myers, Tracy-Ann. 2016. *The Mixed Member Proportional System: Providing Greater Representation for Women? A Case Study of the New Zealand Experience.* New York: Springer.

Jones, Philip E. 2003. *The Pakistan People's Party: Rise to Power.* Karachi: Oxford University Press.

Kahn, Paul. 2012. *Political Theology: Four New Chapters on the Concept of Sovereignty.* New York: Columbia University Press.

Kalhan, Anil. 2013. "'Gray Zone' Constitutionalism and the Dilemma of Judicial Independence in Pakistan." *Vanderbilt Journal of Transnational Law* 46:1–96.

Kalra, Virinder S., and Waqas M. Butt. 2013. "'In One Hand a Pen, In the Other a Gun': Punjabi Language Radicalism in Punjab, Pakistan." *South Asian History and Culture* 4 (4): 538–53.

Kalra, Virinder, and Shalini Sharma. 2013. "State of Subversion: Aspects of Radical Politics in Twentieth Century Punjab." *South Asian History and Culture* 4 (4): 435–42.

Kalyvas, Stathis N. 1996. *The Rise of Christian Democracy in Europe.* Ithaca, NY: Cornell University Press.

Kamran, Tahir. 2015. "The Pre-history of Religious Exclusionism in Contemporary Pakistan: Khatam-e-Nubuwwat 1889–1953." *Modern Asian Studies* 49 (6): 1840–74.

Kang, Alice J., and Aili Mari Tripp. 2018. "Coalitions Matter: Citizenship, Women, and Quota Adoption in Africa." *Perspectives on Politics* 16 (1): 73–91.

Kapiszewski, Diana. 2010. "How Courts Work: Institutions, Culture and the Brazilian Supremo Tribunal Federal." In *Cultures of Legality: Judicialization and Political Activism in Latin America,* edited by Javier Couso, Alexander Huneeus, and Rachel Sieder, 51–77. New York: Cambridge University Press.

Kapur, Devesh. 2015. "Public Opinion." In *Oxford Handbook of Indian Foreign Policy,* edited by David Malone, C. Raja Mohan, and Srinath Raghavan, 298–311. New York: Oxford University Press.

Kazmi, Sara. 2017. "The Marxist Punjabi Movement: Language and Literary Radicalism in Pakistan." *South Asia Chronicle* 7: 227–50.

Keddie, Nikkie R. 1975. "Labor Problems of Pakistan." *Journal of Asian Studies* 16 (4): 575–89.

Keefer, Philip. 2007. "Clientelism, Credibility, and the Policy Choices of Young Democracies." *American Journal of Political Science* 51 (4): 804–21.

Keefer, Philip E., Ambar Narayan, and Tara Vishwanath. 2003. *The Political Economy of Decentralization in Pakistan.* Washington, DC: World Bank.

Kelly, John, and Martha Kaplan. 2001. *Represented Communities: Fiji and World Decolonization*. Chicago: University of Chicago Press.

Kennedy, Charles H. 1987. *Bureaucracy in Pakistan*. New York: Oxford University Press.

———. 1991. "The Politics of Ethnicity in Sindh." *Asian Survey* 31 (10): 938–55.

———.1996. *Islamization of Laws and Economy, Case Studies on Pakistan*. Islamabad: Institute of Policy Studies.

———. 2006. "A User's Guide to Guided Democracy: Musharraf and the Pakistani Military Governance Paradigm." In *Pakistan 2005*, edited by Charles H. Kennedy and Cynthia Botteron, 120–58. New York: Oxford University Press.

Khan, Adeel. 2009. "Renewed Ethnonationalist Insurgency in Balochistan, Pakistan." *Asian Survey* 49 (6): 1071–91.

Khan, Ayesha. 2018. *The Women's Movement in Pakistan: Activism, Islam and Democracy*. New York: I. B. Tauris.

Khan, Bashir Ahmed, and Faisal Bari. 2004. "Economic Challenges for a New Millennium." In *Pakistan on the Brink: Politics, Economics, and Society*, edited by Craig Baxter, 131–54. Lanham, MD: Lexington.

Khan, Feroz Hassan. 2005. "Comparative Strategic Culture: The Case of Pakistan." *Strategic Insights* 4 (10). https://calhoun.nps.edu/bitstream/handle/10945/11241/khan2Oct05.pdf?sequence=1&isAllowed=y.

Khan, Hamid. 2005. *Constitutional and Political History of Pakistan*. Karachi: Oxford University Press.

———. 2016. *The History of the Judiciary in Pakistan*. Karachi: Oxford University Press.

Khan, Lal. 2009. *Pakistan's Other Story: The 1968–69 Revolution*. Delhi: Akbar.

Khan, Maryam. 2015. "Genesis and Evolution of Public Interest Litigation in the Supreme Court of Pakistan: Toward a Dynamic Theory of Judicialization." *Temple Journal of International and Comparative Law* 28:284–358.

Khan, Mohammad Asghar. 2005. *We Have Learnt Nothing from History: Pakistan Politics and Military Power*. New York: Oxford University Press.

Khan, Nichola. 2010. *Mohajir Militancy in Pakistan: Violence and Transformation in the Karachi Conflict*. Oxon, UK: Routledge.

Khan, Nighat Saeed, and Rubina Saigol. 2004. "Sindhiani Tehreek: Rural Women's Movement in Sindh." In *Up against the State: Military Rule and Women's Resistance*, edited by Nighat Said Khan, 192–208. Lahore: ASR.

Khan, Sarah. 2017. "Personal Is Political: Prospects for Women's Substantive Representation in Pakistan." Unpublished manuscript.

Khan Mohmand, Shandana. 2014. "Losing the Connection: Party-Voter Linkages in Pakistan." *Journal of Commonwealth and Comparative Politics* 52 (1): 7–31.

———. 2019. *Crafty Oligarchs, Savvy Voters: Democracy under Inequality in Rural Pakistan*. Cambridge: Cambridge University Press.

Khuhro, Amir Ahmed, and Ali Nawaz Soomro. 2013. "The Role of Benazir Bhutto in the Movement for the Restoration of Democracy: An Analysis." *International Journal of Social Science and Humanity* 3 (3): 274–77.

Kirchheimer, Otto. 1966. *The Transformation of Western European Party Systems, in Political Parties and Political Development*, edited by J. L. Palombara, 177–200. Princeton, NJ: Princeton University Press.

Kirmani, Nida. 2008. *The Relationships between Social Movements and Religion in Processes of Social Change: A Preliminary Literature Review.* Religions and Development Research Program Working Paper 23. Birmingham: University of Birmingham.

Kitschelt, Herbert, and Steven Wilkinson. 2007. *Patrons, Clients and Policies: Patterns of Democratic Accountability and Political Competition.* New York: Cambridge University Press.

Kochanek, Stanley. A. 2010. "Corruption and the Criminalization of Politics in South Asia." In *The Routledge Handbook of South Asian Politics*, edited by Paul Brass, 363–81. Oxon, UK: Routledge.

Kolinsky, Eva. 1987a. "Introduction." In *Opposition in Western Europe,* edited by Eva Kolinsky, 1–8. New York: St. Martin's.

———. 1987b. "The Transformation of Extra-Parliamentary Opposition in West Germany, and the Peace Movement." In *Opposition in Western Europe,* edited by Eva Kolinsky, 318–52. New York: St. Martin's.

Kopecky, Petr. 2011. "Political Competition and Party Patronage: Public Appointments in Ghana and South Africa." *Political Studies* 59 (3): 713–32.

Krook, Mona Lena. 2006. "Reforming Representation: The Diffusion of Candidate Gender Quotas Worldwide." *Politics and Gender* 2 (3): 303–27.

Krook, Mona Lena, and Diana Z. O'Brien. 2010. "The Politics of Group Representation: Quotas for Women and Minorities Worldwide." *Comparative Politics* 42 (3): 253–72.

Krouwel, Andre. 2006. "Party Models." In *Handbook of Party Politics*, edited by Richard S. Katz and William Crotty, 249–69. Thousand Oaks, CA: Sage.

Kumar, Sumita. 2001. "The Role of Islamic Parties in Pakistani Politics." *Strategic Analysis* 25 (2): 271–84.

Kunovich, Sheri, and Pamela Paxton. 2005. "Pathways to Power: The Role of Political Parties in Women's National Political Representation." *American Journal of Sociology* 111 (2): 505–52.

Laakso, Maarku, and Rein Taagepera. 1979. "Effective Number of Parties: A Measure with Application to West Europe." *Comparative Political Studies* 12: 3–27.

Ladinski, Jack. 1963. "The Impact of Social Backgrounds of Lawyers on Law Practice and the Law." *Journal of Legal Education* 16: 127–44.

Lahore High Court. 1954. *Report of the Court of Inquiry Constituted under Punjab Act II of 1954 to Enquire into the Punjab Disturbances of 1953.* Lahore: Superintendent, Government Printing Press.

Lamb, Christina. 1991. *Waiting for Allah.* New York: Viking Penguin.

Lapidus, Ira M. 1996. "State and Religion in Islamic Societies." *Past and Present* 151: 3–27.

———. 1997. "Islamic Revival and Modernity: The Contemporary Movements and the Historical Paradigms." *Journal of the Economic and Social History of the Orient* 40 (4): 444–60.

Larreguy, Horacio, John Marshall, and Pablo Querebin. 2016. "Parties, Brokers, and Voter Mobilization: How Turnout Buying Depends upon the Party's Capacity to Monitor Brokers." *American Political Science Review* 110 (1): 160–79.

Lavoy, Peter R. 2006. *Pakistan's Strategic Culture.* Reston, VA: SAIC.

Liaqat, Asad. 2019. *Representation through Information: Political Responsiveness to Citizen Preferences in Pakistan*. Working Paper, Harvard University.

Liaqat, Asad, Michael Callen, Ali Cheema, Adnan Khan, Farooq Naseer, and Jake Shapiro. 2019. *Political Connections and Vote Choice: Evidence from Pakistan*. Working Paper, Harvard University.

Lieven, Anatol. 2011. *Pakistan: A Hard Country*. London: Allen Lane.

Lipset, Seymour M., and Steve Rokkan. 1967. *Party Systems and Voter Alignments*. New York: Free Press.

Lupu, Noam, and Rachel Riedl. 2013. "Political Parties and Uncertainty in Developing Democracies." *Comparative Political Studies* 46 (11): 1339–65.

Lyon, Stephen M. 2004. *An Anthropological Analysis of Local Politics and Patronage in a Pakistani Village*. Lampeter, Wales: Edwin Mellen.

Mahmud, Khalid. 1958. *Trade Unionism in Pakistan*. Lahore: University of the Punjab.

Mainwaring, Scott P. 1999. *Rethinking Party Systems in the Third Wave of Democracy: The Case of Brazil*. Stanford, CA: Stanford University Press.

Mainwaring, Scott, and Timothy Scully. 1995. *Building Democratic Institutions: Party Systems in Latin America*. Stanford, CA: Stanford University Press.

Mair, Peter. 1997. *Party System Change: Approaches and Interpretations*. Oxford: Clarendon.

Malik, Adeel, and Rinchan Ali Mirza. 2015. *Religion, Land and Politics: Shrines and Literacy in Punjab, Pakistan*. Working Paper No. 030 Pakistan Strategy Support Program. Washington, DC: IFPRI.

Malik, Anas. 2010. *Political Survival in Pakistan: Beyond Ideology*. Oxon, UK: Routledge.

Malik, Anushay. 2013. "Alternative Politics and Dominant Narratives: Communists and the Pakistani State in the Early 1950s." *South Asian History and Culture* 4 (4): 520–37.

———. 2018. "Public Authority and Local Resistance: Abdur Rehman and the Industrial Workers of Lahore, 1969–1974." *Modern Asian Studies* 52 (3): 815–48.

Malik, Hafeez. 1967. "The Marxist Literary Movement in India and Pakistan." *Journal of Asian Studies* 26 (4): 649–64.

Malik, Iftikhar. 2002. *Religious Minorities in Pakistan*, vol. 6. London: Minority Rights Group International.

Malik, Jamal. 1996. *Colonialization of Islam: Dissolution of Traditional Institutions in Pakistan*. Delhi: Manohar.

———. 2007. *Madrasas in South Asia: Teaching Terror?* Oxon, UK: Routledge.

Malik, Muneer. 2008. *The Pakistan Lawyers' Movement: An Unfinished Agenda*. Karachi: Pakistan Law House.

Maniruzzaman, Talukdar. 1966. "Group Interests in Pakistani Politics, 1947–1958." *Pacific Affairs* 39 (1–2): 83–98.

Martin, Nicholas. 2016. *Politics, Landlords and Islam in Pakistan*. Oxon, UK: Routledge.

McAdam, Douglas, and Sidney Tarrow. 2010. "Ballots and Barricades: On the Reciprocal Relationship between Elections and Social Movements." *Perspectives on Politics* 8 (2): 529–42.

Mehdi, Tahir. 2010. *National Assembly Elections in Pakistan, 1970–2008*. Islamabad: Free and Fair Elections Network (FAFEN) and Church World Service Pakistan/Afghanistan.

Meierhenrich, Jens. 2008. *The Legacies of Law: Long-Run Consequences of Legal Development in South Africa*. New York: Cambridge University Press.

Merolla, Jennifer, Laura B. Stephenson, and Elizabeth J. Zechmeister. 2008. "Can Canadians Take a Hint? The (In)Effectiveness of Party Labels as Shortcuts in Canada." *Canadian Journal of Political Science* 41 (3): 673–96.

Messick, Brinkley. 2005. "Madhabs and Modernities." In *The Islamic School of Law—Evolution, Devolution and Progress*, edited by Frank E. Vogel, Peri Bearman, Rudolph Peters, 159–74. Cambridge, MA: Harvard University Press.

Metcalf, Barbara. 1982. *Islamic Revival in British India: Deoband, 1860–1900*. Princeton, NJ: Princeton University Press.

Michels, Robert. 1915. *Political Parties: A Sociological Study of the Oligarchical Tendencies of Modern Democracy*. New York: Hearst's International Library.

Migdal, Joel S. 1988. *Strong Societies and Weak States: State-Society Relations and State Capabilities in the Third World*. Princeton, NJ: Princeton University Press.

Milam, William B., and Matthew J. Nelson. 2013. "Pakistan's Populist Foreign Policy." *Survival* 55 (1): 121–34.

Mills, C. Wright. 1959. *The Sociological Imagination*. New York: Oxford University Press.

Mir, Asfandyar, and Dylan Moore. 2017. "Political Party, Incumbency, Disorder: Evidence from Natural Experiment." Working Paper, Stanford University.

Mitra, Subrata Kumar, Mike Enskat, and Clemens Spiess, eds. 2004. *Political Parties in South Asia*. Westport, CT: Greenwood.

Moj, Muhammad. 2015. *The Deoband Madrassah Movement: Countercultural Trends and Tendencies*. London: Anthem.

Mufti, Mariam. 2011. *Elite Recruitment and Regime Dynamics in Pakistan*. PhD diss., Johns Hopkins University.

———. 2015a. "Pakistan: Ministerial Turnover in the Federal Cabinet." In *The Selection of Ministers around the World*, edited by Keith Dowding and Patrick Dumont, 117–38. Oxon, UK: Routledge.

———. 2015b. "The Years of a Failed Democratic Transition, 1988–1997." In *The History of Pakistan*, edited by Roger D. Long, 633–79. Karachi: Oxford University Press.

———. 2016a. "Factionalism and Indiscipline in Pakistan's Party-Political System." In *State and Nation Building in Pakistan: Beyond Islam and Security*, edited by Robert D. Long, Yunus Samad, Gurharpal Singh, and Ian Talbot, 60–75. Oxon, UK: Routledge.

———. 2016b. "Pakistan Tehreek-i-Insaf: New Phenomenon or Continuation of the Political Status Quo?" *NORIA (Network of Researchers in International Affairs)*, October 22. https://www.noria-research.com/south-asia-5-pakistan-tehrik-e-insaaf/.

Mufti, Mariam, and Farida Jalalzai. 2017. "Subverting the Gender Quota: A Study of Candidate-Selection in Pakistan." Paper presented at the American Political Science Association, San Francisco, September 2.

Mulla, Ayesha. 2017. "Broadcasting the Dharna: Mediating 'Contained' Populism in Contemporary Pakistan." *International Journal of Communication* 11:4181–96.

Munoz, Heraldo. 2010. *Getting Away with Murder: Benazir Bhutto's Assassination and the Politics of Pakistan*. New York: W. W. Norton.

Murray, Rainbow. 2014. "Quotas for Men: Reframing Gender Quotas as a Means of Improving Representation for All." *American Political Science Review* 108 (3): 520–32.

Mustafa, Daanish, and Amiera Sawas. 2013. "Urbanisation and Political Change in Pakistan: Exploring the Known Unknowns." *Third World Quarterly* 34 (7): 1293–1304.

National Archives UK (NA). 1967. Confidential letter received from the British High Commission, February 8, 1967. Records of the Foreign Office, No. 57, SH 1/8, FCO 37/185.

Naqvi, Tahir. 2007. "The Politics of Commensuration: The Violence of Partition and the Making of the Pakistani State." *Journal of Historical Sociology* 20 (1–2): 44–71.

———. 2012. "Migration, Sacrifice and the Crisis of Muslim Nationalism." *Journal of Refugee Studies* 25 (3): 474–90.

Narang, Vipin, and Paul Staniland. 2018. "Democratic Accountability and Foreign Security Policy: Theory and Evidence from India." *Security Studies*, January. https://www.tandfonline.com/doi/abs/10.1080/09636412.2017.1416818.

Nasr, Syed Vali Reza. 1992. "Democracy and the Crisis of Governability in Pakistan." *Asian Survey* 32 (6): 521–37.

———. 1994. *The Vanguard of the Islamic Revolution: The Jama'at-i Islami of Pakistan*. Berkeley: University of California Press.

———. 2000. "The Rise of Sunni Militancy in Pakistan: The Changing Role of Islamism and the Ulama in Society and Politics." *Modern Asian Studies* 34 (1): 139–80.

———. 2001. "The Negotiable State: Borders and Power Struggles in Pakistan." In *Right-Sizing the State: Politics of Moving Borders*, edited by Brendan O'Leary, Ian S. Lustik, and Thomas Callaghy, 168–200. Oxford: Oxford University Press.

———. 2005. "'The Rise of' Muslim Democracy." *Journal of Democracy* 16 (2): 13–27.

Nawaz, Shuja. 2008. *Pakistan, Its Army, and the Wars Within*. Oxford: Oxford University Press.

NDI (National Democratic Institute) and ANFREL (Asian Network for Free Elections). 2013. *The 2013 National and Provincial Assembly Elections in Pakistan*. Washington, DC: NDI and ANFREL.

Nellis, Gareth, and Niloufer Siddiqui. 2018. "Secular Party Rule and Religious Violence in Pakistan." *American Political Science Review* 112 (1): 49–67.

Nelson, Matthew J. 2011. *In the Shadow of Shariah: Islam, Islamic Law and Democracy in Pakistan*. London: Hurst.

———. 2017. "Islamic Law in an Islamic Republic: What Role for Parliament?" In *Constitution Writing, Religion and Democracy*, edited by Asli Ü Bali and Hanna Lerner, 235–64. Cambridge: Cambridge University Press.

Newberg, Paula. 1995. *Judging the State: Courts and Constitutional Politics in Pakistan*. New York: Cambridge University Press.

Norris, Pippa. 2006. "The Impact of Electoral Reform on Women's Representation." *Acta Política* 41 (2): 197–213.

O'Dwyer, Connor. 2004. "Runaway State Building: How Political Parties Shape States in Post-Communist Eastern Europe." *World Politics* 56 (4): 520–53.

———. 2006. *Runaway State Building: Patronage Politics and Democratic Development.* Baltimore: Johns Hopkins University Press.

Oldenberg, Philip. 2016. "The Judiciary as a Political Actor." In *Pakistan at the Crossroads: Domestic Dynamics and External Pressures*, edited by Christophe Jaffrelot, 89–120. Gurgaon: Random House India.

Pakistan People's Party. 1967. Pakistan People's Party Foundation Document. Lahore: privately printed.

Pakistan Tehreek-e-Insaf. 2012. *Constitution of the Pakistan Tehreek-e-Insaf.* Lahore: privately printed.

———. 2013. *An Agenda for Resurgence: The Manifesto of Pakistan Tehreek-i-Insaaf.* Lahore: privately printed.

Panitch, Leo. 1987. "Paper Stones: A History of Electoral Socialism." Review of *Paper Stones* by Adam Przeworski and John Sprague. *American Journal of Sociology* 93 (2): 490–93.

Perlmutter, Amos. 1969. "The Praetorian State and the Praetorian Army: Toward a Taxonomy of Civil-Military Relations in Developing Countries." *Comparative Politics* 1 (3): 382–404.

Pew Research Center. 2014. *A Less Gloomy Mood in Pakistan: Sharif Gets High Marks, while Khan's Ratings Drop.* Washington, DC: Pew Research Center.

———. 2015. *Global Attitudes Spring 2015 Survey.* Washington, DC: Pew Research Center.

Pirzada, Sayyid A. S. 2000. *The Politics of the Jamiat Ulema-i-Islam Pakistan, 1971–1977.* New York: Oxford University Press.

Ponomarev, Yuri. 1986. *The Muslim League of Pakistan.* Lahore: People's Publishing House.

Potter, Allen. 1966. "Great Britain: Opposition with a Capital 'O.'" In *Political Oppositions in Western Democracies*, edited by Robert Dahl, 3–33. New Haven, CT: Yale University Press.

Pruysers, Scott, William P. Cross, and Anika Gauja. 2017. "Candidate Selection Rules and Democratic Outcomes: The Impact of Parties on Women's Representation." In *Organizing Political Parties Representation, Participation, and Power* edited by Susan E. Scarrow, Paul D. Webb, and Thomas Poguntke, 208–33. New York: Oxford University Press.

Przeworski, Adam. 1985. *Capitalism and Democracy.* New York: Cambridge University Press.

———. 1991. *Democracy and the Market: Political and Economic Reform in Eastern Europe and Latin America.* Cambridge: Cambridge University Press.

Przeworski, Adam, and John Sprague. 1986. *Paper Stones: A History of Electoral Socialism.* Chicago: University of Chicago Press.

Qadri, Rida. 2014. "Jumping Ship: The Story of Party Switching in Pakistan." Institute for Development and Economic Alternatives Working Paper.

Qasmi, Ali Usman. 2010. "God's Kingdom on Earth? Politics of Islam in Pakistan, 1947–1969." *Modern Asian Studies* 44 (6): 1197–1253.

———. 2015. *The Ahmadis and the Politics of Religious Exclusion in Pakistan.* London: Anthem.

Qureshi, Mohammad Farooq. 1995. *Nawaz Sharif—Quaid-Hazib-Ikhtaf ki Siyast* [Nawaz Sharif—Politics of the Leader of Opposition]. Lahore: Gora.

Raghavan, Srinath. 2013. *1971: A Global History of the Creation of Bangladesh.* Cambridge, MA: Harvard University Press.

Rahman, Tariq. 1996. *Language and Politics in Pakistan.* Karachi: Oxford University Press.

———. 2010. "Language Problems and Politics in Pakistan." In *Routledge Handbook of South Asian Politics: India, Pakistan, Bangladesh, Sri Lanka, and Nepal,* edited by Paul Brass, 232–46. Oxon, UK: Routledge.

Rana, Muhammad Amir. 2004. *A to Z of Jehadi Organizations in Pakistan.* Translated by Saba Ansari. Lahore: Mashal.

Rashiduzzaman, M. 1997. "The National Awami Party of Pakistan: Leftist Politics in Crisis." *Pacific Affairs* 43 (3): 394–409.

Raza, Ali. 2013. "An Unfulfilled Dream: The Left in Pakistan ca. 1947–50." *South Asian History and Culture* 4 (4): 503–19.

Reetz, Dietrich. 2006. *Islam in the Public Sphere: Religious Groups in India, 1900–1947.* New York: Oxford University Press.

Reyes, Soccoro L. 2002. "Quotas in Pakistan: A Case Study." Paper presented at the IDEA workshop in Jakarta, Indonesia.

Richter, William L. 1979. "The Political Dynamics of Islamic Resurgence in Pakistan." *Asian Survey* 19 (6): 547–57.

Rizvi, Hassan A. 2000. *Military, State and Society in Pakistan.* London: Macmillan.

Robinson, Francis. 2013. "Strategies of Authority in Muslim South Asia in the Nineteenth and Twentieth Centuries." *Modern Asian Studies* 47 (1): 1–21.

Rorty, Richard. 1989. *Contingency, Irony, and Solidarity.* New York: Cambridge University Press.

Rubin, Barnett. 1995. *The Fragmentation of Afghanistan: State Formation and Collapse in the International System.* New Haven, CT: Yale University Press.

Saeed, Aamir. 2007. "Media, Racism, and Islamophobia: The Representation of Islam and Muslims in the Media." *Sociology Compass* 1 (2): 443–62.

Saeed, Sadia. 2007. "Pakistani Nationalism and the State Marginalisation of the Ahmadiyya Community in Pakistan." *Studies in Ethnicity and Nationalism* 7 (3): 132–52.

———. 2017. *Politics of Desecularization: Law and the Minority Question in Pakistan.* Cambridge: Cambridge University Press.

Saigol, Rubina. 2016. *Feminism and the Women's Movement in Pakistan Actors, Debates, and Strategies.* Islamabad: Friedrich-Ebert-Stiftung.

Samad, Yunas. 1995. "Pakistan or 'Punjabistan' Crisis of National Identity." *International Journal of Punjab Studies* 2 (1): 23–42.

———. 2017. "Elections and Democratic Transition in Pakistan: One Step forward and Two Steps Backwards." *Commonwealth & Comparative Politics* 55 (4): 509–30.

Samuels, David, and Cesar Zucco Jr. 2014. "The Power of Partisanship in Brazil: Evidence from Survey Experiments." *American Journal of Political Science* 58 (1): 212–25.

Samuels, Richard. 2005. *Machiavelli's Children: Leaders and Their Legacies in Italy and Japan.* Ithaca, NY: Cornell University Press.

Sanyal, Usha. 2012. *Ahmad Riza Khan Barelwi: In the Path of the Prophet.* London: Oneworld.

Sartori, Giovanni. 1969. "The Sociology of Parties: A Critical Review." In *West European Party System*, edited by Peter Mair, 150–82. New York: Oxford University Press.

———. 1990. "The Sociology of Parties: A Critical Review." In *The West European Party System*, edited by Peter Mair, 150–84. New York: Oxford University Press.

Sayeed, Khalid Bin. 1959. "Collapse of Parliamentary Democracy in Pakistan." *Middle East Journal* 13 (4): 389–406.

———. 1967. *The Political System of Pakistan.* Boston: Houghton Mifflin.

———. 1968. *Pakistan: The Formative Phase, 1957–1948.* 2nd ed. Karachi: Oxford University Press.

———. 1984. "Pakistan in 1983: Internal Stresses More Serious than External Problems." *Asian Survey* 24 (2): 219–28.

Schattschneider, E. E. 1942. *Party Government.* New York: Farrar and Rinehart.

Schneider, Mark. 2019. "Do Brokers Know Their Voters? A Test of Guessability in India." *Electoral Studies* 61.

Scott, James C. 1969. "Corruption, Machine Politics, and Political Change." *American Political Science Review* 63 (4): 1142–58.

Sekine, Kimie. 2014. "Benazir Bhutto: Her Political Struggle in Pakistan." Master's thesis, University of Massachusetts.

Shafqat, Saeed. 1997. *Civil-Military Relations in Pakistan.* Boulder, CO: Westview.

———. 1998. "Democracy in Pakistan: Value Change and Challenges of Institution-Building." *Pakistan Development Review* 37 (4): 281–98.

———. 1999. "Pakistani Bureaucracy: Crisis of Governance and Prospects of Reform." *Pakistan Development Review* 38 (4): 995–1017.

———. 2002. "From Official Islam to Islamism: The Rise of Dawat-ul-Irshad and Lashkar-e-Taiba." In *Pakistan: Nationalism without a Nation,* edited by Christopher Jaffrelot, 138–48. London: Zed.

———. 2009. "The Kargil Conflict's Impact on Pakistani Politics and Society." In *Asymmetric Warfare in South Asia: The Causes and Consequences of the Kargil Conflict,* edited by Peter Lavoy, 280–308. New York: Cambridge University Press.

———. 2013. "Reforming Pakistan's Bureaucracy." In *Development Challenges Confronting Pakistan,* edited by Anita M. Weiss and Saba Gul Khattak, 99–119. Sterling, VA: Kumarian.

Shafqat, Sahar. 2018. "Civil Society and the Lawyers' Movement of Pakistan." *Law and Social Inquiry* 43 (3): 889–914.

Shah, Aqil. 2014a. *The Army and Democracy: Military Politics in Pakistan.* Cambridge, MA: Harvard University Press.

———. 2014b. "Constraining Consolidation: Military Politics and Democracy in Pakistan (2007–2013)." *Democratization* 21 (6): 1007–33.

Shah, Aqil, and Bushra Arif, 2015. "Pakistan in 2014: Democracy under the Military's Shadow." *Asian Survey* 55 (1): 48–59.

Shaheed, Zafar. 1979. "Union Leaders, Worker Organizations and Strikes: Karachi 1969–1972." *Development and Change* 10: 181–204.

———. 2007. *The Labor Movement in Pakistan: Organization and Leadership in Karachi in the 1970s.* Karachi: Oxford University Press.

Shaikh, Riaz Ahmed. 2010. "1968—Was It Really a Year of Social Change in Pakistan?" In *Sixties Radicalism and Social Movement Activism: Retreat or Resurgence*, edited by Bryn Jones and Mike O' Donnell, 73–88. London: Anthem.

Shambayati, Hootan. 2008. "Courts in Semi-Democratic/Authoritarian Regimes: The Judicialization of Turkish (and Iranian) Politics." In *Rule by Law: The Politics of Courts in Authoritarian Regimes*, edited by Tom Ginsburg and Tamir Moustafa, 283–303. Cambridge: Cambridge University Press.

Siddiqa, Ayesha. 2007. *Military Inc.: Inside Pakistan's Military Economy.* London: Pluto.

———. 2019. "Pakistan—From Hybrid-Democracy to Hybrid-Martial Law." *Journal of South Asian and Middle Eastern Studies* 42 (2): 52–72.

Siddiqi, Faisal. 2015. "Public Interest Litigation: Predictable Continuity and Radical Departures." In *The Politics and the Jurisprudence of the Chaudhry Court*, edited by Moeen Cheema and Ijaz Shafi Gilani, 77–130. Karachi: Oxford University Press.

Siddique, Osama. 2006. "The Jurisprudence of Dissolutions: Presidential Power to Dissolve Assemblies under the Pakistani Constitution and Its Discontents." *Arizona Journal of International and Comparative Law* 23 (3): 622–715.

———. 2015. "Judicialization of Politics: Pakistan Supreme Court's Jurisprudence after the Lawyer's Movement." In *Unstable Constitutionalism: Law and Politics in South Asia*, edited by Mark Tushnet and Madhav Khosla, 159–91. New York: Cambridge University Press.

Siddiqui, A. R. 2008. *Partition and the Making of the Mohajir Mindset: A Narrative.* Karachi: Oxford University Press.

Siddiqui, Niloufer. 2010. "Gender Ideology and the Jamaat-e-Islami." *Current Trends in Islamist Ideology* 10: 173–93.

———. 2017. *Under the Gun: Political Parties and Violence in Pakistan.* PhD diss., Yale University.

———. 2018. "Who Do You Believe? Political Parties and Conspiracy Theories in Pakistan." *Party Politics*, https://doi.org/10.1177/1354068817749777.

Sidhwa, Rustam. 1989. *The Lahore High Court and Its Principal Bar: 1866–1988.* Lahore: Maktaba Jadeed.

Staniland, Paul, Adnan Naseemullah, and Ahsan Butt. 2018. "Pakistan's Military Elite." *Journal of Strategic Studies,* August 2018.

Stokes, Susan C. 1999. "Political Parties and Democracy." *Annual Review of Political Science* 2: 243–67.

———. 2005. "Perverse Accountability: A Formal Model of Machine Politics with Evidence from Argentina." *American Political Science Review* 99 (3): 315–25.

———. 2007. "Political Clientelism." In *Oxford University Press Handbook of Comparative Politics*, edited by Carles Boix and Susan C. Stokes, 604–27. New York: Oxford University Press.

Stokes, Susan, Thad Dunning, Marcelo Nazareno, and Valeria Brusco. 2013. *Brokers, Voters, and Clientelism: The Puzzle of Distributive Politics*. New York: Cambridge University Press.

Su, Yen-Pin. 2015. "Anti-Government Protests in Democracies: A Test of Institutional Explanations." *Comparative Politics* 42 (2): 149–67.

Syed, Anwar Hussain. 1992. *The Discourse and Politics of Zulfikar Ali Bhutto*. London: Macmillan.

Talbot, Ian. 1996. *Freedom's Cry: The Popular Dimension in the Pakistan Movement and Partition Experience in North-West India*. London: Oxford University Press.

———. 1998. *Pakistan: A Modern History*. London: Palgrave Macmillan.

———. 2002. "Does the Army Shape Pakistan's Foreign Policy?" In *Pakistan: Nationalism without a Nation?*, edited by Christophe Jaffrelot, 311–36. New York: Zed.

———. 2012. *Pakistan: A New History*. Oxford: Oxford University Press.

Tavits, Margit. 2007. "Clarity of Responsibility and Corruption." *American Journal of Political Science* 51 (1): 218–29.

Thompson, E. P. 1966. *The Making of the English Working Class*. New York: Vintage.

Tirmazi, Syed A. I. 1995. *Profiles of Intelligence*. Lahore: Combined Printers.

Toor, Saadia. 2011. *The State of Islam: Culture and Cold War Politics in Pakistan*. London: Pluto.

Trubowitz, Peter. 1998. *Defining the National Interest: Conflict and Change in American Foreign Policy*. Chicago: University of Chicago Press.

Trubowitz, Peter, and Nicole Mellow. 2005. "'Going Bipartisan: Politics by Other Means." *Political Science Quarterly* 120 (3): 433–53.

Tsubura, Machiko. 2013. "The Politics of Constituency Development Funds (CDFs) in Comparative Perspective." Paper presented at the Annual Meeting of the American Political Science Association, Chicago, September 2013.

Ullah, Haroon K. 2013. *Vying for Allah's Vote: Understanding Islamic Parties, Political Violence, and Extremism in Pakistan*. Washington, DC: Georgetown University Press.

Van Cott, Donna Lee. 2005. *From Movements to Parties in Latin America: the Evolution of Ethnic Politics*. New York: Cambridge University Press.

Verkaaik, Oskar. 2004. *Migrants and Militants: Fun and Urban Violence in Pakistan*. Princeton, NJ: Princeton University Press.

———. 2005. "On Terror and Sacrifice." In *Religion, Violence, and Political Mobilisation in India*, edited by Ravindar Kaur, 165–83. New Delhi: Sage.

———. 2016. "Violence and Ethnic Identity Politics in Karachi and Hyderabad." *South Asia* 39 (4): 841–54.

Volkens, Andrea, Judith Bara, and Ian Budge. 2009. "Data Quality in Content Analysis: The Case of the Comparative Manifestos Project." *Historical Social Research* 34 (1): 234–51.

Von Beyme, Klaus. 1987. "Parliamentary Oppositions in Europe." In *Opposition in Western Europe*, edited by Eva Kolinsky, 31–51. New York: St. Martin's.

Waltz, Kenneth N. 1967. *Foreign Policy and Democratic Politics: The American and British Experience*. Boston: Little, Brown.

Wängnerud, Lena. 2009. "Women in Parliaments: Descriptive and Substantive Representation." *Annual Review of Political Science* 12: 51–69.

Waseem, Mohammad. 1989. *Politics and the State in Pakistan*. Lahore: Progressive.

———. 1994. *The 1993 Elections in Pakistan*. Lahore: Vanguard.

———. 1999. "Partition, Migration and Assimilation: A Comparative Study of Pakistani Punjab." In *Region and Partition: Punjab, Bengal and the Partition of the Subcontinent*, edited by Ian Talbot and Gurharpal Singh, 203–28. Karachi: Oxford University Press.

———. 2001. "Mohajirs in Pakistan: A Case of Nativization." In *Community, Empire and Migration*, edited by Crispin Bates, 245–60. New York: Palgrave Macmillan.

———. 2002. "The Dialectic between Domestic Politics and Foreign Policy." In *Pakistan: Nationalism without a Nation?*, edited by Christophe Jaffrelot, 263–82. New York: Zed.

———. 2006. *Democratization in Pakistan: A Study of the 2002 Elections*. New York: Oxford University Press.

———. 2015. "Constitutionalism and Extra-Constitutionalism in Pakistan." In *Unstable Constitutionalism: Law and Politics in South Asia*, edited by Mark Tushnet and Madhav Khosla, 124–58. New York: Cambridge University Press.

———. 2016. "The Operational Dynamics of Political Parties in Pakistan." In *Pakistan at the Crossroads: Domestic Dynamics and External Pressures*, edited by Christopher Jaffrelot, 62–88. New York: Columbia University Press.

Waseem, Mohammad, and Mariam Mufti. 2012. *Political Parties in Pakistan: Organization and Power Structure*. Islamabad: Asia Foundation.

Weeks, Ana Catalano. 2018. "Why Are Gender Quota Laws Adopted by Men? The Role of Inter- and Intraparty Competition." *Comparative Political Studies* 51 (14): 1935–73.

White, Joshua T. 2008. *Pakistan's Islamist Frontier: Islamic Politics and U.S. Policy in Pakistan's North-West Frontier*. Religion and Security Monograph Series, no. 1. Arlington, VA: Center on Faith & International Affairs.

———. 2012. "Beyond Moderation: Dynamics of Political Islam in Pakistan." *Contemporary South Asia* 20 (2): 179–94.

Wiktorowicz, Quintan. 2004. *Islamic Activism: A Social Movement Theory Approach*. Bloomington: Indiana University Press.

Wilder, Andrew. 1999. *The Pakistani Voter: Electoral Politics and Voting Behavior in Punjab*. Karachi: Oxford University Press.

Wilkinson, Steven I. 2000. "Democratic Consolidation and Failure: Lessons from Bangladesh and Pakistan." *Democratization* 7 (3): 203–26.

Witsoe, Jeffrey, 2013. *Democracy against Development: Lower-Caste Politics and Political Modernity in Postcolonial India*. Chicago: University of Chicago Press.

Wolf, Siegfreid O. 2016. "China-Pakistan Economic Corridor, Civil-Military Relations and Democracy." Paper presented at the 24th European Conference on South Asian Studies (ECSAS), University of Warsaw, July 27–30, 2016.

Wolpert, Stanley. 1993. *Zulfi Bhutto of Pakistan: His Life and Times*. Oxford: Oxford University Press.

Yaseen, Zahid, Muhammad Abrar Ahmad, and Tahir Mahmood Butt. 2016. "Hypothetical Political System of Martial Laws: A Case Study of General Zia-ul-Haq." *Journal of the Punjab University Historical Society* 29 (1): 122–32.

Zaidi, Akbar. 2005. "State, Military and Social Transition: Improbable Future of Democracy in Pakistan." *Economic and Political Weekly* 40 (49): 5173–81.

———. 2008. "An Emerging Civil Society." *Journal of Democracy* 19 (4): 38–40.

———. 2010. "Who Is a Muslim? Identities of Exclusion—North Indian Muslims, c. 1860–1900." *Indian Economic and Social History Review* 47 (2): 205–29.

Zaman, Muhammad Qasim. 1998. "Sectarianism in Pakistan: The Radicalization of Shi'i and Sunni Identities." *Modern Asian Studies* 32 (3): 689–716.

———. 2002. "The 'Ulamā' in Contemporary Islam: Custodians of Change." Princeton, NJ: Princeton University Press.

———. 2018. *Islam in Pakistan: A History*. Princeton, NJ: Princeton University Press.

Zamindar, Vazira. 2007. *The Long Partition and the Making of Modern South Asia: Refugees, Boundaries, Histories*. New York: Columbia University Press.

Zehra, Nasim. 2018. *From Kargil to Coup: Events That Shook Pakistan*. Lahore: Sang-e-Meel.

Zhirnov, Andrei, and Mariam Mufti. 2019. "Electoral Constraints on Inter-Party Mobility of Candidates: The Case of Pakistan." *Comparative Politics* 51 (4): 519–54.

Zigon, Jarrett. 2007. "Moral Breakdown and Ethical Demand: A Theoretical Framework for an Anthropology of Moralities." *Anthropological Theory* 7 (2): 131–50.

Ziring, Lawrence. 1971. *The Ayub Khan Era*. Syracuse, NY: Syracuse University Press.

———. 1998. *Pakistan in the Twentieth Century: A Political History*. Oxford: Oxford University Press.

Contributors

Sameen A. Mohsin Ali, assistant professor, political science, Lahore University of Management Sciences.

Johann Chacko, PhD candidate, School of Oriental and African Studies, University of London.

Ali Cheema, associate professor, economics, Lahore University of Management Sciences, and senior research fellow, Institute of Development and Economic Alternatives (IDEAS), Lahore.

Christopher Clary, assistant professor, political science, University at Albany, State University of New York.

Philip E. Jones, professor, intelligence studies and global affairs, Embry-Riddle Aeronautical University, Prescott, Arizona.

Hassan Javid, assistant professor, sociology, Lahore University of Management Sciences.

Sarah Khan, assistant professor, political science, Yale University, New Haven, Connecticut.

Tabinda M. Khan, independent scholar, PhD Columbia University, New York.

Yasser Kureshi, senior teaching fellow, School of Oriental and African Studies, University of London.

Asad Liaqat, PhD candidate, public policy, Harvard University, Cambridge, Massachusetts.

Anushay Malik, assistant professor, history, Lahore University of Management Sciences.

Shandana Khan Mohmand, research fellow, Institute of Development Studies, University of Sussex.

Mariam Mufti, assistant professor, political science, University of Waterloo.

Tahir Naqvi, associate professor, sociology and anthropology, Trinity University, San Antonio, Texas.

Saeed Shafqat, professor and founding director of the Centre for Public Policy and Governance, Forman Christian University (a chartered university), Lahore.

Sahar Shafqat, professor of political science, St. Mary's College of Maryland.

Ayesha Siddiqa, research associate, School of Oriental and African Studies, University of London.

Niloufer Siddiqui, assistant professor, political science, University at Albany, State University of New York.

Mohammad Waseem, professor, political science, Lahore University of Management Sciences.

Index

Figures and tables are indicated by f and t following the page numbers.

AAT (Allah-o-Akbar Tehreek Party), 231
Afghanistan: political party views of, 262;
    Soviet intervention in (1979), 27, 52;
    voter attitudes toward, 263, 264f. *See also*
    Taliban
Ahle Sunnat Wal Jamaat (ASWJ), 112, 120
Ahmad, Aijaz, 219
Ahmadis, marginalization of, 10, 111, 114,
    117, 120n3
Ahmed, Imtiaz, 53
Ahmed, Saifuddin, 12
Ahmed, Wajihuddin, 69, 70
Alavi, Hamza, 12, 181
Ali, Sameen A. Mohsin, 15, 178, 279
Allah-o-Akbar Tehreek Party (AAT), 231
All-India Muslim League (AIML), 7, 82, 84,
    89n7, 112, 227
all-parties conferences, 28, 208
Al-Zulfikar, 52–53
Anderson, Benedict, 82
ANP. *See* Awami National Party
APP (Azad Pakistan Party), 96
Appadurai, Arjun, 89n8
Army General Headquarters (GHQ),
    215, 217, 222–23, 226, 229–30. *See also*
    military
Article 58 Section 2b, 28, 31–33, 180, 192,
    222, 274
aspirational candidates, 147, 147f, 151, 153,
    158t, 278

ASWJ (Ahle Sunnat Wal Jamaat), 112, 120
Auerbach, Adam, 129, 132
authoritarianism: in civilian governments,
    39, 48; electoral contests in, 112; and
    Islamic populism, 110, 119; judicial
    suppression under, 248; of military, 42, 65,
    72, 152; and regime uncertainty, 198. *See
    also* hybrid regimes; military dictatorships
autonomy: municipal, 80–81; political,
    146–51, 155, 157, 278; provincial, 10, 94,
    96; regional, 94, 96; of sacrifice, 83; of
    ulema, 115
Awami League, 47, 48, 96, 98, 266
Awami National Party (ANP): candidate
    selection by, 145; electoral strategies
    of, 94, 156; ethnic support for, 8; on
    foreign policy, 267; formation of,
    100–101; ideological positioning of, 9,
    267; intraparty elections held by, 60–61;
    literature review, 5; NAP as parent party
    of, 93; origins of, 151; repression of,
    101–2; ticket application fee required by,
    147; underperformance in elections, 91;
    women's involvement in, 165
Awami Workers' Party (AWP), 91, 94, 103
Ayub Khan, Mohammad: domestic policies
    under, 29, 217; economic policies under,
    43–44; instrumentalization of Islam by,
    116; judiciary under, 240–42; military
    intervention by, 24–25, 43, 274; political

Ayub Khan, Mohammad (*continued*)
    parties co-opted by, 2, 219, 227; protests
    against, 6, 25, 46–47, 90, 98; resignation
    from presidency, 46, 90
Azadi (Freedom) March, 207–8
Azad Pakistan Party (APP), 96
Aziz, Sartaj, 30, 33, 35, 40n5
Aziz, Shahid, 257

Bajwa, Qamar, 223–24
Baloch, Naz, 70
Balochistan Awami Party (BAP), 10
Baloch Liberation Army (BLA), 10
Baloch National Party (BNP), 9, 10
Bangladesh: formation of, 41, 47, 98, 109,
    198; left-wing parties impacted by, 98;
    Pakistani military failures in, 48, 258
Bari, Farzana, 168–69
Basic Democrats, 44
Basu, Amrita, 171–72
Beg, Mirza Aslam, 29, 53, 222, 225, 245
Benazir Income Support Program (BISP),
    187
Bhashani, Abdul Hamid, 96–98
Bhavnani, Rikhil R., 170
Bhutto, Begum Nusrat, 164, 221–22
Bhutto, Benazir: assassination of, 55, 57,
    66, 179, 223; corruption allegations
    against, 54–55; foreign policy under,
    256; incarceration of, 52, 53, 221, 222;
    judiciary under, 249; leadership following
    father's death, 51, 171; marriage of, 53;
    military relations with, 53, 222–23; and
    Panama Papers, 55; plot to overthrow, 53,
    222; as PPP chair, 164; as prime minister,
    32, 33, 53, 54, 59; removal from power, 54,
    222, 248; return from exile, 28, 184. *See
    also* Pakistan People's Party
Bhutto, Murtaza, 52–53
Bhutto, Shahnawaz, 52–53
Bhutto, Zulifkar Ali: domestic policies under,
    48, 49, 220; electoral strategies of, 45–47,
    50; emergence of, 44–45, 90; execution
    of, 49, 51, 221, 242, 248; foreign policy
    under, 26, 48; judiciary under, 248; mass
    movement led by, 39; military relations
    with, 219–21, 280; as prime minister,
    47–51, 220–21; self-image created by, 219,
    221. *See also* Pakistan People's Party

Bhutto-Zardari, Bilawal, 53, 56–59, 186, 224
biraderi. *See* kinship networks
BISP (Benazir Income Support Program),
    187
BLA (Baloch Liberation Army), 10
blasphemy laws, 6, 108, 118
BNP (Baloch National Party), 9, 10
Bokhari, Fasih, 228
Bokhari, Saloni, 64
bribery, 50, 53, 185, 186, 227
broker mediated theory of clientelism, 129
brokers, 13, 58, 129–31, 133, 277
"brown sahib," use of term, 64, 73n12
Brumberg, Daniel, 237
Buehler, Arthur, 108
Bugti, Nawab Akbar, 9
Bukhari, Gul, 58
Bukhari, Zahra Basit, 162, 174
Buncombe, Andrew, 204
bureaucratic appointments, 178–94;
    delegation strategy in, 178–79, 183–85,
    191, 279; methodology for study of, 179;
    overview, 178–79; for party loyalists, 181;
    for personal gain, 178–79, 185–87, 191;
    politicization of, 180, 182–83, 186, 188,
    279; in service delivery agenda, 178–79,
    187–92, 279
Butler, Judith, 82, 83
Buzdar, Sardar, 71–72
Buzdar, Usman, 192

candidates, 144–61; aspirational, 147, 147*f*,
    151, 153, 158*t*, 278; charisma of, 150–51,
    157; commitment of, 146–47, 151–53,
    157, 159, 278; dynastic, 149, 171–72, 173*f*,
    278–79; financial resources of, 147–48;
    loyalty of, 145–46; party-switching by,
    151, 157–60, 278; party worker, 147,
    147*f*, 153–54, 157, 158*t*, 278; political
    autonomy of, 146–51, 155, 157, 278;
    recruitment of, 155–57; selection of,
    145, 154–57, 164, 170; social constraints
    on, 152–53, 159; support networks of,
    148–50; typology of, 146–54, 147*f*, 278;
    women as, 164–66, 165*f*, 169*f*, 170–74.
    See also electables; elections; voters and
    voting behavior
catch-all parties: candidate selection in, 157;
    characteristics of, 61–62, 67; detrimental

effects of, 72–73; ticket application fee required by, 155; transformation of, 60, 61, 276. *See also* mainstream parties; *specific parties*

censorship, 2, 58, 222, 274

Chacko, Johann, 11, 105, 277

Chan, Nadeem Afzal, 144–45, 150, 159

Chandra, Kanchan, 171

charisma: authority deriving from, 108, 152; of Bhutto family, 42, 47, 51; of candidates, 150–51, 157; of PTI leadership, 57, 65, 205; of *ulema*, 108

Charter of Democracy (2006), 60, 73n1, 201–2, 205, 209, 229

Chaudhry, Iftikhar, 185, 203, 226, 244, 247, 280

Cheema, Ali, 13, 125, 149, 171, 175, 277

Cheema, Anwar Ali, 144–45, 150, 152, 159

China: acquisition of weapons from, 220; NAP tensions over, 97; political party views of, 261; unconditional friendship with, 44; voter attitudes toward, 263, 264*f*

China-Pakistan Economic Corridor (CPEC), 17, 226, 261

CII (Council for Islamic Ideology), 116, 118

civil war, 47, 98, 109, 198, 256, 266

Clary, Christopher, 17, 253, 281

clientelism: broker mediated theory of, 129; defined, 13; as deterrence to women in politics, 170; voting behavior influenced by, 13. *See also* patronage

Cold War, 76, 92, 95

commitment of candidates, 146–47, 151–53, 157, 159, 278

Communist Party of India (CPI), 94

Communist Party of Pakistan (CPP), 92, 94–96

confessional parties, defined, 107

Congress Party. *See* Indian National Congress

constituency politicians. *See* electables

Constitution: in 1956, 96, 166; in 1962, 43, 166; in 1973, 48, 98, 110–11, 114, 166, 193, 228, 240, 242

constitutional democracy, 113, 235, 240, 248

Convention Muslim League, 227

corruption: bribery, 50, 53, 185, 186, 227; in elections, 1–2, 35, 50–51, 54, 109, 230; in government, 34–39, 183, 185–87;

judicial investigations into, 36–37, 186, 247; kickbacks, 54–55; protests against, 6, 35–37, 230. *See also* clientelism; patronage

Council for Islamic Ideology (CII), 116, 118

CPEC (China-Pakistan Economic Corridor), 17, 226, 261

CPI (Communist Party of India), 94

CPP (Communist Party of Pakistan), 92, 94–96

Dahl, Robert, 195

Dasti, Jamshed, 153

Daultana, Mumtaz, 25

deep state, 49, 198, 200, 204, 206

defection. *See* party-switching

delegation strategy, 178–79, 183–85, 191, 279

democracy: barriers to, 15–17, 196; constitutional, 113, 235, 240, 248; establishmentarian, 17, 273–75, 279, 281; in global environment, 23; institutions integral to, 2, 195; Islamic party support for, 110; and judiciary, 244–47, 249, 280–81; parliamentary, 40, 42; representative, 112; social, 65–66, 151; transition to, 1, 29, 34–35, 199, 202, 247; trust in, 128, 140. *See also* Charter of Democracy (2006); elections; hybrid regimes; Movement for the Restoration of Democracy; political parties

denominational parties: competition among, 105, 108; electoral participation of, 112–13; extended networks of, 110–12; future outlook for, 118–20; political relevance of, 108–10, 277; relationship with state, 115–18; underperformance in elections, 108–9, 114–15, 277. *See also* Islamic parties

dharnas. See sit-ins

dictatorships. *See* military dictatorships

dissonant institutionalism, 237–39, 249, 280, 281

domestic violence, 162, 172–73

door-to-door canvassing, 135–36, 136*t*, 138*f*

dynastic candidates, 149, 171–72, 173*f*, 278–79

dynastic party leadership, 23, 37, 60, 149

East Pakistan. *See* Bangladesh

economic uncertainty, 3, 197

ECP (Election Commission of Pakistan), 2, 5, 70, 162, 164, 192

education: government spending on, 61, 72; Islamic, 110, 116, 117; philanthropic efforts related to, 63; Punjab Education Sector Reform Program, 189–90; teacher selection process, 189–90; World Bank Social Action Program for, 54

Eighth Amendment. *See* Article 58 Section 2b

Eighteenth Amendment, 56, 187, 215, 223

Elahi, Pervaiz, 183–84

electables: bargaining power of, 157; defined, 14, 145; party loyalists vs., 13–14, 273; PTI use of, 15, 61, 62, 67, 71, 230; recruitment of, 155–57; wavering loyalty of, 272. *See also* independent electables

Election Commission of Pakistan (ECP), 2, 5, 70, 162, 164, 192

elections: corruption in, 1–2, 35, 50–51, 54, 109, 230; denominational party participation in, 112–13; in establishmentarian democracies, 274–75; indirect, 43, 169, 170, 217; intraparty, 60–62, 69–70; military interference in, 2, 16, 58, 216; public trust in, 35; reserved seats for women, 165–70, 176, 177, 177n6, 278; results from (1998–2018), 282–83; social media use during, 12; violence in, 50, 58. *See also* candidates; political parties; voters and voting behavior; women in politics

elite. *See* political elites

enlightened moderation, 199

environmental uncertainty, 209

essentialism, 78, 88, 276

establishmentarian democracy, 17, 273–75, 279, 281

ethnic parties: appeal to voters, 6, 276; definitions of, 8; electoral challengers to, 109; military relations with, 222; tribal family politics of, 273. *See also specific parties*

ethnic riots, 76, 79, 89n3

ethnonationalism, 76–77, 80, 81, 88, 97

extremism. *See* religious extremism

Facebook, 12, 60

factionalism: administrative chaos resulting from, 71–72; as barrier to party development, 24, 77; ideological-based, 110–11; in left-wing parties, 92; in political machines, 133

Fair, C. Christine, 256

family. *See* kinship networks

Farooq, Imran, 85–86, 226

Fawad, Fawad Hasan, 191

Federal Security Force (FSF), 49, 51, 221

females. *See* women in politics

financial resources, 30, 147–48

Fish, Stanley, 107

Folke, Olle, 172

foreign policy, 253–71; asymmetric regional consequences of, 265–66; and coethnic affinity, 266–67, 281; distributional implications of, 266; and ideological-based differences, 267; literature review, 254–55; in manifestos, 17, 259–63, 281; nationalism in, 44, 256; and oppositional opportunism, 268; of PML-N, 199; political party influence on, 17, 255–63; of PPP, 26, 48; role of public opinion in shaping of, 268–69; structural constraints on, 253–54, 265; voter attitudes toward, 263–65, 264f

FSF (Federal Security Force), 49, 51, 221

Gabol, Nabil, 157

Gandhi, Indira, 48, 171

gender equality, 170–71

gender quotas, 164–70, 176

genocide, 76, 83

GHQ (Army General Headquarters), 215, 217, 222–23, 226, 229–30. *See also* military

Gilani, Yousaf Raza, 56, 186–87, 247

Gilmartin, David, 82, 118

Ginsburg, Tom, 237

glass ceiling, 171

Government of India Act of 1935, 43, 165

Grzymala-Busse, Anna, 180

Gul, Hamid, 53, 222, 230

Gul, Zartaj, 163

Gulalai, Ayesha, 70

Habermas, Jürgen, 106

Haq, Naeemul, 63

Haqqani, Hussain, 223

Hasan, Mahmud al-, 112

Hasan, Pervez, 63

Hashmi, Javed, 67, 70, 155

Hassan, Mubashir, 97
Htun, Mala, 166, 168
human rights, 72, 90, 103, 111, 220
Hussain, Abida, 148
Hussain, Altaf: blind faith in leadership of,
81, 152; exile of, 77, 80, 86, 225; legal
troubles of, 9; military relations with,
225–26; mobilization of supporters, 79;
on sacrifice, 86; social media use by, 12;
on terrorist safe havens, 262. *See also*
Muttahida Qaumi Movement
Hussain, Shujaat, 153, 183
Hussain, Zahid, 29, 34, 36
hybrid regimes: criticisms of model,
273–74; dissonant institutionalism of,
238; governance pattern in, 215, 237; lack
of research on, 18; manifestations of, 4;
party-voter linkages in, 11

Iftikharuddin, Mian, 96
IJI (Islami Jamhoori Ittehad), 30–32, 53–54,
180, 223, 227, 233n13
IJT (Islami Jamiat-ul-Tuleba), 50, 67
Inayatullah, Sohail, 12
income support programs, 187
independent electables: bargaining power of,
278; commitment of, 147, 147f; party-
switching by, 150; as percentage of total
candidates, 158t; political autonomy of, 147,
147f, 150, 151; recruitment of, 155, 156
India: and Kashmir conflict, 18, 43, 44, 95,
257, 260–61; and Lahore Declaration,
228, 233n33; Muhajir migration from,
76–80, 83–84; nuclear program of, 33,
53, 220; political party views of, 260–61;
Sikh insurgency in, 256; and Tashkent
Declaration, 44–45, 219; voter attitudes
toward, 263–65, 264f
Indian National Congress, 24, 42, 112
indirect elections, 43, 169, 170, 217
Indo-Pakistani War (1965), 44, 45, 266
Insaf Students Federation (ISF), 67–69, 163
institutional uncertainty, 3, 195, 197, 205, 279
Inter-Services Intelligence (ISI): expansion
of domestic role, 49; and IJI, 30, 53;
Islamization of, 52; political interference
by, 58, 230; and PPP, 222, 223; and PTI,
64, 230; on rigged elections, 50–51
intraparty elections (IPEs), 60–62, 69–70

Iqbal, Muhammad, 87–88, 111, 114
Iran: Khomeini revolution in (1979), 27;
political party views of, 261–62
ISF (Insaf Students Federation), 67–69, 163
ISI. *See* Inter-Services Intelligence
Islam and Muslims: education for, 110, 116,
117; excommunication of Ahmadis from,
114; liberal version of, 199; modernist
movement in, 109, 111, 115–18, 121n4;
pan-Islamism, 86; political, 27, 109; *sharia*
in, 6, 26, 29, 119, 277; Shi'a, 107, 110, 112,
256, 266–67, 281; Sunni, 10, 107, 110,
112, 256–57, 266; *ulema*, 108, 110, 113,
115–19
Islamic parties, 105–21; appeal to voters,
6, 107, 114; barriers to advancement
of, 105–6; on foreign policy, 258,
259; military relations with, 231–32;
in Pakistani context, 107–8; role of,
10–11, 105, 273; underperformance in
elections, 108–9, 114–15, 277. *See also*
denominational parties; *specific parties*
Islamic socialism, 97, 99
Islami Jamhoori Ittehad (IJI), 30–32, 53–54,
180, 223, 227, 233n13
Islami Jamiat-ul-Tuleba (IJT), 50, 67
Islamization programs, 29, 52, 100, 246, 275

Jalalzai, Farida, 170
Jamaat-e-Islami (JI): campaign financing
by, 147, 157; candidate selection by, 145;
defections from, 67; electoral strategies
of, 156–57; on foreign policy, 258–62;
intraparty elections held by, 60–61;
judicial upholding of rights for, 241–42;
left-wing influences on, 95, 104; military
relations with, 231; in MMA coalition,
10; organizational structure of, 52;
parliamentary seats won by, 25; patronage
extended to, 100; political orientation
of, 107; protests led by, 50; women's
involvement in, 164
Jamhoori Wattan Party (JWP), 9
Jamiat Ulema-e-Hind (JUH), 112
Jamiat Ulema-e-Islam (JUI): coalitions
involving, 10, 112–13; factionalism within,
110–11; on foreign policy, 259–62, 266–
67; ideological positioning of, 99; military
relations with, 231; parliamentary

Jamiat Ulema-e-Islam (JUI) (*continued*)
seats won by, 25; political approach of, 112, 114, 156
Jamiat Ulema-e-Pakistan (JUP), 25
Janjua, Asif Nawaz, 225, 228
Javid, Hassan, 14–15, 144, 171, 278
Jawaid, Arsalan, 208
Jehd-e-Musalsal (television show), 86–87
Jensenius, Francesca R., 165, 166
JI. *See* Jamaat-e-Islami
Jinnah, Fatima, 227
Jinnah, Muhammad Ali: death of, 24; electoral strategy of, 45; instrumentalization of Islam by, 116; mausoleum of, 206, 210n20; and modernist movement, 121n4; and Muslim League, 42–43, 227; Muslim nationalism of, 84–85, 117; Pakistan Movement initiated by, 66; secular government envisioned by, 54
Jones, Philip E., 8, 41, 275
judiciary, 235–52; appointment process, 238–40, 242–44, 249, 252n55; as arbiter of dissonant institutionalization, 237, 249, 280; during democratic rule, 244–47, 249, 280–81; institutional interlinkages with military, 235, 238–42, 249, 250n6; internal culture of, 238, 240, 244, 248, 280; Islamization of, 52, 246; loyalty of, 238, 240; methodology for study of, 235–36; under military regimes, 240–44, 243t, 280; and political parties, 16–17, 235, 243, 248–50; recruitment for, 238–40, 241f, 249; strengthening of, 200, 201, 243–44, 246–47, 280; transitional period for, 239–40; weakening of, 237, 242, 248–49. *See also* Lawyers' Movement; Supreme Court (Pakistan)
JUH (Jamiat Ulema-e-Hind), 112
JUI. *See* Jamiat Ulema-e-Islam
Junejo, Muhammad Khan, 28, 29, 222, 227
JUP (Jamiat Ulema-e-Pakistan), 25
JWP (Jamhoori Wattan Party), 9

Kalhan, Anil, 204
Kalyvas, Stathis, 107
Kamal, Mustafa, 77
Kapiszewski, Diana, 238
Kapur, Devesh, 268

Karamat, Jehangir, 33–34, 228
Kashmir conflict, 18, 43, 44, 95, 257, 260–61
Kasuri, Fauzia, 64, 67, 71
Kasuri, Raza, 49
Keefer, Philip, 182
Khan, Abdul Hafeez, 63
Khan, Abdul Qayyum, 25
Khan, Agha Muhammad Yahya, 46, 47, 217, 227
Khan, Aleem, 67, 69
Khan, Mohammad Ayub. *See* Ayub Khan, Mohammad
Khan, Bacha, 9, 94, 96
Khan, Fida Mohammad, 29
Khan, Ghulam Ishaq, 30–32, 53, 54
Khan, Ghulam Jilani, 29, 227
Khan, Gul Hasan, 220
Khan, Hamid, 62, 63, 65–66, 69
Khan, Imran: controversy surrounding, 8; criticisms of, 70; electoral strategies of, 61, 70, 155; military relations with, 230–31; personality of, 64–65, 68, 205, 276; philanthropy of, 63, 64, 73n4; popularity of, 37, 38, 66, 216; PPP and PML-N challenged by, 56–57, 60; protests led by, 35–36, 207–8, 230; on Taliban, 64. *See also* Pakistan Tehreek-e-Insaf
Khan, Malik Qasim, 25
Khan, Meraj Muhammad, 90, 98
Khan, Mohammad Asghar, 218, 221
Khan, Nichola, 78
Khan, Sarah, 15, 162, 175, 278
Khan, Tabinda M., 8, 60, 275–76
Khan, Tikka, 51, 220
Khan Mohmand, Shandana, 13, 125, 129–30, 148, 182, 277
Khatm-e-Nabuwwat Movement (KNM), 111
Khomeini revolution (1979), 27
Khosa, Asif Saeed Khan, 246–47
Khudai Khidmatgar, 9, 94, 96, 100
kickbacks, 54–55
king's parties, 25, 183, 184, 217, 229
kinship networks: mobilization of support across, 66, 68, 145, 150; social constraints related to, 152–53; voting behavior influenced by, 12, 114, 149; and women's inclusion in politics, 170–74, 278–79
Kirchheimer, Otto, 6, 61, 67

Kiyani, Ashfaq Parvez, 218
KNM (Khatm-e-Nabuwwat Movement), 111
Kohli, Veeru, 103
Kolinsky, Eva, 195–96
Kopecky, Petr, 181
Kureshi, Yasser, 16–17, 235, 280

Lahore Declaration (1999), 228, 233n33
landownership, 147–49, 219
Lapidus, Ira, 107
Lawyers' Movement, 39, 66–68, 90, 201–5, 274, 279–80
left-wing parties, 90–104; and Bangladesh separation, 98; barriers to advancement of, 91–92, 101–2, 276–77; definitions of, 93–94; factionalism within, 92; future outlook for, 102–4; origins of, 90; regionalism linked to, 96–98; repression and persecution of, 91, 92, 95–102; underperformance in elections, 91, 101–3. *See also specific parties*
Leghari, Farooq, 33, 54
Liaqat, Asad, 13, 14, 125, 141, 277
Long March, 74n24, 202–4
loyalists. *See* party loyalists
Lupu, Noam, 3, 197, 206

Madani, Husain Ahmad, 89n7
Mahmood, Javed, 188–89
Mahmood, Mufti, 50
mainstream parties: appeal to voters, 6; characteristics of, 7–8, 272; electoral allies of, 11; on foreign policy, 258–61; ideological differences among, 6–7; Islamic party influence on, 109, 120; women in leadership of, 164. *See also* catch-all parties; *specific parties*
Mair, Peter, 62
Malik, Anas, 113
Malik, Anushay, 9, 90, 276–77
manifestos: candidate articulation of, 14; characteristics of, 258–59; domestic policy in, 56, 103; foreign policy in, 17, 259–63, 281; leader-centric nature of, 182
maslaki parties. *See* denominational parties
mass-party model, 61, 67
Mawdudi, Abul A'la, 107, 114, 116
Mazdoor Kissan Party (MKP), 91, 94, 100
McAdam, Douglas, 115

media: campaign messaging through, 135; censorship of, 2, 58, 222, 274; liberalization of, 66, 200; for political mobilization, 12, 60, 68; social, 12, 23, 60, 68, 258
megapolitics, judicialization of, 237, 280
Mehsud, Baitullah, 55
Meierhenrich, Jens, 237
Memogate scandal, 223, 229
Messick, Brinkley, 107
Milam, William, 269
military, 215–34; as arbiter of politics, 216–18, 232, 280; authoritarianism of, 42, 65, 72, 152; balance of power with political parties, 2, 179–81, 204, 256; domestic policies under, 28–29, 42; economic policies under, 16, 23, 27, 43–44; election interference by, 2, 16, 58, 216; institutional interlinkages with judiciary, 235, 238–42, 249, 250n6; Islamic party relations with, 231–32; literature review, 4; MQM relations with, 224–26, 280; organizational structure of, 218; overdevelopment of, 198; overview, 215–16; party alignment with, 7, 152; patronage used by, 28, 29, 218–19, 232; PML-N relations with, 7, 16, 23, 204, 227–29, 275; political guardianship role of, 42, 43, 198, 218, 255; PPP relations with, 35, 53, 219–24, 280; professionalism of, 218, 225; PTI relations with, 2, 216, 230–31; superordinate-subordinate dynamic created by, 24–25. *See also* Army General Headquarters
military dictatorships: constitutional engineering by, 180; Islamic credentials for legitimacy, 116; judiciary under, 240–44, 243t, 280; left-wing resistance to, 104; nonparty elections under, 79, 80; political parties under, 154; popular mobilization against, 76, 119; postcolonial, 113; regime uncertainty in, 201; repression under, 99–100
Milli Muslim League (MML), 10
Mirza, Iskander, 96
MKP (Mazdoor Kissan Party), 91, 94, 100
MMA (Muttahida Majlis-e-Amal), 10, 101, 104, 231
Modi, Narendra, 229, 268
moral questioning, 82, 83, 88

Moustafa, Tamir, 237
Movement for the Restoration of Democracy (MRD), 27, 39, 52, 100, 152, 222
MQM. *See* Muttahida Qaumi Movement
MQM-Pakistan (MQM-P), 77, 79, 81
Mufti, Mariam, 1, 13–15, 144, 158, 170, 182, 278
Muhajir Qaumi Movement. *See* Muttahida Qaumi Movement
Muhajirs: ethnic riots involving, 76, 79, 89n3; marginalization of, 85–86, 225; migration from India, 76–80, 83–84; military relations with, 224–25; in narrative of sacrifice, 77–78, 81–88, 276; nationalism of, 77, 85–86; as regulative ideal, 84–85. *See also* Muttahida Qaumi Movement
Muhammad, Tufail, 52
Mulla, Ayesha, 208
Munir, Muhammad, 241
Murray, Rainbow, 169
Musharraf, Pervez: bureaucratic appointments under, 181; delegitimization of regime, 200–201; emergence of, 179, 225; enlightened moderation of, 199; ethnic background of, 225, 228; judiciary under, 243–44, 246; liberalization policies under, 66, 199–201; military interventions under, 33–35, 55, 180, 199, 229, 275; political parties co-opted by, 2, 183, 184, 217, 229; protests against, 102, 202, 218; resignation of, 39, 224; structure of elected government under, 80–81
Muslim Democrat parties, 107–9
Muslim League: AIML, 7, 82, 84, 89n7, 112, 227; Convention Muslim League, 227; emergence of, 24; factionalism within, 24; and judiciary, 245–47; as king's party, 25; military relations with, 226–29; negotiating power of, 4; parliamentary seats won by, 25; PML-F, 217, 219, 227; realignment of, 25–26; removal from power, 28; uncontested governance by, 42. *See also* Pakistan Muslim League-Nawaz; Pakistan Muslim League-Quaid
Muslim nationalism, 78, 80, 84–86, 117, 276
Muslims. *See* Islam and Muslims
Muttahida Majlis-e-Amal (MMA), 10, 101, 104, 231

Muttahida Qaumi Movement (MQM), 76–89; alignment with PPP, 53; campaign financing by, 147, 157; candidate selection by, 145; as confessional party, 107; defections from, 81, 89n6; electoral strategies of, 156–57; emergence of, 6, 76, 79–80, 224; ethnopolitical discourse of, 8–9, 78, 80–82; factionalism within, 77; on foreign policy, 260–62; future outlook for, 81; government operations against, 80; intraparty elections held by, 61; left-wing influences on, 104; literature review, 5; military relations with, 224–26, 280; name change for, 76–77, 80, 86, 276; organizational structure of, 9, 115; origins of, 151; parliamentary seats won by, 32, 77; television dramas released by, 86–87. *See also* Hussain, Altaf; Muhajirs

Naqvi, Tahir, 9, 76, 276
Narang, Vipin, 257
Naseer, Farooq, 171
Nasr, Vali, 107
National Awami Party (NAP), 92, 93, 96–101
National Freedom Front. *See* Qaumi Mahaz-e-Azadi
nationalism: ethnonationalism, 76–77, 80, 81, 88, 97; in foreign policy, 44, 256; ideological discourse of, 78; in Indo-Pakistani War, 45; Muhajir, 77, 85–86; Muslim, 78, 80, 84–86, 117, 276; objectives of, 82; sacrifice as manifestation of, 82–83, 85, 276
National Party (NP), 9–10
National Reconciliation Ordinance of 2007 (NRO), 223, 229
National Students' Federation (NSF), 102
Nawaz, Maryam, 37, 38
Nehru, Jawaharlal, 42
Nellis, Gareth, 7, 267
Nelson, Matthew J., 269
Niazi, Hafeezullah, 72
Noorani, Tasneem, 62, 69, 70, 72
NP (National Party), 9–10
NRO (National Reconciliation Ordinance of 2007), 223, 229
NSF (National Students' Federation), 102
nuclear programs, 31, 33, 48, 53, 220

O'Dwyer, Connor, 180

Operation Midnight Jackal, 53, 222

opposition parties, 195–211; on foreign
policy, 258; incentives for coordination,
197–98; institutionalized, 195; lack
of engagement with, 31, 33, 35, 38;
methodology for study of, 196–97;
PML-N as, 199–205, 209; PTI as, 205–9;
and regime uncertainty, 197–202, 206,
209, 279–80; sites of opposition, 195–96;
strategies of, 15–16, 26, 199, 208–9, 279;
violence against, 50

Pagaro, Pir Sahib, 25, 28, 227

Pakistan: deep state in, 49, 198, 200, 204,
206; as geostrategic flashpoint, 18; income
support programs in, 187; independence
of, 1, 23, 34–35, 43; and Kashmir conflict,
18, 43, 44, 95, 257, 260–61; landownership
in, 147–49, 219; mass migration to, 76–80,
83–84; methodological diversity in study
of, 17–18; nuclear program of, 31, 33,
48, 53, 220; sanctions imposed upon, 31;
transition to democracy, 1, 29, 34–35, 199,
202, 247. *See also* education; elections;
foreign policy; Islam and Muslims;
judiciary; military; political parties

Pakistan Administrative Service (PAS), 181,
183–85, 188, 191

Pakistan Awami Tehreek (PAT), 70, 74n24,
207, 208

Pakistan Constitution: Article 58 Section 2b,
28, 31–33, 180, 192–93n2, 274

Pakistan Movement, 24, 66, 85, 87, 88, 112

Pakistan Muslim League-Functional
(PML-F), 217, 219, 227

Pakistan Muslim League-Nawaz (PML-N),
23–40; bureaucratic appointments by,
178–79, 187–92, 279; candidate selection
by, 145, 157; as catch-all party, 155, 157;
censorship of media coverage on, 2; as
confessional party, 107; corruption in
government of, 1, 35–39, 228; defections
from, 10, 37, 38, 273; electoral strategies
of, 135, 156; emergence of, 24, 30–32,
199; factors in development of, 27; on
foreign policy, 199, 259–62, 268; future
outlook for, 37–40, 227; ideological
positioning of, 7, 29, 199, 201; and

Lawyers' Movement, 201–5, 280; literature
review, 5; military relations with, 7, 16,
23, 204, 227–29, 275; as opposition party,
199–205, 209; parliamentary seats won
by, 32, 35, 38, 54, 55; protests against,
207–8; removal from power, 34, 199, 229;
service delivery agenda of, 187–92; ticket
application fee required by, 147, 155;
voter-initiated contact of, 136t, 137–38.
See also Sharif, Nawaz

Pakistan Muslim League-Quaid (PML-Q):
bureaucratic appointments by, 178–79,
183–85, 191, 279; candidate linkages
with, 144, 152–53, 159; collapse of, 66,
158; defections from, 10, 67, 69, 156;
emergence of, 179, 183; as king's party,
183, 184, 217, 229; military relations
with, 229

Pakistan National Alliance (PNA), 26, 29,
39, 50–51, 227, 248

Pakistan National Party (PNP), 96

Pakistan People's Party (PPP), 41–59;
bureaucratic appointments by, 178–79,
185–87, 191, 279; candidate selection
by, 145, 157; as catch-all party, 155, 157;
as confessional party, 107; corruption
in government of, 34, 50–51, 185–87;
decline of, 8, 41, 42, 48, 50, 275;
defections from, 57, 59; emergence of,
6, 8, 25, 26; on foreign policy, 26, 48,
259–62, 268; founding of, 45–46, 219;
future outlook for, 58–59; ideological
positioning of, 7, 59, 151, 152, 272;
and judiciary, 246, 248–49, 252n55;
and Lawyers' Movement, 202–3, 280;
legislative achievements of, 187; literature
review, 5; mass movements led by, 46, 52,
90; military relations with, 35, 53, 219–24,
280; parliamentary seats won by, 25, 32,
47, 53–58; removal from power, 26–27,
32, 51, 242; and socialism, 45, 97–99, 219;
ticket application fee required by, 147,
155; uncontested governance by, 42, 48;
undermining of support for, 29–30, 58,
221–23; women's involvement in, 164.
See also Bhutto, Benazir; Bhutto,
Zulifkar Ali

Pakistan Taliban. *See* Tehreek-e-Taliban-e-
Pakistan

Pakistan Tehreek-e-Insaf (PTI), 60–75; bureaucratic appointments by, 192; candidate selection by, 145; as catch-all party, 60–62, 67, 72–73, 276; as confessional party, 107; conflict between old and new members, 69–71; criticisms of, 38, 39, 62, 64, 70–72; defections from, 69–70; early years of, 63–66; electoral strategies of, 15, 61, 70, 72, 135, 155, 230; emergence of, 8, 60, 62; factionalism within, 71–72; on foreign policy, 259–62, 266–67; future outlook for, 192; ideological positioning of, 7, 61, 64–66, 272; intraparty elections held by, 60, 62, 69–70; left-wing influences on, 104; military relations with, 2, 216, 230–31; "new" Pakistan promised by, 60, 65–69, 72, 206; as opposition party, 205–9; parliamentary seats won by, 38, 62, 70, 71, 206; PPP and PML-N challenged by, 57, 60; protests organized by, 6, 35, 37, 61, 207–8, 230; social media use by, 12, 60, 68; ticket application fee required by, 147; voter-initiated contact of, 136t, 137–38; women's involvement in, 64, 66. *See also* Khan, Imran

Pak Sarzameen Party (PSP), 77, 81, 226

Panama Papers, 36–37, 55, 204, 208, 230

pan-Islamism, 86

Panitch, Leo, 93

parliamentary democracy, 40, 42

parties. *See* political parties

Partition, 4, 43, 76, 86–7, 91, 94, 111, 117, 148

party heavyweights: commitment of, 147, 147f, 278; party-switching by, 154, 160; as percentage of total candidates, 158t; political autonomy of, 147, 147f, 151; recruitment of, 155, 156; social constraints on, 152–53, 159

party indiscipline. *See* party-switching

party loyalists: bureaucratic appointment of, 181; defined, 13–14; electables vs., 13–14, 273; incentives for, 145–46, 160; in political machines, 132–33; recruitment of, 30

party-switching: by candidates, 151, 157–60, 278; ideological impediments to, 7, 152; and ideological positioning, 7, 152; by independent electables, 150; material incentives for, 121n7; motivations for, 59, 69, 158; patronage as influence on, 158–59, 272–73; prevalence of, 12, 15, 158; by senior leadership, 57, 70, 81

party worker candidates, 147, 147f, 153–54, 157, 158t, 278

PAS (Pakistan Administrative Service), 181, 183–85, 188, 191

Pashtuns, 9, 112, 151, 224–25, 267, 281. *See also* Awami National Party

Pashtun Tahaffuz Movement, 72

PAT (Pakistan Awami Tehreek), 70, 74n24, 207, 208

patronage: in candidate recruitment, 155–57; development funds as, 149, 156; and Islamic parties, 105; and left-wing parties, 91, 100; in military regimes, 28, 29, 218–19, 232; party-switching influenced by, 158–59, 272–73; political parties as instruments of, 23, 180, 277–78; spiritual, 150; through targeted goods, 182, 188, 191, 279; teaching jobs as, 189, 190; voting behavior influenced by, 13, 114, 134, 145. *See also* clientelism

personal gain, pursuit of, 178–79, 185–87, 191

Pew Research Center, 119, 255, 263, 269n2

Pirzada, Abdul Hafeez, 220

PKMAP (Pukhtunkhwa Milli Awam Party), 9

PML-F (Pakistan Muslim League-Functional), 217, 219, 227

PML-N. *See* Pakistan Muslim League-Nawaz

PML-Q. *See* Pakistan Muslim League-Quaid

PNA (Pakistan National Alliance), 26, 29, 39, 50–51, 227, 248

PNP (Pakistan National Party), 96

political autonomy, 146–51, 155, 157, 278

political elites: attributes of, 147–51; expansion of, 25; foreign policy views of, 268–69; influences on policy, 267; landownership of, 147–49, 219; literature review, 4; military relations with, 25, 154, 232; opportunities available to, 120

political machines, 125–43; anecdotal illustrations of, 125–26; closeness with voters, 128, 138–40, 140f, 143n20; door-to-door canvassing by, 135–37, 136t, 138f; factionalism within, 133; information transmission in, 134, 141, 277–78; literature review, 129–30; membership

of, 126–27, 131–32; methodology for study of, 127, 141–42n7, 142–43nn16–17; organizational structure of, 126–27; relationship between political workers and higher-tier politicians, 132–33; in urban Punjab, 130–34; voter-initiated contact outside of campaigns, 136*t,* 137–38, 139*f*
political parties: all-parties conferences, 28, 208; balance of power with military, 2, 179–81, 204, 256; barriers to development of, 23–24; classification of, 5–11; dynastic leadership of, 23, 37, 60, 149; ethnic, 6, 8–10; foreign policy influence of, 17, 255–63; functions of, 2–3, 11–16; as gatekeepers to political entry, 163; governance role of, 15, 178; institutional environment of, 64, 68, 163–65; Islamic, 6, 10–11; and judiciary, 16–17, 235, 243, 248–50; literature review, 4–5; mainstream, 6–8; objectives of, 41; registered, 5, 19n2; relations among, 15–16; voting behavior in relation to, 11–13, 144–45; within-party actors of, 13–15. *See also* candidates; elections; opposition parties; party-switching; women in politics; *specific names and types of parties*
Political Parties Act of 1962 (Pakistan), 241
political violence, 65, 80, 224–25, 231
populism: PPP, 41, 58, 272; PTI, 272; religious parties, 112, 118–19,
PPP. *See* Pakistan People's Party
Pressler Amendment of 1985 (US), 31, 40n4
provincialism, 84, 85, 94
Przeworski, Adam, 93
PSP (Pak Sarzameen Party), 77, 81, 226
PTI. *See* Pakistan Tehreek-e-Insaf
Pukhtunkhwa Milli Awam Party (PKMAP), 9
Punjab Disturbances (1953), 112–13, 121n5
Punjab Education Sector Reform Program, 189–90

Qasim, Malik, 227
Qasmi, Ali Usman, 119
Qaumi Mahaz-e-Azadi, 90, 98, 100
Quaid-e-Azam. *See* Jinnah, Muhammad Ali
Quaid-e-Azam mausoleum, 206, 210n20
quotas, 164–70, 176
Qureshi, Mehmood, 67, 155
Qureshi, Moeenuiddin, 32

Raghavan, Srinath, 90
Rahim, J. A., 45, 48, 97
Rahim, Sajjid, 220
Rahman, Mujibur, 48
Rashid, Ahsan, 63, 69
Rasool, Kamran, 183
regime uncertainty, 3, 197–202, 206, 209, 279–80
regionalism, 96–98
regional parties. *See* ethnic parties
Rehman, Fazlur, 10, 110, 114, 156
religious extremism, 18, 27, 64, 120, 225
religious parties. *See* Islamic parties
religious violence, 7, 267
representative democracy, 112
reserved electoral seats, 165–70, 176, 177, 177n6, 278
Rickne, Johanna Karin, 172
Riedl, Rachel, 3, 197, 206
riots, 76, 79, 89n3
Rizvi, Khadim, 108
Rumi, Raza, 227

sacrifice, Muhajir narrative of, 77–78, 81–88, 276
sahib, use of term, 141n1
Sahibzad, Sadiqa, 64
Sami-ul-Haq, 110
sanctions, 31
Sartori, Giovanni, 93
Sattar, Babar, 64
Schattschneider, E. E., 2
Schneider, Mark, 129
schools. *See* education
Servants of God. *See* Khudai Khidmatgar
service delivery: bureaucratic appointments for, 178–79, 187–92, 279; and party-voter linkages, 129; by political machines, 134; in urban areas, 81, 188; voter contact of politicians regarding, 137
Shafqat, Saeed, 7, 23, 275
Shafqat, Sahar, 1, 15–16, 195, 279–80
Shah, Aqil, 255
Shah, Sajjad Ali, 33, 246
Shaheen, Abdul Jabbar, 190
sharia (Islamic law), 6, 26, 29, 119, 277
Sharif, Nawaz: corruption allegations against, 35–37, 54, 60, 229; criticisms of, 34, 35, 38, 66, 268; on detention during Long

Sharif, Nawaz (*continued*)
March, 203; economic policies of, 30, 31; emergence of, 7, 24, 28–32, 222, 245–46; exile of, 66, 183, 187–88, 200, 229; foreign policy under, 257; go-it-alone attitude of, 31–34, 39; judiciary under, 33; military relations with, 33–35, 227–29, 275, 280; and Panama Papers, 36–37, 55, 204, 208, 230; as prime minister, 30, 32, 34–35, 227–29; protests against, 35–36, 61, 207–8; removal from power, 1, 32–35, 54, 229, 247. *See also* Pakistan Muslim League-Nawaz
Sharif, Raheel, 256–57
Sharif, Shahbaz, 30, 35, 38, 183, 187–89, 210n15
Shaukat Khanum Memorial Hospital (SKMH), 63–64, 67, 73n4
Shi'a Islam, 107, 110, 112, 256, 266–67, 281
Siddiqa, Ayesha, 16, 198, 215, 280
Siddique, Osama, 245
Siddiqui, A. R., 84, 85
Siddiqui, Niloufer, 1, 7, 12, 263, 267
Siddiqui, Saeed-uz-Zaman, 33, 246
Sind National Front, 94
sit-ins, 35–36, 61, 74n24, 202–3, 207–8, 230
SKMH (Shaukat Khanum Memorial Hospital), 63–64, 67, 73n4
Skoric, Marko M., 12
Smith, Daniel M., 172
social constraints, 152–53, 159
social contract, 83
social democracy, 65–66, 151
socialism: international, 93; Islamic, 97, 99; and PPP, 45, 97–99, 219; rhetoric of, 26, 98
social media, 12, 23, 60, 68, 258
social movement theory (SMT), 106
Soviet intervention in Afghanistan (1979), 27, 52
spiritual patronage, 150
Sprague, John, 93
Staniland, Paul, 257
Stokes, Susan, 2, 129
Su, Yen-Pin, 196–98
Suleri, Z. A., 85
Sultan, Haroon Ahmed, 162
Sunni Islam, 10, 107, 110, 112, 256–57, 266
support networks, 148–50

Supreme Court (Pakistan): appointment process amended by, 240; corruption investigations by, 36–37, 186, 247; judicial activism within, 185, 244; legitimation of coups by, 200, 201, 241, 243, 248; under military regimes, 241–44; on presidential dissolution of power, 32, 245–46; prime ministers ousted by, 1, 37, 247, 248
Syed, G. M., 94, 96

Tahir-ul-Qadri, 35–36, 70, 74n24, 207
Taliban: and Bhutto assassination, 223; foreign policy views of, 262, 267, 281; government support for, 256; justifications for, 64; political parties targeted by, 102; voter attitudes toward, 263, 264f, 266. *See also* Tehreek-e-Taliban-e-Pakistan
Tarar, Rafiq, 33
Tareen, Jahangir, 67, 69, 155, 192
Tarrow, Sidney, 115
Tashkent Declaration of 1966, 44–45, 219
teacher selection process, 189–90. *See also* education
Tehreek-e-Labbaik Pakistan (TLP): emergence of, 6, 10–11, 108; mainstreaming of, 120; military relations with, 231–32; parliamentary seats won by, 109; protests led by, 72; social media use by, 12
Tehreek-e-Taliban-e-Pakistan (TTP), 35, 55, 267
terrorism: military as target of, 52–53; political parties threatened by, 59, 101; safe havens for, 262; War on Terror, 18, 65, 200, 253, 259
Thompson, E. P., 93
Tirmazi, Syed A. I., 49
TLP. *See* Tehreek-e-Labbaik Pakistan
TTP (Tehreek-e-Taliban-e-Pakistan), 35, 55, 267
Turab, Anita, 186
Twitter, 12
typology of candidates, 146–54, 147f, 278

ulema (religious scholars), 108, 110, 113, 115–19
Ullah, Haroon K., 113
uncertainty: defined, 197; economic, 3, 197; environmental, 209; institutional, 3, 195,

197, 205, 279; regime, 3, 197–202, 206, 209, 279–80

United Muslim League (UML), 25–26

United Nationalist Movement. *See* Muttahida Majlis-e-Amal

United States: generational transmission of party identity in, 132; military pacts with, 95; nonalignment policy with, 26; partisan divergence in, 265; political party views of, 259–60; pressure for democratic reform from, 201; sanctions implemented by, 31; voter attitudes toward, 263, 264*f*; and War on Terror, 18, 65, 200, 253, 259

Vajpayee, Atal Bihari, 34, 228

Verkaaik, Oskar, 78

violence: in Bhutto regime, 49; civil war, 47, 98, 109, 198, 256, 266; domestic, 162, 172–73; in elections, 50, 58; ethnic, 273; genocide, 76, 83; incitement through social media, 12; in mass movements, 46; political, 65, 80, 224–25, 231; religious, 7, 267; riots, 76, 79, 89n3. *See also* terrorism

voters and voting behavior: closeness with politicians, 128, 138–40, 140*f*, 143n20; contact with politicians initiated by, 136*t*, 137–38, 139*f*; door-to-door canvassing for, 135–37, 136*t*, 138*f*; foreign policy views of, 263–65, 264*f*; kinship networks as influence on, 12, 114, 149; literature review, 12–13; patronage as influence on, 13, 114, 134, 145; political parties in relation to, 11–13, 144–45; and religious ideals, 114; women in politics, attitudes toward, 174–77, 175*f*

Wali Khan, Abdul, 98–100

Waltz, Kenneth, 263, 268

Waraich, Omar, 204

War on Terror, 18, 65, 200, 253, 259

Waseem, Mohammad, 6–7, 17, 84, 182, 272

Weber, Max, 41

Wilder, Andrew, 4, 5, 13, 182

women in politics, 162–77; contact with politicians, 128, 135–38, 136*t*; family and kinship influences on, 170–74, 278–79; future outlook for, 175–77; and institutional environment of political parties, 64, 66, 163–65; leadership roles of, 53, 170; as percentage of total candidates, 164, 165*f*, 166, 169*f*; public attitudes toward, 174–77, 175*f*, 279; reserved electoral seats for, 165–70, 176, 177, 177n6, 278; underrepresentation of, 15, 163, 166, 169, 176, 278

World Bank, 32, 54, 184

World Values Survey, 174, 175*f*

Yahya Khan, Agha Muhammad, 46, 47, 217, 227

Yemen, civil war in, 256–57

Zaman, Muhammad Qasim, 109

Zardari, Asif Ali, 39, 53–60, 66, 179, 186–87, 223, 275

Zhirnov, Andrei, 158

Ziauddin, Muhammad, 230

Zia-ul-Haq, Muhammad: blasphemy laws under, 108; bureaucratic appointments under, 181; death of, 29, 53, 222, 225; dictatorship of, 76, 79, 80, 99–100; domestic policies under, 28–29, 42, 52, 217; elections introduced by, 5, 39, 180, 243; judiciary under, 242–43, 245, 246; legislation passed by, 27–28; military interventions under, 26–27, 51, 274; political parties co-opted by, 2, 224–25; repression under, 99–100, 119; treatment of Bhutto women by, 51–52

CPSIA information can be obtained
at www.ICGtesting.com
Printed in the USA
BVHW030841020821
613054BV00023B/5

9 781626 167704